PRAISE FOR
DISNEY'S LAND

"My favorite new book of 2019 . . . brisk, smart, a delight."
—Richard Brookhiser, *The Wall Street Journal*

"The clockwork of the park—and to some extent, the personality of the man who created it—receives an expert inspection . . . and the whole enterprise is shown as a magnificent amoeba that was as much an accident as a mastered design."
—*The New York Times Book Review*

"Eight hundred million visitors have trekked to the so-called 'happiest place on earth' since its 1955 opening, seeking its carefully scripted brand of excitement and cheer. How and why Walt Disney envisioned a place where people 'could live among Mickey Mouse and Snow White' is carefully detailed in this new book."
—*The Washington Post*, "Best Books to Read in December [2019]"

"An extremely entertaining story . . . *Disney's Land* is Snow's exhaustively researched, jam-packed chronicle of how Walt Disney conceived and created a new kind of amusement park."
—*Newsday*

"Entertaining . . . Mr. Snow [proves] to be as solid a storyteller as Walt Disney himself."
—*The Wall Street Journal*

"Disney fans will enjoy this rendering of the founder and entrepreneurs will find their time well spent inside the covers of Snow's book."
—Associated Press

"A story of astonishing innovation . . . fascinating and delightfully written."

—*Forbes*

"Arrive an hour before your chosen [Disney] park opens with a copy of 'Disney's Land' by Richard Snow, filled with great park tidbits."

—*USA Today*

"Disneyland is rarely mentioned as a milestone American invention, but it should be. . . . The captivating origin story of the 'Happiest Place on Earth' is well-told in *Disney's Land*, the latest work from esteemed historian and novelist Richard Snow. It's a rollicking read befitting the home of Mr. Toad's Wild Ride, chock full of Alice-in-Wonderland-level surprises, with the grandeur of Sleeping Beauty's Castle, and other delightful details (Walt Disney would eat his favorite hot dog lunch from a cart, walk away, and place garbage receptacles at the exact spot he finished his frankfurter)."

—Medium.com

"A rich biography of a place . . . Snow echoes Disney's attention to detail in this lush history of how the theme park came to be."

—*The Christian Science Monitor*

"Every Disney fan needs to read [this]."

—*PopSugar*

"Fantastic."

—*New York Journal of Books*

"This joyful, lavishly detailed account will entertain Disneyphiles and readers of popular American history."

—*Publishers Weekly*

"An animated history of an iconic destination."

—*Kirkus Reviews*

"Snow's smooth narrative spotlights the hard work and heart that the 'happiest place on Earth' required."

—*Booklist*

"Call it what you will: a fantasy, a folly, a country of its own, a city from the Arabian Nights, a giant cash register, a monument to Main Street, a saccharine absurdity, a triumph of urban design. Richard Snow calls Disneyland an invention on par with the Kitty Hawk Flyer and—in the most shapely of narratives—not only convinces us of its magic but somehow reproduces that magic on the page. A witty, wild, wondrous Tilt-A-Whirl of a book."

—Stacy Schiff, Pulitzer Prize–winning author of *The Witches* and *Cleopatra: A Life*

"This is a deeply felt and deeply researched story about the complicated man and his vision to create 'the happiest place on earth.' Snow brings a historian's eye and a child's delight, not to mention superb writing, to the telling of this fascinating narrative."

—Ken Burns

"Richard Snow gives Disney fans everything they could want in a history of the world's favorite theme park, from its nascent phase as a mere faraway look in Walt Disney's eye, to the hysteria of its opening day, with the freshly poured asphalt on Main Street barely set—and beyond. Snow is a great researcher and a terrific storyteller—and no detail is too small, whether it's the landscaping, the design of the rides, or the way Walt Disney did (or didn't) manage the money. As Snow tells it, *Disney's Land* is more than mere history; it's a page-turner of a suspense story, and, even knowing how it all turns out, you'll find yourself wondering if Walt is really going to get his pie-in-the-sky project ready in time for its opening day. I couldn't put it down."

—Brian Jay Jones, *New York Time*s bestselling author of *Jim Henson: The Biography* and *Becoming Dr. Seuss: Theodor Geisel and the Making of an American Imagination*

ALSO BY RICHARD SNOW

The map Herb Ryman created in one frantic weekend

to sell television executives on Disney's idea.

Walt Disney explains his new park while it's still under construction in 1955.

DISNEY'S LAND

Walt Disney and the Invention of the Amusement Park That Changed the World

RICHARD SNOW

SCRIBNER

New York   London   Toronto   Sydney   New Delhi

Scribner
An Imprint of Simon & Schuster, Inc.
1230 Avenue of the Americas
New York, NY 10020

First Scribner paperback edition December 2020

SCRIBNER and design are registered trademarks of The Gale Group, Inc., used
under license by Simon & Schuster, Inc., the publisher of this work.

For information about special discounts for bulk purchases, please contact
Simon & Schuster Special Sales at 1-866-506-1949 or business@simonandschuster.com.

The Simon & Schuster Speakers Bureau can bring authors to your live event.
For more information, or to book an event, contact the Simon & Schuster Speakers
Bureau at 1-866-248-3049 or visit our website at www.simonspeakers.com.

Interior design by Erika Genova

Manufactured in the United States of America

10 9 8 7 6 5 4 3 2 1

Library of Congress Cataloging-in-Publication Data

Names: Snow, Richard, 1947– author.
Title: Disney's land / Richard Snow.
Description: New York : Scribner, 2019. | Includes bibliographical references
   and index. |
Identifiers: LCCN 2019024840 (print) | LCCN 2019024841 (ebook) |
   ISBN 9781501190803 (hardcover) | ISBN 9781501190810 (paperback) |
   ISBN 9781501190827 (ebook)
Subjects: LCSH: Disneyland (Calif.)—History. | Architecture, American. |
   Architecture—Social aspects—United States.
Classification: LCC GV1853.3.C22 S66 2019 (print) | LCC GV1853.3.C22 (ebook) |
   DDC 791.06/879496—dc23
LC record available at https://lccn.loc.gov/2019024840
LC ebook record available at https://lccn.loc.gov/2019024841

ISBN 978-1-5011-9080-3
ISBN 978-1-5011-9081-0 (pbk)
ISBN 978-1-5011-9082-7 (ebook)

For Rebecca Snow and William Snow,
who, although they never shared their father's fascination
with amusement parks—not even Disney ones!—
nonetheless have always generously indulged it.

When he reached middle age . . . it seemed that we were going to witness an all-too-familiar process—the conversion of the tired artist into the tired businessman. When in 1955 we heard that Disney had opened an amusement park under his own name, it appeared certain that we could not look forward to anything new from Mr. Disney.

We were quite wrong. He had, instead, created his masterpiece.

—Aubrey Menen

"I wouldn't ask too much of her," I ventured. "You can't repeat the past."

"Can't repeat the past?" he cried incredulously. "Why of course you can! . . . I'm going to fix everything just the way it was before."

—F. Scott Fitzgerald, *The Great Gatsby*

CONTENTS

DISNEY'S LAND

1

SUNDAY, JULY 17, 1955, 4 A.M.

Walt Disney had been prowling about his park for hours looking for something to do.

Nobody seemed to need help—or else they needed far more than any one person could offer. All around him, hundreds of men were sawing and painting and hammering in the bone-white glare of work lights, dodging the blades of swiveling forklifts, pushing dollies here and there in an endless cursing bustle that made the whole site throb like a wartime munitions factory.

They were putting the finishing touches—or, in some frantic cases, the initial ones—on a fantastic metropolis that stood where, two years earlier, there had been nothing but 160 acres of Southern California orange trees. These had been supplanted by something so radical that the term "amusement park" was too meager a description.

Here, spread about the towers of a fairy-tale castle, were "lands" that recreated the American West of a century earlier and a jungle river fraught with perils, that offered a journey to the moon by rocket, or one to Peter Pan's Never Land by galleon, or along the Mississippi of Mark Twain's youth aboard a stern-wheeler. All these as yet untried diversions were encircled by a railroad—the real thing, live steam, its engines, their fireboxes already lit, hissing and popping as they awaited their debut on the morrow.

Miles away, out in the dark countryside, publicity department people were planting illegal street signs pointing the way toward this new place, this Disneyland.

Its author, Walt Disney, might have been wearing a bathrobe—often his uniform of choice when touring the site—but probably not this night, as he wanted to do some hands-on work, always a comfort to him when he was nervous.

He was nervous now, and his anxiety sometimes crackled into anger. There were so many things that could have been done better. Here and there he would spot a dribble of color leaking down from a hastily painted windowsill—his omnivorous eye took in all such minutiae—and he would lift an eyebrow, a familiar storm warning to everyone who worked for him. Bill Sullivan, one of the earliest Jungle Cruise skippers said, "We all knew this—if he raised that left eyebrow, you knew your ass was in trouble."

He continued his wanderings—or what might have been called wanderings had they been conducted at a slower tempo. He was fifty-three years old, slightly overweight, an incessant smoker, but during the past months he had amazed his colleagues by how quickly he could move about his future park. An employee setting out in a car to check on a mechanical crocodile or a still-dry bend of riverbed would find that Disney had somehow beaten him there on foot.

The scary eyebrow was seen more often in his studio than at the work site. He could be chilly and remote, stingy with praise, but there was nothing of the snob about him. He always liked having a franks-and-beans lunch with his workers in the food tents that had fueled his increasingly large force as the park neared completion.

He eventually came upon one of his art directors, Ken Anderson—who had been on his feet for days—groggily painting an attraction. Disney joined him and picked up a brush.

When they were done, the two walked down Main Street, an exuberant fantasy based on turn-of-the-century commercial architecture, to what had been named Town Square.

They sat together on a curb looking out over the dully gleaming streetcar tracks, which stood on Orange County dirt: the paving around them had yet to be laid. Disney put a match to a Chesterfield, his brand of cigarettes; he was always lighting a Chesterfield. Before he'd finished it, a workman hurried up. "There's no power on the Toad ride! Somebody cut the wires!"

Anderson wearily rose to his feet. "Don't worry, Walt. I'll take care of it." He went off into the clanging darkness.

The air was dense and close; tomorrow would be a scorcher. Well, that was better than the biblical sluices of rain that had recently swamped the site. Disney decided to call it quits for the night. He walked toward one of the Town Square civic buildings, a firehouse, and climbed the stairs behind it to the apartment he'd had built on the second floor. It was small, but prettily decorated in the high-middle-class style of fifty years earlier.

The last of a thousand, ten thousand, decisions lay behind him in the ruckus and dazzle beyond the narrow windows. There'd been a plumbers' strike, and he'd had to make a choice between installing drinking fountains or restrooms. "People can drink Pepsi-Cola," he said, "but they can't pee in the street."

The street was still unfinished. From the distance came the prehistoric grumblings of trucks pouring the asphalt that crowds of people— governors, movie stars, railroad presidents, hordes of children—would be walking come daylight when Disneyland opened its gates for the first time.

Outside, ecstasies of threats and swearing rose between the workers trying to set curbstones and the television crews whose wiring they were screwing up. Not only was Disney inaugurating an amusement park, he was to be the host of the largest live TV show ever mounted. Stations from New York to San Francisco had been stripped of equipment for this extravaganza. The American Broadcasting Company had spent weeks prerecording shows so the station wouldn't have to go dead during the days leading up to the ceremonies.

ABC was Disney's main sponsor. He had twisted the company's corporate arm to make a deal: I'll give you programming if you'll help pay for my park.

That was a deal the better-established stations, CBS and NBC, wouldn't touch. They wanted a Disney show, too, but not enough to get involved with the amusement park industry, which by 1955 had become widely perceived as both dangerous and disreputable.

"Why build an amusement park?" Walt's wife, Lillian, asked him.

They're so squalid and depressing. His brother Roy, an immensely capable businessman, had posed the same question. "Walt will get over it," he'd assured people back in the beginning. But Walt hadn't, and now Roy was in the same boat with him.

Disney went to bed.

He'd come a long way from being the farm boy who had shivered along snowy predawn streets delivering newspapers to help keep his family solvent in Kansas City. He was famous now, had almost single-handedly brought animation from a coarse novelty to a highly profitable art, but at the moment he felt no more secure than he had back in Missouri.

"Why did you do this?" a journalist asked amid the park's scaffolding, and received the simple answer "For twenty years I wanted something of my own." There was a good deal more to it than that. Disney had become tired of animation, had been embittered by a 1941 strike at his studio, and like so many at the end of World War II felt dissatisfied and adrift.

And this man who had so acute a sense of what the public would respond to believed that other Americans shared such feelings—that there was a vast potential audience in need of reassurance.

The present is a bully, always making us think the molten moment we inhabit is the most alarming ever, while the past tends to slip into that specious category of "simpler times." The 1950s now bask in the sunshine of false memory: sock hops, genial Ike, two-car garages, Elvis, and a victorious America, her manufacturing plants unshaken by a single Axis bomb in the war, bestriding the industrial world.

Few saw the decade like that while they were making their way through it. In 1947 W. H. Auden published a book-length poem in which four characters in a New York City bar discuss the cosmos. It won the Pulitzer Prize in 1948, but reading it could be heavy going. Nevertheless, it at once became universally known because of its title: *The Age of Anxiety.* That's what millions of Americans thought they were living in.

And with reason. The war had ended with the thunderclap of two doomsday weapons over Japanese cities, and just four years later Soviet

Russia, recently an ally, now a threat, possessed those weapons, too. American GIs who had never wanted to see another acre of Asian landscape found themselves fighting a shooting war against Communism in Korea and, once that dwindled to a stalemate, were being urged to help the French in Vietnam.

The fear of Communism simmered, a low fever that ran throughout the decade, spiking every few months, as when the Russians matched the new U.S. hydrogen bomb, or when Senator Joseph McCarthy claimed that reds had infiltrated American life at every level.

Nor was all the unrest in other lands; in a few months Rosa Parks would refuse to yield her seat on a Montgomery, Alabama, bus to a white passenger, thereby triggering the first direct action campaign of the modern Civil Rights Movement.

———

Walt Disney envisioned his park as an antidote to an edgy, restless, suspicious era, a concrete affirmation of the better angels of our national nature. Of course it was to be a place where people had fun and spent money, but he believed it could also, by drawing on the American past, give its visitors a faith in a safe and prosperous future.

He'd hocked his life insurance, sold his summer home, and borrowed every dollar he could to build what was a three-dimensional tribute not so much to himself as to how he would like to see the world, and persuade others to see it.

Not surprisingly, this had been a tough concept to sell. The park had struck most as a foolish extravagance at its initially projected cost of a million and a half dollars. The sound of the asphalt at last being tamped down around Town Square must have reminded Disney of the final figure: $17 million—$160 million in today's dollars. Just as he had been after his first big hit cartoon character, Oswald the Lucky Rabbit, got stolen from him in the 1920s, he was broke.

But he had built Disneyland.

If he succeeded in getting any sleep, it lasted for about two hours, troubled by the constant grind and clank of heavy equipment right beneath his window. At six o'clock he rose, got dressed, and headed for the television show rehearsal. He didn't get far. During the night paint-ers had gone over the firehouse, and their work on his apartment had dried so completely that he couldn't open the door. Walt Disney had to call one of his maintenance men to let him out, into the most impor-tant day of his life.

2

How I Got to Disneyland

I believe we divide ourselves early in life into two camps: those who like circuses, and those who prefer amusement parks.

For as long as I can remember, I've been in the latter group. Circuses always depressed me: the bored animals in the menagerie staring out through gummy eyes with a mixture of apathy and malevolence; the mirthless raillery of clowns; the acts, long and loosely conducted, featuring people in bathing suits dangling in the distant murk of the tent's top, imperiling their lives and scaring me for no satisfactory reason.

But an amusement park! Here was a bright little city in which you could roam where you pleased; drive a miniature car; or fly what Theodore Dreiser called "a captive airplane" in a vivifying, self-generated summer wind; surge through the supple wooden bracings of a roller coaster; and listen to the snare-drum rattle of the carousel band organ while awaiting that hushed moment when the shadows disappeared entirely for a pale instant and night came on—a night full of mysterious architecture, cream and crimson buildings with their onion domes and minarets picked out in colored lightbulbs.

My parents were fond of neither circuses nor amusement parks, but they were fond enough of me to make a couple of trips each season to Playland in Rye, New York, which was near Bronxville, where we'd moved from Manhattan in 1948, when I was eight months old.

The village of Bronxville was one of the earlier railroad suburbs, suckled by the New York Central—the trip from midtown Manhattan took just half an hour—and my mother had grown up there with a friend who had become the principal of the well-regarded Bronxville

Public School, which I attended from kindergarten until my high school graduation.

Looking back on my twenty years there, I sense that in some ways the village chimed with the subject of this book. I gradually became aware of all the care that went into making the town a place of insulating and sometimes novel beauty. Trees were everywhere, many of them riding the wide lawns that my friends and I heedlessly scrambled across without their owners ever giving the least hint that we might be an annoyance.

Even Bronxville's two-block business district held much to divert a child, and not only with such obvious splendors as Robert's Toytown. The butcher shop window contained neither a display of chops and sausages nor a chart showing the whereabouts of various cuts of meat on a cow, but a model of an Alpine village with a waterfall that sent *real water* trickling down through blue-white plaster channels to spill onto the nervous surface of a tiny pond. And there was Steinman's Pharmacy, where, in that time when drugstores still had lunch counters, a hamburger and French fries were mine for 30 cents.

There was a further, and subtler, diversion to be had: the domestic architecture. Although in the mid-1950s, nobody had heard the term "theme park" (nor would anyone, until Disney built the first) my town was a superbly realized one.

A designer, a man named Lewis Bowman, had lived and practiced there, and he was omniscient about the architectural past. He built many of the houses I bicycled past, and they were exact in every anachronistic detail. Not only would Bowman get the Tudor half-timbering right; he'd drop the middle of a roof an inch or two lower than its ends to suggest the house's slow settling over the centuries.

The realities of suburban real estate intruded to just the right extent: The Elizabethan manor, with its rosy old brick twisted into intricate chimneys, stood on half an acre of land. A mere hundred yards away rose the gray battlements of a keep built in the reign of Coolidge the Silent. So my friends and I could look out of the same mullioned windows that hawk-faced Elizabethan noblemen had glanced through while they wondered how the Channel fighting was going and see not sopping moorland falling away to a gaunt huddle of peasant crofts, but rather fifty feet of emerald lawn, and beyond it a Good Humor truck pulling up, ready for our business.

The landscape worked in collusion with the houses. A child walking home from the movies across summer yards, with the branches of old oaks heavy overhead and the sharp-cut edges of their leaves silhouetted by lights shining out from under slate eaves, may not learn much about nature, but he will learn a good deal about beauty.

When, years later, I began to hear how artificial and confining the suburbs were, how they represented a dishonorable retreat from real life, I took the lesson seriously, but always with a grain of complacency. If, during the last summer I lived there, in the hagridden Vietnam year of 1969, Bronxville looked reprehensible in the light of the fires that were burning twelve miles down the line in Harlem, the village had nonetheless given me a considerable gift. The lovely artifice of those lawns and houses offered my friends and me purest fantasy, resting on the solid, homely piers of the actuality of our daily lives. Surely youth can have no assurance more comforting than that.

So in a way—and this struck me only lately—I had grown up in Disneyland, or at least surrounded by many of the fixtures that have nourished its enduring popularity.

But I'm getting ahead of myself.

Back in Playland, I especially enjoyed the Old Mill, which put you in a blunt-nosed skiff that jostled gently past briefly lit scenes of miners at work and such before bobbing back out into the daylight through a curtain of water that miraculously dried up the moment the boat passed beneath it.

That was my favorite Playland ride, but it no longer wholly satisfied me, because the Bronxville Public Library had yielded up a copy of *Good Old Coney Island.* I got enough out of that book at the age of ten or so to learn that Coney was the Gibraltar, the Rockefeller Center, the St. Peter's Basilica of American amusement parks.

I started badgering my father to take me there, and eventually he put my friend Ted and me in the Chrysler, and off we went.

My goal was Steeplechase. The earliest of the three great amusement parks that brought a few hundred yards of Brooklyn shoreline international renown (Coney Island was the first place Sigmund Freud wanted to see when he visited America in 1909), Steeplechase was an immense glass and cast-iron shed with a clerestory roof, a cross between a greenhouse and a European railroad station, set in gardens and ringed with the horse-race ride that gave the park its name. It had long outlasted its rivals by the time I got there.

The tall, bright summer Sunday was gorgeous, but Coney was visibly in the hundred-year decline that has only recently begun to reverse itself. Still, there was glitter and clatter, and pitch-and-toss games nobody could win, and four coasters running. And Steeplechase.

I lurched through the rolling barrel that had thrown laughing couples together for half a century and into the underwater light of the Pavilion of Fun, which was clamorous with rides: a roof-high polished wooden slide down which I shot on a fragment of carpet, a magnificent three-tier carousel, and the Steeplechase itself. A sort of hybrid— part roller coaster, part merry-go-round—it sent wooden horses off four abreast on parallel tracks that undulated around the outside of the pavilion.

So away I went, looking not at the sky, or at the sea that had drawn New Yorkers out here for a century, but at the ground beneath me as I glided over enticing heaps of industrial clutter: fragments of rides abandoned or under repair, a mound of greasy machinery, what appeared to be cans of creosote. Then it was back to the Pavilion of Fun, where Ted and I dismounted and rejoined my father.

I enjoyed that day, but nonetheless came away with an empty feeling, because I had gone as a false-hearted suitor. Already Disneyland had colonized my imagination, and Coney's decrepit glories couldn't compete with the far grander park that coruscated behind my eyes.

A couple of years earlier my parents had bought a secondhand television set, a veteran from the dawn of the medium housed in a walnut case pierced with louvers shaped like musical clefs, behind which a scrim of goldish cloth concealed the feeble speaker, all this superstructure supporting a little gray screen the size of an apple. On Wednesday nights—and I don't think I missed a single one—I would sit before it rapt, absorbing more and more about Disneyland.

By the time Walt Disney had come to the end of that harrowing final pre-opening day, he had run, as his agreement with ABC demanded, eight months of his television program. He hadn't named his new show *Walt Disney Presents*, or *The Wonderful World of Walt Disney*, or *The Disney Hour*. It was called simply *Disneyland*, and every weekly episode was an advertisement for the still unborn park.

There'd be a couple of cartoons, some spluttering indignation from Donald Duck, and then twenty minutes about what I'd see during the Jungle Cruise, or in Tomorrowland, or on the firing step of the Frontierland stockade.

The show found a wholly persuaded client-to-be in me, and I set out at once on a campaign to get to Los Angeles. This was a far more ambitious enterprise than driving half an hour to Playland, and it took me some years to prevail. But I won in the end.

One day in 1959 my parents entrusted me, at the age of twelve, to TWA for a rumbling eternity in a prop-driven plane that pulled me across the continent. When I got off, proudly wearing the pilot wings a stewardess had pinned to my shirt, my aunt Gene and uncle Win, who lived in Santa Monica, were there to meet me.

The weather was, as on most Southern California days, sunny; and, withal, it was a sunny epoch, despite the constant subdued thrum of Cold War tensions (the first ballistic missile submarine, the USS *George Washington*, was launched in June). The nation had emerged from a recession the year before—the sharpest between World War II and 1970, but even so lasting only eight months. President Dwight D. Eisenhower had just welcomed Hawaii and Alaska into the union, and my aunt and uncle lived in a section of the country that, thanks to New Deal, wartime, and then NASA spending, was soon to enjoy an economy that stood at sixth among the world's *nations*. Southern California was also inventing new sorts of urban planning that would affect the nation as a whole—Disneyland would have a hand in that—and sending out other emissaries of change: that year, there were 145 McDonald's in operation. One would have had to be clairvoyant to perceive what the deaths of Chester Ovnand and Dale R. Buis in July portended, but they were the first Americans killed in action in Vietnam.

Although a homework assignment on Alaska had taught me the word "tundra," none of these developments made much of an impression on me (my first Big Mac still lay five years in the future). Certainly nothing about our forty-ninth and fiftieth states interested me in the least compared with my imminent trip to Disneyland, which took place two days after I arrived in California.

My expectations could not have been higher; they were met and surpassed.

Right at the outset, I, who had never shown the slightest botanical leanings, was fascinated by the floral Mickey Mouse—seven thousand flowers composed his beaming face—on the hillside that sloped up to the railroad station that, along with the recently completed Matterhorn, was the only substantial part of Disneyland visible from outside the park.

We went inside through one of the twin entrance tunnels, and I found myself in a sun-splashed 1910. A band was playing (although I only identified the song years later) "I Wonder Who's Kissing Her Now," a tune plaintive and moving even when performed at "Yankee Doodle" tempo. A glossy horse-drawn streetcar was taking on passengers for a short trip to provinces that had nothing to do with President Taft's America—fanciful destinations promised by the pennanted medieval castle at the far end of the street. I immediately understood that, wherever I was, it was nothing like any amusement park I'd ever seen. This was its own country.

I'm sure Mickey and Minnie and Goofy were there, but I was a little too old to be interested in them. What thrilled me was being given the run of the place.

Uncle Win had worked on developing acoustic homing torpedoes during the war and, having spent a good deal of time aboard submarines, was curious about Disney's newly christened fleet of them. The boats turned out not to be the predictable composition shells with seats inside, but real metal, obviously the product of a shipyard.

Win was impressed; when the hatches were dogged down, he said, "Gee!—It even *smells* right."

After the brief voyage, he and my aunt turned me loose to explore on my own.

I was lifted in a galleon out through the window of an English bedroom and sailed above nighttime London across an ocean to circle the mountains of Never Land (their peaks lurid with the nacreous shine of Day-Glo paint, the first time I'd ever seen it), where Peter Pan was locked in eternal combat with Captain Hook. After taking a raft across what seemed a wide river to Tom Sawyer Island, I manned the wooden parapets of Fort Wilderness and squeezed off shots with a rifle that made a sharp, satisfying *c-r-aaa-ck* each time I pulled the trigger.

Cruising along that river by Frontierland, I passed a burning settler's cabin, its owner lying dead at his front door, killed by Indians. (This somber scene has long since been replaced by a wise, gentle old sachem dispensing tribal lore.)

In Tomorrowland, the Autopia gave me the chance to drive, for the first time in my life, a gas-powered automobile, a skill my wife believes I have not yet entirely mastered.

The Jungle Cruise was all the *Disneyland* show had made it out to be—the tumbled, overgrown temples of a vanished race guarded now only by swaying serpents, a hippo attack foiled by our skipper's quick pistol work.

On and on—Win and Gene let me exhaust the last attraction before we left.

Despite the temples and the rifles and the flying galleon, what made the strongest impression on me was Main Street, Disney's evocation of the small-town America of his youth. Standing there in the dusk while the lights came on, I watched them limning the busy cornices as a horsecar clopped quietly past, and suddenly I wanted to stay in this place forever. And, in a way, I have. I came home from California fascinated by turn-of-the-century America, and my interest never waned. Instead, it expanded to include other aspects of our country's past, and it has put bread on my table all my working life.

I did not stay grateful to Walt Disney for this bequest. By the time

I was sixteen he embarrassed and irritated me, and in my twenties I felt he represented in its purest form a sterile, institutionalized, self-congratulatory blandness. But people keep outgrowing their outgrowing, and in the 1980s, when the presence of a four-year-old in my life forced me back to Disney's cartoons, I realized that his was a far more imaginative, less sentimental vision than I had come to believe.

So it was with the greatest interest that, thirty years after my first visit, I made my way back to Anaheim. Disneyland is the extension of the powerful personality of one man. It is not, like many perfectly good modern theme parks (of which there would be exactly none without him), a consensus on what might make a nice place. It *is* a nice place, of course—so much so that the standard criticism claims it is altogether too sanitized, too cut off from true experience. This doesn't bother me much; the world serves up no end of true experience whether you want it or not, and I don't mind somebody trying to trick me into thinking otherwise for a day or two. But I was interested to see whether Disney's American past was simply the pap some historians have called it.

Disneyland's reconstructed past begins at the gate. The first building you see as you enter is the Main Street Station, and chances are good one of the trains that serves it will be pulling in. These are the McCoy: three-foot-gauge live-steam locomotives ravishingly polished and painted. And for all the fantasy that lies ahead, there's nothing on earth more real than the lush, brassy call of their whistles.

Beyond the station lies Disneyland's main drag. You get to Fantasyland, Tomorrowland, and the other lands by walking past a couple of blocks of early 1900s storefronts. The models for them can be found in any small midwestern city, but these have been embellished. They seethe with elaborate decoration; half the windows are topped with colorful awnings; Queen Anne exuberance is brought to its final ebullient absurdity. But the overall effect is not absurd. It is amusing and comforting—amusing because it is so cannily done, comforting because the set designers Disney had build his street employed the old stage trick of forced perspective. On the street floor the buildings are seven-eighths full size, the second stories are five-eighths, the third one-half. The result is that your eye says you are looking at full-size buildings, but you feel about them as you do about every revisited place of your youth: it is all so much smaller.

Walt Disney's first Main Street was Kansas Avenue in Marceline, Missouri. His father bought a farm near there in 1906, but before long had to put the property up for auction, and with the proceeds he bought a paper route in Kansas City. At the age of nine Walt was climbing out of bed every morning at three-thirty to go to work. "In the winters there'd be as much as three feet of snow," he recalled toward the end of his life. "I was a little guy and I'd be up to my nose in snow. I still have nightmares about it. What I really liked on those cold mornings was getting to the apartment buildings. I'd drop off the papers and then lie down in the warm apartment corridor and snooze a little and try to get warm." Summers were better. Disney's father didn't believe children should have toys, but "on nice mornings I used to come to houses with those big old porches and the kids would have left some of their toys out. I would find them and play with them there on the porch at four in the morning when it was just barely getting light. Then I'd have to tear back to the route again."

It seems to me that something of that experience—the grueling work, the stolen scraps of rest and pleasure—charges the best of Disney's cartoons and imparts the underlying toughness that separates them from even their most successful rivals. It's what fascinates children about them, too. There is real menace, real danger, along with the comedy.

When Disney came to build his world, he included the occasional show of fangs—Mr. Toad's Wild Ride in Fantasyland, for instance, sends cute ancient motorcars careering along a course that ends with Mr. Toad dead and in hell—but he chose to have his small town be a place of absolute safety, to make permanent the feel of those fleeting moments on the morning porches. His interest in the American past didn't end with his street. He had that steam-powered Mississippi River stern-wheeler constructed from the keel up; he launched a scrupulous reproduction of a 1787 three-masted merchant vessel to share the river with it; built Fort Wilderness in Frontierland; and as soon as the technology permitted him to develop what he called Audio Animatronics, he made a life-size Abraham Lincoln who spoke with eerie, waxen conviction.

But it is still his Main Street that stays with me most strongly. I believe it was a triumph of historical imagination. It was not at all true to the physical reality of the past that Disney knew: Kansas Avenue in Marceline was rutted, raw, shorn of trees. But however crude and unformed those streets look to us today, they revealed something else to the people who lived on them. The architectural styles which Disney artfully elaborated were sufficiently decorative in their original form to mirror the era's confidence in human and material progress. The fact that such optimism is only part of the story does not make it a lie. Sinclair Lewis found his Main Street foul with hypocrisy, cant, and blighted aspirations. He wasn't wrong. But neither was Walt Disney.

From its earliest days, Disneyland has fomented strenuous and articulate hostility. That a California amusement park could summon clouds of scholarly controversy and flaying examination only confirms that here was something new, both in public entertainment and in how it expressed the way millions of Americans want to view their country— more than seven hundred million so far, and they just keep on coming.

The accretion of hostile criticism through the years—it has never ceased—reflects the park's uniqueness, and just as strongly that of the man who built it with a watchmaker's precision, an artist's conviction, and the recklessness of a riverboat gambler.

Disneyland may have begun with a toy train (it enjoys a dozen creation myths), but it indisputably began with a young cartoonist who, having been cheated out of an amusing rabbit, decided to replace it with an amusing mouse: the man Walt Disney's shrewd biographer Steven Watts called "the most influential American of the twentieth century."

3

A Horrible Name for a Mouse

Walter Elias Disney was born in 1901, the fourth son of Flora and Elias Disney. His father incubated a peculiar joyless blend of grim Protestant work ethic and socialism; his mother was softer, an ameliorating presence in the house. Walt's older brother Roy said, "We had a wonderful mother that could kid the life out of my dad when he was in his peevishness." When she couldn't, she did her best to soften things for the boys, sometimes handing them slices of bread buttered on the bottom so their father wouldn't see them being spoiled with such a luxury. Elias soon moved his family away from the urban snares of Chicago to Marceline.

Their farm, like every farm, demanded hard work, which, in this case, was thankless: Elias Disney believed that using fertilizer on a crop was like giving whiskey to an alcoholic. He refused to do it, with the predictable results.

While his brothers worked from "can't see to can't see," Walt was too young to be any help, and he had the run of the place. He loved it. There were animals to play with, a pig to ride, a Maltese terrier that all his life he would refer to as "my pal," and he loved Marceline's modest main street. That happy time ended abruptly in 1911, when Elias transplanted Walt to Kansas City and sent him out to years of predawn drudgery on the paper route. His rural world was gone forever—just as it was vanishing from the nation at large in those years—but his animal pals would populate his cartoons, and his idealized main street would be retrieved as the boulevard that gave access to his future paradise.

He did, however, briefly hold a job he far preferred to delivering newspapers. For a while he worked as a "news butcher" on the Missouri Pacific trains out of Kansas City, passing through the cars selling the passengers papers, snacks, smokes, and sundries, all the while "feeling very important wearing a neat blue serge uniform with brass buttons, a peaked cap, and a shiny badge on my lapel." The job, he said years later, was "brief, exciting, and unprofitable." The excitement more than made up for the dismal wages: "As the train rolled into one station after another, I stood beside the conductor on the car steps to enjoy the envious stares of youngsters waiting on the platform." Like so many boys of the era he was enthralled by the railroad's speed, its power, its ability to conjure fresh scenery every few seconds: "Railroads loomed large in the scheme of things," he said, "and steam engines were formidable and exciting."

Perhaps he didn't mind the drop in wages, but his father would have, and before long Walt was back on his paper route. Worn down by his predawn deliveries, he dozed through his grammar school classes and brought home poor grades. But as he got older, he summoned the energy to take Saturday classes at the Kansas City Art Institute. Perhaps this, too, was a reflection of the remembered pleasures of Marceline: it was there that the boy had been overwhelmed to receive a quarter for his drawing of the much-admired horse that powered his neighbor Dr. Sherwood's buggy.

In 1917 the restless Elias furthered his marginal career by moving back to Chicago to take a hand in running the O-Zell jelly company. In high school there, Walt drew cartoons vilifying the Kaiser for the school newspaper and took courses at the Chicago Academy of Fine Arts.

For one who was to spend much of his working life celebrating the virtues of family, he was eager to get away from his. Turned down by the army because of his youth, he forged an earlier date on his birth certificate, and in September of 1918 the sixteen-year-old joined the Red Cross as an ambulance driver. He arrived in France shortly after the November 11 Armistice put an end to the war, but there was still plenty to do, and he spent a crowded year there, during which he found time to decorate the sides of ambulances and, for ten francs, paint designs on his comrades' jackets.

By the time he returned to the States, in the fall of 1919, his brothers, weary of their father's skinflint socialism, had decamped. Soon, he did, too.

Wanting nothing to do with O-Zell jellies, and failing to land a job at a Kansas City newspaper, he talked his way into an enterprise called the Pesmen-Rubin Commercial Art Studio. For a few weeks he had a fine time making advertising layouts, writing copy, and designing program covers for local movie houses. Then Christmas came and went, carrying away in its wake much of Pesmen-Rubin's business, and Disney was out on the January streets along with another brief hire, who had the unusual name of Ubbe Iwerks.

Disney liked Iwerks and suggested the optimistic idea that they form a partnership. They did: at first it was Disney-Iwerks, and then Iwerks-Disney (this was not modesty on Disney's part: he thought the former name suggested a firm of opticians).

The fetal business foundered in weeks, but Disney wangled a job at the Kansas City Film Ad Company, and soon got the firm to hire Iwerks, who had changed his first name to the thriftier but no less eccentric Ub. Their new employer produced minute-long promotional films for local businesses that ran in the city's movie houses. Even for that morning time of animation, these were crude: black cutouts, hinged at the arms and legs like Balinese shadow puppets, would be shot for a couple of frames against a white background, moved a fraction of an inch, and shot again.

Disney immediately sought more advanced technology, as he would for the rest of his career. He found books on animation, borrowed a camera, and started experimenting, soon settling on celluloid as the best medium for making cartoons. A series of drawings on transparent sheets showing a capering chicken or a running cat would be placed over a static background—a barn, a city street corner—and these cels were photographed in sequence.

Soon he was producing short cartoon ads he called "Laugh-O-Grams," and then he made longer cartoons drawn from fairy tales.

He went bankrupt in 1923 after completing an ambitious project called *Alice's Wonderland*, a blend of live action, on the part of a young girl, and animated figures.

New York was the capital of the young cartoon industry, but Disney moved to join his brother Roy in Los Angeles when an Alice sample he had sent back east drew the attention of a film distributor named Margaret Winkler, who was about to lose the rights to the popular *Felix the Cat* cartoons. She gave Disney a contract for six Alice episodes. With Roy as his business manager—for the rest of Walt's life, as it turned out—he began hiring a larger staff and persuaded Ub Iwerks to join him. One of the new people who came aboard as a secretary in 1925 was an Idaho girl named Lillian Bounds. She and Disney were married a few months later—by all accounts happily, in the main, although Lillian never cared much for Hollywood and was not greatly interested in Walt's movies.

Alice ran out of steam in 1927. Margaret Winkler had by then turned over the distribution business to her husband, Charles Mintz, who urged Disney to come up with something new that he could market through Universal Pictures. Disney responded with Oswald the Lucky Rabbit, which proved so solid a success that early in 1928 he confidently went east with Lillian to meet with Mintz and ask for more money. Mintz offered him less. Disney indignantly refused, and discovered that not only did Universal own the rights to Oswald, but that Mintz had hired away his entire animation staff save for Iwerks. The steely distributor told him, "Either you come with me at my price, or I'll take your organization away from you. I have your key men signed up."

Disney never hesitated, but he and Lillian had a forlorn cross-country trip ahead of them. Who knows what happened on that anxious train ride? The conception of Disney's next character is clouded in contradictory stories. But Lillian said that while she sat brooding, "watching the green of the Middle West change to sagebrush and desert," Walt scribbled out a scenario involving a comical mouse named Mortimer. He read it to her, and all her worries about the suddenly uncertain future coalesced around that name; she found it ponderous, fussy, and pretentious. For all her indifference to her husband's business, Lillian Disney right then made perhaps the single most important contribution to it: "Mortimer is a horrible name for a mouse!"

Disney liked the lilt of "Mortimer Mouse," but after thinking it over for a while, he came up with a friendlier name.

Back in Los Angeles, he and Iwerks began to work up Mickey Mouse: round head, round ears, short pants with two buttons (no gloves, as yet). This was looking good.

Mickey Mouse was introduced to the world as an aviator in *Plane Crazy*, which hoped to capitalize on Charles Lindbergh's recent transatlantic flight, followed by some southwestern scuffling called *The Gallopin' Gaucho*. Both cartoons were initially filmed without sound, and Disney was dissatisfied. The 1927 filmic counterpart to Lindbergh's triumph was Al Jolson's hit *The Jazz Singer*, which was only a talkie partway through but still a novelty powerful enough to transform the industry. For his third Mickey short Disney hired an orchestra and an arranger to produce *Steamboat Willie*, the first sound cartoon.

It was a sensation. As Oswald quietly joined the immense menagerie of forgotten cartoon animals, Mickey—and Disney with him—rose to such heights that just a few years after his birth the gossip empress Louella Parsons could write, "Mickey Mouse has a bigger following than nine tenths of the stars in Hollywood."

The early Mickey was a scruffy reprobate. He knocked back beers and danced lasciviously with Minnie Mouse; he smoked cigarettes; he was mean. As his fame grew, however, his character and his outline softened until eventually he would cease to be a character at all, but rather the benign, denatured spirit that served as a sort of papal ambassador to the vast Disney enterprise.

In the meantime, Disney's cartoons became subtler and more fluent. He added color to them, and began to garner Academy Awards. In 1933 he released what one media historian has called "the most successful short animation of all time," *Three Little Pigs*, whose song "Who's Afraid of the Big, Bad Wolf" became a defiant ballad of the Depression years. Of its success, Disney said, "The main thing was a certain recognition from the industry and the public that these things [cartoons] could be more than just a mouse hopping around." Urged to make a sequel, he declined, his terse refusal a fine show-business apothegm: "You can't top pigs with pigs."

As that suggests, he was tiring of his short films, successful though they were. In 1934 he embarked on making the first feature-length cartoon. He had budgeted a half million dollars for *Snow White and the Seven Dwarfs*; it ended up consuming a million and a half, and four years. By the time it was released, in 1937, it had become known in Hollywood as "Disney's folly."

Snow White was a triumph. The biggest hit of 1938 and the most profitable sound film yet made, it took in $6.5 million and propelled its creator into *Pinocchio* and the wildly complex (and possibly overblown) *Fantasia*. The next couple of years were the most satisfying Disney would know until he began to toy with the idea of an amusement park.

Things soured for him quickly. His next two features performed tepidly at the box office, partly because the war that began with Hitler's invasion of Poland choked off his European market. Revenues dwindled, he had to take his company public, and deep salary cuts triggered an ugly strike at his studio. It only lasted five weeks, but it left Disney with a lifelong grievance. He became increasingly austere (some of his staff thought tyrannical), remote, and politically conservative. The strike, he believed, had largely been a Communist effort.

And the bad feelings the relatively brief fracas engendered might account for the genesis of something darker than a reputation for authoritarian crankiness: many people today believe Disney was an anti-Semite. There is scant evidence for this. He fired two of his lawyers when he overheard them disparaging a pair of his songwriters for being Jews; he was happy to have his daughters date Jewish boys; and he was the 1955 choice of the Beverly Hills chapter of B'nai B'rith as "Man of the Year." When the rumors of such ill feelings reached Kay Kamen, his Jewish head of merchandising (who, with the Ingersoll company, gave his boss and the world the preposterously successful Mickey Mouse watch), he dismissed them with the remark that Disney's organization "had more Jews in it than the Book of Leviticus."

When the war came to America, Disney spent several arid years while his Walt Disney Training Films Unit made shorts with titles such as *Four Methods of Flush Riveting*. By 1945 he was exhausted and in debt. Nor were his spirits improved by a brief postwar flurry of turning out commercial films—*The ABC of Hand Tools*—and he abandoned that in 1946 after issuing only twelve.

As did tens of thousands of others in those postwar months, he felt, he said, that "it seemed like a hopeless thing to begin to pick up again." His daughter Diane wrote, "I think it was just after the war when nothing seemed to stimulate him. I could sort of sense it. I could tell he wasn't pleased with anything he was doing."

One small enterprise did please him, though, and it had little to do with the art he had done so much to invent and of which he was the undisputed master.

In the Christmas season of 1947 he bought himself a gift, "something I've wanted all my life": a Lionel electric train set. He put together the layout next to his office so he could play with his railroad in odd hours. Then he thought it would be nice to add some sidings, and then put in a little landscaping, and then . . . Any collector or hobbyist will recognize the fatal progression.

When, in the early 1950s, the *New York Times* film critic Bosley Crowther visited Disney, he was dismayed to find that the man whose work he had long admired "seemed totally uninterested in movies and seemed wholly, almost weirdly concerned with the building of a miniature railroad engine and a string of cars. . . . All of his zest for invention, for creative fantasies, seemed to be going into this plaything. I came away feeling sad."

4

The Railroad Fair

Of all the influences that helped shape Disneyland, the railroad is the seminal one. Or, rather, *a* railroad, one Disney owned. It had no connection whatever with the Christmas Lionel set. This was an honest-to-god outdoor operation with grade crossings and signals, tracks and a roadbed, its centerpiece a live-steam locomotive powerful enough to haul several adults perched on miniature freight cars over a half-mile right-of-way that wound through the grounds of a new house Disney had built especially to accommodate it.

It came about because of a remark made to Disney by the studio nurse, Hazel George.

Although polo is a sport not readily associated with a midwestern farm boy, Disney was an enthusiastic player in the 1930s, at one point owning a string of nineteen ponies. He liked the game and went at it hard, if not skillfully. (His brother Roy's son, Roy E. Disney, said, "I was watching a match between my dad's team and Walt's team when someone asked me to point out my uncle. 'He's the one who just fell off his horse,' I remember answering.") Disney's doctor became increasingly concerned about the bruises he kept finding on his patient's legs, and finally told him to quit the game when, knocked from the saddle by a hard-driven ball, Disney fractured four neck vertebrae.

He sold his ponies, but the injury pained him on and off for the rest of his life. By the 1940s he was ending his working days prone on a massage table in a room next to his office while Hazel George treated his neck with ice, hot towels, and a vigorous massage.

Disney came to look forward to these sessions for more than the relief they gave him. George, who had come to the studio during the 1941 strike, was tart, sardonic, and quick-witted. She once said, "Walt was more at ease with women than he was with men," and he was completely at ease with George, happily swapping studio gossip with her.

She took good care of him. When he complained that he couldn't get at his day's-end ration of scotch while lying on his stomach, she solved the problem with the simple expedient of supplying a straw. She was loyal, but no pushover. Once, when he gave voice to a timeless entrepreneur's plaint—"After I die, I would hate to look down at this studio and find everything in a mess"—she replied, "What makes you think you won't be using a periscope?" ("Smartass," Disney grunted.)

During their sessions in 1948 George began to sense that her boss was sinking into what seemed to her a dangerous depression, perhaps even heading toward what was then called a nervous breakdown. He'd had one—or something like it—back in 1931. Years later he said of that time, "I had a hell of a breakdown. I went all to pieces. . . . As we got going along I kept expecting more from the artists and when they let me down and things, I got worried. Just pound, pound, pound. Costs were going up and I was always way over what they figured the pictures would bring in. . . . I just got very irritable. I got to a point that I couldn't talk on the telephone. I'd begin to cry."

He had recovered by taking a leisurely cross-country trip with Lillian—"the first time we had been away on anything like that since we were married"—and returned, he said, "a new man."

Now it seemed again to be just pound, pound, pound. Once more the money wasn't coming in: his last successful feature, *Bambi*, was six years in the past, *Cinderella* nowhere near finished, the studio, like the country, in the uneasy postwar doldrums. Disney was often aggrieved, abrupt, and, when not angry, remote.

George told him he had to take a vacation. She had a "perfect" one in mind.

Disney would have spoken with her about his brief stint as a news butcher on the Missouri Pacific, and his Lionel train. She had spotted a newspaper report of a forthcoming all-train pageant: the Chicago Railroad Fair. Under the aegis of the Chicago Museum of Science and

Industry, the New York Central, Northern Pacific, Rock Island, Illinois Central, Great Northern, Erie, and thirty other lines had built exhibits on fifty acres of Lake Michigan shorefront.

Disney, instantly intrigued, said he'd like to go. George suggested he take Ward Kimball along. "Yeah," said Disney, "Kimball is always relaxed. Maybe it's because he's got such a wonderful hobby running that big steam engine in his backyard."

———

The animator Ward Kimball is the only man that anyone ever heard Walt Disney call a "genius." He worked up Jiminy Cricket for *Pinocchio* and developed the affable crows in *Dumbo*, later sometimes denounced as being racist, although they save the film's hero, teach him to fly, and outclass every white in the movie. Kimball was the studio's train man. When a locomotive needed animating, he was usually the first choice for the job. His was the locomotive that Mr. Toad hijacks in *The Wind in the Willows*, and he created the hardworking little Casey Jr. that pulls Dumbo's circus train.

He collected trains, too, and on a heroic scale: model trains, toy trains, and actual trains. Kimball had begun with the toys and models, and then, thinking it might be nice to display them in an authentic setting, acquired, in 1938, a sixty-year-old passenger car from the Carson & Colorado. Few hobbyists can have been more fortunate in their marriage: it was Ward's wife, Betty, who, evidently believing the coach looked lonely all by itself, told her husband he should get a locomotive. They found one built by the Baldwin Works in 1881 that the Nevada Central had long since retired, and bought it for $400. Ward and Betty were drawn to it not only for its battered authenticity, but because it was narrow-gauge.

A railroad's "gauge" means the width between the inside facing edges of the rails that carry the train. Before the Civil War, lines tended to choose their gauges arbitrarily, causing much effort and sorrow: any trip to a destination that was served by tracks of another gauge meant a change of trains; travelers heading south from Baltimore in the 1850s had to board eight different ones before they reached New Orleans. A much-needed rationalization began to come in with the completion of the Transcontinental Railroad in 1869. Its rails were spaced (rather mysteriously) at 4 feet, 8½ inches; other roads followed its powerful example, and today this is the standard gauge throughout North America.

Standard gauge carried the heavy freights and fast passenger trains between cities, but for lighter, less-demanding work, a network of narrow-gauge railroads grew up. Usually three-footers, they were far cheaper to maintain, useful for big plantations, logging and mining operations, and connecting thinly populated communities. The gauge naturally dictated the size of the rolling stock, and so the locomotives and cars were much smaller. That gave them considerable charm: here was real, working equipment that nonetheless had about it a beguiling feel of the toylike.

Kimball spent years restoring his locomotive, which he christened the *Emma Nevada* after a celebrated California-born operatic soprano, spiked down nine hundred feet of track, and had it running by 1942. Before long his Baldwin was joined by a second engine, a wood-burner that had served a Hawaiian sugar plantation. The Kimballs' unorthodox honeymoon had taken them on an exploration of parched, half-forgotten logging and mining towns in the Sierra Nevada, and there they came upon the single remaining building of a long-vanished hamlet: a post office bearing the name Grizzly Flats. They brought the name home with them and bestowed it on their line. The Grizzly Flats Railroad gave Kimball the distinction of being the only American to own a full-size, operating train in his backyard.

A gregarious couple, the Kimballs often held "steam-ups" where they fed their friends and gave them rides. Disney first saw the Grizzly Flats Railroad at work in the fall of 1945. Kimball gave him a turn at the throttle; it was the first time Disney had been in the cab of a locomotive since his Missouri Pacific days. Kimball said, "I'm sure that I never saw him smile wider than that evening when he pulled the throttle on the *Emma Nevada* as she steamed out of the enginehouse with her bell ringing and whistle blowing."

That enthusiasm had clearly stayed with him, for after George planted the idea of the Railroad Fair he got on the phone at once.

"Hey, Kimball, this is Walt."

"Walt who?"

"Disney!" ("Walt who?" was a joke, one Kimball played again and again; he claimed his boss never caught on.) "There's a swell train show they're opening in Chicago down by the lake. It's supposed to be the biggest event in railroad history and I want to go."

So did Kimball, whose boss "said we would have to leave in two days to make it in time. I had been reading about the rail fair in the papers; how all the famous, historical railroad locomotives were refurbished, reboiled, retubed, and put in running order by the big railroads. I replied to Walt, 'Wow, I want to see that.' Here was my chance. So, I told him I'd be happy to go along."

A couple of days later Kimball and Disney boarded the Santa Fe's crack *Super Chief* and headed east. Disney established himself as the senior partner of the duo at their first dinner. The railroad-omniscient Kimball knew just what he wanted long before he saw the menu. "I was looking forward to that famous selection, 'Santa Fe Beef Stew.' They had a way of preparing the dish where they would sear the meat before they put it in with the vegetables and potatoes. It had a wonderful flavor. All my railroad friends talked about it, and I was looking forward to this moment on the *Super Chief*, going over the Cajon Pass through the San Bernardino mountain range, eating Santa Fe's delicious stew."

Disney told the steward, "I'll have the filet mignon steak, rare." Kimball said, "I'm having your wonderful and famous beef stew."

Nothing doing. "Beef stew, for God's sake!" Disney snorted, and countermanded the order: "He means he really wants the filet mignon."

This was a surprising exercise of Disney's executive power, because he was not a filet mignon man. His years on a short financial tether had given him a lifelong fondness for lunch-wagon cooking.

In 1956 his daughter Diane wrote, "He likes fried potatoes, hamburgers, western sandwiches, hot cakes, canned peas, hash, stew, roast-beef sandwiches. He's not keen for steak—or any of the expensive cuts of meat." When he came home for dinner in the 1950s, Diane said, he'd ask Thelma, their cook and housekeeper, what's for dinner. "If it's steak, he'll say, 'Oh, steaks,' with a falling note in his voice to indicate disappointment."

But possibly at that moment on the *Super Chief* he was living the railroad life of his youth, when the high rollers in the dining car would settle for nothing less than a porterhouse that overlapped its platter.

In any event, that night the two had filet mignon, and so it went, with Disney calling all the shots. During the forty-hour trip, he would knock on the wall between their adjoining roomettes and shout, "Kimball, come in here, let's have a drink."

The drink was scotch, poured from the cut-crystal decanter in Disney's leather travel bar, and Kimball hated scotch: "It was like drinking some kind of lye solution."

There were compensations. Kimball, like almost everyone who encountered Disney, said he was a superb storyteller. He rarely developed friendships with his employees, and became even more distant from them after the strike. Now though, cut loose from his company, he talked and talked, reminiscing about his past, formulating plans for the future, and assessing that newcomer, television. He did chew over his bitterness about the strike—"He couldn't give that up," Kimball said—but for the most part he was happy and relaxed.

The railroad companies had allowed themselves only six months' preparation time to, as their promotional brochure put it, "give America its first great outdoor exposition since the war." They'd come through impressively. The fair's main event, "Wheels a-Rolling," took place on a 450-foot-wide stage fronting the lake. Two-story-high panels at either side served as the wings, from behind which a century's worth of rolling stock emerged twice daily to encapsulate the rise of American motive power.

The promoters did their best to herald an expansive future. The Chesapeake & Ohio presented "a full-scale model of a passenger car designed for its new, lightweight 'Train X' . . . designed to permit speeds up to 150 miles an hour," and the show ended on a note of triumphant modernity, richly described in the fair's guidebook: "The pulsing music of Modern America soars up to the heavens and out across the fleeting whitecaps of beautiful Lake Michigan. Nowhere, nowhere today is there a frontier! Modern transport has met the supreme challenge of the horizon! And so, an epic of progress—an adventure in speed and growth—comes to a close . . . as two of railroading's newest miracles—a giant steam locomotive and a magnificent new diesel—slowly, majestically form the final curtain."

Nevertheless, the feel of the entire fair was one of elegy. The giant modern steam engine was indeed imposing: some American locomotives had grown to be eighty-five feet long and weigh three-quarters of a million pounds; but, like the dinosaurs, they became their largest on the eve of their extinction. The fair was really about the past, and the "Wheels a-Rolling" tableaus were, all but the final one, historical: locomotives from the 1830s, the *Pioneer* that steamed into Chicago in 1848, Lincoln's funeral train, the driving of the Golden Spike completing the Transcontinental, the New York Central's tall fleet 999, built in 1893 and said to be the first wheeled object to exceed one hundred miles per hour.

All this of course was deeply appealing to Kimball and Disney. When Lenox Lohr, head of the Museum of Science and Industry, discovered they were there, he opened the whole backstage area to them. "We could do anything we wanted," said Kimball. "They let us run the steam locomotives around the three or four miles of trackage." He was allowed to drive the *DeWitt Clinton*, a replica, created for the 1893 Chicago World's Fair, of the fourth locomotive made in America. For Kimball, "It was like shaking hands with George Washington."

The two watched "Wheels a-Rolling" several times. Disney wept at each appearance of Lincoln's funeral train, and he put on an 1870s top hat and frock coat to join the extras in the scene where "steel flows straight and guitars play sweetly as Fred Harvey introduces wholesome waitresses and wholesome food to the rough and tumble frontier towns of the old Southwest."

But what most impressed him were the fair's ancillary exhibits.

One can see some of the spores that would blow into Disneyland in the guidebook's description: "In its acres of exhibits the Railroad Fair offers hours of fascinating enjoyment, intriguing pageantry, invaluable education. Taken back to that early day when an unbelieving American looked askance at the first wood-burning locomotive, you will move rapidly forward to the mammoth streamliners that beckon the way into our own tomorrow. . . . Each exhibit will prove an exciting and entirely different chapter in a stirring melodrama. While one railroad in truly duplicated surroundings will take you into the primitive Indian country it serves, another will carry you away to the playgrounds of Florida or the romantic old French Quarter of New Orleans . . . [or the] colorful old time western dance hall and other attractions capturing the exotic romance of the southwest."

Disney would have been especially drawn to the Chicago & Northwestern's display, which "re-created Chicago's first railroad station. Interior of the station replica is a popular Fair ground playhouse. Studying the quaint old building from the outside, however, you find it easy to imagine unheralded Chicago of a century ago, a muddy frontier outpost serving as a trading center for miners, merchants, farmers and Indians." He rode the "Deadwood Central" narrow-gauge from the fair's entrance to "Gold Gulch," a replica of a nineteenth-century mining town, and explored a miniature Yellowstone Park where Old Faithful spewed on an accelerated schedule.

There was gumbo to be had in the recreated French Quarter; and the people who served it were dressed in period costume, as were the miners and dance-hall girls in Gold Gulch. The exhibits added up to a coherent whole, the growth of America told in three dimensions, a history lesson you could walk through. Although the term still lay in the future, Walt Disney was visiting a theme park.

Kimball and Disney stayed at the fair for several days, and made another crucial stop on their way home, at Henry Ford's twenty-year-old Greenfield Village outside Detroit. Ford had shared both Disney's fondness for rural America and his intense dislike of the kind of labor that supported it. His "village" was a tribute to the nation's agrarian past, but even more to the industrial age that remade it. As the richest American, he was able to collect on a titanic scale. He brought Thomas Edison's Menlo Park laboratory (and seven freight car loads of the New Jersey earth it had stood on), the boardinghouse that had put up Edison's workers, the Edison Illuminating Company in Detroit where the young Ford had tended the massive dynamos. He collected the homes of people he admired—Noah Webster's, the slave cabin where George Washington Carver was born, Harvey Firestone's childhood farm—and a courthouse where the young Lincoln practiced law. He acquired not only the Wright brothers' house but the bicycle shop where they conducted their momentous experiments. Ford also shared Disney's respect for detail; he had the mortar that had bound the stones of the Wright house's foundation reground and reused.

Ford was not recreating the past as John D. Rockefeller had at Colonial Williamsburg; instead, he was building a vision of what most appealed to him about it (three watchmakers' shops in his town, and none of the banks he despised), equipped with a Florida river sternwheeler and a steam railroad.

Ford's town was an entirely personal reflection of the man. So would Disney's be "the road map of Walt Disney's life," as one of his colleagues was to say.

5

THE *LILLY BELLE*

The two travelers left the Midwest with Disney full of plans about his own Greenfield Village, his own Railroad Fair. Over the homeward-bound scotches he talked about it incessantly and scribbled down notes. "Disneyland was already forming in his mind," said Kimball. "Of course he thought [it] should have a full-size steam train that he could have fun operating himself on days when the park was closed."

A couple of days after returning to the studio, on August 31, he drafted a memo describing what he called "Mickey Mouse Park."

"The Main Village, which includes the Railroad Station is built around a village green or informal park. In the park will be benches, a bandstand, drinking fountain, trees and shrubs. It will be a place for people to sit and rest, mothers and grandmothers can watch over small children at play. I want it to be very relaxing, cool and inviting.

"Around the park will be built the town. At one end will be the Railroad Station, at the other end, the Town Hall. . . . Adjoining the Town Hall will be the Fire and Police Stations. The Fire Station will contain practical fire apparatus scaled down." There would be an opera house and movie theater, a toy store, a hobby shop, a magic store, and "an old-fashioned candy factory where we would sell candy that is no longer obtainable. We would use only the best materials and stress the fact that it is the old-fashioned kind that can't be bought today.

"The Horse Car. The car would start at the Main Entrance and pick up those who did not want to walk. The car would take them down the street to the Railroad Station. . . .

"The Western Village. A general store with a soda fountain and lunch counter. . . . We might also put in some kind of a Western museum.

"We will have a pony ring, set up in a corral, where the kids can ride.

"The Stage Coach. The coach would leave the Western village, pass through the farm, go through the Indian village and pass the old mill. This would be by a special road.

"The Donkey Pack Train. The donkeys would be all hooked together and handled by one man. This would take ten kids."

A surprising number of the ideas in this inaugural memo would come to pass, but the most immediate result of Disney's visit to the Railroad Fair was his determination to build a railroad of his own.

Roger Broggie, who had joined the studio in 1939, was head of its machine shop, and he had helped Disney set up his Lionel train. The boss told Broggie, "This is an electric train, now what's for real?"

That was a rhetorical question, one to which Disney had already received the answer in Chicago. Live steam was for real. Live steam is, after all, *live*—or at least simulates life as vigorously as Disney's cartoons do. Disney found out from Kimball that there was a fraternity of West Coast enthusiasts who had built and were running such operations. Kimball introduced him to one of them, a man named Dick Jackson, who, having made a fortune in selling after-market automobile accessories—luggage racks, spare tire mounts, horns, headlamps—had spent much of it on a one-twelfth scale (one inch on the model equals one foot on its full-size prototype) railroad in the yard of his Beverly Hills home.

Disney went out to see it, and Jackson, having explained that the scale was large enough to accommodate grown-up passengers, let him drive the locomotive, a model of a 1920 B&O passenger engine that its owner had built from the original plans. Yes, this was what Disney wanted.

He found out that there was a small industry producing miniature steam trains, but all of its products seemed drab to him—somber and gray, drearily representative of this dying time of steam railroads in North America.

Broggie, who was also interested in the hobby, took Disney to meet another fan: Jerry Best, a Warner Bros. sound engineer who not only built models but was one of the nation's leading railroad historians, with an immense collection of photographs, drawings, and models. Best introduced him to the Central Pacific's No. 173. Disney fell for it at once. Best said, "It was those pictures and my little model that sold Walt—he said that it was the most beautifully proportioned locomotive ever built, and the one he wanted for his model. He had a great eye for design."

Disney's eye hadn't failed him. The 173 was handsome as a clipper ship—long, lean, glinting with brass brightwork. Shipped around Cape Horn in pieces to California, and at work on the West Coast when the Transcontinental Railroad was completed, it was a passenger locomotive of the era, so typical that its pattern was known as the American Type, a 4-4-0—which, according to the universally used Whyte system of classification, meant that it had four pilot (leading) wheels, four larger driving wheels, and no trailing ones.

The morning after Best had loaned him photographs of the 173, he brought them to Roger Broggie's office: "I've found the design I want to build."

The Central Pacific had been absorbed by the Southern Pacific years earlier, but had kept 173's blueprints in its archives. Broggie got hold of them, and began breaking them down into working plans for a one-eighth scale model, a chore that took four months. From these were drafted thirty-five engineering drawings that scrupulously showed every gear and driving rod, and Broggie assigned various chores to his twelve-man staff, some parts to be cut in the machine shop while the studio's prop shop carved smooth wooden patterns from which castings would be made. All the finer work went to men who maintained the watch-work intricacies of the studio's animation equipment.

Disney stopped by every day to check on progress, and on one of these visits said to Broggie, with unusual diffidence, "I don't want to interfere with what the boys are doing, but I don't think it is fair that they're having all the fun. I'd like to help."

Broggie cleared off a workbench, and the next day began conducting a master class in machining for his single pupil. Disney proved a good student. "He surprised all of us," Broggie said. "In many ways Walt [was] a temperamental guy. Most of the boys didn't think he'd be much good in the shop. But he had a high aptitude for machine work."

The machinist, too, was a temperamental guy—he was known around the shop (when well out of earshot) as "the Prince of Darkness"—but the two men worked harmoniously together. "You only had to show Walt once," Broggie said, "and he got the picture." They had an affinity that went beyond Disney's being a quick study. Any good machinist— and Broggie was the best—is a perfectionist, and he saw the same in his pupil.

As Disney turned the small whistle on a jeweler's lathe, bored holes with a miniature drill press in the stanchions that would support the handrails that ran along the boiler, he took a pleasure approaching joy at seeing how exquisite his baby version of No. 173 would be, how rich with the detail he would someday demand for every aspect of his park.

Number 173 was not destined to be a mere ornament; it was to power a railway system, and Disney needed a place to run it. Early in 1949 he drove Lillian out to see a five-acre undeveloped hilltop in Holmby Hills, between Beverly Hills and Bel Air. It seemed time for a new, larger house—their two daughters, Diane and Sharon, were soon to be teenagers—and Lillian liked the site. So did her husband, although she had little idea of what chiefly drew him to it: varied terrain, a broad lower outcropping of land, fine views that would be finer still when seen from a moving train.

The Disneys bought 355 Carolwood Drive on June 1, set an architect to work on a seventeen-room house, comfortable but by no means grand by Hollywood magnate standards, and Disney took a topographical map of the property to Broggie to work out where the tracks would go. He gave the job to one of his draftsmen, Eddie Sargeant, another railroad enthusiast, who scratch-built model locomotives in his spare time. He worked up a track plan, but his first pass was too timid for Disney: "No, that's not what I want. You show track only on the lower shelf. I want the line to run completely around the house. That's why I bought five acres of land, so I'd have plenty of running room!"

Sargeant's next try was more like it: 2,615 feet of track connected with eleven switches so cunningly laid out that a train could steam along for nearly a mile without passing over any stretch of the line twice in the same direction. This won Disney's instant acceptance, but there was a problem.

Walt's track plan did not sit well with his wife. He complained to a colleague that "Lilly has made up her mind that I shouldn't run my railroad completely around the house because it was going to run right through the middle of her garden. She wanted to have a large window put in so her friends can look out at her flowers while they're playing Canasta."

Disney explained this impasse to Jack Rorex, who was in charge of construction on the studio back lot; he suggested a tunnel that, at ninety feet, would be long enough to allow the train to pass under the garden. The card players would never have to see it.

This was an expensive solution, made the more so because Rorex had suggested it be dug in the shape of an elongated "S" whose curves would prevent riders entering at one end from seeing the light at the other. Once construction was under way Rorex had second thoughts: was the sense of mystery those curves would impart really worth the trouble? He suggested to Disney it would be prudent to make the tunnel straight.

"Hell, it's cheaper not to do it at all," Disney said. Back at the studio he gave his secretary an order: "I don't want you to tell me any of the costs for the Carolwood tunnel."

The trestle proved even more extravagant. At forty-six feet long and nine high, it was large enough to bring itself under the authority of Los Angeles building codes; it demanded the same standards as any public bridge in the city. The trestle was a wooden one, made of two- by four-inch redwood beams, because, as Broggie said, "We had a goal in the shop. Everything was to be built in the same manner as the 1880s."

That rule fell apart when it came to laying the tracks. The prospect of hammering them down to the ties, yard after yard after yard, with clothespin-size spikes was too daunting. They were built by what Broggie called, with purist scorn, the "Lionel Method." That is, ten-foot sections were prefabricated—ties, spikes, and all—and set down the way they would be on a toy train layout.

The first track was laid in December of 1949, the final rails the following May. Disney named his line the Carolwood Pacific (he liked the fact that it had the same initials as the Central Pacific where the original 173 spent its working life).

The locomotive also got christened. A week before Christmas Disney came into the shop and told Broggie, "I think I have the perfect name for the locomotive. I'm going to call her *Lilly Belle*. It's for Lillian, and I think she'll be pleased. Besides, she's been a good sport about this whole railroading project."

Broggie also had some news. That morning he'd had the engine going for the first time; he had tested it with compressed air, and all the running gear functioned smoothly. Now it only remained to fire her up.

Disney startled him: "We could hold the steam-up during the Christmas party next Saturday." Broggie was not at all enthusiastic about giving the virgin locomotive its first run in front of the staff: steam was far more powerful than compressed air, and all sorts of flaws might reveal themselves.

So began a busy few days. The cab wouldn't be finished on time, but the tender had to be, as it carried not only the fuel and water, but the engineer. Broggie's men attended to the final touches while the prop crew laid a three-hundred-foot circle of track in Sound Stage 1. On Christmas morning Broggie trundled the engine and tender—seven feet long, 350 pounds—over from the machine shop and set them on the track.

Special scale-size coal, ordered from Pennsylvania, went into the firebox; water was pumped from the tender to the boiler, the fire lighted. The engine creaked and pinged as pressure mounted; when it reached its maximum of 120 pounds per square inch, the safety valve did its job, lifting and slobbering out excess steam. Disney reached down and tugged the whistle valve; it's four-note voice filled the cavernous hall with surprising authority.

No question of who would get the first ride. Disney sat on the tender, braced his feet on two pegs that extended from its forward sides, and cracked the throttle. Steam punched into the cylinders, the pistons slid, and the driving wheels began to turn. For a moment they slipped on the rails, then gained traction and, hissing and chirping and spilling pungent coal smoke, the *Lilly Belle* steamed forward with tiny majesty past the cheering staff and the deeply relieved Broggie.

———

The *Lilly Belle* went to work the next May, when she arrived in Holmby Hills from the studio and was, for the first time, mounted on the road that had been prepared for her. Surrounded by landscapers still at work on the grounds, Disney spent some time admiring his creation. She made a brave sight: bright red driving wheels, blued-steel jacket held to the boiler by polished brass bands that blazed in the California sunshine, and teeming with Disney-delighting detail. Railroad headlamps, for instance, were elaborate affairs in the 1860s, and so was the *Lilly Belle*'s: scarlet and gilt, with side panels bearing appropriate scenes painted by a studio artist showing a view of the Yosemite Valley on one, a bull elk on the other.

The locomotive's minute precision spooked Salvador Dalí, who was in a short-lived but cordial collaboration with Disney. He darkly imagined small-scale disasters "or even sabotage . . . like miniature train wreckers! Such perfection did not belong to models."

The *Lilly Belle* was joined by equally perfect freight cars, a yellow caboose that Disney built entirely by himself—it took him a full year—and six passenger-carrying gondolas. Unlike the other cars, which were made solely from the same materials that went into their nineteenth-century prototypes, these latter were molded aluminum. But care was taken that the wood grain on the patterns showed up in the metal, which, once painted, was indistinguishable from wood until you touched it (a technique that would show up again in Disneyland).

Once up and running, this spectacular plaything proved immensely popular. The Disneys weren't much for going to Hollywood parties, but they enjoyed holding gatherings at which the Carolwood Pacific was the main event, and now a good deal of Hollywood came to them: Frank Sinatra, the six-year-old Candice Bergen with her famous ventriloquist father Edgar, the producers Walter Wanger and Hal Wallis, the durable doyenne Mary Pickford, Kirk Douglas (who had a leading role in Disney's *20,000 Leagues Under the Sea*, and rather churlishly sued the studio for $415,000 for invasion of privacy when a clip of him aboard the train appeared later in a Disney television show). Every guest went for a ride, eleven to a trainload—the muscular *Lilly Belle* could haul two thousand pounds—peering down from a berm into what Disney named the Yensid Valley ("Disney" spelled backward), perhaps being a bit alarmed by the trestle, which looked a good deal higher from the cars than it did from the ground, and pleased by the disorienting blackness of the costly tunnel. Sometimes they stopped for refreshment at a fully equipped ice cream parlor Disney had set up near the house's swimming pool.

The Carolwood Pacific attracted attention well beyond Hollywood. *Look* magazine ran an article on it that generated so much interest that Disney established a micro-business selling working drawings and even castings based on the *Lilly Belle*. More and more strangers showed up just to have a look at the train.

So it went for two years, with almost every weekend regularly punctuated with the *Lilly Belle*'s whistle and the bright chime of her bell. Then, on a spring day in 1952, a guest who had been given a turn at the throttle managed to flog the train up to forty miles an hour. The *Lilly Belle* jumped the track, and lay on her side jetting high-pressure steam from where her whistle had been snapped off.

A five-year-old girl ran over to see what was happening, and got her legs scalded. The injury was minor; Disney's response to it was not.

"That's it," he told Broggie. "I want it outta here. Take it back to the studio and store it in the machine shop."

Disney had not been planning an abrupt end for the Carolwood Pacific. He had ambitious plans: a turntable, a block signal system that would allow several trains to run at the same time, a roundhouse. Broggie had already been machining parts for a freight locomotive, and Disney had acquired two eighth-scale British locomotives to give an international flavor to his line.

But that was that. The *Lilly Belle* went under a drafting table, the rolling stock into storage.

The day after the accident, when he and a colleague went out to collect the *Lilly Belle*, Broggie walked a stretch of track and mused aloud about how Disney had "created a fine layout here and we've all learned a lot designing and building it and the rolling stock." By the time the Carolwood Pacific was done, Disney had spent $50,000, half of it for the roadbed and landscaping, half for the *Lilly Belle* and the cars on which he had expended so much affectionate care. How strange that the boss should just drop it. "Walt doesn't give up," said Broggie, "so he must have something else in mind."

Broggie was right. There was more to the sudden abandonment than that derailment. Disney had loved his railroad, but evidently now discovered it had done all it could to help with his larger plans. The Carolwood Pacific had ceased to be a satisfactory answer to his long-ago question to Broggie, "This is an electric train, now what's for real?"

Disney had indeed, as Broggie said, learned a good deal from building his train. But he'd perhaps learned more from creating a full operating system so carefully landscaped that it gave his guests an experience—a narrative, really—of shifting scenes, one blending smoothly into the next: the highly literal but small-scale trestle; the mysterious wiggle through the dark tunnel; and the sudden flash of daylight at its end. Here was a whole little world, with him in absolute control, and one in which visitors weren't sitting back and watching a screen but rather were full participants.

A few years later Marvin Davis, an art director whom Disney had hired away from Fox to help in his still barely conceived amusement park, told of visiting his new boss, who wanted to show off the train. "I was pretty thrilled about all of this. I got the impression that he was trying to give us the idea of what he wanted for Disneyland. He used his Carolwood Pacific railroad as an example of what he wanted to do next. There was a definite line between Walt's train at his home and what he went on to do at Disneyland."

6

WORLD'S FAIRS, CONEY ISLAND, AND THE DECLINE OF THE AMUSEMENT PARK

Beyond the certainty of a railroad, Walt Disney had many half-formed ideas of what he wanted for his park; and a firm one of what he didn't. In the early 1950s he visited New York City's most famous seaside attraction, and had a strong reaction to it. He told Lillian, "I'm almost ready to give up the idea of an amusement park after seeing Coney Island. The whole place is so run-down and ugly. The people who run it are so unpleasant. The whole thing is almost enough to destroy your faith in human nature."

In touring Coney during its long, tawdry decline, he would not have known he was surrounded by the ghostly spires and vanished music of a public amusement empire that in many ways prefigured what he hoped to build.

So, too, did the nineteenth-century legacy of the great world's fairs, which was still vigorous during his early years. His father had worked as a carpenter on one of the grandest of them, the 1893 World's Columbian Exposition in Chicago, and often spoke about it. There is no evidence that Walt attended the most ambitious one of his adulthood, the 1939 New York World's Fair, but he came of age in a nation whose expectations of a stirring public experience had been shaped by the exhibitions. Designed to entertain while promoting civic uplift, they had penetrated the consciousness of even those who had never been to one.

Millions had, however. Despite its taking place in a pre-automotive age, one out of every four Americans managed to get to the 1893 Chicago fair. The historian Neil Harris wrote, "American expositions provided visions of a higher life set amid heavenly landscapes. Enveloping in their scale, their novelty, their string of surprises, they punctuated their decades like giant exclamation marks."

The world's fairs, an entirely urban phenomena, had been preceded by a movement to establish public parks. The most famous of these was Central Park, created in 1857 in what was then northern Manhattan by the landscape architect Frederick Law Olmsted and the architect Calvert Vaux. Striving for an enclave of greensward and rocky gorges that would look as if nature alone had put it there, Central Park was in fact as thoroughly man-made a work as the Brooklyn Bridge, a huge sculpture whose trees and glades were to serve as a serene retreat from the hot, struggling lives of close-packed New Yorkers. Its enormous success polluted it in Olmsted's eyes: just twenty years after it was finished, he complained that it was "going to the devil." The problem was with its beneficiaries; yes, they liked the calm surroundings, but they wanted to have fun in them, too, which inevitably led to rowdiness and what Olmsted saw as general dissipation and despoliation.

The international expositions also looked to elevate their attendees, and had better luck keeping them in hand. The 1876 Philadelphia Centennial Exhibition, the first official American world's fair, saw the construction of two hundred pavilions in Fairmount Park, with the 21½-acre Main Exhibition hall being, for its short life, the largest building in the world. Here, and in the fairs that followed, the visitors were easily controlled. It cost money to get in, everything was done at the highest architectural level, with richly planted promenades leading to displays of the era's technology and acres of ormolu and statuary that represented "the fine arts."

The fairgoers tended to be sedate. One observer wrote of the 1893 Chicago fair, "Courtiers in the garden alleys of Versailles or Fontainebleau could not have been more deferential and observant of the decorum of place."

But as the century advanced, these elevating enterprises grew raucous offshoots, sometimes even on their grounds, which ballyhooed racy shows, scary rides, exotic food, and spectaculars offering an immersion in the souks of Marrakesh or a recreation of whatever war was on at the time. The Chicago fair's rakish stretch was the Midway Plaisance (which, when the fair closed, left behind the word "midway" in the American language); the 1915 Panama–Pacific International Exposition had the Zone; the Pike enlivened St. Louis in 1904, the Pay Streak the 1909 Alaska–Yukon–Pacific Exposition; the Warpath added louche sparkle to the 1907 Jamestown Exposition. The exposition managers were more than tolerant, as the midways never failed to bolster the receipts. The official history of the 1901 Buffalo Pan-American Exposition said, "We may as well admit the main reason, which is that people want to have some fun, and there is no reason why they shouldn't have it to the profit of the undertaking." There was no doubt that the public enjoyed these more strenuous diversions: the closing of the most famous attraction of the Chicago fair, the 264-foot Ferris wheel, sparked a riot.

The world's fairs, for all their imposing scale, were *fairs*—that is to say, they were evanescent: they came and went. And because they represented the efforts not of a single impresario, but of whole cities, while they ran there was plenty of money to keep them immaculate.

Not so with the amusement parks to which they helped give rise, although for a little while Coney Island, which Disney so detested, came close to echoing their extravagance. The first decade of the last century saw the construction of three lavish mini-cities there that might be called Disneyland's harbingers. Steeplechase Park, Luna Park, and the most effulgent of them, Dreamland, all had single entrances, charged admission fees just to get on the grounds, and offered increasingly elaborate attractions in carefully monitored environments.

Two showmen named Frederic Thompson and Elmer Dundy gave the Pan-American Exposition a ride called A Trip to the Moon, in which the airship *Luna* carried thirty passengers at a time up past Niagara Falls and above the earth's curvature to disembark them in spackle grottoes where they could visit the Man in the Moon's palace, appreciate his dancing "moon maidens," and come away with souvenir chunks of green cheese. This extravaganza cost 50 cents (the equivalent of $14 today) to take in, and drew more than four hundred thousand customers. At fair's end it went east to Luna Park.

Dreamland also had many attractions that suggest the Disneyesque. A 1907 seasonal publication called *'Round the Beaches* described one: "Coasting thro' Switzerland . . . is a magnificent production placed in a vast building, which shows the alpine heights of Switzerland in all their beautiful reality. The proscenium Arch which frames the great entrance to this building will in itself give the visitor an idea of the beauty of this attraction. The lobby display is a most wonderful miniature reproduction of the Alps with its snow clad peaks, its roaring cascades, its vast glaciers, its rushing torrents and waterfalls. . . . The mountains of Switzerland are reproduced in the interior with striking reality, the effect of distance being obtained by reducing the scale, and [the] trip itself is as refreshing as a breath from the vine clad foothills of the Alps."

All three parks made perfunctory genuflections to the educational. A Steeplechase brochure celebrated its electric plant, whose "ceilings and walls are covered with costly oil paintings depicting historical electrical events from [the] time of Franklin and Morse and studded with jewels." The "engines and dynamos are enameled in white with gold mountings. A Vernis-Martin curio table holds the tools, and a beautiful mosaic table, the oil cups." The engineer—who went about his tasks wearing white gloves—"is a college graduate, qualified to lecture upon his plant as well as to operate it."

Dreamland actually *looked* like a world's fair, with a central court of sugar-white buildings ranged around a 375-foot tower solemnly patterned on the Giralda in Seville.

But economics worked against such extravagance. The Coney season was short—Memorial Day to Labor Day—so the buildings couldn't be built like war memorials. They were lath and plaster, vulnerable to hard winters and highly flammable. Dreamland burned to the ground in 1911, putting an end to the decade of Coney's greatest splendor.

The subway got to the island after World War I, giving New Yorkers entrée for a nickel, and the summer crowds grew from a quarter million a day in earlier years to a million during the 1920s. They had less money to spend, and lesser enterprises arrived to cater to them. Then came the Depression and the war, and by the time Walt Disney made his disgruntled visit, Coney was again pretty much what it had been half a century earlier, when *Pacific Monthly* magazine, taking a jab at the East Coast, described it this way: "A jumble of old dilapidated shacks, thrown together in haste and negligence: dirty little shops, smelling of sausage and sauerkraut: low-class saloons of every variety: vulgar dance halls, reeking with the odors of stale beer and sweating humanity: a mass of 'fake' shows, with boisterous 'spielers': a perfect bedlam of fakirs and tricksters, the very quintessence of the crass and the vulgar."

But as Coney shone at its brief zenith, it helped spawn perhaps as many as twenty thousand lesser imitators across the country. These were what are remembered today as traditional amusement parks, and with their mighty eastern progenitor they shared carousels and roller coasters, fun houses and Ferris wheels, and cataracts of electric light, still in itself something of a novelty a century and a quarter ago.

The one fifteen blocks north of Walt Disney's Kansas City boyhood home was actually called Electric Park. Like most of its fellows, it was a child of the trolley car. The new traction companies all faced the same problem: ridership dropped away to next to nothing on the weekends, but they had to pay the power companies for electricity every day, no matter how few fares they collected to offset its cost.

To give people a reason to travel on Saturday and Sunday, they built amusement parks—in groves, beside lakes, by the seashore—out at the end of the line. During the early decades of the century, these trolley parks prospered, and as they did, most spent money to keep up their amenities. *Play*, a newsletter published by the Philadelphia Toboggan Company, a leading manufacturer of carousels and roller coasters, published what it called "A Beauty-full Editorial" that began, "Yes, I know; you're all fed up on this idea of *Beauty* in your park. You've had it poked at you in the columns of this terrible publication; in the editorial and news departments of the trade press; at the annual conventions, and in person by this, that or t'other park man. . . . But where there is so much smoke there must be some fire. . . . Yes folks want something of the circus attractiveness, too. Give them amusement. That's where the money comes in. It's a complex, strenuous, nerve-trying age in which we live, and if people can't relax they can't keep going. It is taken for granted that your park will contain amusements. The thing that isn't taken for granted, somehow—and that's why you can cash in on it in the long run—is Beauty.

"Green grass, well kept, is Beauty. Flowers are Beauty. Clean toilets and inviting benches and shaded walks are Beauty. Fresh paint is Beauty. Honest concessions are Beauty. And so is the element of safety in rides, and plenty of drinking water, and courteous attendants, and dining facilities, and many other things.

"BEAUTY PAYS."

This exhortation ran in *Play*'s May 1929 issue. A little more than month after that operating season came to a close, the stock market crashed, and in the straitened decade that followed the parks suffered along with everything else. And when better times came, they came to a country that was swarming with fresher, more urgent diversions: movies, air travel, television, and the all-conquering automobile. Like the trolley lines that gave them birth, the parks began to wither.

"Beauty" was an early casualty. So, too, were "honest concessions." The Chicago firm of H. C. Evans—the country's foremost manufacturer of gambling devices—in 1933 published its *Park and Carnival Equipment* catalog, a remarkably frank compendium of ways to cheat the customer: "The Evans' Cast Aluminum Milk Bottles . . . are a decided improvement over the old style wood bottle. They are indestructible and nicely painted to represent an ordinary bottle of milk. The bottles are placed on a twelve inch board in a pyramid, the player endeavoring to knock all the bottles off the board with three baseballs. This would appear very simple, but due to the special construction of the Evans' Bottles can only be accomplished when so desired by the operator." So, too, with "Evans' Cat Rack." The four feline targets "are made of extra heavy duty canvas, 18 inches in height and are under the operator's control at all times but can be demonstrated to the players as they are not weighted."

Another Evans catalog featured the "World's Fair Striker," a countertop miniature of the midway game where the customer swings a mallet and tries to knock a "chaser" up a wire to the bell at the top of a plank.

It was "one of the most practical hand strikers or 'bingers' ever produced and one that can be depended on to do the work"—meaning that it was "very easily controlled, the regulator being set as the indicator is lowered after every strike."

No such thing as a game of chance with H. C. Evans: the "Circulating Fish Pond," the "Automatic Devil's Bowling Alley," the "Mexican Six-Arrow Spindle," the "Chinese Dice Box," the "Hooligan Dice Game," the "Silver Wheel Spindle," the "Rolling Log Game"—all were "gaffed," which is to say, rigged.

Paintless seasons gave an air of squalor in the parks, while deferred maintenance added actual danger to the make-believe risks of the thrill rides. The park-goer was likely to get bilked, and possibly damaged, too.

In his wonderful 1946 novel *Mister Blandings Builds His Dream House*, the author Eric Hodgins recounts the travails of his hero as he joins the postwar exodus to the suburbs, in this case a Connecticut one. Four years later Hodgins published a sequel, *Blandings' Way*, about Mr. Blandings adjusting to life in exile from the city. It contains a passage that perfectly reflects how most Americans viewed amusement parks at the very moment Walt Disney proposed to build one.

"Lake Shamalaug was about three miles long and three-quarters of a mile across at its widest point. It lay in a complex fold of hills six miles from the center of Landsdale Town, and its waters were clear and cold. Mr. and Mrs. Blandings were conscious of it mostly at those times when [their daughter] Betsy was at home; at one end of it was a sagging and decayed amusement park set in a huge, handsome pine grove that provided unexampled opportunities for adolescent lovemaking. Mrs. Blandings wished it was in hell."

7

Dwarf Land

Mrs. Disney would have agreed with Mrs. Blandings. Her husband told a reporter that she had once asked him, "Why would you want to get involved in an amusement park? They're so dirty, and not fun at all for grown-ups. Why would you want to get involved in a business like that?"

He fielded the question the way he would countless times during Disneyland's germination: "That's exactly the point. Mine isn't going to be that way. Mine's going to be a place that's clean, where the whole family can do things together."

Cleanliness was the least of the ways his park was going to differ from its predecessors. Long before he built the Carolwood Pacific, Disney had made gestures toward the sort of attractions he would someday mount. Attendees at the 1937 Christmastime premiere of *Snow White and the Seven Dwarfs* got to see the first example.

The movie opened at the Carthay Circle Theater in Los Angeles on December 21. The NBC radio announcer covering the event—which had drawn nearly forty thousand spectators—said, "Well, believe it or not, ladies and gentlemen, Dwarf Land was moved to Hollywood. Down at the corner of Wilshire Boulevard . . . Walt Disney built a replica of the dwarfs' cottage that appears in this picture. . . . The cottage is only ten feet high and not quite that wide, so I had a little bit of difficulty trying to get inside, but every kid in this here now town has been through it, believe me. Outside are giant mushrooms three feet tall painted yellow and blue and pink, and then there are weird-looking trees with eyes that light up and long arms that reach out and grab at you just the way they grab at Snow White in the picture.

"Then there's a little dwarfs' millwheel there, and a diamond mine sparkling in the spotlights that illuminate the entire scene. Then there's a dwarfs' garden that stretches for about two blocks, I believe. It's filled with all sorts of strange-looking statuary, not to mention stumps and toadstools and flowers by the hundreds and hundreds. A stream flows through the garden that turns the millwheel, of course, and the crowds stand around watching the antics of the seven little dwarfs—actual dwarfs, too, in quaint medieval fairy-tale costumes—who are working the diamond mine and raking the garden and running in and out of the house, putting on a great show and singing and dancing for children and grown-ups alike."

One of the animators who worked on the film found the exhibit unsettling. His "most vivid memory of the evening . . . was the dwarf costumes. To help create some atmosphere the company made one of its first attempts at costumed characters. They must have been an after-thought because they weren't close to the model sheets. It's a wonder they didn't scare people away."

Far from it. After the film had left the Carthay Circle, *Movie Mirror* magazine reported on "Snow White Island": "Since so much interest was aroused by travelers to the dwarfs' country, we delved into the matter and came up with some pertinent information. The Island is a park, surrounded by a road, which is owned by the Native Sons and Daughters of California. It is almost 900 feet long, and on this was built the land of the seven dwarfs. It cost nearly $10,000 to erect, and bills for lighting and watchmen (there were four) ran $6500.

"You could see the mountain, the wishing well, the fantastic forest—all real as life and twice as exciting. The first day it was finished, a guard counted 1,010 cars circling the display in one hour."

Dwarf Land's citizens decamped after the premiere, replaced with plaster figures; when these proved too fragile (children kept prodding Dopey in hopes of getting him to talk), Disney had them recast in concrete. *Movie Mirror* expressed the transformation from spectator to participant that was the foundation on which Disney would build his park. "Maybe you think the dwarfs' cottage, their work, the mountain climbed by the wicked queen, and all the strange scenes you saw in *Snow White and the Seven Dwarfs* exist only on paper, just so many colored lines drawn by a cartoonist. Actually all these things existed to be touched, felt, and photographed by some half million people who visited The Island during the four months' run of the movie at Carthay Circle."

A decade later Disney followed his foray into three-dimensional public entertainment with another effort that, although on a smaller scale, was more ambitious.

Disney had been drawn to miniatures well before the *Lilly Belle*. Visitors to the 1939 Golden Gate International Exposition in San Francisco were charmed by an exhibit of the Thorne Rooms. These were the hobby—actually, too narrow a word to describe an intense and meticulous exercise in architectural history—of a Chicago artist named Narcissa Niblack Thorne. In 1932 she started commissioning and overseeing the construction, on a one-inch scale, of domestic interiors. Executed with exquisite realism, they recreated rooms—parlors, kitchens, bedchambers, foyers—from Europe, Asia, and America between the thirteenth century and 1940. Her husband, James Ward Thorne, being an heir to the Montgomery Ward mail-order fortune, she was able to employ a team of thirty master craftsmen who milled matchstick floorboards and cut real crystal pendants the size of grains of rice for chandeliers.

The Thorne Rooms enchanted Disney (as they have millions of others over the years: today, sixty-eight of the rooms comprise the most popular exhibit at the Chicago Art Institute). He began to collect miniatures with such enthusiasm that in 1951 he would write a friend, "My hobby is a life saver. When I work with these small objects, I become so absorbed that the cares of the studio fade away . . . at least for a while." Before long he began making them, too. After being especially pleased with a five-inch-tall cast-iron stove he fashioned for the Carolwood Pacific caboose, he wrote, "I had a pattern made up and it turned out so cute, with the grate, shaker and door, and all the little working parts, I became intrigued with the idea. I had a few made up: one was bronze, another black, and I even made a gold one! Then we made more and started painting them in motifs that fitted the period of the turn of the century."

Eventually, as with the working drawings of the Carolwood Pacific, he turned them into a miniature business, putting some on sale for $25 in a Manhattan antiques shop. He must have felt he'd passed a kind of master's exam when the exacting Mrs. Thorne bought two for her own collection.

In 1948 Disney released a live-action film that proved the jumping-off point for a new venture. *So Dear to My Heart* is about a spunky midwestern lad named Jeremiah Kincaid and his mischievous black lamb, who together carry a plot wispy to the point of nonexistence. Although to a cold eye a movie wholly devoid of interesting incident, Disney loved it, perhaps because it was set in the era he was later to incarnate in his park's Main Street. (He gave the movie's rural depot to Ward Kimball for his Grizzly Flats Railroad. Kimball's initial delight quickly waned when he discovered—as his boss was to in a few years—the very different demands of a movie set and a working building. When Disney asked for the depot back to put in his park, Kimball, remembering all the money and effort he had to spend making it permanent, refused outright.)

Not long after the film came out, Disney told one of his animators, "I'm tired of having everybody else around here do the drawing and painting. I'm going to do something creative myself. I'm going to put you on my personal payroll. I want you to draw twenty-four scenes of life in an old Western town. Then I'll carve the figures and make the scenes in miniature. When we get enough of them made, we'll send them out as a traveling exhibit." It would be called Disneylandia.

The first scene he built was "Granny Kincaid's Cabin," the home of Jeremiah's sage, peppery grandmother. "I think he did all of that himself, or most of it," said his colleague Fred Joerger. "I remember him telling me he picked up the pebbles out at Palm Springs to do the little fireplace. There were pieces of furniture that he had made, beautiful reproductions. On the captain's chairs, he made Lilly pretty upset because he steamed the wood in her pressure cooker so he could bend it." "Granny Kincaid's Cabin" would have passed muster with Narcissa Thorne: all its elements—spinning wheel, flintlock on the wall, family Bible by the rocking chair—were perfectly scaled and crafted. Granny, however, wasn't there. When Disney tested the waters by displaying the cabin at the Festival of California Living in the winter of 1952, she was represented purveying homespun wisdom in a two-minute narration recorded by Beulah Bondi, who had played her in the movie.

One of Disney's associates, sent to gauge the public's reaction, said, "People would watch and watch. They wouldn't go away. They saw the whole show and stayed for the next one. So the show had to be stopped for twenty-five minutes to clear out the audience. Walt knew it was a success."

While the next scene—a barbershop quartet—began to take shape, Disney was planning how to send Disneylandia on the road. He envisioned a twenty-one-car train that would park in cities across the country while paying audiences walked through it being entertained by what Disney described as "visual juke boxes with the record playing mechanism being replaced by a miniature stage setting."

Disney had the idea—a rather sentimental one for that canny businessman—that towns and railroads alike would so warmly welcome Granny Kincaid's world that they would cover the expenses of moving it about. Fat chance. The best offer he could get was of a "Disney spur line"—a siding in the rail yard of one town to the tune of $13,000 per month. A couple of visits to freight yards gave him a dispiriting vision of children picking their way through a maze of dangerous machinery to get to the exhibition train.

Well, perhaps then set up the dioramas in department stores and generate revenue by having viewers deposit coins. Roger Broggie said no likely amount of coins would cover the cost of maintenance.

And maintenance would be costly, because Disney now wanted the interiors populated: the four members of the barbershop quartet were to be mechanical puppets that, powered by a cat's cradle of wires and cams, would, with operatic gestures, sing "Down by the Old Millstream."

Disney's love of miniatures never faltered, but he began to feel that deploying them in this fashion was too minor and fussy an effort. Roger Broggie was on hand at Disneylandia's abrupt demise. He was working on the barbershop scene: "We got as far as building the guy in the chair and the barber behind him . . . then the whole job was stopped."

Walt told Broggie, "We're going to do this thing for real!"

8

GETTING STARTED

With his trains, Disney's "for real" had meant live steam. This time, it meant bigger: bigger than Disneylandia and, Disney came to realize, bigger than what was in the hasty memo about Mickey Mouse Park that he'd written after coming home from the Railroad Fair. In his restless imagination, the branch of Main Street was sprouting "lands": a land devoted to the Old West; one that would take the visitor down a jungle river; one devoted to that elusive quarry, the future; and one given over to fantasies based on his cartoons.

Disney began, almost surreptitiously, recruiting people from the studio to help him. One of the first proved among the most valuable.

Harper Goff drew well from the time he was a boy in Colorado, and in his twenties was earning a good living in New York as a magazine illustrator. He began to earn a better one out in Hollywood, where he designed settings and executed continuity sketches for Warner Bros.: *Captain Blood, Sergeant York, Objective Burma!, Casablanca.*

In 1951 Goff and his wife went to England on vacation, and being a railroad enthusiast, as soon as he reached London he made for the Bassett-Lowke store in High Holborn.

Bassett-Lowke was Britain's foremost manufacturer of model trains, everything from fifteen-inch-gauge live steamers to Lionel-scale electrics. "They were famous for their locomotives," Goff said. "I saw this one old-time locomotive I liked and I said to the guy in the store, 'That's the one I want.'"

The clerk informed him with polite regret that another gentleman had already spoken for it. Naturally, this made the engine all the more attractive to Goff, and he persisted. It turned out his competitor wasn't quite sure; he had the locomotive on hold until that afternoon when he would return and make his decision. Perhaps Mr. Goff would like to speak with him?

"We came back that afternoon and we saw this fellow in the store, and he had purchased the locomotive. He turned to me and said, 'I'm Walt Disney. Are you the man that wanted to buy this engine? I have trains—do you have trains?'"

Goff "almost fell over. He asked me what I did for a living. I told him that I was an artist. I told him about the *Air View* picture series I had done for Douglas Aircraft Company showing the various battles with their planes during the war. Disney concluded the conversation with 'When you get back to America come and talk to me.'"

Goff did. "By the time I went to see him at the studio he was aware of my artwork in *Coronet* and *Esquire*." Disney offered him a job. Goff was puzzled. "I said, 'I'm not an animator—what can I do here?' He explained that he was planning to go into live-action filming, and do motion pictures with actors and sets. This fit in with my experience at Warner Bros."

As Goff's first assignment, Disney asked him to work up storyboards for a film that left the illustrator cold. "Walt explained to me about his plans to do a short subject about fish. . . . He said, 'I want to film whales and so forth with underwater cameras, and I've got a name for it. I want to call it *20,000 Leagues Under the Sea*. That's the name of a famous story, but that's what I want to call it and we'll show all these beautiful underwater scenes.'"

Disney left for a business trip to Europe, and Goff started right in—on a completely different tangent. "It happened that *20,000 Leagues Under the Sea*—the silent version—was my favorite movie as a kid." No playful porpoises for Goff; he cheekily set about filling eight four-by-eight-foot storyboard panels with scenes for a live-action movie of Jules Verne's novel.

Goff was fortunate that he was so good at what he did. An associate said, "Harper had a way of placing you inside the environment he created in a piece of art," and he was especially adept at evoking the high

Victorian era. Goff reported that when Disney returned he was (small wonder) "kind of angry since all that time I hadn't made the sketches that he'd asked me to do."

But as his exasperated new boss looked over Goff's interiors of the *Nautilus*, its lavish Belle Époque upholstery wedded to ornate mid-nineteenth-century ironwork, and the menacing whimsy of the submarine itself, he was gradually won over. At first he protested that he didn't have a big enough soundstage, but one day Goff got a call from him: "Come on up—we're going to do the *20,000 Leagues* motion picture."

The movie was still in preproduction when Disney assigned Goff to Disneylandia—it was he who came up with the aborted barbershop quartet—and he hadn't been back on *20,000 Leagues* for long when Disney came by his desk and, without preamble, asked, "Have you ever been to Knott's Berry Farm? It's fun, isn't it?"

Knott's Berry Farm, in nearby Buena Park, had begun in the 1920s with Walter Knott and his wife, Cordelia, selling boysenberry jam and preserves from their farm. Eventually Cordelia expanded the bill to include her chicken dinner, which her neighbors held in high regard. So, it seemed, did the rest of California, and in the 1940s Walter started adding buildings from Western ghost towns to keep the crowds occupied while they were waiting for a seat in the restaurant. The imported attractions became increasingly elaborate, and by the early 1950s Knott's was a thriving tourist draw.

It was not, however, a staple of conversation in the Disney studios, and Goff had no idea what to make of his boss's seemingly irrelevant pleasantry. Disney went on: "I've been thinking I'd like to have something like that." He took Goff into his office to discuss it. Goff started out sketching possible Main Street buildings, and he felt right at home with the assignment: "I was born . . . in Fort Collins, Colorado. My dad owned a newspaper there, the *Fort Collins Express Courier*, and I grew up there. It was a very prosperous town. We had banks that looked like banks, you know, and there was a Victorian city hall. I was born in 1911, and these buildings were around when I was a kid. When I started working on Main Street, I had photographs of Fort Collins taken. I showed them to Walt and he liked them very much. Disneyland's City

Hall was copied from Fort Collins . . . so was the bank building and some others."

Goff's testimony notwithstanding, the indefatigable Disney chronicler Jim Korkis (so far, he's published twenty-eight books on the subject) reports that company researchers now believe the actual model was the Bay County Courthouse in Bay City, Michigan. Both are similar—husky Beaux-Arts buildings with a central tower—but there's no question that Bay City's looks more like its Disneyland descendant.

Whichever its progenitor, Goff's city hall stands today in the park, one of the earliest Disneyland schemes to come to fruition. Disney was pleased with Goff's work, but not much else was going smoothly. One elemental decision—where to put Mickey Mouse Park—was especially troublesome.

Disney first lit on the studio back lot, where old sets and other cast-off odds and ends were stored. He told his studio production manager not to put anything else on it: "I'm going to build my park there." The lot was all of two and a half acres, so that plan didn't last long.

He next decided on sixteen acres of scrub that lay across the street from the handsome modern Burbank studio he'd built with the profits from *Snow White*. Disney took to pacing the property, kneeling now and then to get a child's perspective. One of his colleagues said, "I used to work at a window in my studio . . . and it overlooked that bare space between the Disney Studio and the river, down by Riverside Drive. I'd often work over the weekends, and one Sunday I looked up and saw Walt out there pacing an area, with his long three-foot strides. I knew he was measuring space for something—he'd walk a certain direction, then walk another way. I remember asking him: 'What in the hell are you doing across the street, tramping around in those weeds?' And so he told me about his ideas for a park."

At about this time, the name Mickey Mouse Park was coming to seem too juvenile and limiting to Disney. Nobody knows exactly when it became Disneyland (although that was an obvious evolutionary step from Disneylandia); one early recruit remembered that "the name was suddenly said by Walt, and it sounded good, and that was that."

That was the name the public saw when the first mention of the park appeared in the press. Under the headline "Walt Disney Make-Believe Land Project Planned Here," the March 27, 1952, issue of the *Burbank Daily Review* told its readers Disneyland would contain "various scenes of Americana, rides in a space ship and submarine, a zoo of miniature animals and exhibit halls." Walt was quoted as saying, "Disneyland will be something of a fair, an exhibition, a playground, a community center, a museum of living facts and a showplace of beauty and magic." It would cost $1.5 million to build.

The article concluded with the surprising claim that "Disneyland is not intended as a commercial venture, park board members have been assured. The facilities are to be instantly available for youth groups, Parent-Teacher Associations and other organizations devoted to civil and social welfare."

This was a sop—or, more accurately, a lie—to placate the Burbank City Board of Parks and Recreation. The park board immediately embraced the project; not so the city council.

Disney and Goff went before the latter body with maps and sketches drawn by Goff, which Disney explained with all his considerable powers of persuasion: Disneyland would be educational with its authentically recreated buildings from the American past, clean and prettily landscaped, and small and friendly rather than operating "on a full-bore moneymaking scale."

Disney, who rarely had trouble reading an audience, sensed the council wasn't with him. After he'd made his pitch, he sat back down, tapping his fingers on the arm of his chair—a warning, like the lifted eyebrow, that all who worked closely with him had come to recognize and dread—while the city fathers conferred. He was not surprised when one of them announced their decision: "We don't want a carny atmosphere in Burbank. We don't want people falling in the river, or merry-go-rounds squawking all day long."

Disney did not enjoy being instructed about the necessity of wholesome public entertainment by a bunch of municipal hacks, but he didn't argue. He didn't say anything, just gestured to Goff—who felt the council "sneered at us"—to pack up his drawings, and the two left the room without another word.

———

Disney could have spared himself the humiliating meeting, because he was already beginning to doubt that the Riverside Drive property would work. It was simply too small to contain his expanding vision.

That's what his architects had told him from the start. They were Charles Luckman and William Pereira, whom he had hired, for $3,000, to create an overall plan based on the sketches Goff and other early insiders were producing.

Finding suitable architects was not easy: no model existed anywhere for what Disney wanted to build. He chose Luckman and Pereira because they were designing Marineland, which was to be the world's largest oceanarium when it opened in 1954. It was nothing like an amusement park, but Disney thought it demanded more imagination than a supermarket or an office tower.

Luckman said of their first meeting, in the spring of 1952, that Disney "had this vivid mental image of it all—the streets and stores from other eras, the parade of Disney characters led by Mickey Mouse, the bright lights, the bands playing, the variety of restaurants, the scenes and sets of his cartoons to serve as backgrounds for the concessions, water rides through enchanted lands, the mechanized people who could speak, the birds who could sing, the monorail which he would drive on opening day."

Where would all this be? Luckman wanted to know. Disney pointed out the window toward Riverside Drive. "I've got the site right next door."

Luckman thought it too small, and said so. Disney breezily reassured him: "You and Bill can do it."

They couldn't. "As the weeks went by," Luckman said, "the proposed size went from ten to twenty acres, then to thirty. Walt was screaming."

When he'd screamed it up to fifty acres, Luckman backed off. A project this large, he said, required a much bigger site, one beyond the studio neighborhood, and probably beyond Los Angeles itself.

The three parted amicably. Disney had come to believe that what he needed couldn't be supplied by architects. Another architect, a friend of his named Welton Becket, told him, "No one can design Disneyland for you. You have to do it by yourself."

That is, his studio people would have to do it. What Disney sought had more to do with movies than with architecture. His staff might not know anything about stress factors and site locations, but they understood color and pacing, how to go from one scene to a very different one without jarring the audience. Disney's buildings, his lands, would be the work of set designers.

Despite their brief tenure, the architects did make two vital contributions to the park. Pereira insisted on the supreme importance of a single entrance. With that, you could control what your visitors experienced beyond it. "If you had more than one entrance," he told Disney, "you would never be a success."

And Charles Luckman put him in touch with the Stanford Research Institute.

After they'd parted ways, Disney ran into Luckman at a cocktail party. He said he was still fretting about finding a site. Luckman replied that when he'd been stumped in his search for the best place to build a football stadium in Hawaii, SRI had found the perfect spot. He wrote down the phone number of the firm's Los Angeles office.

The next day, Disney passed it along to an assistant on the park project named Nat Winecoff. He wasn't a Disney Studios type, being cut to a slightly earlier Hollywood pattern, a loquacious promoter with shoe-polish hair, a Cesar Romero mustache, and scarlet vests, who went headlong at his assignments. When he called SRI, Winecoff opened the conversation with "What the hell do you guys do for a living anyway?"

He was talking to an economist named Harrison "Buzz" Price, who was tempted to reply with the old joke about the zebra asking the stallion what he did, and being told: I'll be glad to show you if you take off those fancy pajamas. Instead, Price, even before asking what was *wanted* done, said he'd come down the next day and discuss it. By the time the conversation was over, Price had learned that Walt Disney was planning a weird-sounding amusement park, and needed a place to put it.

9

Buzz and Woody

Winecoff's blunt question could have drawn forth an elaborate answer. The Stanford Research Institute had been founded in 1946 by the trustees of Stanford University to conduct research—scientific, economic, technical—that would benefit the rapidly developing West Coast. The company's first job was to determine whether the guayule plant might become a domestic source of natural rubber; its initial economic study, commissioned by the U.S. Air Force, assessed the service's potential for rapid expansion in an emergency (not good, it turned out). SRI addressed the growing problem of smog, and in 1949 had held, in Pasadena, the First National Air Pollution Symposium. Where its efforts fit with Disney's was the SRI economics division's study of all the factors that went into finding locations for firms wishing to establish new West Coast branches.

Amid such lofty enterprises, SRI was soon viewing the Disney job with amused condescension—it was "Project Mickey"—but Buzz Price took it seriously from the very start. Despite the zippy informality of his nickname, he took everything seriously.

Numbers were high and holy things to him, and had been since his earliest years. "My first love has always been the numbers. I loved their digital specificity. As a child record collector, I tallied 'times played' on my album covers. I knew how many ski runs I made at Mammoth Mountain (465), and there were many other compulsivities appropriate to this bent." Years later, as a jogger, he clocked the distance of his every run and computed the cost of "club dues, track suits, socks, parking, and three pairs of Adidas" to calculate that his hobby cost him 74 cents per mile.

Born in Oregon in 1921 and raised in San Diego, he took a degree at the California Institute of Technology, and got a job at Ingersoll Rand as a mechanical engineer. Despite self-doubts ("At 21, I was younger than my age, insecure, frightened, a loser at cards, desperate for peer approval.") he did well. He got a first taste of the sort of work that would occupy the rest of his life as an air force private on the United States Strategic Bombing Survey, formed to assess the impact of the American air campaign on German industry. This was an unusual posting for a private, but Ingersoll Rand was America's largest machinery maker, and that got him the job. "My part of it was to draft reports on machine tools, capital equipment, and ball bearings, their production rates, interdiction, and recovery. I did not know at the time that I was learning a future craft, writing reports by the numbers."

At war's end he went back to Ingersoll, and reinforced his already more than satisfactory credentials by attending the Stanford Business School. He'd thought of then returning to what he called the "Mother Corporation," but found himself instead drawn to "a new kind of place—a new kind of consulting, data-based applied research, really a new profession." That was the economics division of Stanford Research Institute—devoted to the practice of what one of Buzz's professors called "Engineering Economics." Price loved it: "Our job at SRI, on each assignment, was to prove our consulting opinions *by the numbers* [the happy italics are his]."

He worked up some numbers as soon as he got off the phone with Winecoff, drafting not one but two preliminary reports: the first on finding a location for the park, the second on its "economic feasibility"— that is, how likely were people to go there and spend money?

Price met Walt Disney in the park-to-be's offices, housed in a wooden structure so modest that he remembered it as a "trailer." There was another SRI man present: C. V. Wood—but "Call me Woody," he demanded in a Texas-drenched accent. Woody was Price's boss, and was the opposite of his colleague. Tall, restless, noisily affable, and looking a decade younger than his thirty-three years, he was the "presenter," whose innate confidence would counterbalance Price's diffidence. Price said that Wood, who claimed to have an engineering degree, was "the quickest numbers man" he ever worked with: "He could estimate space, time, velocity, volume, revenue, cost, and frequency and other physical variables and relationships with a mental arithmetic that was quick as a flash." He was strongest, however, as a salesman, and he exuded friendly certainty, a whiff of oil money, and, along with the dusty glamor of longhorn cattle, a hint of polish applied by good schools back east.

Disney took to him at first. This was not surprising, as everything Woody heard about the park seemed to delight him. Not so Price: "It sounded strange, unlike anything you would expect in an amusement park. At a time when most parks were planned as a grid with four-side access, [Disney] outlined a design concept of a single park entrance passing through a turn-of-the-century main street, which would end in a circular plaza or town square. This area would feed off radially into four thematic activity areas, the World of Tomorrow, Fantasyland, Frontierland, and Adventureland. Whereas most amusement parks wanted all the street visibility they could get, Walt's entire park would be hidden from the outside world by a high landscaped berm. . . . He was talking about customized rides, exhibits, and attractions instead of the standard off-the-shelf Ferris wheel and tunnel of love. . . . Rides would be subordinate to story and setting. Most shocking, there were no thrill rides." Price could not imagine such a place without that monarch of all amusement park rides, the roller coaster; but most alarming, this entertainment anomaly had to open in just two years.

Woody thought it all sounded great.

They discussed the few Disney mandates: the land must be flat, relatively unpopulated but easily accessible to automobiles, and nowhere near the water. Disney did not like the idea of sand-encrusted vacationers slopping through his park in beach dress; nor did he want to compete with the Pacific Ocean: Disneyland was to be its *own* attraction. Beyond this, he offered few specifics: just that he needed about 150 acres somewhere in Southern California.

Price asked, "Do you have any bias, any opinion, on where it should go in Southern California? The study area you are talking about is big. The greater Los Angeles five county area is at least four thousand square miles."

Disney wasn't much help. "No, you tell me."

"You own the Golden Oak Ranch out in Saugus, is that a consideration?"

"No, you tell me where it should go."

That was all Price and Wood could get out of their client; that and a contract. When Price explained his second proposal—that they "study market behavior in other amusement parks and public attractions and use it as a basis for judgment in developing an economic feasibility model"—Disney at once agreed. There was a good deal of talk about the necessity of secrecy so as not to drive up land prices. Then the deal was struck: for twelve weeks of SRI's services, Disney would pay a consulting fee of $10,000 for the site study and $15,000 for the feasibility report.

Price and Wood immediately started visiting potential sites—they'd hit seventy-one before they were through—in five counties: Los Angeles, San Bernardino, Ventura, Riverside, and Orange. Woody lounged in the car spinning yarns with Lone Star relish. He'd be valuable once it came to dickering with property owners, but at this early point it was Price who did most of the work. "I had a precise assignment," he recalled half a century later, "and I didn't burden myself with the idea, is this crazy?" He worked out "the center of gravity of the residential market (the point which is the shortest distance to all the people)" who would become Disneyland customers, and found it to be three miles east of the railroad yards that served downtown Los Angeles. Too close to the city, too dreary, and far too expensive.

So Price and Wood embarked on a more difficult calculation: Where would the population center be in ten years' time? It was shifting quickly, driven by a number of social and technological pressures.

More than any other state in the Union, California had been enriched by World War II: the government had pumped in $35 billion by 1945, and although the shipbuilding boom would dwindle after V-E Day, other military spending on the Cold War that lay ahead, and the growth of NASA, would keep the state burgeoning (in a decade its economy would outpace Japan's). A national westward migration was bringing California into competition with New York as the most populous state—a palm it would seize in 1962. Los Angeles was spreading in random, helter-skelter ways that eastern cities had never known, far flung conurbations fed by new highways.

Price and Wood studied the routes of nascent freeways, which to Price "indicated we could move northwest to the San Fernando Valley, out east toward Pomona, or southeast toward Santa Ana." Santa Monica had promising aspects, but that brought the unwelcome beach into the picture, and in any event the freeway wouldn't reach it until at least five years after the park opened.

Although Price had grown up in Southern California, he'd had no idea of its climatological differences; the San Fernando and Pomona Valleys lay inland and were twelve degrees hotter than the coastal areas in summer, seven degrees colder in winter. That was no good.

The two men determined that the population center was already moving southeast toward Orange County. As they closed in on it, they began to call their shifting goal "the amoeba." In the end, the amoeba revealed itself to them as the town of Anaheim.

10

ORANGE COUNTY

Many Americans had heard of Anaheim, but only through the comedian Jack Benny's popular radio show, whose progress was often interrupted with a running-gag announcement: "Train leaving on Track Five for Anaheim, Azusa, and Cuuuu-ca-mon-gaaa!" That is, nowhere towns with funny names, three Podunks.

Anaheim could not have been more different from the loosely held quasi-communities that were erupting to the north, where Los Angeles County was laying out some thirty-eight thousand subdivided lots with single-family homes each year. It was founded by two German immigrants, a violinist named Charles Kohler and John Frohling, a flautist, whose Germania Concert Society brought them to San Francisco in 1850. There, they were enough taken with the local grapes to abandon their musical pursuits in favor of viniculture. Although lacking any experience whatever with winemaking, the partners raised $12,000, bought a vineyard at what is now the intersection of Seventh Street and Central Avenue in Los Angeles, and, amazingly, prospered from the start. By 1857, they were producing one hundred thousand gallons annually, and that year, along with fifty German-American families, they established a winemaking cooperative twenty-five miles south of their original vineyard, where they bought up 1,165 acres for a price of $2 an acre.

The Santa Ana River flowed nearby, and, combining the Old World with the New, they took the German word *heim*—"home"—and married it to Ana to form the name of their town. The extraordinary run of success continued: within thirty years Anaheim was the capital of American wine production.

At that bright moment, all the square miles of vines began to die, done in by a bacterium named Xylella fastidiosa, which causes what is today known as Pierce's disease, for which there was then (and is now) no cure. The vintners scrambled to find substitutes—walnuts, dates, olives, pistachios—but it was another crop that salvaged the fortunes of what would, in 1889, split off from Los Angeles to be consolidated under the name of Orange County.

The Spanish first brought the orange to California, and Franciscan missionaries were cultivating them by the 1700s. But they were a minor part of the region's agriculture until, in 1873, Eliza Tibbets, the wife of a Riverside farmer named Luther, wrote a friend in the U.S. Department of Agriculture seeking advice about what would grow best in Southern California. The friend sent her two cuttings of a seedless orange he had recently found in Brazil; he called it the Washington navel. The trees those cuttings eventually produced bore fruit so sweet and meaty that people traveled for miles just to see the orchards; Luther—who gained the cumbersome nickname of Seedless Orange Tibbets—had to string barbed wire to keep visitors from plundering the buds.

The Washington navels, however, fared poorly near the humid coastal regions. William Wolfskill, a New Mexico fur trapper who turned husbandman when he moved to California in the 1830s, was successfully producing wine, lemons, and oranges when the 1849 Gold Rush brought on the largest internal migration in American history. The miners, Wolfskill discovered, would pay the phenomenal price of a dollar for a case of oranges. In meeting this demand, he developed the Valencia orange which, unlike the Washington, was to be largely used for juice.

The Valencia was as great a success as the Washington; before long the massive Irvine Ranch had given over half of its 120,000 acres to Valencia orange groves. By 1880, despite the lingering fevers of the Gold Rush, agriculture had eclipsed mining as California's main industry.

Technology had a good deal to do with the shift. At first Southern California was mostly feeding San Francisco; fruits and vegetables rotted on the long journey east. The refrigerated freight car changed that. The first California oranges were shipped east in a state of chilled preservation in 1877. By the early years of the twentieth century twelve million crates went east annually, borne along by effective use of the nascent advertising industry. In 1908 the California Fruit Growers Exchange inserted the word "Sunkist" into the language, and soon it was the world's best-known brand of fruit. The orange came to represent health and vitality, an edible ambassador from a land where perpetual sunshine warmed the anodyne air. Americans who in their youth had never seen an orange were now consuming forty of them annually, which meant $60 million a year to the growers.

Right in the middle of this verdant empire lay Anaheim. By the time Buzz Price put the town in his sights, the area was still forested with Valencia orange trees, but as with so much else in American life, postwar prosperity was working a change on it. Housing was coming in at a rate that caused one local newspaperman to complain, "Pretty soon it will be Orange Country no longer. It will be 'Tract County.'" Speculators began buying up land, a process that accelerated when a blight like the one that had befallen the vineyards three-quarters of a century earlier killed off fifty thousand acres of trees. The rising land prices, and consequent higher taxes, made raising oranges an increasingly costly business. Those prices would keep on going up as the area became more accessible, and that would happen soon. Planned in 1939, and being built since 1947, the Santa Ana Freeway was about to connect Los Angeles with Orange County.

Still, Anaheim remained a quiet, provincial town, its four square miles and fifteen thousand citizens served by a forty-two-man police force whose members had to supply their own cars. The city's two jail cells (the worst, one visitor said, outside of Tijuana) were sufficient to handle any troublemakers. Such visitors as there were had a choice of five hotels and two motels offering among them a total of eighty-seven rooms. There were, however, stirrings of ambition in Anaheim. Keith Murdoch, the city manager, said, "We were looking to improve the status of the city by attracting new industries." He had no idea of the scale—and the radical novelty—of the industry that was heading his way.

11

BUYING ON THE SLY

In early August 1952 Price and Wood met with Walt and Roy Disney in SRI's Los Angeles offices. Price laid out what he had found. He reviewed two promising sites, and then a third he'd just discovered. It was a 139-acre plot at the juncture of Ball Road and Harbor Boulevard in Anaheim, planted with four thousand orange trees thriving in a climate that had fewer swings of temperature than the other places they'd been considering, very little "haze," no significant industrial presence, no nearby oil wells, and was soon to be invigorated by the Santa Ana Freeway. True, the land was in the hands of seventeen different owners, but Price had learned that they were considering selling to subdividers. At $4,800 an acre, the price was more than Disney wanted to spend, but the area had a friendly tax rate of 5.26 percent, as opposed to 6.95 in nearby ones.

Disney said: "Let's go have a look." A few days later he, Wood, and Nat Winecoff were driving along narrow roadways that seemed far more than twenty-five miles from L.A. Among the orange trees they saw a scattering of farmhouses, chicken coops, and windmills. Disney liked it. At one point, they pulled over and stood for an hour on a lightly traveled byway talking strategy, most of which centered on secrecy. The land had to be optioned surreptitiously; just one of the seventeen owners bridling would wreck the plan. And until they had it sewn up, nobody in Anaheim must know. Of course they'd need to have extensive dealings with the city managers, but not until their own position was unshakable.

Disney hired Coldwell Banker to serve as shield and purchaser, and two of their real estate people began feeling out the owners in what the would-be buyers were calling the Ball Road site. Their overtures were driven by thrift as well as secrecy. The land they wanted was worth as much as $5,000 an acre, but they seemed to be having some success at offering $4,000, until they came to the Viking Trailer Manufacturing Company. It occupied not only the largest holding, but one that lay directly next to the future path of the Santa Ana Freeway. Here, Disney authorized Coldwell to pay $5,300 an acre as well as a steep $100,000 for the trailer company itself. Viking agreed to the offer, and Disney put down a $10,000 option on the land.

Almost immediately, a speculator, probably tipped off by someone at the trailer company, bought up twenty acres adjoining the Viking land. The interloper could have had no idea that it was Disney he would be putting the screws to; he merely guessed that anyone who wanted that land enough to pay such a high price would do the same for the parcel he'd just bought.

Walt Disney, feeling bruised and something of a sucker, walked away from his $10,000 deposit and the Ball Road site. Price and Winecoff and Wood expanded their searches, again and again finding that all the nearby desirable land was more expensive and more heavily freighted with high tax and utility rates.

Anaheim remained the most attractive goal, and Disney decided he had to form an alliance with the city government sooner than he had planned. He had one advantage. Some months earlier, the city had come up with a plan to draw commercial attention with a Halloween festival, and asked the Disney Studio to contribute floats for a parade that would open several days of festivities. Disney came through handsomely with six floats based on his features *Peter Pan*, *Pinocchio*, and *Snow White*, along with one that bore an early iteration of the Sleeping Beauty Castle that was to become as familiar to the world as the Eiffel Tower.

When the scope of the film company's contribution became clear, the grateful city asked Disney to appoint an honorary judge for the pageant. He chose Nat Winecoff, and on October 31, there he was, bustling about in his ringmaster's red vest, choosing the owner of the most copious beard as the winner of the Wiskerino contest, kidding around with the beauty pageant contestants, and generally ingratiating himself. But he was there as more than a goodwill ambassador.

Toward the end of the day, Winecoff approached Earne Moeller, the executive secretary of the Anaheim Chamber of Commerce, and told him in strict confidence what Disney hoped to build in Orange County. He wondered if Moeller might be able to help. Moeller at once asked if he could bring Keith Murdoch, the city manager, in on this. Winecoff agreed, Moeller hurried off to find Murdoch in the crowd, and soon the three men were sitting together in a car parked behind the chamber of commerce building.

Moeller and the thirty-four-year-old Murdoch, who was just three years into the job he would hold for more than a quarter century, listened eagerly as Winecoff described the property Disney was seeking, and told how the first effort to get it had been stymied. When he described the park, both Moeller and Murdoch were astonished by its size and complexity. But if this fantasy was actually going to materialize, they wanted it in Anaheim.

Just a week later the two had Disney and Winecoff in a station wagon touring properties they had chosen. The drive started out badly; right outside the first area stood an overgrown graveyard. Disney, who always had a strong aversion to death and funerals, balked at once. Moeller and Murdoch assured him it could be tidied up, but he wanted nothing to do with this reminder of where all amusements end. "I wouldn't bring my guests past this for love nor money," he said. "Do you have another site?"

They did. It was on La Palma Avenue: flat, all but empty save for the orange trees, crossed with a few unvisited dirt roads. Moeller said it could be had at a friendly price.

The mood in the station wagon changed. Disney was delighted, and they drove to Knott's Berry Farm to celebrate over a chicken dinner.

During the meal Disney talked enthusiastically about his plans for the park, and what he'd be doing to the property to accommodate it.

A local real estate agent, who recognized the personage at the next table, picked up enough of the conversation to understand what was in the wind, and within days he had options on much of the land.

When Disney found out, Murdoch said, he was "infuriated." Twice this had happened! That was it for Anaheim. They'd start scouting Garden Grove, miles away.

Moeller didn't give up. Instead, he said, "the threat of competition for the location . . . elsewhere acted as a catapult, for my office became more resolved than ever to hold on to the most promising prospect for putting Anaheim on the map."

Murdoch came up with the solution. On an empty Sunday morning two weeks later, he sat in his office brooding over a map that showed all the properties in northern Orange County and the names of the families that owned them. "I kept looking at that doggone map, thinking where can we locate it?" As he stared at the original Ball Road site for the hundredth time, he noticed something that had escaped him. The beneficiary of the trailer company tip-off had bought only twenty acres at the northern edge of the land Disney wanted. Cerritos Avenue ran across the southern boundary of that land. Below Cerritos, however, lay acres of family farms that Murdoch thought might go for a modest price.

He did some quick homework and discovered that although there were any number of obstacles, it was possible to close a public road.

A week later Moeller and Murdoch were with Disney and Winecoff in the Burbank studio. Murdoch laid out a map, and said that if they extended their property beyond Cerritos Avenue, they would have what was basically the original Ball Road site, only shifted south by about a block.

Disney told Moeller and Murdoch, "If you can close that street, we've got a deal." They shook hands on it.

———

Disney dropped the Coldwell Bank Realtors and chose two local men who knew the area and its residents, and had already acquired land for industrial developers with satisfactory secrecy. They went to work securing the Ball Road properties, and here Wood's salesmanship came into play. He not only launched an effective disinformation campaign, leaking to local papers that Disney was planning an amusement park in the San Fernando Valley, fifty miles away, but was wily and persuasive with the owners. One of his colleagues said, "He was young and charismatic, and he could charm farmers out of their orange groves with his Texas talk. I don't know . . . and I don't even want to know . . . about some of the ways borders were changed and people were persuaded to sell their land to Disney."

Buzz Price had estimated that much of the Ball Road property could go for as much as $6,200 an acre, but Wood was bringing it in at less than $4,600. He made concessions when he had to, some bordering on the absurd: the Claussen family would sell only if their daughters could live on in their house even while the park was built around them.

Moeller and Murdoch proved good as their word: Cerritos Avenue was closed. Now, though, there was a fresh difficulty. A good deal of the property was not in Anaheim but in unincorporated Orange Country, where taxes were significantly steeper. Disney said the land had to be incorporated, which Moeller and Murdoch skillfully brought about amid a din of thwarted lawsuits. It remained only to persuade Anaheim landowners and residents to vote on the annexation. The former enthusiastically passed the measure 56 to 2; the residents were more leery of the deal, but in the end 56 percent voted in favor.

Disney had his land.

––––––––––

For years Walt Disney had been good friends with that font of bonhomie, Art Linkletter, whose television show *People Are Funny* had made him one of the most popular entertainers in America. One afternoon, while the last of the Anaheim properties were being nailed down, Disney asked Linkletter to come for a ride in the country with him. "We drove about twenty-five miles through orange groves and fields in a sparsely populated area of Orange County," Linkletter wrote. There "we turned off the main road and drove along some groves until we came to a large expanse of land, uninhabited except for a few grazing horses and some abandoned sheds." Disney pulled the car over and stopped on the shoulder of a silent roadway. "We got out and Walt began vividly describing Disneyland: the acres of colorful buildings in places called Tomorrowland, Jungleland, and Fantasyland, the thousands of people parked in huge parking lots . . ." and a swatch of small-town America of the McKinley years, frontier stockades, flying pirate ships, a tall-stacked stern-wheeler churning down Western rivers . . .

"While he talked, becoming more and more enthusiastic by the minute, I began to grow more and more concerned. Who in the world, I mused, is going to drive twenty-five miles to ride a roller coaster?"

As Disney drew his arabesques in the still air, "I hardly knew how to tell him that, for once, he was making what would probably be the biggest, most ruinous mistake of his life."

Then Disney said why he'd brought his friend there. "Art, financially I can handle only Disneyland itself. It will take everything I have as it is. But the land bordering it, where we're standing now, will in just a couple of years be jammed with hotels and motels and restaurants and convention halls to accommodate the people who will come to spend their entire vacations here at my park."

He ended with "I want you to have [the] first chance at this surrounding acreage, because in the next five years it will increase in value several hundred times."

Linkletter was flummoxed. "What could I say? I *knew* he was wrong." He began polite evasions: he said he was a little strapped for money at the moment (he wasn't), but of course he'd look into the investment later on.

"Later will be too late," Disney said. "You'd better move right now."

They started back to the car. "I well remember that short walk along the dry, sandy road because that little stroll probably cost me about a million dollars a foot."

In later years Linkletter could console himself with the knowledge that he'd had the prescience to get in on the hula hoop craze, but he never forgot that "I decided against an investment that would have netted more millions than I care to think about."

But who can blame him? He'd just learned that his friend had spent $879,000 to buy a lot of orange trees and a few decrepit farmhouses.

12

ROY

So now Disneyland consisted in its entirety of sheaves of hopeful drawings and some farmland, and Disney was out of money.

He had been financing the park on his own, and he'd "spent over $100,000 that I borrowed on the insurance I'd been paying for twenty years." He had recently bought a vacation home in Palm Springs; he sold it. If Lillian had been alarmed by the loss of Oswald the Lucky Rabbit, she was truly frightened now: "My wife raised the dickens with me. She wanted to know what would happen to her if something had happened to me."

From the start, the studio had been no help. Walt had lost overall control of Walt Disney Productions in the cash-parched year of 1940, when it went public. He had recently established another company to carry forward work on the park, becoming the sole owner of stock in Walt Disney Incorporated. The name drew immediate shareholder wrath, along with Roy's: How could there be *two* Disney companies?

Walt came up with another title, sneaking in his name anyway under the cover of his initials: WED Enterprises. The new entity was incorporated on December 16, 1952; the legally mandated newspaper announcement that ran for four weeks unmasked his modest deception:

CERTIFICATE OF BUSINESS
UNDER FICTITIOUS NAME

The undersigned, WALT DISNEY INCORPORATED, a California Corporation, hereby certifies:

1. That it is transacting, or will transact, business in
California under the fictitious name of

WED ENTERPRISES

such business being in part the designing of amusement
parks and the designing and manufacture of amusement park
equipment and other products of an entertainment, amusement
and educational nature . . .

All during these early maneuverings, Walt kept after his brother for
support.

———

Roy Disney once told of an incident that had happened back in the
Marceline days sixty years earlier. "Walt found a pocket knife. He was
five years old, and I was thirteen. I said, 'Look, you can't trust yourself
with a knife. You'll cut yourself, and I took the knife away from him.'"

Roy was remembering this because the brothers had recently had
a squabble, and Walt "accused me of bullying him and throwing my
weight around and he says, 'You've been doing that since I was born. I
remember you took that knife away from me. . . .'"

Roy saw the fraternal equation differently: "When Walt and I were
on the farm in Marceline, we had to sleep in the same bed. Now Walt
was just a little guy, and he was always wetting the bed. And he's been
peeing on me ever since."

These two stories represent the extremes of the relationship. The
brothers actually got along well—surprisingly so, given the perpetual
anxieties of their shared business. There was one stretch when they
refused to speak to one another for a full two years, keeping their company going like a couple of haughty Renaissance city states conducting
diplomacy through lower-level courtiers.

But for most of its long run, theirs was a warm partnership. Walt,
of course, was the creative one; but he could not have brought forth his
creations without Roy's business acumen. No Roy, and Mickey Mouse
would most likely be in cartoon Valhalla with Oswald.

A colleague of Roy's said, "Walt was the front man, and Roy was in the background. In a way he was as much a genius as Walt was. They shoved their last chips in the pot a couple of times. Roy always saved the day."

Walt Disney lives in the national memory as the relaxed, amiable personage who welcomed you into the world he'd invented, a fellow who loved pursuing his—the word invariably attaches itself even to his most nakedly commercial efforts—"dreams." And business is business: stern, hard, free from whimsy. But although Roy shunned any public presence, his colleagues found him to have more of the personality that we ascribe to Walt.

Buzz Price saw "*tremendous* mutual rapport and closeness. Different styles . . . Walt was more intense, Roy was more laid back. . . . I felt tremendously at home with Roy. You could tell him exactly what you thought. You didn't have to fart around or play politics or try to manage information; you could say anything." Price even believed Roy had a livelier sense of humor than his brother: "I think Roy had a little more funny bone. Walt was almost too busy at that time [building Disneyland] on a day-to-day basis. But that's an overstatement. He could relax and laugh, but he was always driven. Roy could laugh real quick. I've always been a joker and a smart-ass, and it was old home week with Roy. He liked to laugh."

As one animator saw it, "You could put your arm around Roy's shoulder, too, and did. Not with Walt."

In 1957, at a benefit dinner for the Big Brothers of America, Walt, who almost never spoke openly about family matters, said, "I was fortunate. I had a big brother. And he's still with me. And I still love him. I argue with him. Sometimes I think he's the stubbornest so-and-so I ever met in my life. But I don't know what the hell I'd do without him. . . . We started in the business here in 1923, and if it hadn't been for my big brother, I swear I'd've been in jail several times for checks bouncing. I never knew what was in the bank. He kept me on the straight and narrow."

That straight and narrow led to the greatest prosperity. Not always, though, and not easily. Walt, crossed, could be scathing. Late in 1936, with *Snow White* production at its pressured zenith, he wanted to shift distributors from United Artists to the larger and more influential RKO Radio Pictures. Roy thought it prudent to stay with United Artists and, after defending his choice, received a stinging, sarcastic rebuke from his brother. "If you would resign from U.A. and come over and work for Disney for a while we might be able to make some headway. . . . In repentance, I suggest you give them the plant, our trademarks patents and copyrights, and work for them on a salary—or if perhaps they are not satisfied with this I can go and get a job with Mintz and you can sell vacuum cleaners, again."

Walt Disney Productions went with RKO.

———

Roy Oliver Disney was born eight years earlier than Walt, in 1893. He spent more time looking after the infant than did his two older brothers, and they became close. No one had an easy time of it in the Disney household, and in his mid-teens Roy had to run the family farm while his father was laid up with diphtheria.

After the move to Kansas City, he worked for a while on the newspaper route, but, like all the Disney boys, got away from his father as soon as he could, first as a bank teller, and then, after America entered World War I, in the navy. He made three trips to France on convoy duty—dangerous work; ships around him were lost to U-boats—and came home to be diagnosed with tuberculosis. He spent a gray, desolate period in veterans' hospitals in the Southwest before moving to Glendale, California, just north of Los Angeles. There, as his brother later reminded him, he sold vacuum cleaners, an occupation he so enjoyed that in the middle of one weekday he walked off the job forever, calling the office to say on which Glendale sidewalk he'd left the demonstration model (in that law-abiding age, it was still there when the company came to retrieve it).

Soon afterward, his disease put him back in a veterans' hospital, this one in West L.A. Years later he wrote, "That was when Walt came to Hollywood. He came out here in June of '23 [he meant July]. I was in the hospital at Sawtelle. By correspondence he sold somebody in

New York on a series of pictures. One night he found his way to my bed which was on a row of beds on a screened porch. It was eleven or twelve o'clock at night, and he shaked me awake and showed a telegram of acceptance of his offers. He said, 'What can I do now? Can you come out here and help me to get this started?' So I left the hospital the next day and I've never been back since."

Thus began the company in which Roy at first played every possible role its understaffed needs demanded: bookkeeping, naturally, but also scrubbing clean the animation cels for reuse and running the camera. He wasn't much good at this last chore. His brother said Roy "never could master the cranking rhythm a cameraman must learn. As a result we ended up with a fluctuating tempo on screen." The distributors complained, "so finally I had to hire a real cameraman and that did cost more money."

So did new animators, but they had to hire them, too, because Walt had a surprising deficiency. Roy said, "Walt was never a good artist in executing. He was a Rube Goldberg type of an artist. Walt always put a meaning in his pictures, but the technique was [poor]. . . . He was always conscious of it and would certainly turn to a better artist if he had one around." He stopped drawing for good after 1924, saying years later, "I was never happy with anything I did as an artist."

As the studio grew, and Mickey Mouse cast his ever-strengthening spell upon America, Roy came to devote all his time to managing the company's finances, with a growing assurance that was to make him one of the most successful businessmen of the twentieth century. During the 1930s he adroitly negotiated a series of loans from the Bank of America that allowed *Snow White* to continue its exorbitant genesis.

He never lost his calm understanding that the company's prosperity rested not on the rock of conventional business practices, but on the churning, extravagant, perfectionist imagination of his younger brother.

Still, he could get scared. His low point probably came in the spring of 1936 when he had to hit up the Bank of America for $630,000 to stoke the *Snow White* furnace, which was burning up $20,000 a week. Walt said, "Roy was very brave and manly until the costs passed over a million. He wasn't used to figures over a hundred thousand at that time.

The extra cipher threw him. When costs passed the one and one-half million mark Roy didn't even bat an eye. He couldn't; he was paralyzed."

When Roy first heard his brother was fomenting an equally daunting project (not from Walt, who didn't mention the park during its first stirrings), he said, "Junior's got his hand in the cookie jar again." He may have said it fatalistically, because he knew that a determined Junior was almost impossible to dissuade. Roy voiced in a letter what must have represented a hope rather than a conviction: "Walt does a lot of talking about an amusement park, but really, I don't know how deep his interest really is. I think he's more interested in ideas that would be good in an amusement park than in actually running one himself." It was, he said, just one of "Walt's screwy ideas."

For a while, Roy did his best to ignore the subject. Walt said, "I couldn't get anybody to go with me because we were going through this financial depression and whenever I'd talk to my brother about it, why he always started to get busy with some figures so, I mean, I couldn't bring it up."

In fact, once he'd broached the subject with Roy, he brought it up all the time. With scant effect: when his plans had advanced to the point where he believed the park would cost $1.5 million, Roy offered to put $10,000 of studio money into it.

Then came WED Enterprises, and Walt increased the pressure. Hazel George organized an internal company campaign to support Disneyland, getting the staff to make small donations—five dollars here, ten there—to help pay for the park. This touching display of grassroots faith in the boss's vision was in fact devised by Walt as a psychological gambit to shame his brother into playing a larger role.

Disneyland wasn't going away. Roy may have reminded himself that he'd been frightened by the prospect of making *Snow White*, and that had turned out magnificently. But even the most successful gamble doesn't make a cautious person eager to throw the dice again, and so far Walt's most ambitious forays all had to do with motion pictures. He'd never yet stuck his neck out in real estate or, worse still, the generally despised business of amusement parks.

Roy became increasingly anxious about how his brother was paying for the architects and the endless sketches. "But I didn't ask," he said. "It was his baby."

Finally, he gave in to his curiosity, called a banker Walt knew, and asked if his brother had tried to borrow money from him. "Yes, he did," the man said. "And you know what? I loaned it to him." Roy went on to discover that, along with taking out $100,000 in personal loans, his brother had borrowed a quarter million dollars against his life insurance policy.

Sometime during the tussling with the Burbank City Council, Roy Disney gave in. As Walt was complaining to him about the difficulties with the Riverside drive site, Roy interrupted him. "Oh, we can't do that," he said (and Walt would have noticed the "we"). "We should do it in a bigger way."

13

LIKE NOTHING ELSE IN THE WORLD

On a September Saturday in 1953, Herb Ryman was in his studio working on a painting when the phone rang. He answered it and heard Walt Disney say, "Hi, Herbie. I'm over here at the studio." On a Saturday? Ryman asked. That made Disney testy. "Yes, it's my studio and I can be here anytime I want." Then he changed his tone. "I wonder if you could come over here. Just come the way you are. I'll be out front waiting for you." Ryman "was curious and flattered that he picked up the phone and called me. I had no idea what he wanted."

Herbert Ryman had been set on becoming an artist since he was a child in Vernon, Illinois, but he'd had to nearly die first. "I loved to draw, and everybody looked on it as a harmless hobby." It didn't seem so harmless by the time he was in college. His mother was adamantly opposed: Ryman's father had been a surgeon, killed on the Marne in the First World War, and she was determined that her son honor his memory by becoming a physician, too. But when a severe bout of scarlet fever brought Herbert close to the grave, she relented and, once he'd recovered, sent him to the Chicago Art Institute, where he graduated cum laude.

In 1932 he joined the art department at Metro-Goldwyn-Mayer, and rose to help design *David Copperfield*, *A Tale of Two Cities*, *Mutiny on the Bounty*, and the Emerald City of Oz. This last assignment especially reflected his strengths. He was a first-rate illustrator who painted with dash and brilliance; he could create moody evocations of fantastic places: Grimm Brothers forests, future cities, enchanted castles.

In 1938 Walt Disney saw a display of his work at the Chouinard

Art Institute in Los Angeles and at once hired him away from MGM. Ryman flourished at the Disney Studios, becoming an art director for *Dumbo* and *Fantasia*.

He left Disney in 1946 to go to Twentieth Century-Fox. "I had deserted Walt, which was a very criminal act (or at least he thought it was)." So when he got the call, Disney hadn't been his boss for years, and possibly held a grudge against him. Still, a summons from Walt Disney was not easily flouted. He went at once.

Disney met him and shook his hand. "Hi, Herbie, we're in the Zorro Building." Once there, Ryman asked what was going on. Disney told him, "We're going to build an amusement park."

"That's interesting," Ryman said. "Where are you going to build it?"

"Well, we were going to do it across the street, but now it's gotten too big. We're going to look for a place."

"What are you going to call it?"

"I'm going to call it Disneyland."

"Well, that's a good name. What is it that you want to see me about?"

Disney explained that the project had been germinating in his mind for a long time. Disneyland would be different from any other amusement park ever built. And it would cost plenty, far more than Disney could afford. But he'd had an idea of how to raise the money. The obstreperous new medium of television had alarmed most moviemakers, but Disney saw in it valuable possibilities for advertising, and for raising capital.

That Monday his brother Roy was going to New York to pitch a Walt Disney television series. He expected a warm reception—there had been a good deal of interest in a Disney TV show—but there was a hook. Any station that signed on for the show would also have to pay for the park.

Disney fully realized that TV executives might not be eager to enter the faded and ramshackle outdoor amusement industry. Still, the show was bound to be good, and Roy would have with him a powerfully persuasive rendering of an aerial view of the proposed park.

Intrigued, Ryman asked to see the drawing.

"You're going to do it."

The artist was appalled. "No. I'm not. You're not going to call me on Saturday morning at ten a.m. and expect me to do a masterpiece that Roy could take and get the money. It will embarrass me, and it will embarrass you."

Disney started to plead, his visitor said, "like a little boy who wants something." With tears in his eyes, "Walt paced back and forth. Then he went over into the corner and he turned his head around with his back to me and said coaxingly, 'Will you do it if I stay here with you?'"

Ryman gave in. "I knew I couldn't do a good job, but if he wanted to stay up all Saturday night and all Sunday night, I figured I could do it, too."

Ryman started to draw and Disney started to talk. "This is a magic place. The important thing is the castle [the studio was in the early stages of filming *Sleeping Beauty*]. Make it tall enough to be seen from all around the park. It's got to keep people oriented. And I want a hub at the end of Main Street, where all the other lands will radiate from, like the spokes in a wheel. I've been studying the way people go to museums and other entertainment places. Everybody's got tired feet. I don't want that to happen in this place. I want a place for people to sit down and where old folks can say, 'You kids run on. I'll meet you there in a half hour.' Disneyland is going to be a place where you can't get lost or tired unless you want to."

Ryman sketched a rough triangle on a big sheet of tissue—forty-three by seventy inches—and started to fill it in with hills and rivers; he put Mississippi stern-wheelers and an ancient square-rigger on the waterways, added a castle with a carousel in the courtyard, and, running from the park's single entrance to the castle, a broad street lined with late-Victorian buildings. He blocked out various "lands" with their potential names: Frontier Country, Holiday Land, Mickey Mouse Club, Fantasy Land, Lilliputian Land, World of Tomorrow, True-Life Adventure Land.

Fueled by milk shakes and tuna fish sandwiches, the two worked through the weekend in the blue haze of Disney's Chesterfields. Ryman could do bold cityscapes with an almost expressionist palette, but this drawing was crisp and literal, delicate and full of appealing specifics. Forty hours after Disney's phone call, Ryman set down his carbon pencil. The two men looked at the finished work.

What they had conjured from Disney's vision and Ryman's patient skill was remarkably close to what, two years and many millions of dollars later, would rise from the vanished orange groves of Anaheim, California, to tease the imagination of the entire world.

Frontier stockade and spaceport, jungle river and carousel were marshaled together within a steel border demarcated by the salient instruction Disney had given his artist at the outset: "Herbie, I just want it to look like nothing else in the world. And it should be surrounded by a train."

14

THE ALMOST BROADCASTING COMPANY

Roy was fully committed to the project by the time his brother had decided the best way to fund it was through television, and it was he who would go east with Herb Ryman's drawing to pitch a Disney show to the networks.

Walt had been interested in television for as long as television existed. While he was working on *Snow White* in the mid-1930s, he made his way to Camden, New Jersey, to watch David Sarnoff, the head of RCA and the founder of NBC, display gray little figures jittering on a cathode-ray tube.

One of the reasons Disney broke with United Artists in 1936 was their pushing for the television rights to his films—something he refused to consider even at a time when there were perhaps two thousand television receivers in the entire world.

Roy, too, saw television's potential, and in 1947 he ordered sets for all the company's executives. The next year Walt spent a week in New York for the sole purpose of watching TV "day and night." He returned from this awful vacation convinced, he told Hazel George, that "television is the coming thing."

By 1948 he was saying publicly that the newcomer would help rather than harm the motion picture industry, a view that proved highly controversial in the next few years when the studios came to regard television as a homeowner does termites. Still, Disney was cautious enough to hire a research firm named C. J. La Roche to study the wisdom of getting involved with the new medium. La Roche delivered its report, "Television for Walt Disney Productions," in September of 1950. Start small, it said; test the waters not with a series, but a single show. Two months later Disney announced a Christmas Day special.

Bill Walsh remembered that he was going through a period of frequently running into his boss in hallways and parking lots, when one day Disney stopped him and said, "You! You be the producer of my TV show."

Walsh was dumbfounded. "Huh? But I don't have any experience as a television producer."

"Who does?" Walt said, and that was that.

The startled new producer had been in show business for most of his life. "I was born in New York City on September 13," he said. "The year escapes me somehow [it was 1913]. It always goes sort of blank there. I lived there about two weeks, I could see the city was starting to fall apart, so I moved to Cincinnati, Ohio, where I grew up with an aunt and uncle who were in a tent show." He barnstormed around the Midwest with them during the summers, selling candy and tickets, and after graduating from Purcell High (leaving behind the rousing legacy of the school song he had composed, "Onward Cavaliers") he attended the University of Cincinnati on an athletic scholarship. His grades were abysmal from the start, but while still a freshman he wrote a show for the school's musical club that was good enough to catch the attention of the Broadway stars Frank Fay and Barbara Stanwyck, who were playing Cincinnati in a revue called *Tattle Tales*.

They offered Walsh $12 a week to join their company as a rewrite man, and that was the end of his formal education. "I thought Fay was under some kind of influence or something. Twelve bucks a week! This was the Depression, so I left that night with the Stanwyck-Fay troupe."

Tattle Tales went on to Broadway, where, Walsh said, it lasted for only five weeks, "despite the Cincinnati touch." Fay and Stanwyck headed for Hollywood, and Walsh went with them. He landed a job as a press agent: "I publicized everything from the Brown Derby restaurants to Technicolor to diamonds to Elizabeth Arden face cream, and a group of people such as Irene Dunne, Loretta Young, and Edgar Bergen."

Bergen thought Walsh's work showed a sense of humor sharp

enough for him to become a joke writer, and had him try his hand at it. Soon Walsh was turning out gags for the ventriloquist and his monocled dummy, Charlie McCarthy, and the equally popular team of George Burns and Gracie Allen. When Bergen got a role in Disney's 1947 film *Fun and Fancy Free*, Walsh contributed jokes to the movie and cowrote a song for it. The filming over, he stayed on with the company writing the Mickey Mouse comic strip (he enjoyed that work, and kept doing it well into the 1960s, long after he'd become one of Disney's highest lieutenants).

Disney's choosing him for the television job wasn't entirely impulsive, though it was slightly strange, as Walsh had recently sent a memo urging him to keep away from a project whose chances of success in a medium that seemed largely given over to "the roller derby and a lot of wrestling" were "something like going to the moon."

But Walsh was energetic and flexible—jokes, songs, PR, comic strips—and he started right in on the Christmas show, although, he said, "it was kind of stuck together with glue and chicken wire, very cheaply."

One Hour in Wonderland aired on Christmas afternoon of 1950. It opens with Edger Bergen and Charlie McCarthy driving to a holiday party where they are greeted by a roomful of teenagers. We first meet their host sitting astride the *Lilly Belle*, demonstrating its whistle. "So you see," Disney is saying, "this is the result of being a good boy for thirty years."

He goes on to summon the slave in the magic mirror from *Snow White*, and orders him to grant any wish for one of his guests. As the show was sponsored by Coca-Cola, she asks for "a pause for a little refreshment," and a table bearing Coke bottles under hillocks of shaved ice appears to a rapturous reception. But in fact the entire show is one long commercial for Disney's forthcoming feature cartoon *Alice in Wonderland*. The second wish the mirror slave grants is for a preview.

In that seedtime of the medium, the self-referential hard sell was happily accepted by critics and audience alike. The columnist John Crosby wrote, "The kiddies and the adults, too, could hardly ask for more of a

Christmas afternoon. Mr. Disney captured 90 per cent of the available television, and he put in a nice play for his upcoming movie. I hope he decides to do it again."

He did, this time confident enough to jettison Edgar Bergen and serve as the sole host of *The Walt Disney Christmas Show*, which was, like last year's, an extended commercial; and, like last year's, a great success. All the networks had long been eager to sign up a weekly Disney series, and Roy had been negotiating with them. Negotiating slowly and cautiously, for he knew a show would put a strain on the studio. A full television season ran twenty-six weeks at that time, and although the company had an immense archive, drawing on it too heavily would quickly pall. Most of the material would have to be new, which meant filming twenty-six little movies in half a year.

Now, though, Disneyland had given Disney a reason to do just that. Actually, two reasons. The first, he explained, was that "every time I'd get to thinking of television, I would think of this Park. And I knew that if I did anything like the Park that I would have to have some kind of medium like television to let people know about it. So I said, 'Well here's the way I'll get my Park going. It's natural for me to tie in with my television.' So it happened that I had a sort of say whether we went into television or not. I had a contract that had a complete say over what we produced. So I just sort of insisted that my Disneyland Park be part of my television show."

The second reason, of course, was that the network that signed on for a Disney program would have to help pay for the park. Disneyland speeded up negotiations that might have run their leisurely course for months, even years. Instead, there came the pressure-cooker weekend when Herb Ryman penciled Disney's vision of the park, and on that Monday Roy flew east to pitch it.

Despite his shrewdness, and his essential friendliness, Roy was perhaps not as good an emissary as his brother would have been when it came to selling a skeptical audience on a radical scheme.

In any event, he didn't sell it. He unfurled Ryman's elegant drawing to CBS and NBC, and got no takers. CBS's president, William Paley, invoked the familiar bugaboo: Disneyland would be "just another

Coney Island." David Sarnoff said, "I want your television show, but why the hell do we have to take that damned amusement park?"

That ended the first meeting, and Roy went back to California empty-handed. But then Sarnoff warmed—or seemed to warm—to the partnership, and Roy was encouraged by the time he turned over the negotiations to Joseph McConnell, the president of RCA. McConnell, however, strung things along for months, and after a particularly galling meeting Roy left the RCA Building, walked back to the Waldorf-Astoria, where he was staying, and called Leonard Goldenson, the president of ABC.

There was a reason Roy had saved the American Broadcasting Company for a last resort: ABC was the Anaheim of television. Founded as a radio network in 1943, the station had done well with such serials as *The Lone Ranger*, *The Green Hornet*, and *Sergeant Preston of the Yukon*. But after moving into television in 1948, it faltered, and by 1949 was on the edge of bankruptcy. An industry-wide joke had its initials standing for the "*Almost* Broadcasting Company," and the comedian Milton Berle said, "If the Russians ever drop a bomb, let's all run over to ABC because they've never had a hit."

Leonard Goldenson remembered that his famously farsighted rival David Sarnoff had finally brushed off Disney with one of the least accurate predictions of all time: "Cartoon films? Television will never be a medium of entertainment." When Disney at last gave up on NBC and called the ABC executive, he said that Goldenson asked, "Roy, where are you? I'll be right over."

Goldenson had preceded Disney into television by only a couple of years. He was a motion picture man who had come up through Paramount and was running its chain of theaters when, in 1948, the government ruled that studios could not also own movie houses. "I was hell-bent to get into television," Goldenson said; he saw it as an "irresistible tide." He had bought ABC in 1951 and found the business rough going. Surveying the field, he wrote that "ABC's network had only fourteen primary affiliates. By then CBS had seventy-four, NBC seventy-one. Since the number of viewers exposed per message determines the price of advertising, this meant one hour of CBS programming brought in five times as much as an hour on ABC. But the cost to create that programming was about the same for all networks."

He believed he knew the answer—"My position was we had to . . . bring Hollywood to television"—and headed west on a campaign to form alliances with the studios. In a time when Warner Bros. forbade its executives to have TV sets in their offices, and no movie would include a television among the furnishings of a prosperous home, he was everywhere rebuffed. At a luncheon with MGM he was told, "You're being a traitor to the motion picture industry. You'll take all our directors, producers, and talent over to television, and we won't have anybody to carry on ourselves."

"That's silly," said Goldenson. "If I were able to put a trailer of your next picture into every home in the United States, how much would you give me? A million dollars? Well, I rest my case."

His case rested alone. "I was trying to sell television as an opportunity to rejuvenate the movie business. Nobody was buying. Television was the enemy. I came back to New York empty-handed."

He didn't give up. "I had to find a way to get Hollywood into production. Otherwise we'd be dead pigeons." By the time he sat down across from Roy Disney at the Waldorf, he was willing to risk entangling himself in an expensive amusement park. He'd known that was probably what he'd have to do: friends at other stations had already warned him that the price tag for Disney programming came attached to something called Disneyland.

Right off, he asked Roy what it would cost. "Walt figures from two to five million to get started," Roy said. "But I figure maybe ten million." Goldenson figured maybe fifteen million: "After construction they would have to staff it, train people, and operate at a loss for some time."

Goldenson didn't like the idea any more than Paley and Sarnoff had. But he and Roy realized that each was the other's best hope. After two days of discussion they shook hands on a deal.

Months passed before that handshake ramified into signatures. Not until the following April did Disney announce the pact. ABC would invest half a million outright in the park, and purchase a weekly hour-long television program, paying Disney $50,000 a show during the first year, $60,000 in the second, and $70,000 in the third. In addition, the network would guarantee $4.5 million in construction loans. "In exchange," wrote Goldenson, "we took 35 per cent of Disneyland and all profits from the food concessions for ten years. I knew that could be a gold mine. And of course there was the programming. That's what I really wanted from them. We agreed to a seven-year deal, with an option for an eighth, at $5 million a year. At $40 million, it was the biggest programming package in history."

Reassured by this mounting cumulus of capital, Western Printing and Lithography, which had long published Disney books and comics, came up with another million. When all the paperwork had settled, the Disney company owned 34.48 percent of the park, ABC another 34.48 percent, Western Printing 13.8 percent, and Walt himself 16.56 percent, with options to buy out the other investors after two years.

Mindful of the worry the deal was causing his fellow moviemakers, Disney made sure to insist that he was "convinced of the compatibility of films and TV." After all, he said, he was currently in the midst of the three most expensive features his company had ever made—*20,000 Leagues Under the Sea*, *Lady and the Tramp*, and *Sleeping Beauty*—and they were bound to be consecrated to movie theaters, as all were being shot in CinemaScope, the new technology that permitted a wider image than TV screens could then accommodate.

That didn't mollify Spyros Skouras, who ran Twentieth Century-Fox: "We have been approached [by television networks] and we have refused because we believe the future is in the theater. If we were to sell our pictures today to television it would hurt the box office. It would be very disastrous at this time to destroy the theater business." The *New York Times* was more prescient than Walt Disney about the effects of his becoming "the first leading Hollywood producer to enter a formal alliance with television." The newspaper predicted exactly what was going to happen: "The end result could, indeed, change the complexion of the entertainment business."

As for Disney's part of the bargain, he—and Bill Walsh—had only the most shadowy idea of how he was going to fulfill it.

In their April 2, 1954, joint press release announcing the partnership,

ABC and Disney promised "an entirely new concept in television programming," with the "use of both live action and cartoon techniques in
a series of programs based on variety, adventure, romance, and comedy."

All this appealing blend had to support it was a scatter of haphazard
notes Walt had scrawled for Goldenson, of which the following is a fully
representative fragment:

- Half hour T.V. show presenting Disney hits of the past—
- Something of the present
- And things to come
- Special TV films to be produced
- HISTORY OF THINGS
     Fun with Facts
- MUSIC FOR THE LOW BROW
     You and Me
- WE CAN ALL DRAW
     It's a Cinch
- THE LOWDOWN ON ART
     A Good Cook's an Artist
- THE ORIGIN OF FABLES
     Aesop-LaFountain [sic]-Grimm

These offerings came with "Drawing Contests," "Story Contests," and
"Disneyland Contests," with "Plenty of Prizes" (the plan, perhaps not
a surefire parent pleaser, was to "give away ponies bred and raised in
Disneyland").

Sparse though this palette might be, Walt was sure of one thing: the
title of the new series—*Disneyland.*

15

SELLING THE IDEA

In planning, at least, Disneyland the park was far more advanced than *Disneyland* the show. Now, with the land nailed down and the financing in place, Disney felt it was time to present the park to his staff.

Of course there had been rumors—everyone knew something was up—but given how the park colonized his thoughts night and day, Disney had discussed it with surprisingly few of his employees. Possibly no more than twenty people in the studio had heard about Disneyland from the boss.

Disney knew the project would not be an easy sell. Buzz Price had been working on the other part of SRI's commission and getting scant encouragement from what he was finding.

Compared with scouting out the land, he said, "our second assignment (still in the fall of 1953), the feasibility study to be presented as a workbook or planning manual, was more intangible. We lacked comparable role models."

They went looking for them. Harper Goff said, "My wife and I traveled thousands of miles, all over the United States, trying to find information about, for example, what proportion should there be of men's toilets to women's toilets. . . . How much thievery? How many people came in a car? How big a parking lot?"

They clocked the duration of dark rides, those attractions where electrified cars fizz along a twisting path while amusing or alarming scenes flare into brief life. At the Pike, Long Beach's amusement zone, the Honeymoon Trail crackled from gate to gate in one minute and thirty-eight seconds; Laff in the Dark offered its patrons one minute and thirty-four seconds of lafter.

Buzz Price believed he gleaned the most valuable information not from any amusement park but at the San Diego Zoo: "a paradigm with good comparability, a good predictor of market penetration, attendance, and seasonal variation." It ran all year, as would Disneyland, and "shed light on economic performance and could be used for modeling."

Southern California's leading tourist attraction, Forest Lawn Memorial Park, was helpful chiefly in ratifying Disney's belief that his park should be lushly planted.

Price was disappointed by the result of his calculations on the performance of traditional amusement parks: "The average visitor was good for a stay time of two-and-one-half hours and a $1.50 expenditure."

Whitney's Playland at the Beach, a ten-acre operation in San Francisco, struck Disney as just another park, but his visit there proved fruitful. He'd expected to meet the owner, a vigorous entrepreneur named George Whitney. But "the Barnum of the Golden Gate," as he liked to be known, was too busy to see Walt, and sent his son, George K. Whitney Jr., to take him around. Although Disney wasn't interested in any of the standard rides Whitney showed him, he was impressed by his grasp of the business and his crisp, lucid explanations of how the park kept the crowds moving, entertained, and fed. Disney had said, "I don't want anyone hired who has anything to do with an amusement park," but he lured his guide away from Playland to oversee ride operations for him; Whitney was Disneyland's seventh employee, and the only one with any prior park experience.

As Price summed up many weeks of work, "We visited all sorts of attractions in the U.S. and Tivoli [gardens and amusement park] in Copenhagen looking for a model, any appropriate fix on numerical guidelines on what was being invented. We studied attendance peaks and seasonal variations, per capita visitor expenditures, on-site crowd densities, required ride capacity as a function of attendance, and investment levels. At the time we did not have names for these things. They had to be invented."

Invented. Price uses the word twice in that passage, and he uses it correctly. This park was more than an exercise in crowd flow and economic projections and architectural solutions. It was unlike anything ever before attempted, as much an invention as the Wright brothers' Kitty Hawk Flyer.

At the time Herb Ryman was sweating over his persuasive drawing, Bill Walsh was composing what current business parlance would call a mission statement to accompany it. In its steady inspirational tone, it reflects an entity entirely different from a place where plywood skeletons light up in the dark and bumper cars assault one another and you try to knock over an invincible pyramid of wooden milk bottles.

> *The idea of Disneyland is a simple one. It will be a place for people to find happiness and knowledge.*
>
> *It will be a place for parents and children to share pleasant times in one another's company; a place for teachers and pupils to discover greater ways of understanding and education. Here the older generation can recapture the nostalgia of days gone by, and the younger generation can savor the challenge of the future. Here will be the wonders of nature and man for all to see and understand.*
>
> *Disneyland will be based upon and dedicated to the ideals, the dreams, and the hard facts that have created America. And it will be uniquely equipped to dramatize these dreams and facts and send them forth as a source of courage and inspiration to the world.*
>
> *Disneyland will be something of a fair, an exhibition, a playground, a community center, a museum of living facts, and a showplace of beauty and magic.*
>
> *It will be filled with accomplishments, the joys and hopes of the world we live in. And it will remind us and show us how to make these wonders part of our own lives.*

This, then, was the essence of what Price presented at "the highlight of our feasibility analysis." That took place in November 1953 at the annual amusement park convention and trade show, held at the Sherman Hotel in Chicago. "There we cornered four of the nation's leading amusement park owners and fed them Chivas Regal and caviar in our suite." His audience, Price said, "were all important people in the industry, William Schmidt, owner of Riverview Park in Chicago; Harry Batt of Pontchartrain Beach in New Orleans; Ed Schott of Coney Island (the one in Cincinnati); and George Whitney of Playland at the Beach in San Francisco."

To these princes of the outdoor amusement industry Price, Nat Winecoff, and C. V. Wood explained the park-to-be for two hours, referring to Ryman's aerial view, which was fortified with many supplemental drawings. They told of the Rivers of America, plied by a full-scale Mississippi stern-wheeler, of a tropical waterway where visitors in motor launches would float past living jungle animals on its banks, of electrically powered rides that would whisk through the dwarfs' diamond mine and fly over London to Peter Pan's Never Land, of a lake with a pirate ship in it, of the still-vague Tomorrowland; they explained the turn-of-the-century main drag that led to the central hub, which would be dominated by a castle; they said everything would be immaculate, and richly landscaped.

The reaction was unanimous: Disneyland would not work.

Price took careful notes of the negative remarks—there were no positive ones—beginning with "all the proven moneymakers are conspicuously missing, no roller coasters, no Ferris wheel, no shoot-the-shoots [*sic*] . . . no carny games like the baseball throw," and several other things Disney didn't want, winding up with, "without barkers along the midway to sell the sideshows, the marks won't pay to go in."

There wasn't "enough ride capacity to make a profit," but that was irrelevant because "custom rides will never work" anyway: too costly to build and liable to break down. "And besides, the public doesn't know the difference or care."

Many of Disney's favorite projects made no sense at all: "Things like the Castle and Pirate Ship are cute but they aren't rides so there is no economic reason to build them," and Main Street "is loaded with things that don't produce revenue."

The single entrance would be another kiss of death: "This will create a terrible bottleneck. Entrances should be on all sides for closer parking and easier access."

Price's audience was particularly hostile to the Jungle Cruise, which "will never work because the animals will be sleeping and not visible most of the time."

Finally, "Walt's screwy ideas about cleanliness and great landscape maintenance are economic suicide. He will lose his shirt by over spending on things the customers never really notice."

One of the owners left Price with the advice "Tell your boss to save his money. Tell him to stick to what he knows and leave the amusement business to people who know it."

The dire litany didn't frighten Walt Disney.

That audience, those guys who called a paying customer a "mark," couldn't grasp what he had in mind.

He'd weathered equally discouraging criticism back in the *Snow White* days. And, as with *Snow White*, he would do his best to pitch Disneyland to his staff.

His best could be formidable. Ken Anderson had been there at the birth of *Snow White*, and he never forgot Disney's introduction to the project. Born in 1909, Anderson studied architecture at the University of Washington in Seattle, and did well enough to land a scholarship to the École des Beaux-Arts in Paris and the American Academy in Rome. After a brief stint designing sets at MGM, he joined the Disney Studio in 1934. At first he wasn't drawn to his new boss: "He didn't welcome me with open arms or anything like that. I was just one of the group, but I was horribly impressed by him. He was a very dictatorial guy." Nor did Anderson think him a very funny one. "I had a secret notion the he didn't have the best taste in these gags and things like that." There was too much barnyard humor, "all kind of countrified." This initial distaste didn't last long: "I found out that I was wrong and Walt was right." By the time *Snow White* was germinating, Anderson admitted that his feelings had evolved into something close to reverence. "I became a devotee of Walt's. I think probably I was his greatest admirer in the studio."

One afternoon in the mid-1930s Disney surprised his animators by giving them fifty cents to go to dinner and then come back and gather on the studio's soundstage. "That was a wonderful thing to get fifty cents because that's the same as five bucks now," Anderson said. "So I went over to this mom's greasy spoon and had a damn fine dinner for 35 cents and then had a good pie and dessert. . . . Waddling back to the studio, we went to the soundstage. . . . Not suspecting anything from Walt or anything at all, we came in and were all having a hell of a good time. . . . Anyway, Walt got down on this floor below in front of us at about eight-thirty or a quarter to nine and he started telling this story. No introduction at all, he just started in telling this thing and he acted all the parts. He did a fantastic job! He cooked me into such a tremendous stew that I would have killed for this guy. This was fantastic this thing we were going to do. Absolutely unbelievable! It was just marvelous! All these characters came to life while Walt talked. . . . He had most of the dwarfs down cold . . . and he told the whole story. It was midnight when we got out of there, and we were just really stunned. All of us, we walked out of there in a stupor and went home. The next morning we came in and then we didn't have our regular jobs to do, the thing was we were going to work on *Snow White*."

Twenty years and innumerable successes later, Disney put on an equally rousing show. He filled the studio's main projection room with renderings and models—the trains, the steamboat, the castle, the rocket ship that was the only sure Tomorrowland feature, and, of course, Herb Ryman's aerial view. After hundreds of employees had fifteen minutes to look these over, they took their seats and Disney came onstage and began to talk.

The audience heard the same thing the amusement park men had, but from Walt himself, not his executives. The effect was all he could have wished, and his listeners left ebullient at the prospect at working on this unprecedented undertaking.

That didn't last for many of them. Disney had concluded by explaining how he was going to pay for the park, and one of his animators said, "After our initial shock wave wore off, the full impact of what Walt said began to sink in. Our workload would increase dramatically. We'd have to turn out more film in a week than we had been doing in a year to support this TV schedule."

But few in the audience doubted Disney would get his park built. Anderson said, "I didn't have any extra money, but, boy, I sure would have put money down if he was going to build a place."

———

Now that his plans were fully in the open, Disney began selecting staff to work on Disneyland. Ken Anderson was part of it from the very earliest days. He would have described it as being shanghaied into working on the park: Disney "didn't ask me how I would like to—he just decided I *would* work for him, on his own, and cancel my Disney check . . . and be paid by Walt."

His new job worked out well for Anderson, but not at first, because "Walt forgot to pay me." Used to getting a weekly check, Anderson began to fret as day after day went by with no sign of his salary.

He was deeply nervous by the time Disney asked him absently, "Hey, Ken, I didn't pay you last week, did I?"

Anderson took the bull by the horns. "You didn't pay me the last three weeks, Walt."

"Oh, really? Jeez, that's bad."

On the spot, Disney wrote him out a check for all his back pay— multiplied by a factor of four.

"He would have been mad if I had said, 'Oh, God, this is too much.' I just had to be quiet. So I was quiet and accepted it. From then on he paid me every week, but he paid me three times what I would have gotten at the studio."

Several people had, like Anderson, trickled onto the project already— Herb Ryman, Harper Goff—but perhaps Disney's first real hire was Richard Irvine. A Stanford graduate and art and architecture student, Irvine had worked for Disney briefly during World War II before going to Twentieth Century-Fox as an art director. Best known for *Miracle on 34th Street*, and nominated for an Academy Award for his work on the

1941 adventure film *Sundown*, he had no plans to leave the studio when he got a call in 1952.

Disney had been in touch with Twentieth Century-Fox, a promising breeding ground for people likely to understand what he was after. Fox's back lot, four times larger than the Anaheim acreage Disney had bought, was an amalgam of many of the elements that would go into his park: Western log forts, recreated corners of nineteenth-century Chicago and New York's Lower East Side, country depots and bandstands, haggard cow-town streets silent between gunfights, even a full-scale (although landlocked) stern-wheel steamboat.

Disney called Lyle Wheeler, the Fox art director who had won an Oscar for *Gone with the Wind*, explained the difficulties he was having, and asked, "Who have you got available?"

"I've got this guy," said Wheeler, "he's perfect. He's got an architectural background from USC. He studied at the Chouinard Art Institute. He's a great combination of architect-artist. Dick Irvine."

Pleased with the coincidence that he already knew Irvine, Disney got him on the phone and explained what he wanted—someone with a solid movie background to serve as a liaison with the architects. Irvine said he'd come.

The liaising didn't last long. Disney, said Irvine, "decided that if he were really going to do his ideas and get them developed that he probably could start out with his own staff, so that we could jell the ideas before he could go with an architect. And then, finally, when he started to jell the ideas, the momentum started to build and he got excited about it, and went ahead and did it in-house, so to speak."

The house in question was the Zorro Building, where Disney had taken the startled Herb Ryman at the beginning of their big weekend. He'd bought the rights to a series of stories written, beginning in 1919, by Johnston McCulley about Don Diego de la Vega, an effete, cowardly nobleman in Spanish California who, masked and fearless by night, conducts an unceasing war against all sorts of evildoers. Douglas Fairbanks had made a hit out of this material in 1919, but although Disney would later put it to television use, he wasn't much interested in it at the beginning. So far, he had a few screen treatments, and a slapped-together approximation of Don Diego's hacienda that contained some gloomy, vaguely Spanish-colonial-looking furniture Disney himself had scavenged.

To his art director Marvin Davis, it was "a ramshackle, wallboard thing, very temporary, hot in the summer and cold in the winter." Once Irvine saw the architects were out of the picture, he hired Davis, who had worked with him at Fox and there developed skills that would prove useful: "I worked on the *Titanic* with Barbara Stanwyck. We did a lot of miniatures, on the back lot, with a huge scenic backdrop about seventy feet high. We had a lake in front of that for the three-fourth-inch model. They were that size so we could create realistic water. You shoot scenes at water level, and they look fairly realistic."

Still, "it was quite a departure for me to come with Disney and work on Disneyland. I was scared to death of the thing, and I was convinced that there was no way it could work. But by God it did. I started on Disneyland, in 1953, from scratch. I never had much to do with interiors of rides or structures. My planning always had to do with outsides, and areas." However frightened he may have been, Davis didn't often show it: he soon gained a reputation for being as mulish and demanding as Disney himself, and in 1955 he got a foot in the family door, marrying Marjorie Sewell, Walt's niece.

He first met Disney when Irvine introduced the two men in the Zorro Building. Disney "invited both Dick and I up to his house to take a ride on his train, which was impressive for me because it was Walt Disney. I was pretty thrilled about all of this. I got the impression that he was trying to give us the idea of what he wanted for Disneyland. He used his Carolwood Pacific railroad as an example of what he wanted to do next. There was a definite link between Walt's train at his home and what he went on to do at Disneyland."

Davis set to work in his uncomfortable office. "I did a hundred and thirty-three different drawings and designs, because we had no idea where the park was going to be, or anything, to begin with. I just started out putting together the ideas that we had all talked about . . . the idea of the train circling everything, in a kind of oblong shape. Then we started using the pear shape, because it seemed to accommodate all the things we needed."

Both Irvine and Davis would prove invaluable to Disney in the months and years ahead. They were the nucleus of the WED team that would acquire a name as firmly rooted in Disney tradition as Donald Duck's.

16

IMAGINEERING

Wilson Follett's *Modern American Usage*, published in the mid-1960s, includes an entry on "telescopings," what Lewis Carroll called "*portmanteau words*, because they packed several meanings into one container, like one's belongings in a suitcase or portmanteau." Follett doesn't like them. He grudgingly acknowledges that Band-Aid and Frigidaire are relatively "sedate," but after forty years "the cleverness of these manufactured names is beginning to seem tawdry, even for articles of trade." He decries "*travelodge, transistor, selectric*, etc.," and contemptuously adds that "the *Wooletin* is published by the American Wool Council."

Follett does not mention the compound that attached itself to the WED staffers, but there is no doubt what he would have thought of it. They were applying imagination to engineering problems: they were "imagineers."

Besides being one syllable too long for comfortable pronunciation, the word carries a whiff of arrogance (as though ordinary engineers *didn't* require imagination to build, say, a Titan II rocket). Although Disney once surprised Buzz Price by thanking him for originating the term, it was not born in Disneyland, but in the 1940s, when the Alcoa Corporation coined it. A 1942 *Time* magazine ad proclaimed: "For a long time we've sought a word to describe what we all work at hard here at Alcoa . . . IMAGINEERING is the word. . . . Imagineering is letting your imagination soar, and then engineering it down to earth." The term migrated to Union Carbide, whose in-house publication explained in 1957 that "BRAINSTORMING IS IMAGINation engineERING." A couple of former Union Carbide employees evidently brought the word with them to WED, where it began to crop up with increasing frequency. By 1989 it had become so inextricably bound to the company that Disney trademarked it (serial number 73803332, registration number 1584097), and WED Enterprises became Walt Disney Imagineering.

Though he wasn't yet calling them imagineers, Disney now needed a lot of them, and he got them summarily. Gone was the easy affability with which he'd introduced the park to the staff. A week after his presentation he walked past John Hench's drafting table and, without breaking stride, tossed down a command, "I want you to work on Disneyland. And you're going to like it," before hurrying out of the room in search of other draftees.

Hench went to work on Disneyland, and he *did* like it. In a way, his inclinations had been prompting him toward such an exercise, even though he didn't know it. As an art student in San Francisco and New York he'd proved himself a gifted draftsman, but he was also deeply interested in what made paintings work, about precisely how the visual mechanisms they contained could both convey and shape emotions. His teachers had little time for this: Just follow the long-established laws of color and balance and perspective, they told him, and don't brood about what goes on in the viewer's mind.

His frustration with that arid response led him to the movies, a medium that communicated through images more kinetically than did painting. He came to the Disney Studio in 1939, and went to work on *Fantasia*, which allowed him to indulge a fascination that went back to earliest childhood: "Color has always been of special interest to me. I remember going on a fishing trip in the mountains as a little boy with my father. I caught two trout from a running stream. I was struck by how elegant they were as their iridescent colors shone brightly in the sunlight. They were so beautiful—so colorful, I thought—that I just couldn't keep them. My dad wanted to cook them for dinner, but I persuaded him to let them go."

Fish and color got him started at Disney. While trying to create an undersea atmosphere for the "Arabian Dance" sequence, he noticed that "the wall in the bedroom where I worked was plastered with a sandy finish, and by holding black paper up against it and rubbing pastels over the paper it produced a sparkle effect suggesting unusual underwater lighting." Then, "when they found out I could draw sexy girls, they told me to take a stab at sexy fish. After a lot of work, we were finally able to get something satisfactory."

Better than satisfactory: Hench drew so well that in 1953 Disney entrusted to him the "official" twenty-fifth anniversary portrait of Mickey Mouse. Hench loved his subject, and thought hard about the hold the mouse had on the world. "As a graphic representation, Mickey is a symbol of life. He is a series of round shapes that have a distinctive relationship characterized by the flow of one curve into another, creating lines that relate to each other in the musculature of a human being. Curves typically indicate movement typical of the living human figure. I see Mickey as a record of dynamic movement." And more: those curves suggested fecundity, regeneration, babies and breasts, the lost safety of the womb, the life impulse itself.

Hench spoke that way, his conversation peppered with Freudian allusions and Jungian archetypes. This wasn't mere chatter; he was seriously interested in just how it was that Disney's fairy tales had such power to enthrall. The innocent wayfarer through life, beset by perils and escaping them, went back, he believed, to the bedrock foundational myths of the race. "I think our pleasure comes from survival. The first thing we strive for as an infant is the kind of life experience, and it's the last thing we want to give up. We strive for . . . the experience of being alive." And when you've escaped the darkling wood, outwitted the murderous witch, you feel most alive. "Pleasure is sweetest when we are triumphant, when we have survived. The implication is that we have one struggle behind, and we are that much stronger for the next one."

He believed that the power of the visual was part of our Darwinian legacy. "The better you use your eyes, the further away you can size up a situation and relate it to survival or its opposite, the better off you are. So those of us who are here today, whose ancestors survived, are very good at relating images together." When it came time to create Disneyland's castle, Hench saw the building as something more potent than a picturesque architectural fantasy. "We carry these so-called myths, and they're part aspiration, part dream, and it's something we share, on a fundamental basis, of course, with every living person. The castle was a strong point, and I suppose it actually has something to do with the relationship with mountains, too—with a high point in the landscape. It's a place of safety. I think the medieval churches also played up that same kind of feeling. It was a large architectural statement, and it said something to people about a rallying point, a safe place, a protector." To stand beneath the battlements of Disney's castle, he believed, would make the visitors feel secure, secure in a dimly understood way that they had yearned for since the mists of infancy.

Disney might have seen these constantly expressed musings as so much gaseous piffle, except that Hench was extremely good at what he did. And he did almost everything: "I guess I've been in most departments. I didn't get a chance for character animation, but I did do effects animation, and I worked through story and layout, background painting, and multiplane background painting. Then I wanted to go down to Camera and see what happened to all this stuff, so I spent three years in Camera and Special Effects. And the studio, at that point, was able to do things like that. I asked Walt, and he said, 'Sure, go ahead.'"

Such praise as Disney gave usually took the form of an absence of criticism. Once, having gone over some sketches with one of his artists, Samuel McKim, he said, "Sam, you did a good job." Sam's boss, Jim Algar, was there at the time. "Jim asked me to come into his office afterwards," McKim said, "and asked me to close the door because he wanted to have a private chat. He said, 'You know, Walt just complimented you, and I want you to know something. In all my forty-six years here, Walt has complimented me twice. You remember this . . . it doesn't happen very often.'" That's why Disney's pronouncing Ward Kimball a genius was so well remembered around the studio, and why he startled those who heard him say of John Hench, "Johnny has never let me down."

Nor would Hench let Disney down now. He understood from the start that Walt wanted something more akin to a motion picture than an amusement park. "In designing Disneyland, we thought of the park as if it were a three-dimensional film. We wanted *everything* that guests experience, not only the shows and rides, to be an entertaining part of the story. This was a new idea: we took the most basic needs of guests and turned them into attractions."

Disney continued to prowl through the studio tapping people for his park—some for a few weeks or months, and some, as it turned out, for years. Before long he had so eaten into his workforce that the disgruntled staff members left behind began referring to WED's dilapidated hacienda as "Cannibal Island."

17

THE ADMIRAL

While Walt was busy recruiting, Roy made a hire of his own.

"I remember him with some awe as a baby-faced gangster," a high school classmate of C. V. Wood's said years later. "He smoked, drank gin, did unspeakable things with girls, and stole his folks' car for joyrides. But then strangely at the other end of the pendulum he was an Eagle Scout."

That last wasn't a figure of speech: Wood really *was* an Eagle Scout. The rest of it was true, too, save that the things he did with girls were far from unspeakable: he spoke of them constantly to admiring friends.

He'd always had admiring friends. Woody lived for approbation and learned early how to get it. He was born in Oklahoma in 1920, the son of a brakeman and conductor on the Santa Fe. The railroad must have been a strong family influence for a long time, as his father was named Commodore Vanderbilt Wood, and so, too, apparently was Woody, although he denied it, always insisting he was "C-for-nothing V-for-nothing Wood."

His family moved to Amarillo before he entered elementary school, but he had already formed an identification with the state he would say had nurtured him. While still in Oklahoma, at the age of five, he had fallen under the spell of Tom Mix's cowboy movies, and especially the hero's rope handling.

He set about learning the ways of the lariat with the intensity that would mark him all his life. His grandfather gave him some instruction, and so did the cowboys who often blew through town, but basically he taught himself, and by the time he entered first grade in Amarillo he had mastered the Wedding Ring, the Merry-Go-Round, even the demand-ing Texas Skip that had him bouncing in and out of the spinning loop.

He made his debut in his new neighborhood in full Texas regalia: Tom Mix chaps, leather vest, holsters at his waist. Given the brutal vaga-ries of small boys this splendor might have earned him a pummeling. But he had the moves to back it up.

One of the first friends he made, a boy named Eugene Lemmon, said, "To my complete surprise and envy he began to twirl the rope and jumped through it as he spun it from side to side." That Lemmon was still on hand to talk about this years later suggests Wood's knack for making lifelong friends. During his lackluster high school career—he was smart enough to figure out complex mathematical problems in his head, but never worked hard—he formed a cadre who called themselves the Bombers. They stayed loyal to him, and he to them: many would follow him from job to job for decades.

Wood brought a mixture of dedication and raffishness to all he did. During the Boy Scout career that he pursued to the high plateau of Eagle, he'd routinely set out on hikes with a canteen full of wine.

So it went in college, which was, strangely, a religious one: Hardin-Simmons, a Baptist school in Abilene. He avoided expulsion only because his lariat was an ornament to the Hardin-Simmons University Cowboy Marching Band. A classmate of his said, "He was a trouble-maker from the day he hit school. He was smart enough. There wasn't any real doubt about that. . . . The only way he ever made it through college was because he could throw that goddam lariat. . . . His conduct was bizarre. He'd do everything from paint the dean's house to blow up the barn. He was constantly up to pranks. He just had that look about him: that sweet, kind face, and the mind of a goddam criminal."

After two years as scholastically lackadaisical as they were socially strenuous he transferred to the University of Oklahoma in 1939, aim-ing, or so he said, for a degree in petroleum engineering. He seems to have hung on there until December of 1940, but the next spring, with overseas war orders strengthening the American aviation industry, he applied for a job at the Consolidated Aircraft Corporation. He was aim-ing for an hourly salary as a riveter, but at some point during the interview the con artist in him stirred, and he persuaded the Consolidated personnel people that he had a degree in engineering. He didn't, but he landed an engineer's job in Consolidated's inspections department.

This meant he had to leave his spiritual home state for Consolidated's San Diego plant. There he threw himself into work that was leagues above any training he had received for it, drawing on his Eagle Scout's energies and not his paint-the-dean's-house ones. Early in his new post he finished, within forty-eight hours, a satisfactory report that his boss had thought would take upward of a week.

Perhaps more important, his Texan persona began to ripen under the California sun. Whatever sunken genius he had for instinctively grasping complex mathematical concepts, he had a greater one for making friends: hearty handshakes, yips of delight, penetrating eye-to-eye looks of sympathetic understanding, artless country ways (his boss was tickled by how Wood called a Coke "so*dee* pop") that never quite hid what he presented as a first-rate education, his confident energy, his ability to assert his leadership without abrading the feelings of far better qualified colleagues, an effortless authority in the boardroom, and a contagious relish for shepherding companions through Mexican whorehouses on the occasional weekend blowout. His soft, faintly childish features, brightened by a limitless arsenal of dirty jokes, gave him the air of a debauched cherub; he radiated a combination of louche intimacy and professional decisiveness that most men and many women found hard to resist.

Wood rose at Consolidated until, at the age of twenty-seven, he was appointed the chief industrial engineer overseeing construction of the B-24 Liberator bomber. This post brought him to Washington, where his carefully groomed personality won him close friends in the Pentagon. By now he had the authority to hire from his old gang; half a dozen Bombers, including Eugene Lemmon, who had been dazzled by his rope tricks two decades earlier, joined him at Consolidated.

The war over, SRI recruited him, and all during the forced-draft acquisition of Anaheim orange groves, Roy Disney kept an eye on Wood. In early April of 1954 Roy took him to a Los Angeles bar for a drink and a talk. Walt, of course, was in charge of the creative side of the amusement park; Roy was responsible for much of the construction and the finances. He liked all the things about Wood that everyone else did, and he saw something else there, too: Wood clearly understood the park as primarily a moneymaking enterprise. No matter what gorgeous new entity Disneyland might lay in the grateful lap of Southern California, it had to pay. Roy told Wood that he needed a general manager who would serve as a counterbalance to Walt's more extravagant visions. This person should of course understand construction—and, after all, hadn't Wood built long-range bombers?—but most important, he must keep a sharp watch over the till.

Would he like the job?

Wood didn't hesitate. "I can promote it," he said. "I can get the money for it. I can build it. I can manage it. And you and your brother can do all the dreams that you want."

A couple of days later the agreement became final: C. V. Wood was executive vice president; as he exuberantly told Lemmon, "I got the job of building Disneyland."

He believed, quite naturally, that Walt had fully backed his brother in hiring him. That wasn't quite the case.

Although during their land scouting days, Walt had enjoyed Wood's unflagging enthusiasm, especially as compared with Buzz Price's skeptical caution, he was one of the few immune to the new vice president's charm. Never a glad-hander himself, Disney rarely responded warmly to one. And this man who had built an empire by making people laugh loathed jokes, especially dirty jokes. He found the buildups tedious; to him they were all shaggy dog stories, sterile exercises that lacked the crucial component of the visual. "He was prudish yet he was earthy," said Buzz Price. "He was a fierce editor of humor in his environment. His brother Roy once told me, 'You'd better watch it, your funny bone will get you in trouble.' Herbie Ryman told me after I got a fierce reaming out over a mild joke about death statistics. . . . 'Everybody knows you don't tell an off-color joke around Walt, and death is not an acceptable topic under any circumstance. Let him tell the joke.' I did not repeat the mistake."

Nor would Disney have warmed to Wood's easy assumption of equality with anyone he was speaking to.

The official word was that Walt had welcomed his new executive vice president with some hearty encouragement along the lines of "Since you helped plan this park, get it built!" In fact, Disney concluded a brief and rather cool conversation with the acrid observation that Wood's new position "doesn't leave much room for advancement."

Wood was never quite in tune with the budding Disneyland ethos, but right at the outset he laid hands on a person who would prove essential to the park's success; indeed, to its very existence.

———

From the start, Disney had been particularly interested in how crowds flow through public spaces. He wanted to ensure that Disneyland visitors were constantly tempted to keep moving. To draw them along, he envisioned a series of attractions to which he gave the rather undignified name of "wienies" (current park employees are discouraged from using the term).

All his life he remained fond of hot dogs, and when he came home from work he'd often pull two raw frankfurters—wieners—out of the refrigerator and eat one while sharing the other with Duchess, his poodle. He dispensed it by increments, walking from room to room with Duchess following him, always after the next morsel.

Just as the hot dog lured Duchess, so would his wienies beckon his customers. The first of these "visual magnets," as John Hench called them, and the only one that could be seen from outside the park, would be the railroad station at its entrance, enlivened by the constant passage of gleaming steam locomotives. Inside, the castle would pull the crowds along Main Street. Disney knew from the start what his Frontierland wienie would be: the tall stacks and lacy wooden scrollwork of a Mississippi River stern-wheeler.

The vessel would be a scrupulously accurate steam-powered recreation of the sort of riverboat no American shipyard had produced for more than half a century.

Disney told C. V. Wood about this, and as it happened Wood was friendly with Rear Admiral Joseph W. Fowler, a man who knew a good deal about building ships.

Fowler had graduated from Annapolis in 1917, and having been second in his year, was one of two academy men from his class invited to do postgraduate work at the Massachusetts Institute of Technology. He took a master's degree in naval architecture in 1921, and put it to work in Shanghai, designing and building Yangtze River gunboats, a tour of duty that left him with a lifelong detestation of the future Chinese president General Chiang Kai-shek. He was designing submarines at the Mare Island Naval Shipyard in Vallejo, California, when the bombs fell on Pearl Harbor. His duties ballooned, and soon he was running the San Francisco Naval Shipyard with forty thousand workers under him, along with all the other West Coast yards throughout the war.

He retired in 1948, but was back in uniform a few years later, smoothing naval supply systems during the Korean War, and then, out of uniform but not out of service, he worked to cut waste in fifty-seven government branches.

It was during this stint that he met C. V. Wood, who was in charge of an SRI study on how to set up uniform procedures for guided missiles among the three services.

In 1954 the fifty-nine-year-old Fowler was out of government for good, living in Los Gatos and managing the construction of Bay Area tract houses, which, though profitable, seemed mundane after sending new warships into battle.

That April his friend Woody telephoned him, and after a good deal of ribald banter (unlike Disney, Fowler enjoyed a joke), Wood said, "Joe, I'd like to come up and see you. I'm bringing a friend."

Joe said that would be great, and on April 17 Wood appeared at the door of his ranch house. He'd actually brought two friends; one was Nat Winecoff, and the other was Walt Disney.

They sat down over drinks, and early into the conversation Disney told him about the steamboat, and went on to describe the park that was to house it. Everyone got along fine; there was no discussion of any specific job, but as the visitors made their farewells Disney said, "Joe, I'd like to have you come down next week and have a look at Disneyland. We'll send you a ticket."

It arrived quickly. The next Monday the admiral, having packed a single change of clothes, set off for Los Angeles, telling his wife, "I don't know anything about the motion picture business. I'll be back tomorrow night." Mrs. Fowler wouldn't see her husband again for three weeks.

In his Burbank studio office, Walt talked about Disneyland for half an hour, then excused himself: he had to see the rushes from the previous day's filming. "I'll be gone for maybe an hour," he said. "Help yourself to anything you want. Push the button—get coffee. Here's a copy of the *Wall Street Journal.*"

Disney never returned.

After a while a secretary appeared in the doorway.

"Are you Joe Fowler?"

"Yes."

"Will you come with me?"

"Sure."

They went down the hall past several doors, and then the secretary stopped and opened one. "This is your office. There's some contractors in the office opposite we want you to talk to." She remembered something and handed him an envelope. "Here's the keys to a car."

"That was my introduction," said Fowler. "Nothing was mentioned about salary for about a week."

Nothing was mentioned about the steamboat, either, not at first. Plunged into a round of meetings, Fowler came to realize that this job, whatever it was, would involve more than a single stern-wheeler. But he was not a man intimidated by complex work, and he knew right away that whatever lay ahead was worlds more interesting than tract houses.

He finally did get a job description from his new boss: "Now Joe, I will create in my mind all the things we're going to do, and your job is to make engineering realities out of them."

Put in more concrete terms, he was to be the construction boss for the park, which had to open in a year. Well, he was used to wartime schedules, and wartime exigencies. "I don't think," he said, "that I ever had a complete set of plans of anything I undertook at Disneyland."

Disney had been set on having a riverboat in his park for nearly as long as he had on having the encircling steam trains. Ward Kimball said, "To Walt Disney the *Mark Twain*"—there had never been any doubt about the name, either—"and the Disneyland trains were like the seventh and eighth wonders of the world." Fowler started right in on it.

The hull was laid down at the Todd Shipyard in San Pedro. It was 106 feet long—the vessel was designed on a five-eighths scale—and unlike those of its forebears, the *Natchez* and the *Robert E. Lee*, was made of steel. The rest of the boat would be of mid-nineteenth-century materials, but built to the most rigorous twentieth-century specifications, with all castings and forgings meeting the standards of the American Bureau of Shipping. The vessel would look just like an 1850s craft, but not be prey to the manifold weaknesses of its dangerously volatile and combustible predecessors (some five hundred riverboats were destroyed by boiler explosions; the *Mark Twain*'s namesake had stood at the bedside as his younger brother, Henry Clemens, died from one).

One hears the voice of an earlier era in the descriptions of the boat's makeup: the planking above the hull "caulked with three threads of yacht cotton and the decking with two threads," the fir upper deck sheathed in cotton duck of "approved weight, laid over a coat of marine glue, made smoother with ends turned and tacked to the edges."

Mississippi riverboats burned wood for fuel; the *Mark Twain* had oil-fired boilers, but steam would drive her. The two big, slow-breathing horizontal engines, each with a brass lubricator to inject oil into the cylinders, took shape not at Todd but in the shop of Disney's steam savant, Roger Broggie. Doors, banisters, and the bar on the promenade deck were made in Sound Stage 3 in the Burbank studio. Fowler, wanting work done closer to Anaheim, insisted that the opera house be one of the first Main Street buildings completed so that he could have a machine shop in the park itself; the *Mark Twain*'s carefully researched scrollwork was cut there.

That search for historical accuracy extended to every fitting. Century-old running lights had to be found, and for the first time in decades craftsmen turned out fire buckets with rounded bottoms to hang along the ship's main deck (because these couldn't stand upright on their own, they discouraged deckhands from grabbing them for other chores and leaving their brackets empty when danger struck).

Although this marine archaeology was new to Fowler, he had no trouble taking it in stride, and work on the *Mark Twain* proceeded smoothly on schedule. But his riverboat-building forerunners had one great advantage over the admiral: Fowler had to supply the river as well as the boat.

18

THE INSTANT JUNGLE

The initial step toward giving the stern-wheeler something to float on took place on July 12, 1954, when a bulldozer started scraping at Disney's acreage. For a place that was going to produce continual pageants, the work commenced with surprisingly little fanfare. An official groundbreaking had been scheduled for August 26, but there were, among the Anaheim citizenry, enough holdouts still worried about carnival disorder to cause fears of a public protest, and the idea was dropped. Besides, it had become clear that the schedule allowed little time for extraneous festivities.

Disney had hired McNeil Construction, a third-generation operation that had been helping build Los Angeles since 1868, as the prime contractor. What McNeil's bulldozers' blades turned up, said Morgan "Bill" Evans, "was sand. It was almost ball-bearing sand. You could have used this stuff for a good grade of concrete. It wasn't contaminated with any soil. It was just sand. This isn't the best prescription for horticulture."

The sand concerned Evans because he and his brother Jack had been hired to landscape the park—as Bill said, "to put a green frame around all those adventures and rides."

The Evans brothers had grown up around plants. Their father cultivated a three-acre garden given over to unusual greenery, and a 1920s tour of duty with the merchant marine allowed Bill to harvest exotic seeds from lands as distant as South Africa and Australia. Home from the sea, he nurtured his seeds and in 1931 began wholesaling rare plants to local nurseries. Five years later he and Jack opened a landscaping business. Their unusual inventory gained them a Hollywood clientele that included Clark Gable, Greta Garbo, and Elizabeth Taylor.

Walt Disney brought them to Holmby Hills to dress up the Carolwood Pacific right-of-way, and was so happy with the result that he gave them their largest job. "We landscaped all of Disneyland," said Bill, "in less than a year with a maximum of arm-waving and a minimum of drawings."

The Evans brothers' intimidating challenge was that from the day Disneyland opened, the park had to look as if it had been there forever. This meant they needed mature trees. "We superimposed a drawing on an aerial photograph of Disneyland over the trees on the land and endeavored to salvage whenever possible the existing orange trees. We did this because they represented to us the equivalent of about five hundred dollars a tree, which was a lot of money in 1954. Wherever the grade remained at the original elevation, we could keep the trees." Still, they needed far more of them than their $360,000 budget could accommodate, which led to a working routine that often seemed more a scavenger hunt than a horticultural project.

Bill Evans was friends with the head of landscape architecture for the California Department of Transportation, and thus got advance word when a new road was about to cut down the trees that stood in its path. "The Santa Monica Freeway, the Pomona and the Santa Ana Freeways all yielded trees for Disneyland. We paid twenty-five dollars for each tree to the contractor who was going to bulldoze them and take them to the dump. That fee was so he'd stay away from those trees and not bruise them, while he was wrecking everything else. As fast as we could, we'd get in there and put a six-by-six box around the roots, which was anywhere from five to ten tons a unit, and then pick up the tree and drive it down to Anaheim and give it a new home."

Evenings they spent cruising through prosperous neighborhoods with Harper Goff, the art director for Adventureland, knocking on the doors of houses whose yards contained promising specimens and offering to buy them outright. Sometimes they got lucky. In Beverly Hills they came upon a magnificent banyan shading the lawn of an equally magnificent house, a tree easily worth several thousand dollars.

Goff rang the doorbell and, when the owner answered, nervously asked if he might consider parting with his tree. The man laughed. "That big old son of a bitch there? I'm so tired of that thing." Goff and Evans got it for the cost of installing a small tree in its place.

They scored at least one coup closer to home. A Canary Island date palm stood on the land Disney had bought. "Planted in 1896 by an early rancher," said Bill, "it was a stalwart and revered resident of his front lawn, admired by three generations of children and adults. One member of the family was married beneath it. When the owner of the land sold his acreage . . . he requested that this venerable palm be preserved. Walt was more than happy to oblige, but since the tree stood in the middle of Section C of the projected parking lot, he ordered that it be carefully 'balled,' lifted tenderly from its old home, and trundled, all fifteen tons of it, to Adventureland." The tree stands today near the Indiana Jones ride, the oldest living thing in the park.

The landscaping that would matter most, and prove most difficult, had to ape a jungle's dense tangle. There were to be two main waterways in the park, the Rivers of America, in Frontierland, along which the *Mark Twain* would glide, and, in Adventureland, the Tropical Rivers of the World. The latter had evolved from Disney's initial idea for a "River of Romance," a boat ride through the Everglades. By 1953 this had rotated halfway around the globe to become a waterborne safari that would take visitors from a dock out into a lake, there to steam around a tropical island.

Harper Goff realized that wouldn't work. He told Disney, "What you've got is everybody on that boat if you go counterclockwise around the island, having to look to the left. The boat isn't going to go sideways, so half the people will have to look over the shoulders of people beside them." Better to cut a river through the island so there'd be things to see on both sides.

Disney worried it would take too long to load the boat, get to the island, cruise through it, and then return to the dock. Goff suggested that racing boats could speed to the island, then slow down for the river. Disney rejected this out of hand. Goff finally countered with a ride that followed a circular route through heavy foliage, ending where it began. That became the Jungle Cruise.

To encourage jungly growth, the brothers drenched the coarse, sterile soil with fertilizer, and planted it with anything that would look convincing. They were not attempting a true jungle; Bill Evans had been in several, and found them boring: "Turns out when you really plod through an authentic jungle you are apt to travel for a day or two and the scenery doesn't change much." Instead, "we were trying to capture this armchair traveler thing and get all kinds of textures and all kinds of effects. The palms. The tree ferns. The philodendrons. You get a kind of 'man-eating' atmosphere. The giant bamboo was not actually a jungle denizen, but it fills a role conveniently. You might discover a rather pedestrian castor bean plant, but the effect is good and it adds to the texture.

"We picked material from Brazil, material from Africa, material from India and Asia and Malaysia. We pushed it all together. It's all quite compatible in the sense that it all has that lush, vigorous growth. What we attempted to do in planting the jungle was to make it look as though we had nothing to do with it."

Harper Goff came up with an ingenious idea for using the definitely non-tropical walnut tree. He "had the inspiration of turning them upside down to get a kind of mangrove effect [from the gnarled roots] onto which we grafted the top half of the orange truncated also to get branches. It was a pretty good illusion."

The orange trees they'd worked into the mélange would make trouble for years, as Disney gardeners beat their way through the jungle every morning before the park opened making sure that nobody on the cruise would see the anomalous fruit glowing through the undergrowth of the Mekong Delta. But in the end, the Evans brothers' efforts proved remarkably successful. As Bill said years later with justifiable pride, "That two-acre man-made jungle is the best damn jungle this side of Costa Rica."

There was more to the Evans' job than planting. "There's another very important thing we accomplish with landscaping," Bill said. "In order for Walt Disney to take his guests by hand through an Indian Village, or a Missouri wilderness, or an African jungle . . . what he doesn't need is a high-rise building or transmission tower, or freeway interchange in the background. We have to shut all that out. We have to bring the guest in from whatever circumstances he left behind when he passed beneath the Disneyland Railroad tracks and entered the park. We don't want any visual intrusion. In order to accomplish this, we build a berm to shut out the sound outside. Trees alone won't do it. It takes about a hundred feet of dense trees to block sound, but you can do that with about twenty feet of earth. Then we garnish the berm with all the landscaping we can afford, and in this way we exclude the twentieth century."

———

The berm was finished early, a naked earthworks guarding the yet-to-appear city-state, its flanks formed with dirt gouged from the riverbeds of the Amazon and the Rio Grande.

The berm was relatively easy, the work of a few bulldozers. Furnishing its enclosure was not. While Disney's designers drew elevations of the spirited storefronts and public buildings of Main Street, his animators were struggling to create a new kind of kinetic architecture, amusement park rides that told stories the same way that movies did.

The movies, of course, were Disney movies—*Snow White*, *Peter Pan*, *The Wind in the Willows*—and the animators began by storyboarding scenes, making a sort of highly evolved comic strip in which each panel showed how the action advanced. This was a familiar, decades-old chore; but nobody had ever tried to storyboard something that would end up in three dimensions while unfolding a coherent narrative. To be sure, the dark rides Coney Island mounted during its glory days in the first decade of the twentieth century had sent boats or electrically powered cars past elaborate scenes of Venetian palaces, Swiss chalets, coal mines, and, in one oddity, the crimson chambers of hell. No Coney entrepreneur, however, thought to string together such shadow-box tableaux into any kind of story.

The outdoor amusement industry offered no help. Just as Disney had been discouraged by the parks he'd seen, so was he by the manufacturers he visited. He had already decided against a roller coaster for Disneyland, so what he viewed were mostly flat rides, those that flung the customers around in erratic circles on a horizontal plane. The Tumble

Bug, the Caterpillar, the Tilt-A-Whirl, the forty-year-old Whip and the brand-new Scrambler, the Flying Scooters, the Loop-O-Plane and its descendants the Roll-O-Plane, the Fly-O-Plane, and the Rock-O-Plane, the Octopus . . . beyond the shrill splash of decoration on their cars, all Disney could see were armatures and linkages, chains and grease-caked sprockets, an industrial clutter that seemed to him the antithesis of fantasy.

So when Dick Irvine urged him to travel to Mountain View, 350 miles to the north, and drop in on a small manufacturer, he only grumpily complied. His reluctant visit would have crucial results for Disneyland, and for the amusement industry worldwide.

19

ARROW

The Arrow Development Company had been founded in 1945 by two California boys, Edward Morgan and Karl Bacon. Both of them had been fascinated by invention since childhood, and had suffered the usual fiascos of the mechanically inclined youth. At sixteen Ed built a rooftop roller coaster shut down by parental fiat after it broke a playmate's collarbone; Karl's interest in chemistry had led him to build a hydrogen generator that exploded in his kitchen and gashed his grandmother's hand. The two met during the war, at a navy plant where they were working on torpedo launchers.

After V-E Day, they decided to go into business together. "We met with an attorney in town," Bacon said, "and he asked what the name of our business would be. Ed looked down at his tie and he had a stickpin. Ed said, 'Arrow.'"

The attorney approved: "That's good; it puts you at the front of the phone book." When he went on to ask what Arrow was going to do, neither of the founders had any idea.

"Fabrication and machine work was all we knew at the start," said Karl. "Ed and I built our first shop. We laid the brick ourselves, built the whole thing." In it they installed a decrepit lathe and mill, and began to pick up commissions from Hewlett-Packard which, however welcome, were always demanding. "The way HP usually worked," said Ed, "was if they were buried or had problems that they really didn't want to face, they'd give it to us. When we got things going well, they'd take it back and do the manufacturing themselves and keep it in-house."

Karl said, "We made *everything*," and given that catholic franchise

the partners paid attention to a newspaper story about a San Jose amusement park soliciting bids for a twenty-foot carousel. Morgan's sole experience with the amusement business had been that rooftop coaster; he
had no idea what a merry-go-round cost. He wrote the venerable carousel firm of Allan Herschell in upstate New York asking the price of a
twenty-foot machine and, with that information in hand, subtracted the
hefty shipping cost from the East and bid the job in.

"We knew nothing about merry-go-rounds at that time," said Bacon.
"But we did know a fellow at a carnival in Palo Alto." He let them spend
a day with one of his carousels to "measure the shaft and gears and see
how the thing worked." They returned to Arrow and recreated it—in
steel. "Everything had been wood up until then," said Morgan. "This
was the first of the all-steel carousels."

San Jose liked it, and Arrow was in the amusement business to stay.
A couple of years later the partners made a forty-five-foot metal merry-
go-round for a park in Fresno, but, said Ed, "we mostly made portable
carousels, and portables are plain because most of the baroque castings
[on a traditionally decorated merry-go-round] were plaster, and you
can't have that on a portable. Now they're fiberglass. They'd tear these
things down after three or four days and move on, so everything had
to be extremely portable. They were, from the mechanical standpoint,
very advanced. But from the aesthetic standpoint, I am really ashamed
of them."

Arrow began to diversify. Postwar shortages made things tough—the
only truck they could lay hands on in those early days had been through
a fire; it ran, although it never did get new floorboards—but the partners found that the sudden quenching of the vast national military flow
could work to their advantage. Morgan was delighted to discover a near-
infinite supply of surplus airplane fuel tanks: "You could buy them for
ten bucks each or something like that. You couldn't create anything like
it for a pile of money. They came in crates so they weren't all beat up. We
had templates [that showed] where you could cut a well out of them. We
suspended them and made little rocket ship rides out of them. It was an
inexpensive ride, and we sold a lot of them."

They began to make and sell miniature sheet-metal trains, which came out so nicely that in 1952 the city of Oakland commissioned an excursion boat to cruise around Lake Merritt. This resulted in the *Lil' Belle*, a stern-wheeler powered by a gasoline engine and decorated with a pair of oversize show stacks, a pilothouse, and a large brass bell.

The *Lil' Belle* was at work on Lake Merritt when, Morgan said, "I read in the newspaper about Disneyland. We thought, boy here's a chance to get in on this thing." They sent a letter describing their boat. "The newspapers were very sketchy as to what Walt Disney was going to do. But they did respond."

The response came from Dick Irvine, and on January 6, 1953, Arrow replied, on letterhead that advertised "TRAINS. MERRY GO ROUNDS. AUTO RIDES. PLANE RIDES": "Thank you for your inquiry on our stern wheeler boat. I regret that we do not have the photographs and information on it worked up as yet. However we are having these things prepared and will forward some to you as soon as they are completed."

When the additional information came, it persuaded Irvine that Arrow might be able to supply Disney's riverboat (Admiral Fowler had not yet arrived, and the *Mark Twain* lay months in the future).

Disney and Irvine headed north to Mountain View, along with Bruce Bushman, one of Disney's animators who had been kidnapped to Cannibal Island. Bushman, who'd worked on *Fantasia*, had already shown what Disney believed to be an instinctive grasp of the rides that would best suit Fantasyland, and he was adept at envisioning the cinematic flow of the attractions.

Morgan and Bacon had done their best to present the *Lil' Belle*: they were so excited, said Morgan, "that we got permission from the city of Oakland to dry-dock the boat, truck it down, wash it, polish the brass, and put it on a stand."

The visitors arrived. They approached the *Belle*, and, to Morgan's dismay, "they walked right by it and didn't even slow down. Talk about a sinking feeling!"

The pictures hadn't conveyed its small scale. The boat was just over twenty feet long, and its nod to historical fittings looked tacky despite the fresh paint and polish. While Bacon and Morgan stood disconsolately to one side, Disney walked around the workshop giving cursory glances to the half-assembled rides, and the gas-powered trains that had nothing to do with the steam-driven ones he had in mind. He paused only once, to examine a small car patterned after the Model T Ford. It was a far more literal Model T than the *Belle* was a riverboat—boxy snout, brass radiator, high wheels. Then he made ready to leave.

Bushman stopped his boss and took him aside. He had been working on what would become Mr. Toad's Wild Ride. Drawn from *The Wind in the Willows*, it would allow the driver to become the car-infatuated Toad and pilot his automobile on a reckless spin first through Toad Hall and then out into nighttime London, narrowly avoiding catastrophe at every turn. Bushman had brought sketches of Toad's vehicle as he imagined it. He told Disney that they didn't yet have anybody who could actually *build* a car, and that Model T was pretty nice. He asked to show the partners his drawings.

Disney, at his least encouraging, sullenly told him to go ahead if he wanted to.

Bushman went over to Bacon and Morgan. "Well," he said, "I think what we'd like you to do is have you make one of the cars from the sketches I've brought with me. Don't assume these are final. But they pretty much show what we're looking for."

That was it: No talk of payment, no assurances that, once produced, the prototype would be followed by further orders. And nothing like a working drawing. What the partners were looking at was a breezy caricature of an Edwardian touring car that resembled their Model T only in that it had four wheels.

Still, this opportunity—if opportunity it was—would not return.

"Yes," said Morgan. "I think we can."

In his sudden and unanticipated role of sculptor, Morgan set to work with sheet metal and aviation shears to create a functional vehicle that retained the whimsy of a cartoon. When he was satisfied that he had something that might pass muster, he called Irvine, who returned with Disney and Bushman.

They examined Morgan's car. It was all raw new metal—paint would go on at the Disney studios—but the proportions were there: the scooped-out, downward-sloping hood familiar to 1910 motorists, headlamps that gave the amusing suggestion of a face, a wide, cheerfully out-of-scale passenger seat.

The three men conferred while, as before, Morgan and Bacon nervously kept out of the way. After a long few minutes Bushman came over to the partners. "Walt is very pleased," he said. "If you feel your company can handle this, we'd like to have your company build the vehicles and support system for this ride."

There was more. Bushman produced drawings for another ride, the Casey Jr. Circus Train that fights its way up the mountainside in *Dumbo*. It was far more complex than the Toad car. Bacon immediately said that they could handle the job.

But that was distant. Probably feeling pangs of nostalgia for those slapdash portable carousels, they started in on the Toad cars. "We just went from the original sketch by Bruce Bushman," said Morgan. "No drawings were ever made of the car. Not a single drawing. I lofted one [drew full-size patterns], and when that was lofted I took templates from it, and from the templates we built the subsequent ones. With the templates, we were able to cut out the sheet metal parts. The templates, which were cut out of plywood, showed the line of the fender and the line of the hood. We went directly from a handmade prototype to templates and to the parts."

This swift, rough-and-ready approach occasionally made Morgan jealous of the Disney shops. "That was the big difference between us and Disney. Everything they did was superb. Their welders were artists. They could write a book on the subject. Everything they turned out was like that. There were times we did things just because it was necessary for survival. Poor folk have poor ways."

They would not be poor folk for long; Arrow and Disney would work closely together for the next twenty years.

1

Disney works on a cartoon with Edith Moore, one of his artists, in 1944. Still vexed by the 1941 studio strike, and worried that he had gone about as far as he could with animation, he was already beginning to think about an amusement park.

2

Ward Kimball and his wife, Betty, aboard the *Emma Nevada*, one of the three narrow-gauge steam locomotives they collected for their Grizzly Flats Railroad.

3

Partly inspired by the Kimballs, Disney built the powerful little *Lilly Belle*, seen here at work with Walt at the throttle on the Carolwood Pacific line that encircled his home.

4

Park map in hand, Disney talks with his highly valuable lieutenant John Hench—possibly crossly, as Walt's infamous raised eyebrow seems to be in evidence.

5

Walt's brother Roy basks in the commercial glow of 3,000 company-licensed items in 1953. Without his formidable business acumen, Disneyland might never have come about.

6

Fess Parker and cardboard clone: the *Davy Crockett* show helped Disneyland stave off bankruptcy.

7

Used in the first Disneyland television show on October 27, 1954, this model shows City Hall, the firehouse where Disney had his private apartment, and, in the foreground, the endlessly troublesome bandstand.

8

Disney views a miniature Sleeping Beauty Castle.

9

The castle's spire takes shape in early 1955.

10

Two privileged early visitors with holstered cap pistols
assess progress on Admiral Fowler's *Mark Twain.*

11

The TWA Moonliner
noses onto the
construction site just
eleven days before the
grand opening.

12

July 17, 1955: The unprecedented television special about the park's opening
day, *Dateline: Disneyland,* begins with Walt and Mickey steaming
into the Santa Fe and Disneyland railroad station.

13

Disney about to open the castle "in the name of the children of the world."

14

With the drawbridge lowered,
children stream through the gate.

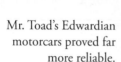

15

Bob Gurr's temperamental Autopia cars: by the end of the park's first week, just two will still be running.

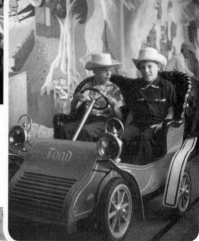

16

Mr. Toad's Edwardian motorcars proved far more reliable.

17

In the beginning, the popular Mad Tea Party ride made almost as much trouble as Autopia.

18

Vice President Richard Nixon enjoys the Snow White ride in August 1955, while his daughter Julie checks to make sure the witch isn't in pursuit.

By 1956 the fully populated Rivers of America featured rafts to Tom Sawyer Island, at left, and, in the foreground, a replica of an 1830s keelboat.

Disneyland unveiled three big attractions in 1959:
the Matterhorn, the Monorail, and the submarine voyage.

Walt Disney in an uncharacteristically empty Town Square, possibly musing about what his $17 million has bought, and definitely planning how to improve on it.

20

HARRIET AND THE MODEL SHOP

While the Arrow crew was learning to hammer together Toad's Edwardian motorcars, Disney likely had already been on the ride itself—skidded through the Toad Hall library, swung past teetering crates of explosives, got a nighttime glimpse of Tower Bridge before being caught in the headlamp glare of an onrushing locomotive—in a pasteboard simulacrum six inches high.

This miniature adventure would have taken place in the WED model shop, which was housed in quarters that made the Zorro Building seem palatial by comparison: a derelict boxcar parked on the Burbank lot. Despite its cramped and splintery disorder, this was one of Disney's favorite places. "When Walt got up to his eyeballs in company politics, he'd tell his secretary Dolores, 'I'm going to take a walk on the back lot,' meaning that he would come visit us. That gave him a little breather. He could just walk down the back lot, and there we were. Then he could relax. It was like his toy shop."

That is Harriet Burns reminiscing. She was the first woman hired by WED in a creative rather than a secretarial job. A child of the Depression whose father had told her he would send her to college only if she majored in home economics, she went, and defiantly shifted her major to art. After graduating, she got a job working on displays for Neiman Marcus, and edged toward show business when she was taken on by a company named Dice Display Industries to make props for television and Las Vegas floor shows. When Dice went under, she heard that Disney was hiring, and applied. At the interview she was told there was no position open for a woman, but she persevered, and got a job (maybe, she liked to say, she was granted that first interview because they thought her name was Harry).

She painted props for the future Disney television shows until the boss noticed the delicacy of her work and moved her to the model shop. A confident woman, she had no trouble trading racy wisecracks with her male colleagues—and she could work a drill press with the best of them—but "it was the 1950s. I wore color-coordinated dresses, high heels, and gloves to work. Girls didn't wear slacks back then, although I carried a pair in a little sack, just in case I had to climb into high places."

Burns was the second hire for the model shop. The first, her immediate superior—with whom she always enjoyed a close collegial relationship—was Fred Joerger. He had graduated from the University of Illinois in 1937 with a bachelor's degree in fine arts, and was working on model sets for Twentieth Century-Fox when, in 1953, he heard that Disney, getting ready to make *20,000 Leagues Under the Sea*, needed someone who could build miniature versions of Captain Nemo's submarine. The movie is testament to what a good job he did. Although Harper Goff, production designer on the film, had never met Joerger, he remembered the fine little *Nautilus* he'd made, and asked him to stop by for an interview. Burns said, "Harper Goff was a great guy, but crazy as a loon! When Fred was sent down to Disneyland prior to the opening, he saw a man sitting in a boat in the load area of the Jungle Cruise. He had a red beard, wind blowing his hair all over, and was playing a banjo. Fred thought, 'Boy, that must be somebody's idiot son. . . .' It was Harper! He was a brilliant man, and he got Fred his first job at WED."

Joerger's initial task was making a model of the *Mark Twain*. It was a beauty, and all the work that followed was just as good. One might think devoting a lifetime to tiny, intricate constructions, often under intense pressure (Burns said Joerger would "get blueprints from the art directors as 5 p.m. . . . and he'd have to have a model ready by 9 a.m."), would make for a fussy and intractable temperament. Not at all: Joerger gained the reputation of being the most sunny-natured of all Disney's lieutenants. "Fred was a super and easy person to work with," said a colleague. "I think anybody that you talk to will say that Fred was one of the very few persons who never yelled, never raised his voice, and no matter what critical situation he was in, he was unflappable. He was always smiling, always pleasant. That's the kind of person you want to work with."

Disney had lost none of his initial enthusiasm for the Thorne rooms, remembered with pleasure crafting his little stoves, but the model shop was more than a hobby. As one who had made trees dance and ducks talk, he distrusted the reliability of renderings, and he disliked the chilly indigo distance of blueprints. They can lie, he said; models don't. And they'll save you money: "A model may cost five thousand, but it's sure less expensive than fifty thousand to fix the real thing."

As Joerger put it, "If you don't get it into three dimensions first, you may have a disaster. Well, my job was to create the model to avert disaster, which was fun, but a challenge."

Burns said, "Most anything at Disneyland, Fred created a model first. He constructed several versions of Sleeping Beauty Castle, for instance, changing each design, moving the turrets around, changing colors."

They started on the castle with several models no more than eight inches high, "then we had Herb Ryman and Eyvind Earle [at the time a studio background artist] paint them. Eyvind did a very unique one, all trimmed in black, red, and gold. Ultimately Walt decided to go with the one Herbie did, with pastels. He felt it would look better against the blue sky that way."

Next Burns and Joerger built a larger model out of plywood and Masonite. They were both clever extemporizers. While the Evans brothers were counterfeiting a jungle with real foliage, the two modelers discovered how to fake the miniature greenery around the castle's ramparts. "We would take little tiny manzanita branches," said Burns, "and we had lichen from Florida. It was from a swamp and they would send us a gunnysack full of it, all dried up. We would soak that stuff in alcohol and glycerin, and it would fluff up beautifully. We would always have a bucket of that going. Then we could shake it in a bag of pigment— green and brown—it just looked terrific. It made great bushes or trees or anything."

Disney did all he could to insert himself into the midst of their miniatures. Fred Joerger put some of them up on stilts so the boss could see them at eye level; and when this proved insufficiently intimate, Roger Broggie helped develop a reverse periscope that let Disney explore Main Street by bending down and examining it from above through a mirrored tube that put him right in among the shop fronts and hitching posts.

All this went on in the unsatisfactory confines of the boxcar. "Back then, everything we had was junk!" said Burns. "Sometimes we'd set up a sort-of plywood table to show the models on. My 'desk' was a table saw with a piece of plywood over it, and I had an old bent-up stool. So when we needed to use the table saw, it would take Wathel [Rogers, who made up the third of the trio of modelers] and Fred to lift the plywood off, and we'd make the needed cut, and then put the plywood back down. This was just like working with your neighbor in your garage."

After about a year of that, Disney told Fred, "I've been looking around and trying to find you more space. I don't know, Fred, that big warehouse back there . . . the plasterers used to cast up back there, but they stopped using it because it was too hot."

The warehouse was hot because it was two stories high and made entirely of corrugated metal, and apparently there was no airconditioning system potent enough—or cheap enough—to overcome the drawback. But it was enormous. Disney warmed to his idea. "If you want it, Fred, there is a lot of room. You can work back there, and I'll put big fans up. I'll have pipes put on top of the roof and fill them with water. That should cool it off."

So they moved into the warehouse, and found it not much better than the boxcar. Burns said, "When we got our bigger model shop in the back, we were always getting just crummy furniture, whatever was thrown away, the crud, because we had a concrete floor and were using all sorts of crude things from paint stuff, polyester . . . and we had it all over the place. We wore smocks and we were all crudded up. So they just gave us whatever was left over. Each of us had a desk, supposedly. I came back one time and they'd painted mine titty pink."

The stifling place immediately gave her heat rash. "And the water on the top—he had sixty-seven pipes put up there, but the water sprayed all over! It was like a waterfall at the door. . . . But the funniest part was—it didn't work. None of the water worked. It made it slightly cooler, but it steamed everything up inside. Our paint wouldn't dry and we were just like broccoli in a steamer."

They told the maintenance crew to "shut off the pipes—but please don't let Walt know." He'd meant well, he'd tried, and they didn't want to hurt his feelings.

In the early months, Disney was an almost daily visitor. The modelers liked this signal that he valued their work, but he was not always a helpful presence.

Some months after the move to the drizzling warehouse, Burns was laying out a stained-glass window for a rural English church. "I was doing all the leading, and working out all the window designs and color. I got to work with the metal shop. I worked the machinery with my foot, and cut the lead pieces and then beveled them. I really enjoyed that. I love lead because it's so malleable. We didn't really need to do that—we could have just put celluloid behind Plexiglas. But at the time, since Walt loved model making, and he loved detail, we did it that way."

Midway through her medieval labors, she had 360 pieces of lead for a single window arranged on her workbench. Disney stopped by, was intrigued, snatched up the assemblage—"and I hadn't soldered it together! It just scattered everywhere!" The modelers "finally learned that if Walt was coming in—have everything glued down because he wanted to play with it so badly."

Despite its uncomfortable quarters, the model shop was productive. In 1954, *Reader's Digest* sent a writer named J. P. McEvoy to interview Disney. Most of his article is given over to the successful nature films the studio was then making. Having witnessed "as many as 24 automatic cameras at a time watching one flower open," McEvoy wrote, "in other buildings we waded through a fascinating jumble of miniature worlds— the frontier land of the past, the rocket-space world of the future, the never-never fantasy land where the fairy-tale Disney characters all live together happily ever after. Maps covered the walls, tables overflowed with contour models and scale drawings, and the floors of the studios, shops and hallways were knee-deep in models of old-time locomotives, paddle-wheel boats, Wild West saloons, Sleeping Beauty Castles and gleaming, jet-propelled spaceships to the moon which looked quite capable of making it. This was the chaotic chrysalis of 'Disneyland'— Walt's newest practical dream, a ten-million-dollar permanent playground fair scheduled to open in July, less than an hour's drive from Hollywood."

21

REAL TRAINS

Disney did not ask the shop for a model of the attraction that most interested him. He didn't need to; he already had a perfect one in the *Lilly Belle*.

Banished from the Carolwood right-of-way, she had been passing the months of Disneyland's birth in exile beneath the machine shop drafting table, a forlorn object, perhaps, but not a forgotten one: a colleague of Disney's remembered, "Once in a while Walt would wander in and look at his engine. He would always touch it in a special way making sure it was all right."

He had—literally—big plans for the *Lilly Belle*.

In December of 1953, the Norfolk & Western outshopped (the locomotive maker's unlovely term for completing a new one) the S1a-class No. 244. A modest 0-8-0 switch engine, she carried the distinction of being the last standard-gauge steam locomotive produced for a mainline road in the nation her 175,000 predecessors had done so much to create.

While No. 244 was learning her yard duties, Walt Disney was building a factory to keep the once-titanic tradition alive.

Initially shrunk to its one-eighth scale backyard size from the Central Pacific prototype, the *Lilly Belle* was now going to expand to five-eighths scale. This meant the new locomotive would be more than two-thirds full size and run on three-foot-gauge track; she would in every way look and behave like the real thing. The *Lilly Belle*'s tipping over on Disney's lawn could be remedied by Walt and Roger Broggie heaving her upright again; any such grief befalling this new locomotive would require cranes and winches to repair. And, backing them up, signals, sidings, a round-house, water tanks, all the paraphernalia of any grown-up railroad.

Disney announced the *Lilly Belle*'s ambitious postmortem career to Broggie without any preamble: "We need to get started building the rail-road for the park. Do you think the boys can do it here in the studio?"

Broggie, fresh off having helped conceive and build the immensely complicated giant squid whose attack on the *Nautilus* feels as though it takes up a quarter of the film (and won *20,000 Leagues Under the Sea* an Oscar for special effects), might have been relieved to return to a ratio-nal world of cylinder heads and cutoff valves. "Since we have the *Lilly Belle* locomotive and have all the information on the trains already, we can just take the drawings and blow them up for the park locomotives."

That was quite a "just." Disney was proposing a railroad line that would be carrying thousands of passengers day in and day out year-round.

At least he understood he'd need a roomy machine shop to build it in. That job fell to Broggie's fellow Carolwood Pacific alumnus Jack Rorex, who was given a site behind the studio's ink and paint depart-ment. "Just tell Purchasing to order the equipment and materials you'll need," Disney told him, adding, probably unnecessarily given all that was going on, "Don't get anything extra—budgets will be kinda tight around here for quite a while." Rorex had the new machine shop ready in less than three months.

What would be made there began with a huge blackboard bearing the chalked outline of the *Lilly Belle* blown up to full three-fifths scale. Despite his skepticism about working drawings, this one looked fine to Disney; "That's it. That's the right size for the park," he said. Broggie told him the cab had to be larger: after all, it needed to contain a full-size engineer and fireman. Accepting the slight loss to *Lilly Belle*'s elegant proportions, Disney agreed.

As work went forward on the first locomotives—there would be two of them—they deviated some from absolute fidelity to their pro-totype: slightly shifted placement of bell and steam domes, somewhat smaller driving wheels, and so forth as various engineering difficulties cropped up.

None of these confounded Ed Lingenfelter, who had behind him a lifetime as a draftsman for the Pennsylvania Railroad and the Southern Pacific, and was making the construction drawings for the Disney engines, while Roger Broggie and Richard Bagley saw to their design. Dick Bagley was a mechanical engineer whose colleagues believed his abilities bordered on the eerie: when Disney gave him a sketch of how he thought the *Mark Twain*'s engines should look, Bagley turned it into a working reality dense with double inlets and intricate exhaust valve gearing. Edward Sargeant, who had originally drawn up the *Lilly Belle*, was in charge of the designs for the rolling stock the locomotives would pull. Disney had complete trust in Eddie but also, being Disney, knew exactly what he wanted from him. Walt had already found a favorite passenger car.

One of the many springs that watered the Disneyland idea flowed from Griffith Park, the 4,300-acre oasis in the Los Feliz neighborhood of Los Angeles. Griffith is home to a magnificent 1926 Spillman Company carousel, and in one of Disney's several varying origin stories, he said, "Disneyland really began when my two daughters were very young. Saturday was always Daddy's Day, and I would take them to the merry-go-round and sit on a bench eating peanuts while they rode. And sitting there, alone, I felt there should be something built, some kind of family park where parents and children could have fun together." (The bench on which he sat is currently on display in the Disneyland Opera House on Main Street.)

Now Griffith Park made another contribution to Disneyland. In December of 1952 a group of Los Angeles steam enthusiasts had dedicated Travel Town there, a museum of Western railroad history that had locomotives and rolling stock on display. Disney was a frequent visitor, and his eye—which missed little—told him one of the exhibits would be right for his railroad. It was a three-foot-gauge day coach built around 1900 in the shops of the Oahu Railway & Land Company, a typical car of its era, with its slightly shrunken size accentuating the features that made it so: the high spine of its windowed clerestory running the length of the roof, which curved down over the open platforms. Disney would pattern his passenger cars on it.

Back to the chalk to work out the scale. "We drew a full-sized car on the blackboard," said Broggie. "Railroad cars are ten feet wide, so we drew a ten-foot car with a standard six-foot, eight-inch door. Then we reduced the size until we got down to a six-foot doorway." The reduction narrowed the car to seven feet. At that point, Disney had a plywood mock-up built in what was five-eighths scale, and stepped into it. "Well, I can go through a six-foot doorway. That ought to be enough." Naturally he had no trouble: he was five feet, ten inches tall. His was a sound call, though; there have been no recorded complaints about the door heights on the Disneyland railroad.

The cars would be built from scratch, but the makers had a surprising stroke of luck when it came to the hardware and fixtures. There were still enough narrow-gauge roads operating in the country to keep in business the C. M. Lovsted Company of Seattle, which was able to supply most of the metal fittings in five-eighths scale.

The coaches were made entirely in one of the Burbank studio's sound stages, but the locomotives needed to have some larger components contracted out to local companies. The boilers went to the Dixon Boiler Works, the wheels and frames to the Wilmington Iron Works. When the boilers and frames were ready to be joined, Disney got a call from Wilmington's manager. Dixon was not a union shop, he said, and Wilmington was: the boilers could not cross his threshold.

Broggie brought this substantial problem to Joe Fowler. In one week the admiral had the foundation for a roundhouse poured on the Anaheim site, track laid, and enough of the building up for the frames and boilers to be mated on Disney soil.

The good fortune that had brought Fowler Disney's way was still at work when a letter arrived at the studio from a man who knew railroads and railroading every bit as well as the admiral did ships and heavy construction.

Disney had assembled a crew whose knowledge of steam machinery could not be surpassed anywhere in the country. But a locomotive, however perfectly functioning, is only one small element of a railroad, a machine that is part of a much larger machine; to do its job, it needs a far-flung infrastructure of thousands of interrelated parts. Earl Vilmer understood all those parts.

Born in 1906 in Pittsburg, a Kansas town that had itself been born when a rail line came through the area thirty years earlier, Vilmer was working for the Kansas City Southern when he was barely into his teens. Beginning as a machinist, he'd risen to roundhouse foreman by the time he was twenty-three, and held that post until he enlisted twenty years later, in 1943.

The army had needed seasoned railroaders, and Vilmer came in on a captain's commission, in charge of a battalion that sent ten million tons of materiel from the Persian Gulf to the Eastern Front: "We hauled the stuff to Tehran, where the Russians took over." He ended the war a major, overseeing the reconstruction of French rail lines that had been all but obliterated during the Normandy invasion and the subsequent Allied push north.

The war over, he returned to Kansas, but things seemed pretty quiet to him there, and when, in 1952, the Bechtel Corporation wanted a railroad to serve their iron holdings in South America, Vilmer took his wife and five-year-old daughter, Judith, to live in the Venezuelan jungle while he built it. This was good for two years, but he realized Judith needed a better education than she could get in a remote tropical village summoned into existence by a mining operation.

The Vilmers went back to Pittsburg. Bechtel had evidently paid its supervisor well during his jungle stint, for he seemed in no hurry to get a job. Answering to the same spur that prodded so many in those hopeful, restless postwar years, he moved his family to California, and there, in the fall of 1954, in his Pasadena apartment, he picked up his morning copy of the *Los Angeles Times* and saw an article about Walt Disney's plans for a new amusement park. He read it with mild interest, which abruptly turned intense when he got to the steam train.

He would write the Disney people. And what he wrote had to look professional. That same morning, he went to a pawnshop, bought a portable typewriter, and on September 22, 1954, sent Roger Broggie a letter that began, "Dear Sir: In a manner of introduction, I am greatly interested in the Disneyland project and would like to offer my well-rounded experience in railroading and railroad equipment." He went on to explain that experience to Broggie in great detail, an engineer talking to an engineer. But he closed with a flash of passion that would have helped win Disney over: "I have always been a firm believer that the steam locomotive would never become useless—Disneyland will substantiate my belief."

Broggie invited Vilmer to lunch; by the time he called for the check, his guest had agreed to oversee the construction of the Disneyland railroad, and the horsecar tracks that were to run two-thirds of a mile along Main Street. The locomotives were well under way when Vilmer arrived, but he got there in time to draft construction plans for their tenders. He took charge unobtrusively—he was a calm and quiet manager—and his operation ran so harmoniously that the railroad was to be the first completed Disneyland attraction.

It was also one of the most expensive: before a yard of track was taken into account, the engines and rolling stock cost just under a quarter million dollars.

———

Disney was all too aware of the money that was going out, and was disappointed with what it had bought. Again and again he asked his WED people when Disneyland would begin to look like "something other than a hole in the ground."

Already 350,000 cubic yards of earth had been moved, and 12,500 orange trees, 700 eucalyptus trees, and 500 walnut trees replanted or done away with. But McNeil Construction had to install four thousand feet each of sewer lines and gas piping, two thousand feet of storm drains, and a mile and a half of water mains before anything substantial could be built aboveground. The schedule had that preliminary work done by September, but deep in October the job remained uncompleted. This wasn't entirely McNeil's fault. F. M. Franz, the company's manager of operations, who was overseeing sixty subcontractors, said, "From the standpoint of construction this project certainly has been unique. We feel sure there has never been anything like this built in

Southern California, or elsewhere in the United States." Because the project was indeed unique, plans kept shifting.

When Joe Fowler arrived, and his vision expanded beyond the *Mark Twain*, he realized that the Main Street buildings would need stronger underpinnings than the architects had specified (eventually, the site would drink up five thousand cubic yards of concrete). Moreover, there was something that had never occurred to the non-nautical planners. The *Mark Twain* weighed 150 tons, and, said Fowler, "we couldn't lift that ship out and take it to the shop." She had to have a dry dock for repairs and the occasional overhaul. This was a serious facility, and Disney didn't want to pay for it. He knew better, however, than to turn down a man who had spent his life building ships. Still, the substantial excavation galled him, and whenever he passed it he'd say—half-amused, half-aggrieved—"Aw well, here's Joe's ditch." (Today it continues to do its job under the more respectful title of Fowler's Harbor.)

One day, Disney took Harper Goff up a temporary wooden observation tower his crew had knocked together in the middle of the site, and the two stood looking out over a landscape as desolate as the Western Front. "I have half the money spent," he told Goff, "and nothing to show for it." Goff saw tears in his eyes as he repeated, "Nothing."

22

KING OF THE WILD FRONTIER

In the meantime, Disney was busy honoring his bargain with ABC to pay for his sloping fields of dirt.

For months the studio had been working to come up with a feasible series. Back in March, Disney said at one of the many, many meetings, "The format of the show is America. We can mingle fantasy, we can dream and be fantastic. There is no one over here telling us we cannot—I think this is part of America. We can show Frontierland and Main Street as part of that package."

That is how the program began to evolve. Each week would have a different topic, but all the topics would be anchored in one or another of the park's four lands.

Disney was nervous when it came time to sell this package to the network. It was, after all, patently self-serving; would the ABC brass see the proposed show as an endless succession of commercials for the new park?

Disney made his presentation to Robert E. Kinter, the president of ABC, on April 22, 1954. He needn't have worried. "It is a very exciting concept," Kinter said. "I think this would be great. I accept it." He added, "I hope you have a large mail department."

The probable recipient of the anticipated fan mail was of two minds about the role he would play in the series. There had been a good deal of discussion around the studio about who might serve as the host, but as the time drew near Disney realized that if there was one, and it was not a cartoon character, it would have to be Walt. He announced this in a lengthy and, for him, introspective talk at a publicity meeting for *Lady*

155

and the Tramp. "I don't consider myself an actor or anything, but in try-ing to get hold of these things I can introduce them, get them going. I'm myself, good or bad, I'm still myself; that will be the gimmick. It's the safest bet to get under way, then we can develop ways and other people can take over. If we over-use me, I'll be the first to recognize it; I know my limitations. If it's right for me to be talking about it, if it's my busi-ness I can talk about it; if it's what we do here at the studio, the group the individuals and the staff—it would be no problem to do that.

"I stumped myself, worrying about being in too much of it. I haven't got a good voice to carry narration, got a nasal twang, I know. I'm not being immodest, just being practical. But I just think it's the way to get this thing off. We've been avoiding it, but I think I have got to do it until we've established other personalities that mean something to the audience."

No such other personality would emerge in Disney's lifetime, but he never came to enjoy being on television. "I'm as big a ham as anyone, but actually it's an ordeal for me to be in front of the cameras. They wanted me to smile, to be warm. All I could see was that cold eye of the camera and the glum faces of the crew staring at me." Sympathiz-ing with his stage fright, the resourceful nurse Hazel George said, "I had heard of egg beaten in sherry." The potion would both smooth his throat and lessen his anxiety. "He liked that," George reported.

Disney's introductions were to be filmed on a set purporting to show his office. The effect was a bit surreal, as the window of the set looked out on the studio's Animation Building, which contained the actual office. As usual, Disney was a stickler for detail, and he wanted all the awards and knickknacks and pictures in his office to be in the set—and then wanted them returned to the real office as soon as the shooting was over. This meant a good deal of exasperating work trundling loads of personal effects back and forth, but their familiar presence added to what ease Disney could summon.

The first show aired on October 27. It was called "The Disneyland Story."

The program opens with the legend "DISNEYLAND" floating alone on the screen. A comet of light circles the word and resolves itself into Tinkerbell. The pixie from *Peter Pan* was carefully chosen for her introductory role: she was appealing and popular, yet not in the top tier of the studio's characters. If the show failed, Disney didn't want it taking Donald Duck or Mickey Mouse down amid the wreckage.

Tinkerbell scatters a sparkle of pixie dust and "DISNEYLAND" becomes "WALT DISNEY'S"; curtains draw back to reveal, again, "DISNEYLAND," this time in front of a painting of the park in an aurora of celestial radiance. "When You Wish Upon a Star" begins to play, and an authoritative voice—not Disney's—proclaims, "Each week as you enter this timeless land, one of these many worlds will open to you: Frontierland, tall tales and true from the legendary past [flintlock rifle, powder horn, Tinkerbell, first dressed as an Indian, then as a pioneer]; "Tomorrowland, the promise of things to come [Tinkerbell sketches an atom and its nucleus, a rocket lifts off]; Adventureland, the wonderworld of nature's own realm [a turning globe]; Fantasyland, the happiest kingdom of them all [Tinkerbell summons up the Sleeping Beauty Castle and flits away]. Presenting this week—the Disneyland story."

A helicopter descends toward the Burbank studio to give an overhead view of a busy Mickey Avenue, its main thoroughfare. The announcer says, "To all outward appearance it's just another working day here"— shots of Kirk Douglas and Peter Lorre getting made up for their roles in *20,000 Leagues* and James Mason stabbing at the giant squid—"but the truth of the matter is, something unusual is going on in the studio today, something that never happened before. Here now to tell you about it is Walt Disney."

He's standing beneath John Hench's twenty-fifth anniversary portrait of Mickey Mouse. "Welcome. I guess you all know this little fellow here. It's an old partnership. Mickey and I started out that first time many, many years ago. We've had a lot of our dreams come true. Now we want you to share with us our latest and greatest dream." He turns from Mickey to a painting of the park, not Herb Ryman's rendering, but a fuller-bodied oil study by Peter Ellenshaw, a studio artist who would win an Academy Award for his work on *20,000 Leagues*.

"I want to tell you about it because later on in the show you'll find that Disneyland the place and Disneyland the TV show are all part of the same."

Despite the camera's cold eye, he seems relaxed, warm, friendly, earnest, the incarnation of the adjective "avuncular." He is clearly excited by the park he's about to explain, but he's no pushy salesman; he speaks as if he and the viewer are in this together: Sure, you all want this place, and, sure, I'm doing my darnedest to give it to you. The "nasal twang" he fretted about is not evident.

"Now on the site of two hundred and forty acres near the city of Anaheim in Southern California, right about in here, we've begun to build Disneyland the place. We hope it will be unlike anything else on this earth. A fair, an amusement park, an exhibition, a city from the Arabian nights, metropolis from the future—in fact, a place of hopes and dreams, fact and fancy all in one."

He moves over to a quarter-inch-to-the-foot scale Main Street. The model shop has done itself proud; the row of buildings is completely persuasive, and immediately recognizable to anyone who has been to Disneyland and walked the street they prefigure. Disney starts to give a tour.

"When you come in the main gate, past the railroad station, down the steps, and across the band concert park, straight ahead lies the heartline of America, an old-fashioned main street, hometown USA just after the turn of the century.

"America was growing fast, towns and villages were turning into cities. Soon the gaslight would be replaced by electricity, but that was still in the future. At that time little Main Street was still the most important spot in the nation, combining the color of frontier days with the oncoming excitement of the new twentieth century.

"Now, at the foot of Main Street, about where you're sitting, is the Plaza. The Plaza, or the Hub, is the heart of Disneyland. Shooting out from here, like the four cardinal points of the compass, Disneyland is divided into four cardinal realms, the four different worlds from which our television shows will originate [this never happened]. They are

Adventureland, Tomorrowland, Fantasyland, and Frontierland [Indian drums, a drawing of a stockade with a riverboat in the background].

"Behind the gate of Frontierland is the inspirational America of the past century. Here is the treasure of our native folklore, the songs, tales, and legends of the big men who built the land. Some of them were completely legendary, like Paul Bunyan the woodchopper with his blue ox Babe. Then again we find that true stories about real people can be fabulous, too. Now, in our series from Frontierland we're going to tell about these real people who became legend, like Davy Crockett, the first coonskin congressman. Now, Davy's life was so fantastic it was hard to tell where fact left off and fancy began.

"Now here's Norman Foster, the director of the unit who's going to shoot the story of Davy Crockett on Davy's own home ground, the Great Smoky Mountains of Tennessee."

Norman Foster is sitting in a director's chair in front of a camera, a battery of lights, and several technicians. He's as relaxed and friendly as Walt. "Well, tomorrow we push off for the Davy Crockett country. When we were back there looking for locations, I noticed a funny thing—people back there still talk about Davy. They sing songs and they tell stories that have been handed down from generation to generation. In the hearts of these people, old Davy Crockett is still very much alive. Now we're about to shoot a little test here that's just as good a way as any for you to meet the young man who's going to play Davy. His name is Fess Parker. He'll tell you a little about it in a song. You ready, Fess?"

Fess is. A rangy young man in buckskins and a fur hat, backed up by a trio of rustics on the porch of a log cabin, strums his guitar and sings a ninety-second ballad about a Tennessee frontiersman who killed a bear when he was three years old, fought Indians, went to Congress, and fixed the crack in the Liberty Bell, then headed for the Alamo.

The song ends (leaving behind it the first breaths of a brewing cyclone); there follows the sequence from Adventureland, which shows Disney cameramen in far places of the world—the Falklands, the Galápagos—filming wildlife, and then comes Tomorrowland with Ward Kimball, far removed from his transportation of choice, talking about manned space flight. As the show moves toward Fantasyland, more and more padding appears. Disney reminds the viewers that it all started with a mouse, and shows clips from a quarter century of Mickey cartoons. Fantasyland is briefly described as a "laughing place," which brings on a fragment of the 1946 *Song of the South* in which Uncle Remus, played by James Baskett, mentions the laughing place, and then dissolves into a cartoon about Br'er Rabbit outwitting Br'er Fox and Br'er Bear. The hour concludes with scenes from Disney's not very successful 1951 *Alice in Wonderland*, a segment, lengthy in itself, which turns out to be merely a preview of what the show has in store for next week.

———

This miscellany was an immediate hit, both with the public and with critics, and instantly put ABC in the television empyrean with NBC and CBS. A nine-city survey revealed that it had captured 52 percent of viewers (with CBS lagging behind with 26.5 percent and NBC at a dismal 14 percent). Arthur Godfrey, whose CBS show had long dominated the Disneyland time slot, found his ratings put him in thirty-fourth place. He was a good sport about it: "I love Disney. I wish I didn't have to work Wednesday night and could stay home and watch his show." Just a month and a half into its life *Disneyland* won the then-prestigious Sylvania TV Award for the best series.

Even better was coming.

Shortly after receiving the Sylvania award, on December 15, 1954, *Disneyland* opened with Tinkerbell leading the viewer to Frontierland, and Disney returning to one of its citizens: "It's characteristic of American folklore that most of our favorite legends and fables are based on the lives of real men—like Davy Crockett of Tennessee."

And then the song began.

Disney had made cartoons about folk heroes in the past—Johnny Appleseed, Pecos Bill—and for at least a decade had been thinking about doing something with Davy Crockett. A few years earlier he'd gone so far as to try to sign up Thomas Hart Benton, perhaps the most American of the American regionalist artists, to take part. Benton did a few sketches before writing an amiable letter of resignation: "Walt Disney's stuff is good enough for my money as it is without a lot of damn painters getting in it."

Once the program was in the works, Disney pressed his Frontierland crew for ideas. He had some rules: "I don't want any picked-over heroes. There will be no outlaws or bad men glorified—no Jesse James or the Daltons." The producer, Bill Walsh, told how they hurried to come up with a suitable hero. "We were planning to do a series on American folk heroes—like Johnny Appleseed, Daniel Boone, and Bigfoot Wallace. And the first one we pulled out, by dumb luck, was Davy Crockett."

Despite his earlier enthusiasm for the Tennessean, Disney began to complain as the storyboards developed; the boss "was not too thrilled by Davy Crockett—too much fighting Indians. After all, how many ways can you kill Indians, or learn anything new about it? So we did some boards on Davy Crockett, and may I tell you, we put everything but the kitchen sink in those boards. Like there he was fighting the Indians, Seminoles, down in Florida, fighting tomahawk duels with Red Stick. Then he went to Congress and raised hell, then he fought Andy Jackson who was doing something bad to the Indians and Davy stalked out of Congress because Andy Jackson was stealing from the Indians, and he didn't want to hear about it. In fact, he fought Andy tooth and nail. Then he went out west and had a lot of adventures going out west and he had a lot more Indian fights there. Then he got into trouble with the cowboys—early Texans—and then he got to the Alamo and then he lasted through the Alamo for fourteen days—and the last day of the Alamo they broke the joint wide open. He died as he had lived, swinging his rifle around, and there was this pile of seventeen dead Mexicans piling up in front of him.

"Walt looked at all of this, and he said—I'll never forget his classic line—'Yeah, but what does he *do*?'"

And who would play him? James Arness seemed right for the role. He was then starring in *Them!*, a nervous product of the era in which nuclear tests unleash giant ants on humankind, and Disney had it screened. He showed little interest in Arness, but at one point jabbed a finger at a bit player and said, "*That's* Davy Crockett."

He'd singled out a thirty-year-old University of Texas graduate who had taken a detour from his American history major to see if he could make a living as an actor. Fess Parker had given himself exactly three years for the experiment, and the thirty-sixth month was on him when Disney called.

He was tall (his six feet, six inches had kept him from becoming a pilot in the war), good-looking, and said he could sing a little. Disney asked him to. He owned a guitar: "I paid forty dollars for it in a pawn shop back in 1951 or 1952. I just happened to have it with me when I auditioned, and I played a couple of songs on it for Walt, and he said, 'Okay.' The next thing I knew I had the job." He was the first adult actor to sign a long-term contract with the Disney Studio. Parker didn't yet know how to ride a horse, but he learned fast and headed south to begin shooting.

There were to be three hour-long episodes: "Davy Crockett—Indian Fighter," "Davy Crockett Goes to Congress," "Davy Crockett at the Alamo."

When these came in edited, each ran short. Disney suggested that Walsh stretch them out, as bread crumbs do a meat loaf, with some storyboard sketches accompanied by a voice-over. That expedient satisfied the time demands, but Disney found the result too static. It needed something extra, he said—some kind of music, a song.

Walsh said, "In a flash I was on the phone to Tom Blackburn, who had written the script. I told him we had to have a song of some sort to accompany the drawings. Could he write one?"

Blackburn was horrified: "Hell, I never wrote a lyric in my life."

Walsh said they didn't need much, but they had to have *something*.

"Okay, if you're that desperate," said Blackburn. The studio had recently brought on a new composer, George Bruns, and he and Blackburn went off to confer.

Bruns proved a lucky hire. In half an hour the two were back with a song that began with a line from the narration—"Born on a mountaintop in Tennessee"—and whose chorus ran: "Daveeee, Davy Crockett, king of the wild frontier."

Bruns sang it for Walsh, who said, "My first reaction was, 'That's supposed to be a song?' I thought it sounded pretty awful, but we didn't have time for anything else." Bruns performed it for Disney the next morning. "I can't tell much from your singing," he said, "but it sounds okay. Bring in a small group and make a demo."

Bruns did; Walt gave the result his approval, and then watched in growing astonishment and delight as it became the ballad of a national infatuation.

————

The song had made a stir when it briefly appeared in the first *Disneyland*, and once it had accompanied the Crockett series it climbed to first place on the *Billboard* Top 100 and stayed there. The initial version, sung by Bill Hayes, sold over two million records. Hayes was soon joined by Burl Ives, Mitch Miller, Tennessee Ernie Ford, Fred Waring, and a dozen others, adding another four million sales to the tally, which eventually grew to ten million.

Everyone who had a hand in the show was astounded as, Bill Walsh put it, "the whole country became unglued." Walsh never did understand the show's success: "It was just a story about some guy shooting at Indians, but all hell broke loose."

As Davy Crockett and his sidekick George Russel (Buddy Ebsen, whose career was made by the series) went from the Seminole Wars to Congress to the Alamo, he became a cultural figure, embodying the virtues Americans liked to ascribe to themselves: self-reliant, freedom-loving, unpretentious, slow to anger but implacable in a showdown. The nation embraced him, and Fess Parker.

When Disney sent his new star on a twenty-two-city promotional tour, Parker was greeted with the same frenzy that assaulted the Beatles a decade later. After he landed at the New Orleans airport, his car inched along the twenty-five miles to the city, every yard crowded with yelling fans.

A dozen new biographies of Crockett came out as 1954 turned to 1955. The fearsome hyper-patriot Martin Dies, first chairman of the House Un-American Activities Committee that played such havoc with

Hollywood, declared that if only the sentiments that animated Davy "are practiced by you and me, the security, the liberty and happiness of the Republic would be insured for all generations to come."

The U.S. Army got on board by deploying the first of 2,100 Davy Crocketts—a recoilless spigot gun that threw a tidy little fifty-pound atom bomb, meant to discourage Soviet armor from entering West Germany.

The Duchess of Windsor named her three Pug puppies Trooper, Disraeli, and Davy Crockett.

Not everyone was swept away by the king of the wild frontier. To the newspaperman and social observer Murray Kempton, Crockett was a loudmouth saloon brawler "who profited far less than other promotes from the fraudulent character of his legend, and who certainly, in life as he has in death, served American industry well." Most Americans, however, sided with the conservative commentator William F. Buckley Jr., who wrote that such cavils merely represented the "resentment by liberal publicists of Davy's neurosis-free approach to life. He'll survive the capers."

However well Crockett might have served American industry in his lifetime, he certainly gave it a tremendous posthumous boost. In a matter of months Americans bought $300 million worth of Davy Crockett items: "buckskin" jackets, plastic Kentucky long rifles and their powder horns, which the owners filled with talcum from their parents' medicine cabinets, table lamps, bath towels (one ad promised "your bathtime struggles are over. . . . They'll run to use Davy Crockett towels"), bathing suits, lunch boxes, moccasins, guitars, and, of course, coonskin caps.

Disney's merchandising people were caught off guard by the specificity of the craze. They'd been expecting to sell merchandise branded with Frontierland symbols, but here was a sudden voracious market that wanted Davy and Davy alone. Philip Sammeth, who was in charge of the Disney character merchandising division, and at least as much a boon to the company right then as was George Bruns, looked at what Fess Parker had on his head and thought a cap with that picturesque dangly tail might sell. Sammeth did some speedy research on the fur-hat industry, and learned that it had fallen on hard times in America. Red

China was looking to buy raccoon skins, but there was a trade embargo on, and Sammeth found a West Coast warehouse full of skins. He persuaded an operation with the unfurry name of Welded Plastics to turn them into headgear, and coaxed a fur-hat maker out of retirement to keep Welded in line. To sell the product, he found a struggling California toy maker that would have perished years earlier had it not been for one 1947 hit, a plastic ukulele called the Uke-A-Doodle. So Mattel came into the profitable mix.

Sammeth got there just in time: the warehouse quickly emptied, the price of raccoon skins rose from 50 cents a dozen to $5—costly enough so that some of the many coonskin cap competitors now in the market found it more profitable to use American mink.

Before the craze burned itself out, ten million had been sold. Not all the profits went to Disney. The company had immediately insisted that anyone selling Davy Crockett merchandise would get in legal trouble, but most grown-ups knew you couldn't trademark Davy Crockett any more than you could the Alamo. Still, Disney alone was able to sell an item emblazoned with "Walt Disney's Davy Crockett," and bearing the briefly irresistible visage of Fess Parker. At least $30 million came the company's way.

The money didn't arrive all at once, of course, but Disney knew that he—and his park—were moving toward firmer financial ground. Not fast enough, though. If he hadn't already blown through his ever-increasing budget, which had inflated itself to $11 million, he soon would.

23

THE STRUGGLE FOR SPONSORS

He felt pinched as Christmas 1954 approached. Usually when the holidays drew near, he'd go through the studio handing out cash bonuses. This year, his employees had to get what seasonal cheer they could from a bottle of Old Forester bourbon.

C. V. Wood believed he could help, and began to use his verve and salesmanship to bolster the revenue by getting corporate sponsorships.

He had moved his offices from the studio to the upper floor of the Dominguez house, whose original owners had ensured the survival of the venerable Canary Island date palm. The team he'd recruited joined him there—many from Oklahoma and Texas, a few Bombers among them. They were a congenial lot, but there was always a slight chill between them and the studio people on the first floor.

Disney had taken up occupancy there, along with many of his artists, and the two floors represented two different managerial worlds. For all his freewheeling expansiveness, Wood was a businessman, steeped in the standard practices of the day, a tightly run conservative fabric of reports, assessments, balance sheets, projections, and clear lines of authority.

Disney, on the other hand, said, "I don't ever want to see an organizational chart." He definitely never saw one in those days. Interviewed years later, a veteran of these early months said, "You asked the question, 'What was your process like?' I kind of laugh because process is an organized way of doing things. I have to remind you, during the 'Walt Period' of designing Disneyland, we didn't have processes. We just did the work. Processes came later. All of these things had never been done before. Walt had gathered up all these people who had never designed a theme park, a Disneyland. So we're in the same boat at one time, and we figure out what to do and how to do it on the fly as we go along with it and not even discuss plans, timing, or anything. . . . We just worked and Walt just walked around and had suggestions."

Disney made fun of the rigidity of his upstairs neighbors, whom he accused of "aircraft thinking"—a reference to so many of them having come from Consolidated—instead of "show thinking." Roy Disney could move comfortably between these polities of art and commerce, and so could Joe Fowler, but for the most part the two camps eyed one another with suspicion.

Disney realized, however, that he needed Wood to sell for him. From the start, he had been interested in leasing space to large corporations, taking as a model the 1939 World's Fair (that distant Deco paradise was then only fifteen years in the past) with its costly exhibits mounted by companies whose sole reward was a name on a pavilion.

He and Nat Winecoff had gone after such giants as Coca-Cola and Hallmark, and were rebuffed. Disney did not want to go lower down the corporate hierarchy, but Wood argued that this was no time for commercial purity: whatever the size of the sponsors, if they could spend money, Disneyland needed them. After all, the famous General Motors Futurama had shared fair space in 1939 with Dave Irwin's Eskimo Village—some papier-mâché igloos and a team of huskies that, claimed Irwin, thrived on "Ken-L-Ration and Ken-L-Biskit exclusively"—not to mention the "Nudist of the Nude" contest, which one critic said was turning the fair into a "temple of filth."

As soon as Wood got his Disneyland job, he went after Fred Schumacher, his first boss at Consolidated and a sometime corporate representative at the World's Fair. Schumacher said, "He came over to my house on the same day he was hired, as best as I can remember. He said, 'How would you like to go work for Disneyland?' And, hell, I didn't know what that was."

Woody the salesman had him aboard within two weeks. As the year drew in, they set off around the country campaigning for sponsors.

It was a barren journey. Despite the success of the new TV show, the whole Disneyland scheme seemed so farfetched that they got to meet only junior executives, all of whom were appalled when their visitors demanded costly commitments that would run for years.

An early, much-desired target was the Atchison, Topeka & Santa Fe Railway, a great name, celebrated in a hit song that had won an Academy Award, and the source of Wood's father's salary. Wood and Schumacher worked up a proposal: the park's line would be called the Santa Fe and Disneyland Railroad (note the precedence of the AT&SF), and the name would appear on every piece of rolling stock; the road's familiar logo, a cross in a circle with "Santa Fe" in the horizontal bar, would emblazon the water tanks; and Santa Fe travel posters would decorate the Main Street Station, where a kiosk sold tickets to visitors who wanted to sample the real thing.

This time Schumacher and Wood were able to break through the crust of junior executives, only to be told by one of the senior ones, when he'd learned they were looking for something like fifty thousand a year, "Goddamn. Sometimes we furnish the paint to put our name on the trains at these kiddie parks. But that's all we've ever done."

They kept trying, and failing. By the time they approached Swift & Company in Chicago, they had nothing to show for their efforts but an unbroken chain of disappointments and a whopping travel bill.

Schumacher knew that Swift had gone all out for the World's Fair: as the official guidebook reported, "Resembling in form a gleaming super-airliner, the Building (Skidmore & Owings, architects and designers) . . . is divided into two principal sections; one constituting the body of the plane, the other the wings . . . while within . . . a great hall resembles the nave of a Gothic cathedral. In the two wings, manufacturing processes of products, including Swift's Premium frankfurters, are demonstrated. Among other exhibits, a marionette show dramatizes typical scenes in retail shops . . ." If Swift could build a temporary food-processing plant in Flushing Meadows, perhaps the company wouldn't flinch at financing a display in Anaheim.

Schumacher said, "The economics were such that the entire project stood in jeopardy. It was an effective do-or-die day. . . . Not a single tenant or lessee had been signed up. We worked our way up through the entire Swift organization, trying to come to some kind of understanding so that we could at least have one major tenant in the park."

They made it to the president's office. Wood gave the pitch: he spread out pictures of Disneyland, and said that people already having a wonderful time there would be delighted to sample Swift products—so much better than just seeing them in a TV or magazine ad—and keep them among their other happy memories of the park.

At first, both Wood and Schumacher thought they had their audience with them. The president liked the idea of a Disney amusement park, and remembered that Swift believed its World's Fair display had justified the investment. Then Wood's sales instincts seemed to falter; he began to press too hard, and realized this only when the president interrupted him with, "I've heard enough, gentlemen. Would you kindly leave the office?"

They went back down to the lobby, but couldn't bring themselves the leave the building. The two hung around there for twenty minutes while Schumacher talked about devising a new strategy.

Wood, who'd been half listening, suddenly said: "I'm going up again."

"How can you? You were thrown out of the office."

"Wait and see."

Wood headed back toward the elevators, Schumacher in reluctant tow. On the executive floor Woody charmed his way past the secretaries, then barely tapped at the president's door before pushing it open to a cold greeting: "What are you doing back here?"

Wood pointed across the office. "Oh, I forgot my briefcase." Sure enough, there it was. Wood was lucky; the effrontery of his manufactured forgetfulness amused the boss, and he laughed.

Perhaps he had been regretting turning Disneyland down; whatever the reason, the tenor of this second meeting was very different from half an hour earlier. The mood in the room was cheerful now, the president asking questions rather than simply absorbing Wood's enthusiasm. Wood and Schumacher went away with a commitment from Swift to build and operate a restaurant on Main Street, paying a yearly lease of $110,000 for the privilege.

The agreement resulted in the Red Wagon Inn ("Swift's Quality

Meats Served Exclusively"). Swift paid, but WED made sure the restaurant got executed to Disney standards. The contract, the same one that would be signed by every subsequent lessee, stipulated: "All interior architectural drawings are to be done by a competent registered architect or approved display house of the lessee's choice. All designs submitted by lessee's architect whether the buildings or construction of interiors in Disneyland must be approved as to the theme and general plan of Disneyland as established by WED Enterprises. Three sets of preliminary drawings are to be furnished to Disneyland Inc. as soon as possible after signing of the lease. Two sets are retained by Disneyland and one set is returned to the lessee's architect with any revisions."

The outcome for Swift's Red Wagon Inn was described in the company's advertising copy as being "resplendent in the elegance of a by-gone area, reminiscent of the famed eating houses of yesterday. All appointments are authentic mementoes of the gay and glamorous 90's—including the stained glass ceiling, entrance hall and foyer taken from the St. James home in Los Angeles, one of the West's most noted old mansions. Atmosphere, however, is not confined to the building alone. The menu itself brings back visions of historic good eating—featuring steaks and chops."

As in a Disney movie, that first successful meeting broke the spell. Main Street would get a Carnation Ice Cream Parlor, a Coca-Cola Refreshment Corner, and a Maxwell House Coffee shop. No Hallmark, but the Gibson greeting card company came in. Fritos, which had grown from an operation founded in 1932 in the Doolin family's San Antonio garage to owning fifty production plants, underwrote the Casa de Fritos Mexican cantina in Frontierland.

Annual rents were $20 a square foot on Main Street, and $15 everywhere else in the park. WED would help with the design of the buildings, but all construction costs—and staff salaries once the park opened—were up to the sponsor. Kaiser Aluminum joined for $37,500 a year, after being assured that the metal would be used lavishly throughout Disneyland; Trans World Airlines and Richfield Oil agreed to annual fees of $45,000; Kodak, $28,000. Almost all the leases ran five years, with the first and last year's rent paid upon signing.

The Upjohn pharmaceutical company eventually paid $37,720 for its yearly lease, so getting into the spirit of things that it dismissed the WED team's plans for a 1900s drugstore as historically inaccurate, and hired its own designer. Upjohn was so scrupulous that when their exhibit opened it was staffed by two actual pharmacists who had nothing to do but wear striped shirts with sleeve garters and look picturesque. A pamphlet handed out to visitors explained, "The pharmacy adds its note of realism to Disney's nineteenth century scene. It is also one of the most elaborate museums of authentic pharmaceutical wares, furnishings and equipment in existence. Well over 1000 antiques were collected by the personnel of the Upjohn Company, in a search that took them to auctions, attics, old pharmacies, dealers and historians in New Orleans, Chicago, New York City, South Carolina, Michigan and New Jersey. The showcases, fans, counters and other equipment were designed by experts and faithfully reproduced."

StarKist and Chicken of the Sea actually got into a fight about which company would sell its tuna fish sandwiches in the park, but Wood had approached the latter first, and Chicken of the Sea won the concession.

Even with such big companies in the fold, Wood went after smaller fry. The Hollywood-Maxwell Brassiere Company of Los Angeles rented space on Main Street for its Intimate Apparel store, which would offer a display documenting the evolution of the brassiere, presided over by a talking mechanical sorcerer called "the Wizard of Bras."

And finally the Santa Fe capitulated, agreeing to an annual fee of $50,000, its famous name giving this new world of fantasy an anchor—as all good fantasy must have—in quotidian reality. The two locomotives then under construction would be named the *C.K. Holliday*, after Cyrus Kurtz Holliday, the line's founder, and the *E.P. Ripley*, for Edward Payson Ripley, its first president after its 1895 reorganization.

Around the time these sponsorships were falling into place, Disney received a letter that began, "Dear Walt, I feel somewhat presumptuous addressing you in this way yet I feel sure you would not want me to address you any other way. My name is Ray A. Kroc. . . . I have very recently taken over the national franchise of the McDonald's system. I would like to inquire if there may be an opportunity for a McDonald's in your Disneyland Development."

Disney sent Kroc a cordial reply saying that he had passed along his letter to C. V. Wood. But Wood never responded, and Kroc founded his first McDonald's in Des Plaines, Illinois, three months before Disneyland's opening day. Perhaps it is too bad that these twentieth-century juggernauts did not start out in harness together.

That run of sponsorships represented C. V. Wood at his forceful best. But there was also a darker Woody. Chafing at his salary—"What I'm making is an insult"—he asked for a raise, and Disney turned him down flat, making clear that the request had annoyed him.

Wood set about augmenting his income with a system of kickbacks. He left the top tier of sponsors, the Kaisers and the Kodaks, alone, but went after the smaller lessees with a larcenous directness that came close to being a protection racket. He worked with one of his longtime associates, Bob Burns. After he got, for instance, Dickinson's Jams and Jellies settled in on Main Street, Burns showed up and demanded extra payment to ensure that all went smoothly.

Burns split the take with Wood, and that take was considerable. One of the Disney executives said Burns "had to borrow money from Fred Schumacher when he first landed in Santa Ana. After only six months, he owned an expensive, prestigious home. Kickbacks from lessees paid for it."

At this distance, it is impossible to tell how much Walt knew of these goings-on, but he was obviously uneasy about Wood, for he and Roy hired a lawyer, Luther Marr, to look over the sponsorship deals. That didn't sit well with Wood, who, Marr said, "was a very impetuous, dishonest kind of a person. Devious, I'd say. So anyway, he didn't like it that I was hired. I could see that from the beginning. Because that meant that the establishment was going to get in his tent and look around and see what was going on."

Wood tried to keep Marr at bay by showing him innocuous contracts like the one that specified how the lessees should design their buildings. When Marr began to push him, Wood one day handed him a forty-page contract along with a truculent "Look that over and give me your approval."

It was late in the afternoon. Marr said, "Well, yes. I'll take it home tonight."

"No, I mean now."

"Well, there's no way. It would take hours and hours."

Marr left the office, and Wood went directly to Roy and asked him to fire the lawyer. After Marr told Roy about the exchange, the brothers sided with him.

24

VAN ARSDALE FRANCE FOUNDS A SCHOOL

Despite this brackish undertow in Wood's character, his value to the park remained undiminished. For all Disney's scorn of "process," he knew there was one area where it was crucial. "You can dream, create, design and build the most wonderful place in the world," he said, "but it still takes *people* to operate it." And not just willing people. This was no regular amusement park where you could hire a couple of high schoolers to run the Tumble Bug during their summer vacation. The people Disney wanted had to be as appealing as the rides and the buildings, and to be at home in an intricate enterprise whose smooth functioning depended on every element working with the same precision as its railroad. And they had to be ready the day the park opened; learning on the job—as all the WED staffers were doing—wouldn't serve here.

Disney needed a training program. Wood knew who should run it.

One August day in 1954, Van Arsdale France had gotten a call from Wood. The two were good friends. "We'd worked together for four years in Fort Worth, Texas," France wrote. "He was the director of Industrial Engineering at the Consolidated Vultee Aircraft Corporation, and I was in charge of training."

Born near Seattle in 1912, France went with his family to San Diego when he was twelve. He graduated from San Diego State, and found a job dismal even by Depression standards: working in a kelp processing plant for 43 cents an hour. A New Deal agency called the National Youth Administration rescued him from the kelp, discovered that he had organizational abilities, and made him an administrator. That led to Consolidated, and his friendship with Wood. The two parted ways

when the war came. "From deep in the heart of Texas, I'd gone overseas as a training specialist with the Army in England and Germany,
and he'd gone West to eventually join the Stanford Research Group.
Our careers had occasionally crossed paths during that ten-year period,
and I'd recently worked for him on a consulting job with a company
which made the Whirlpool Brassiere, an interesting job." (And one that
explains the Wizard of Bras coming to Main Street.)

Wood told France that he'd left SRI to become a vice presi-
dent of Disneyland. To the inevitable question—"What the hell is
Disneyland?"—he replied, "Why don't you drop out to my office and
I'll tell you about it."

Interested, France left his Wilshire Boulevard office, where he was
struggling "to set up an organization called Small Plant Management
Company," and drove out on the Hollywood Freeway. When he found
the Buena Vista Street entrance to the studio, a guard checked his name
on a clipboard and gave him directions. "I parked in the visitor's lot
and set off on foot down Snow White Lane, past Dopey Drive, until I
came to Mickey Mouse Avenue and the studio's three-story Animation
Building."

There he found Wood in a posture of Lone Star insouciance, his
shoeless feet up on his desk. France was not surprised. "Woody has
always been a bundle of energy wrapped in a deceptively laid-back personality. Without moving his stockinged feet from the desk top, he told
me how he had come to Walt Disney from Stanford Research." As he
talked, the energetic Woody overtook the laid-back Woody; he jumped
out of his chair and began to pace around. "Walt and his brother Roy
liked the [SRI] study, and we were enthusiastic about Walt's dreams.
Walt is a wonderful guy, Van, and this studio is nothing like any place
you or I have ever worked. It's like a family, and Walt treats me like
a son.

"We have *four million dollars* to build this place called *Disneyland*
down in Anaheim."

France wrote, "Since that time I've heard other figures told about the
original financing, but for me, in 1954, four million bucks seemed like
all the money in the world, and that's the way I heard it. He was warm-

ing up about Disneyland when a dapper looking fellow in a sport shirt entered the office and plopped down into a chair. Without any introduction, I knew I was sitting next to Walt Disney."

Wood introduced him, and they shook hands. "I'll always remember that handshake. Somehow I'd imagined that Walt Disney would have the soft, delicate hands of an artist drawing Mickey Mouse. But my hand met the firm grip of a man who had grown up doing hard farm labor and working for his father in construction."

Disney took out a cigarette. "I was dying for one, but I was afraid to light up. He talked about the problem of explaining Disneyland to some people at the Studio, and even to his own wife. The conversation was interrupted when a small, smartly dressed man carrying a book dropped in. We were introduced; his name was Nat Winecoff. With his book he explained the day's transaction for buying and breeding horses and ponies for the proposed park. As I listened to the report, and the ensuing conversation, I was struck by the sense of excitement Disney felt for this project. He even turned to me, an outsider, to present his thoughts."

France sat, a thoroughly entertained onlooker, for two hours. At six o'clock, Wood, feet back up on his desk, "dismissed me, saying, 'Thanks for dropping by. I'll see ya.'"

Driving home, France thought over the visit. "It was great seeing Woody again, and exciting to meet Walt Disney. I could hardly wait to tell my daughter. Yet like so many others, I really didn't understand what this Disneyland was all about. I certainly didn't know it was a day which would change my life."

That change didn't come right away. Six months passed without France giving any further thought to the meeting. He had "forgotten about Woody and this thing called 'Disneyland,' and was occupied with hacking out a living as the Savior of Small Businesses. I wasn't doing too well, I'll admit, when Woody called me to ask if I'd like a consulting job setting up a training program for this venture." Wood said he'd been talking with Disney about the necessity of educating the men and women who would run the park. "I told Walt about your work in Texas, and he agreed that you sounded like the guy for the job."

France thought back to the war. "I suppose Woody felt that if I could convert 65,000 cowboys, farmers, and homemakers into dedicated air-craft workers, then I could mold a group of diverse Californians with no business experience into producers of the 'Disneyland Dream.'"

France went to the studio the next afternoon. "This time Woody didn't have his feet propped up on the desk or his shoes off when I entered his office. There was a sense of urgency about the place."

No two-hour chat this visit. They were continually interrupted by people dropping off architectural drawings, rifling through piles of papers to find this or that vital document, getting signatures, asking questions, complaining about various crises. During what conversation France had with his host, "Woody continued to stand as he talked, which was a signal that I shouldn't even think about sitting down." Wood's "country boy drawl had speeded up to match his mood of hustle," as he explained how things stood: "We have deadlines on top of deadlines, Van. We have a firm opening date of July seventeenth. We're concentrating on getting the place built and finding the money to build it. It's a tough enough job just keeping the construction on schedule. We know damn well that people have to be trained to operate the place. I know you can handle the job."

France agreed on the spot. "Protocol dictated that I think it over for a bit. But . . . there wasn't much time to play games." Wood asked him, "How about two hundred a week?" That sounded fine: "In 1955, two hundred was a good rate for a forty-hour week. I didn't know, however, that I was signing on for about fourteen hours a day, seven days a week, which worked out to about three dollars an hour." But "even as the magnitude of my task became clear to me, I didn't regret my decision, and I never have."

For one thing, there was the studio itself. "Springtime in just about any place is a good time of year, but this one in Burbank made a special imprint on my memory." Used to "the structured environment of an aircraft plant, aluminum reduction plant, or an auto assembly line," he found himself in a tree-shaded factory that many of its workers referred to as "the Campus."

"There were people playing ping-pong, volleyball, basketball, softball, and some just lying on the grass. During lunch I could hear the Firehouse Five Plus Two, made up of animators and other creative sorts, playing music which they would later perform at Disneyland. I could eat lunch in a cafeteria where I might see celebrities who were working on Disney films, sharing the space, if not the table, with Walt Disney himself. Along with the usual cafeteria soft drinks there was, honestly now, BEER!"

He underwent a "major change in my thinking about artists and art directors. I'd imagined such people as flamboyant in dress and with fiery temperaments. Quite the contrary, the highly creative Disney artists could pass easily at any Rotary Club. Those I met were uniformly considerate, moderate in dress, and friendly."

Nevertheless, France was "a bit scared. I was 41 years old, in a totally new environment having to instantly learn a business which was totally foreign to me. I was surrounded by studio people who knew what they were doing. They all had their own groups of friends, and working relationships. I didn't have anyone to eat lunch with."

The only employee he knew was Wood, who was far too busy to pal around with him. But Wood did find the time to introduce the neophyte to several people who not only helped him do his job, but became lifelong friends.

First was Fred Schumacher, who initially alarmed France. "Fred was about six feet two, thin, prematurely grey, ramrod straight, with a moustache which fit as though he'd been born with it. . . . No more unlikely relationship could have been created. Fred was tall, I'm not [true: some of France's colleagues would take to calling him "Jiminy Cricket"]. He was precise and well-organized; I'm sloppy and moderately disorganized. He loved procedures. I hate them. He didn't drink, I do [Schumacher used to, until, he said, "I got sick and tired of waking up sick and tired"]. Yet we established a working relationship which endured for years." It began in a corner of Schumacher's office, where he made room for the newcomer; and with a corner of Schumacher's drafting table, which became France's first desk.

Jack Sayers "was as tall and thin as Fred, with sandy hair and a sense of humor." Disney had talked him into leaving the vice presidency for the entertainment division of the Gallup opinion polls to serve as director of entertainment and guest relations.

Dorothy Manes, even more newly arrived than France, had managed an Oakland attraction called Children's Fairyland; Disney had spotted her on one of his amusement park tours and, France said, "hired her to set up youth activities at the park, working with the Boy Scouts and such organizations." He "understood why Walt hired her. She had a classic look, and beneath the charming exterior was a sharp, cultured mind with a certain toughness. She was not one to be pushed around." Another virtue, though not one that would have appealed to Disney: "She had delightfully good taste in earthy jokes."

As those three helped him begin to create his training program, France told Schumacher he'd need a designer for the visual part. Fred introduced him to Jack Olsen, an artist hired to create the merchandise Disney hoped to sell in the park. Jack at once gave him a piece of advice: "Spend all the money you can on your training handbook. Then, if it doesn't work, Walt will know that money was not the problem. Walt can be a pinch penny if he thinks money is being wasted. Perhaps at some time he had a project that failed, and lack of money was used as an excuse."

Hoping that this seemingly paradoxical counsel was less dangerous than it sounded, France decided to splurge on his first handbook.

"I would meet other pioneers," he said, "make other friends, but Woody, Fred, Dorothy, Jack Sayers and Jack Olsen were the key friends who helped me through those early days."

He knew he needed all the help he could get. "I had created training programs for Rosie the Riveter and other people in heavy industry, but here I was developing a program for people operating a crazy dream."

With the handbook taking shape in his mind, he asked Schumacher if he knew of any material that might guide him. Schumacher sent him to the personnel department, and he came away with *The Ropes at Disney*, a booklet prepared some years earlier for studio employees. "It showed Goofy and Mickey pulling the ropes backstage in a theater, and it covered the rules in a light way. Since Walt had obviously approved it, I felt that I could get by using a light touch in the Disneyland handbook." He did his homework. "I read everything that I could find about Walt and the Disney organization. I was a packrat for anything I could take to my room at night." A fast "if woefully inaccurate" typist, he'd clatter out ideas overnight and show them to Manes and Sayers the next morning.

When he reached the point where he needed illustrations, Schumacher sent him to Ken Peterson, Disney's head of animation. France explained what he wanted. Peterson responded with a weary smile. "Van, I have seven hundred artists, and the reason I have seven hundred artists is that I *need every one* of them."

France persisted until Peterson surrendered the résumé of a young artist named Ned Jacobi who looked promising. France accepted this Hobson's choice, and Jacobi "turned out to be perfect for the assignment."

France had been staying in a small hotel called the Sterling Arms, with the Olive Branch, a welcoming bar and grill, nearby, both within a pleasant ten-minute walk to the studio: "It was the best of times." But now he had to move to Anaheim, to the place where the workers rarely mentioned the future park's name: "It was never called 'Disneyland'— only 'the site.'"

France needed somewhere to train his recruits—he couldn't do it in a hotel room—and he was worried there would be no place for him. "From past experience I knew that space for training was the last priority in most organizations."

Again, Schumacher steered him to the right man. Earl Shelton was, so far as anyone on the project had a firm title, the site coordinator. One of the Bombers, and an army pilot during the war, he was the opposite of Wood, taciturn and grim-looking to France; but he also possessed "a brilliant mind behind the gruff exterior, and a memory like a computer."

Shelton first took France on a tour, by Jeep, of the swarming site, "an anthill of activity, if you credit the theory that ants know what they are doing. Tractors, earth moving equipment and craftsmen of all kinds were working against a deadline six months away." Impressive, but France "couldn't have cared less about the earth movers and construction. My mind was on 'territorial possession.'"

He explained this to Shelton during their bouncing ride. The site manager turned away from the anthill, drove out on West Street to the farther reaches of the Disney property, and came to a stop in front of a sagging two-story house badly needing a new coat of the white paint that was scabbing away from its clapboards; this, he told France, had been the Vandenburgs' home. "It looked old and dusty, ready to be torn down—but beautiful."

France said it was perfect. Shelton gave a grunt and a nod, which France hoped represented some sort of assent. It did. Shelton "worked without notes, but he always followed through. By the time I returned to the studio, he had called Wood, who approved this beachhead on the perimeter of confusion."

———

Not long after, France got an ally to help hold his beachhead. "My workload was building up. After seeing The Site and the abandoned home where we would do the training, I knew I needed some help." Once again, he went to Schumacher; once again, Schumacher came through, handing him an application: "This guy looked pretty good, but we can't reach him by phone." The guy did indeed look good: his application was so strong that France wondered why he hadn't already been snatched up for some other park job. Then his knowledge of Los Angeles telephone exchanges supplied the answer. In those days of alphabetical phone prefixes, France figured out that Schumacher had been dialing PL for PLeasant rather than PR for PRospect, and soon he was talking with Richard Nunis. He made an appointment to see him.

"In came this six-foot, two inches tall, blond, aggressive ex–football player. At the time I didn't know he was a legend at USC, an Academic All-American because of his football record and a 3.6 grade average. I would have hired anyone, but I hired him in five minutes." Not without a pang of hesitation, though, for the twenty-one-year-old candidate was wearing new suede shoes: "At the time I associated these with pimps, con men and used car dealers." And there was to be a disagreement over salary: Nunis believed he had been promised $2 an hour; France always maintained that he'd offered $1.80. They would argue over that 20 cents on and off for thirty years, long after Dick Nunis had become president of Disneyland.

France told "Dick to report to the dirty home which hadn't been lived in for a year, in his working clothes"—not, in slang that had already become musty, "his fancy duds." Nunis didn't worry about the yawning pay gap or the pimp shoes: "Since I was mostly doing other things," France wrote, "he worked one of his first miracles by turning that old house into an attractive training center."

On his endless rounds, Earl Shelton noticed what was going on and, with no fuss, pried a squad of craftsmen away from an equally needy project. "They painted the place inside and knocked out the wall between two bedrooms, giving us a training room, into which we would later squeeze forty people." They washed windows and scrubbed floors and drenched the house with fresh white paint. ("Since few of us foreigners could pronounce that German name, it soon became 'the White House.'")

France was to write more than one memoir about his Disney years, and all of them are told with understated modesty. But across four decades his pride in this, his first work in Disney territory, bursts forth with soldierly bravado: together, he and Dick Nunis had "transformed an Orange County home into something that had the firm imprint of DISNEY. If you'll pardon a self congratulation, I'll have to admit scrounging that old home for training was a lot of good luck combined with pure genius. Many of the people arriving later couldn't find a place to light. We had space, and fortunately Dick proved to be as good a scrounger, liar, and thief as I was."

Nunis was so valuable an asset that he inadvertently gave France a useful lesson in Disney company politics. "Dick was such a damned good worker that people wanted to borrow him, and I would loan him out if it seemed politically prudent. I didn't plan it that way, but it helped us to become something more than a 'Training Department,' and Dick and I had a chance to find out how to move around and get things done in the pre-opening sea of confusion."

While Nunis was away putting people in the new program's debt, France finished his training manual. He'd followed Olsen's advice to be profligate, and the handbook came in at $3.73 a copy; that's a little over $34 in today's terms, and it appalled Fred Schumacher. There was another problem, too. When the manual was ready for printing, France took it to show Schumacher, who would be paying the bill. After glancing through the pages enlivened with Ned Jacobi's drawings of Disney cartoon characters, he said it had better be cleared with the legal department. France sent the booklet over with Dick Nunis, who returned shaken by an unexpected dressing-down. Walt Disney might have been cavalier about flowcharts and the like, but he'd had Oswald the Lucky Rabbit stolen from him, and he was grimly determined to keep tight hold of his other progeny.

The lawyer had taken one look at the book and started to pound his desk, again and again barking out a puzzling incantation: "Circle C, WDP! Circle C, WDP! Circle C, WDP!" Nunis discovered that a "C" inside a circle stood for "copyright," and WDP, "Walt Disney Productions." This had to accompany every single drawing of what was, after all, strictly an internal document.

Every hour of France's work over the past months, his researches in the company archives and his exploration of the Disney ethos, came down to a meeting on Thursday, May 25, 1955: "It was the morning that I was to present the orientation program for the people who would operate Disneyland on opening day, July 17th."

Walt himself wasn't there, but Roy and Wood were, along with the vice president of the Bank of America, representatives from Kodak and Swift, the head of Disney marketing, the head of legal affairs, and a host of other intimidating corporate presences.

France and Nunis faced their audience with a carousel slide projector and that long-forgotten visual aid, a felt board.

France started off with some mild jokes, and his allies—Dorothy Manes, Jack Sayers, Fred Schumacher—obligingly laughed at them. "After the group relaxed a bit, I introduced Dick, who gave a slide presentation of an artist's renderings of what Disneyland would be. He may have been worried along with me, but it didn't show. He brought those slides to life, and made a confident, motivational presentation. I was proud of him."

France offeréd a brief history of the company, "and then prepared to present what would forever become Disneyland's basic policy for serving those who would come to Walt's dream park. I was worried more about this presentation than any I'd ever done before, or since, and the fear was more than justified."

He stuck the first of the cards he'd had made to the felt board. It "depicted a dream castle with blocks showing Disney traditions of Art, Music, Adventure and Fantasy. Then I pointed out that the entire history of Walt's life had been to entertain and educate, a tradition of family entertainment. Now, as Walt's twenty year dream was to open in a few weeks, we at Disneyland were going to follow that tradition. The theme of our joint effort would be, 'WE'LL CREATE HAPPINESS.'"

How to manufacture that elusive, intimate commodity? "At Disneyland I wanted people to feel they were involved in something more than parking cars, serving food, or sweeping up popcorn." He told a parable. Two men are laying bricks. Somebody asks one of them what he's doing, and is told, "I'm laying bricks." To the same question, the other man answers, "I'm building a cathedral."

France put up the next card. It showed a quotation of his own which he'd audaciously attributed to Disney. "Welcome to Disneyland. To make the dream of Disneyland come true took the combined skills and talents of artisans, carpenters, engineers, scientists and planners. The dream they built now becomes your heritage. It is you who will make Disneyland truly a magic kingdom and a happy place for the millions of guests who will visit us now and in future years. In creating happiness for our guests, I hope that you will find happiness in your work and in being an important part of Disneyland."

France went on to give specifics. First, "it all started with a mouse." Jack Sayers had said that in passing one day, and France picked it up for his presentation; it suggested that, just as the Disney empire had begun with the agitations of the scrawny, mildly disagreeable Mickey, big things could grow from the smallest seeds.

One of the most important seeds in this new park would be a smile.

"Dick came up with the idea that a smile is a 'magic mirror,' creating smiles from others." That smile must come "with 'smiling phrases.' Dorothy Manes came up with a response for when we are thanked. 'It's been my pleasure.'" A little formal and unwieldy, but it beats the effortless condescension inherent in the current "no problem."

More cards: "WE DON'T HAVE 'CUSTOMERS,' WE SERVE 'GUESTS'"; "WE ARE 'HOSTS AND HOSTESSES'"; "THERE'S NO SUCH THING AS A DUMB QUESTION"; "WE DON'T HAVE 'CROWDS,' WE HAVE AN 'AUDIENCE'"; THE DISNEYLAND LOOK" (in essence, dress like a prep school graduate, and don't do anything tricky with your hair); "WE WORK WHILE OTHERS PLAY," meaning always act as if you're having as good a time as the "guests," and don't ever try to.

If this bouquet of courtesies seems obvious today, that is only because France's initial program would be refined at Disneyland and spill over into other theme parks and then into the nation at large. When the cashiers at my local grocery store summon the next customer in the checkout line, they call out, "Following guest, please."

To grasp how radical this program was for an amusement park, just imagine the man running the Cyclone Coaster at Coney Island in 1955 (or today) sending a trainload up the grade thinking of himself as a host entertaining his guests.

Every bit as nervous as he had been when he began, France finished his pitch "with the essential need for teamwork between everyone, including all lessees. Together we would be pioneers in one of the great dreams in Disney's history."

Applause.

Roy Disney walked up and thanked Nunis and France with what the latter remembered as "his good sense of humor." If so, it had a barb in it: "Now Van, we are going to create a lot of happiness, but we're also going to have to make money to get Walt's life insurance out of hock. In fact, I'm leaving right now to borrow some more money to meet the payroll."

Never mind; the program had been a hit. France knew it when Wood shook his hand with obvious relief.

"Dick had been sweating it out right along with me. We had been approved by a jury of our peers." After their audience had left the White

House, France and Nunis had a celebratory drink. Despite his success, France felt a trickle of melancholy just then. "We had a neighbor, Mrs. Mohn, who still had chickens which would cluck around. . . . The evenings were aromatic and soft."

He and Nunis, sipping their scotch on a porch still surrounded by orange trees, were enjoying the final vestiges of a way of life that would disappear from that corner of America not in years but in weeks. "It must have been a wonderful place to live . . . to grow up . . . to raise a family. I didn't see how those who sold out could have found any other home, and life style, which could compare."

Nunis finished his drink and left. France sat alone "smelling the fragrance of the orange trees and watching Mrs. Mohn's chickens scratch for their evening meal."

A quarter century later, he wrote, "I was not, of course, naïve enough to feel that Walt Disney didn't want to pay off the money he owed for Disneyland and make a profit. And, there were detractors I knew would question the 'happiness' theme.

"And I was convinced then and I am now that Walt was *not* in it for the money."

His program had made at least one convert. "In selling others on the importance of creating happiness, I think I had convinced myself."

25

THE PONY FARM

Another training course was under way at the site. Unlike France's spanking-new experiment, this one was as old as agriculture.

Frontierland's showpiece riverboat was steam driven, but everything else that pulled a vehicle or carried a person in Disney's Trans-Mississippi West had to be powered by animal muscle. This patch of his manufactured landscape would be populated with pack mules, burros, full-size horses, and miniature ones. All of them had jobs to do, and all were under the tutelage of a Texan named Owen Pope.

By the time Pope met Disney, he had spent his entire life with horses, and twenty years of it with his wife, Dolly. Both of them were skilled trainers, and Pope had also become known for the excellent horse trailers he built. He was an accomplished harness maker, too, and a successful showman.

Harper Goff saw Owen and Dolly putting a dozen horses through their turns at the Pan-Pacific Auditorium in Los Angeles, and suggested that Disney see the show. He did, and asked the Popes to lunch on March 1, 1951. Early as that was in his park's plans, he already knew he'd need livestock, and the couple looked good to him.

The Popes sat down at the table thinking their host wanted horses for a movie. They left it being among the first people to hear of Disneyland.

That meal took the Popes off the show circuit forever. Over the Thanksgiving weekend of 1951, they drove the thirty-foot van that had for years been their home onto the Burbank studio lot, where Pope built stalls for the first ten of the park's horses. A few months later they moved to the site and quit their van for a house overlooking ten acres that came to be known as the Pony Farm. Their new home gave them the distinction of being the only people ever to have lived both in the Disney Studios and in Disneyland.

By the time the Popes were in Anaheim, the Pony Farm corrals held 220 animals, from the miniature horses to the big ones that would pull the two horsecars along Main Street.

Van Arsdale France wrote that his "only failure in getting people to attend orientation was with the men who would operate our horse-drawn vehicles and drive the mule pack." When France urged Pope to show up, he said, "Van, you deal with *people* people. Out here we are *horse* people."

Besides, Pope had his own orientation program to run. For centuries horses had been trained not to be spooked by heavy city traffic, or to quail in the face of musketry. Those days were gone, and Pope had to start from scratch. He strung speakers across the rocky knobs and hollows of the Painted Desert landscape that was taking shape, and led his horses through a cacophony of recorded crowd shouts, band music, and the metallic spatter of shooting galleries. A reporter visiting the site wrote, "It's a little unusual and eerie in the vacant open spaces of the Disney corral to listen to a playback that sounds like the half-time noises of a SC–UCLA football game!" Once the animals were inured to the aural tumult, Pope pelted them with balloons (a particular trigger of equine anxiety) and paper streamers.

If this hazing might seem to carry a tinge of brutality, it is worth remembering the judgment of an officer from the Society for the Prevention of Cruelty to Animals who inspected the park not long after it opened: "If there is anything in this reincarnation stuff, I'd like to come back to Disneyland as a horse someday!" None of the animals, then or now, worked more than four hours a day.

While he was hectoring his charges through their indoctrination, Pope also took charge of Frontierland's stagecoaches—Disney said there *had* to be stagecoaches in his West—and covered wagons. The prairie schooners suffered from the same maddening slowness with which their ancestors had crawled across the Great Plains; they bored their riders, and would soon be abandoned. Bill Martin, whom Disney had hired from Twentieth Century-Fox to work on the Frontierland buildings, said, "The Wagon Train was a dumb ride. It was slow motion, and we had some Indians out in the sand dunes there. Walt never cared for that stuff."

He cared about the stagecoaches. They were faithful reproductions of the famous Wells Fargo Concord Coaches that were everywhere in the American West for half a century, but built on a scale small enough for the miniature horses to pull them.

They were among the first of the park's attractions to be finished, but the pressure of time was already weighing on everyone. One day John Hench stopped by to check the progress on the coaches and had an idea, which he brought to his boss. "Why don't we just leave the leather straps off, Walt? The people are never going to appreciate all the close-up detail."

The same scrupulousness that had recently made Disney refuse to license a Davy Crockett Colt revolver because the firearm hadn't existed in Davy's day treated Hench to a tart little lecture: "You're being a poor communicator. People are okay, don't you ever forget that. They will respond to it. They will appreciate it."

Hench didn't argue. "We put the best darn leather straps on that stagecoach you've ever seen."

Pope might have had less time to devote to stagecoach building had he not hired an authentic wrangler. Born in Kansas, Frank Pfannenstiel was working on a Colorado ranch by the time he was seventeen, when he joined the Marines to serve a machine gun on Guadalcanal, and was back in Colorado riding herd on a 2,200-acre spread when he crossed paths with Pope.

Nobody would have mistaken Pfannenstiel for a graduate of Van Arsdale France's charm school. Although he came to his profession late in its history, his temperament was that of the cowhands of the previous century.

Back in the 1880s, when scions of the British aristocracy ran some of the larger ranches in the American West, a visiting ducal nephew leaned down from his carriage to ask a hand who was fixing a fence, "Can you direct me to your master?"

The fence-mender briefly glanced up from his work. "He ain't born yet."

That might have been Pfannenstiel speaking. He was so ornery that at the end of his ninety-two-year life a friendly obituary writer felt he had to point out that his subject was "irascibly rubbing the right people the wrong way till the end."

He could get away with that because there was no horse he couldn't bend to Disneyland's needs. Like his colleague Earl Vilmer, he was the master of a dying art, and as spring brought a cascade of woes down on Disneyland, Walt knew that at least his trains and animals would be ready.

26

DEMANDS OF THE JUNGLE CRUISE

The one land expected to have the largest population of living animals turned out to have none at all. The Disney crew came to agree with one item in the amusement park barons' enumeration of inevitable money losers: it would be too difficult to stock Adventureland's Jungle Cruise (the attraction's original name, "Tropical Rivers of the World," had been jettisoned as too bulky) with actual tigers and elephants.

Much as Disney wanted them, Harper Goff talked him out it, knowing enough about zoology to believe the creatures would spend most of the day sleeping as far inland from the riverbanks as they could get. And even if they happened to be active, they wouldn't be reliable performers. Herb Ryman said, "If some boatload of people see a crocodile, they'll say, 'Oh, wasn't that beautiful. We saw a crocodile.' And somebody else in another boat didn't see any crocodile, so they're going to sue."

This was by far the smallest of the park's lands: just four acres, and the only one in which the public could wander. It would largely be given over to stores selling souvenirs: the Hawaiian Shop (shirts, of course); the Island Trade Store (bamboo spears with harmless flexible blades, rubber shrunken heads); Tiki Tropical Traders ("South Sea Islands apparel in a colorful assortment of unusual fabrics"); Here and There Imports (brass vessels, jewelry); Curio Hut (pretty much anything). The shoppers could refresh themselves in the Pavilion Restaurant and the "Sunkist, I Presume jungle watering hole." All this commercial activity would take place in an atmospheric main building—Moorish arches, blistered plaster, faded whitewash—and a cluster of bamboo huts with African shields and grinning skulls pegged in here and there.

But what about the actual attractions? There was only one, and it had better be good.

Ryman, having dismissed the live animals, nonetheless at first had scant faith in their replacements: "We had to simulate animals, which disappointed me, because I thought it would look phony. But the talents of the men involved made it look convincing."

Disney went to Bob Mattey, who had helped build the *20,000 Leagues* squid, and who twenty years later would traumatize half the nation with the shark he unleashed in *Jaws*. The initial sculpting of the animals went to Chris Mueller, who had first conceived the squid. He carved them in clay, which served as molds for their fiberglass carapaces.

It was up to Mattey to make them move in convincing ways: "Walt said he wanted mechanical animals that looked real, animals that wiggle their ears and open their mouths."

He divided his cast of creatures into three parts: those that would merely stand stationary by the river; those that would twitch a nose or flick a tail; and those that would actually advance on the audience. For his mobile subjects, Mattey developed intricate machines, cams, and rocker arms that would pivot the hippos' ears, lift the crocodiles' maws, make the giraffes nod their heads. All would be half-hidden by water or foliage; the giraffes would not walk, and the hippos would slide back and forth through the river on eight-foot transits supported by invisible submerged platforms.

Even these limited movements demanded closely knit arteries of rubber hosing and thickets of spring steel. The hippos alone needed three different sets of cams and electric motors to power them through their ponderous gambols.

Harper Goff knew how he wanted to bring the spectators—guests— past this wildlife. He'd been strongly impressed by the doughty little steam launch that had borne Katharine Hepburn and Humphrey Bogart through their adventures in the 1951 movie to which the boat had given its name, *The African Queen*.

Early thinking held the optimistic notion that the river's current alone would carry the boats along. It couldn't, and Disney didn't want gasoline engines for fear of fire. Goff thought diesel power would be more tractable, and designed a twenty-seven-foot, two-ton boat to be built, like the animals, of fiberglass—one of the first extensive uses of the still-new material. ("We had the navy watching us all the time," said Goff, "and when we put the boats in the water, they got permission to come out and they took pictures of everything. That was really pioneering in those days!") The vessels were suitably antiqued with mahogany-stained wood, bright brasswork, and black dummy stacks. Each was shaded by a striped canvas canopy, which imparted a touch of gaiety and, more important, prevented the passengers from looking up to discover how low the young fronds of the supposedly primeval jungle really were. The boats would be driven by forty-horsepower Gray Marine diesels, and kept on course by a guide rail laid along the river bottom.

They initially had a single entrance, cut into the starboard side, but George Miller, Disneyland's sole amusement park veteran, said that two would save time loading and unloading. Each boat could hold up to thirty-six passengers, and there would be seven of them (named by Bill Cottrell, the first head of WED Enterprises: *Ganges Gal*, *Congo Queen*, *Suwanee Lady*, *Amazon Belle*, *Mekong Maiden*, *Nile Princess*, and *Irrawaddy Woman*); if all went smoothly, the fleet could carry twenty thousand explorers through the jungle each day.

Laying out the course of the river proved as challenging as populating it. Goff and his colleagues had earlier designed its 1,640-foot path, but the contractors had trouble with this unusual task, and kept asking for better specifications.

Goff, realizing he wasn't entirely sure of his own calculations, borrowed a Jeep and built on its squat body a framework of spars the length and breadth of his boats. Then he drove slowly through the sandy, twisting path, making sure the stern would clear this outcropping, the bow negotiate that bend, while up on the banks workers drove in stakes as he passed. The bulldozers followed, cutting the channel that had been pegged out.

Meanwhile, far from the Irrawaddy-to-be, a complex acoustical project was under way. The jungle had to *sound* like a jungle. In Los Angeles, James Hervey, in charge of the Jungle Cruise noises for the Ralke Company, which had gotten the contract for the park's audiovisual effects, was mixing chirps and trills and growls in a system that now sounds nearly as antique as a Victrola, but then represented the state of the art.

A trade journal called *Radio and Television News* reported a year after Disneyland opened, "One entire section of the park is a simulated African jungle in which three types of sound effects are required. They are: intermittent localized effects which must come in 'on cue' such as the trumpeting of a mechanical elephant as visitors approach on one of the five-eighth scale riverboats; continuous localized effects such as a constant chattering of monkeys in one area of the 'jungle'; and, continuous over-all effects which would be heard virtually anywhere in the jungle at all times such as the roar of lions, bird sounds, and the noises of crickets and frogs at night. . . . One particular device, especially devised for the 'Disneyland' project, 'moves' the background noises from one section of the jungle to another quite realistically. This is a 'continuous automatic fader.'

"How the sound effects are handled in this section of the park, called 'Adventureland,' are [*sic*] of particular interest, especially the various effects that come in on a specific cue. For example, a typical sequence of events producing an intermittent localized effect goes something like this: as the riverboat nears the 'rhino land' area of the jungle tour it interrupts a photocell beam reaching across the river. Infrared filters keep the beam invisible.

"The signal from the photocell trips relays which are located in the mechanical rhinos, thus setting them in motion, and also starting the tape in one of the 150 cartridge-type repeating tape players in the control room for the jungle area.

"Sound from this continuous-loop tape is fed into a 30-watt amplifier and in turn to a camouflaged loudspeaker at the rhinos' location.

"When the rhino tape has run its sequence (this takes but a matter of seconds) the tape player automatically stops. However when the rhino tape player had originally started, it also activated a relay for the next sound effect, thus providing a specific delay during which time the boat moved farther down the river. After the delay a second tape player producing sound for a mechanical elephant located on one side of the river is started as soon as the elephant begins to move. . . .

"The repeater units provide continuous local sound effects, but here there is no control or switching involved. The tape loops . . . simply run continuously. . . .

"The third type of sound effect used in the park is the continuous over-all effect providing jungle sounds for the entire area. . . . Used on a self-reversing tape player it [this tape] is fed into a 50-watt amplifier and then, sequentially, to five groups of loudspeakers (eight speakers to a group) by means of the 'continuous automatic fader' designed for that purpose.

"This device was developed especially for use at 'Disneyland.' "

And here is Disney with his ceaseless striving for reality in his realm of artifice: "To heighten the illusion, a different sound track is used during the evening, this second track was actually taped in the African jungle at night and brings authentic sounds to the listener."

27

MILKING THE ELEPHANT

The animal that caused the most problems was not in Adventureland but in Fantasyland.

Disney wanted Dumbo in his park: huge-eared flying elephants would revolve and could be raised and lowered by the rider during the flight. Compared with the dark rides that were in the works, this was a fairly conventional amusement park device. But it was not conventional enough to be easily realized.

The initial plans called for pink elephants drawn from the bravura drunken dream sequence in the cartoon, but Disney decided such a prominent advertisement for alcoholism would send the wrong message, and so the elephants became Dumbo himself. Chris Mueller took a break from his Adventureland labors to sculpt the prototype. In the movie, the elephant flew by flapping his ears, which made trouble right away: each Dumbo had a system of gears in his head to keep the ears moving, and the fussy machinery never worked properly.

That wasn't the worst of it. Each elephant weighed seven hundred pounds, and Ed Morgan and Karl Bacon—Arrow had been commissioned to build the ride—had a terrible time getting them aloft. This was a far cry from the warplane fuel tanks they'd converted into their simple circle swings, and they had to hire an engineer. Morgan said, "The guy's idea was clever and we didn't have enough experience to gainsay it." It was a hydraulic system in which "you could cut the horsepower that it took to lift the elephants way down by putting oil under the pressure of nitrogen" in a sealed tube. "It was a wonderful idea, but he didn't know that in order to do that, you had to have a piston that separated the gas from the oil. So what happened was that the rapid movement of the oil would mix the nitrogen and the oil and make foam. The foam threw the whole thing out of stability and it was too late to change it."

What this meant was that after a few minutes of operation the ride would eject quarts of white goo—Bacon described it as "shaving cream"—and required constant cleaning and replenishment of the oil, a job Morgan and Bacon referred to as "milking the elephant" while they tried to come up with a better system.

Arrow was eye-deep in Disneyland now. With Toad's cars completed, they had moved on to Casey Jr. "We mocked up the engine," Morgan said, "and it was a lot of work because of all the oddball shapes that you're not used to. We thought it was great. Disney came, and he looked at it and walked around and looked again. Then he's over in the corner talking to the art director, Vic Greene. Vic comes over and says, 'Walt thinks that if you fatten the boiler up just a little bit it might give it a little more feeling.' And then he'd say, 'Walt thinks that the steam chests, if they were just tipped a little more . . .' So what it amounts to is that by the time they'd leave, I'd be thinking, my God, we've been working our butts off, and there's really nothing here that we can use. You just can't make the boiler over, so you start with another engine next to it and build it up. But I was told by Roger Broggie somewhere along that time, 'Well you better get used to it, because that's the way it's going to be if you work with movie people . . . ,' he looks around to see if anyone was listening, '. . . and particularly with art directors.'"

This unsettling visit took place in mid-March. Despite having casually ordered the complete overhaul of Casey Jr., Disney was pleased with what he saw, and felt the Arrow partners understood his belief in the very different aesthetics of a midway ride and a Disney ride.

After dismantling Casey Jr., Disney moved on to examine the prototype car for the Snow White ride. It was much simpler than Toad's automobile: a two-seat cart presumably made by the dwarfs for their mine, with a pair of wheels in the rear and a single one up front so it could snap around the tightest turns.

It was supposed to be small, but Disney worried it was too cramped when he climbed in and squirmed about on the seat checking the knee room. He beckoned Broggie aboard so he could see how well two grown-ups fit. Tight, but that might be all right; Disney had decided the seats should comfortably accommodate one adult and one child.

He got out, struck with a small inspiration. Bruce Bushman was there, and he was a very large man who came into his own every Christmas, when he played Santa Claus without needing an auxiliary pillow stuffed under his costume to simulate St. Nick's generous rotundity. Disney called him over and told him to sit in the car. "If it fits you, Bruce, it'll fit anybody."

It did fit him, and Bushman good-humoredly added to his duties being a sort of human crash-test dummy for the new rides.

28

AUTOPIA

The attraction that needed the greatest number of cars also demanded the most literal ones. Tomorrowland was more problematic than any other Disney domain, for unlike Main Street and Frontierland it had no models from the past to draw on; nor did it have the cartoons that supplied Fantasyland with its subjects.

Plans remained so vague and shifting that back in September Disney had decided not to open it with the rest of the park. But the future wouldn't let him alone; it was an integral part of his design, and his park would be maimed without it. Fowler said, "The original plans called for completing only the Main Street area, Adventureland, Frontierland, and Fantasyland in time for opening. By the time January 1955 rolled around, however, it was decided that we would build Tomorrowland and have it as part of Disneyland for the opening."

Only one Tomorrowland attraction seemed obvious from the start. The park was being built in a piece of America where tomorrow was already imposing itself on today. Citizens of the future would be driving on the freeways that were, the civic planners promised, soon to throw over Southern California a concrete net with mesh so fine that no home would be more than five miles away from an on-ramp.

So from the start, Tomorrowland was scheduled to have the Autopia Freeway, a mile-long road with cloverleafs and overpasses on which children could learn about life in the internal-combustion era behind the steering wheels of small sports cars.

Autopia, which would turn out to be perhaps the most popular of all the park's attractions, was in the hands of a twenty-three-year-old who had been something of a child prodigy.

Bob Gurr began his 2012 memoir with a proud statement. "Trained as a car stylist, I contributed to ventures worth over $175 million, all without ever obtaining an engineering degree. In fact, my training was free, all learned on the job. No one ever asked for my qualifications. If I had no experience in a new task I'd keep my mouth shut and go full speed ahead."

Gurr's early years carried echoes of Disney's. He had a paper route that called for the delivery of forty-four copies of the *Hollywood Citizen News* six days a week, "plus 1,000 Shopping News, 1,000 Advertisers in the mornings, twice a week before school. After all the papers were delivered, I'd ride my bike home to milk the goats before riding on to school."

He did not distinguish himself there. Mr. Gordy, his geometry teacher, gave him an F, but passed him anyway, explaining, "I never want to see Robert Gurr again."

Rather than concentrating on cosines and tangents, Gurr had been doodling automobiles. In another course, he struck a deal with the more sympathetic Mr. Gullard: "He'd let me design cars in his class on architecture, providing I finish the class assignment first."

Along with looking over his student's architectural assignments, Mr. Gullard took the time to study his car drawings, and urged him to enroll in automobile design at the Art Center School in Los Angeles (now in Pasadena and called the ArtCenter College of Design). He went there on a General Motors scholarship.

Thereafter, everything happened quickly. One of his teachers at the Art Center sent him to Dan Post, who a few years earlier had started publishing the first books on custom cars. He enlisted Gurr to illustrate an opus called *How to Draw Cars of Tomorrow.* By the time he graduated in the spring of 1952, the book was ready to go to press.

GM wanted him in Detroit a month before his graduation. This was a common practice among car designers to get the best first, but even so Gurr was poached away from GM in a deal engineered by a Ford designer named Frank Hershey, who was three years away from helping create the Thunderbird.

This should have been pretty heady for someone who had just turned twenty-one, but Gurr had published a car design book before he'd ever designed a car, and "within two weeks I could see that being a Detroit car stylist doing just hub caps and hood ornaments would be a dead end job."

He went back to Los Angeles and found work at a small design firm named Cumming Wallace Gibson. He had a rubber stamp made up— "R.H. Gurr Industrial Design"—and waited for something to happen.

When something did, it came from an unexpected quarter. Gurr was friends with Ub Iwerks's son David, and often joined the family for Sunday dinner. "One day Ub described a little car running around on the studio backlot . . . no body on it, just a bare chassis." At the end of this not especially stimulating anecdote, Iwerks asked if Gurr did outside work. "I did not, but said yes anyway."

A few days later he got a call. Could he come over to Disney and see someone named Dick Irvine? "On the way to the studio I wondered— do you suppose the little car needs a body designed? Would this be for that new amusement park?"

Irvine, who had laid out the Autopia roadway, met him at the gate and confirmed his speculations: Yes, the little car needed a body; and yes, it was for that new amusement park. "Dick introduced me to some business folks, then showed me the little bare car chassis. A welded steel frame, pivoting front axle, rear axle assembly, and a hot ten horsepower engine from the latest scooter-bike craze, the Mustang Colt. Just as simple as could be, but bare naked. I took some dimensions, then went home to sketch some body ideas."

He still had his regular job so he drew at night, and returned on the following two Saturdays to show Irvine what he'd been doing.

He patterned his design on what he believed was the closest contemporary example of the Car of the Future. The first Ferrari imported to America—a 166 Spyder Corsa—had made landfall in the country that would become the make's most important market just five years earlier.

Like its British counterpart the Jaguar it was gorgeous in its every evolution right from the start.

On one of his visits to the studio Gurr showed his renderings to Roger Broggie, who had some of Disney's peremptory spirit. "On a following Saturday I received a call at (ye gads) 7:00 AM."

"Do you draft?" Boggie wanted to know.

"Yes."

"Get your tools and get over here." Before Gurr could reply, "Silence, dial tone."

Broggie was waiting when he got there, and took him over to the now-familiar little car, "which slowly collected four guys with their feet on each tire, discussing what was to be done. One guy, slightly rumpled with a Roy Rogers wooden bullet belt, had his foot on one tire." Gurr thought "he was the father of one of the night guards" until somebody called him Walt.

Gurr's misapprehension was understandable because there was "no formal introduction, just get to work. Walt was collecting a lot of new folks on the studio lot. We were all gonna design Disneyland."

Despite the improvisatory nature of their jobs, Gurr thought most of those new folks had to know what they were doing. He wasn't so sure about himself. He had complete confidence in the exterior of his mini-Ferrari, but "Roger wanted me to draft the little car's mechanical parts so they could be produced in quantity. I was comfortable drawing up the body, but to be production engineer on a whole car? I was trained as a car stylist, not as a mechanical engineer." But Walt "saw me draw the body, he figured I did mechanical stuff too. I was too afraid to 'fess up that I didn't know how."

"R.H. Gurr Industrial Design" had his hands full, drawing car bodies and, with less confidence, car innards at home during the evenings and spending weekends at the studio—like so many of his peers he was in the Zorro Building—and learning "just how much I didn't know."

Gurr gradually came to realize he wasn't the only employee trying to cope with unfamiliar duties. "All the rest of Walt's guys were in the same boat, nobody had ever designed a Disneyland before." And all of them had to learn how fast: "It was November 1954 and Walt said Disneyland would open in eight months. Oh my gosh."

The torrent of interesting work made his weekdays at Cumming Wallace Gibson begin to pall. That would soon cease to be a problem.

"Walt was seen everywhere," Gurr wrote of that frenetic winter season. "Not just meetings, but wandering into everybody's room, no matter how scattered over the lot. No system of organized vice presidents, project managers, and coordinators like modern times. These guys just stepped up and solved conflicts on the spot."

The WED rooms *were* scattered, a wide circle of outposts haphazardly defending "no real company center other than Dick Irvine's office." Disney patrolled them constantly, and came back from one of his tours to have a word with Broggie about his newest employee. A few days before Christmas, Broggie stopped by Gurr's desk and said, "Walt was in here last night, and told me to keep you real busy."

Gurr took this bait, and asked—perhaps somewhat disingenuously— if "maybe I should quit my regular day job and draw cars every day here." This did not lead to further discussion with Broggie. "Without a word he led me to the personnel department and I hired on minutes later."

Gurr was still "too scared to say 'I don't do mechanicals,'" but this child of the automotive age was saved by the nineteenth century. Now that he was a full-time employee, Broggie assigned him a drafting table in Earl Vilmer's shop, where he found himself surrounded by "interesting 'old tyme' characters from America's past—steam freaks I called them. We seemed worlds apart, they were mostly in their 50s to 70s while I was a green kid. . . . Steam railroads were their passion, sports cars and airplanes were my big thrill."

There he had the good luck to fall in with Ed Lingenfelter, "the fellow who took me under his wing and mentored me into 'the world of steam,'" introducing him to a realm of massive driving rods and sand domes and Johnson bars that could not be more different from the tight tolerances of the compact internal combustion plants that had put the steam engines out of business in the working world. More important, though, he became Gurr's "engineering professor," teaching him the basic principles that did not change with the changing equipment. He "was there to help me every day with the things I didn't know. Roger surely would have glared at me if I'd asked him all the little engineering questions."

Lingenfelter put up "a big chart on his wall explaining the essence of good design communication. He showed me how many ways there were to explain something to a machinist with a blueprint." Gurr, a quick learner, became as capable of drafting what went inside a car as he was rendering the stylish sheet metal that covered it. "To this day, I cherish the knowledge I learned from those wonderful wizards whose world was so far from mine."

Once Gurr and Broggie had finished working out the Autopia car's chassis, they turned to its body. That had to begin with a full-size clay model from which to make the production molds.

Disney had struck an advantageous deal with Gurr's alma mater, the Art Center School. The students would build the model, and because collegians rarely get paid for their classwork, the labor would be free. Then the school decided the arrangement was too one-sided, and backed out. But Joe Thompson, the center's model shop teacher, believed his employer had scuttled a great opportunity for his students: here was a chance to do some real-world work for Disney and be there when Walt himself criticized it. Thompson volunteered to have the model sculpted in the garage of his North Hollywood home.

His charges worked quickly. A week or two later, Gurr learned that the model was ready, and "Walt put me in his brother-in-law Bill Cottrell's old Cadillac and the three of us drove to Joe's place."

Cottrell's car was not only old but disintegrating. At one point in the trip, Disney draped his arm over the seat back, and drew it away decorated with tufts of padding that were leaking from the upholstery.

"Dammit Bill, I pay you enough. Get your car fixed."

They arrived at Thompson's, where Irvine and Broggie were waiting. Disney walked around the model, then climbed into it and rested "his sleeve on the clay. Now he had brown clay rubbed into the white stuffing." This didn't bother Disney at all; he thought the car looked fine, and approved it at once.

The next day the model was in the studio, with the production molds under way. The cars would be made of fiberglass—the new material was cropping up all over Disneyland—and the Glasspar Company in Costa Mesa began producing the first of forty shells, which were sent to Mameco Engineering in Newport Beach for final assembly.

The first of them, though, went to the studio, where it was mounted on a hand-built chassis. Broggie and Gurr now had a complete car, ready for testing. It lacked only bumpers.

At this point Mel Tilley intervened. He was the salesman for Kaiser Aluminum, and seemed to believe that everything in Disneyland outside of the concession food and the window glass should be made of his alloy. He persuaded Gurr to use it for the bumpers, which would encircle the entire car. "Not being an engineer, I didn't know any better."

Before the bumpers went on, Gurr took his prototype "on the local streets of Newport Beach, out for a spin. I got carried away showing how the car could lay rubber with the speed governor disconnected. I soon lost it and smashed into a parked car behind the police station. The fiberglass hood just exploded all over us in a shower of little red bits."

This was not how the miracle material was supposed to behave. When Gurr put that forcefully to the Glasspar people, he learned how perilous it can be to flirt with the future. The sheepish explanation was that Glasspar had been experimenting with "a 'new' plastic resin for the production bodies."

With the resin subtracted from the recipe, the completed cars started arriving. Van Arsdale France had already graduated some freeway recruits, and "in a circus tent set up in the backstage area the new Autopia ride operators helped me install the bumpers."

Disney thought they were getting too close to the wire for crash tests, but Gurr went ahead with them anyway. He set up a simulation of the ride in which the cars jostled one another, as they inevitably would on the freeway. "I quickly observed that the aluminum bumper material deforms and does not return to its original position, such as sheet metal would."

This coolly stated summary does not suggest how the trial struck onlookers not involved with the Autopia Freeway. Gurr went on to acknowledge that "the bumper crash testing looked like a bunch of wild kids smashing cars in clouds of dust." Word of an ongoing demolition derby quickly reached headquarters, and Admiral Fowler "drove his ugly old '54 Plymouth [old? This was April of '55] all the way from the administration building to our test area to personally order a stop to the perceived mischief."

Despite a chewing-out from the admiral, Gurr surreptitiously continued with limited testing on his own, and none of it pleased him.

The aluminum bumpers revealed all sorts of failings, from crumpling up like shirt cardboard when encountering anything much firmer than a beach ball to leaving behind bright scribbles of shaved metal whenever they brushed a curb.

Gurr faced the fast-approaching summer with dread. "Opening day was imminent, and thousands of real test drivers were going to do the REAL testing."

29

THE MOONLINER

Only one element of Tomorrowland came about with relative ease. The *Los Angeles Times* reported on July 6, "Early risers along a twenty-mile route between Hollydale and Anaheim were startled this morning to see an 89-foot rocket ship moving through the streets." They were very early risers, because, in order to avoid an immense traffic jam, "the 'Air Ship of Tomorrow' was trucked before sun-up, from Hollydale where it was built to Disneyland where it will become part of the TWA exhibit as well as the theme of the Tomorrowland section of the park."

C. V. Wood had sold a sponsorship to Trans World Airlines, which became "the Official Airline to Disneyland" and would put its name to a simulated trip to the moon (which was causing much grief) and this "Moonliner" (which was causing comparatively little).

The spaceship had been designed by John Hench, and it looked like the V-2 rockets launched against England by Germany late in World War II. That's hardly surprising, as their father, Wernher von Braun, also worked on the Moonliner (interestingly, he declared Walt Disney the most intelligent man he had ever met). Von Braun, who would have gone on trial in Nuremberg had not the urgencies of the budding Cold War welcomed him into the American space program (when a movie about him called *I Aim for the Stars* came out, someone suggested a subtitle: *But Sometimes I Hit London*), took part in the *Disneyland* episode "Man in Space," which aired that spring. Hench made the Moonliner look like the innocuous passenger vessel it was supposed to represent by adding portholes and a pilot's cabin, along with three graceful twenty-two-foot pylons that curved out from the lower third of the ship to form a tripod that kept it upright.

"The building was actually kind of subtle," Hench said. "We used the same methods they use to manufacture boilers at a boiler works. The hull didn't have that elegant shape exactly, but we bridged with a lot of little changes. And it worked all right, particularly when we got the curved sections up where perspective helped."

Bob Gurr disagreed with Hench about the subtlety of the structure: "They had this horizontal frame laying on the ground, with all these plywood rings, and all this aluminum. It was a crude way to build it, but it was built very quickly." Seventy-six feet tall, the Moonliner was sheathed in fifteen thousand square feet of aluminum laid over a steel skeleton. Here again Mel Tilley's favorite metal made some trouble, although less than it had with Gurr's bumpers. "They got the entire rocket together in Tomorrowland," Gurr said, "and then discovered what they had done wrong. As soon as they had it put in place, the aluminum started expanding in the sun, while the steel and the wood interior structure didn't. You'd hear this thing going 'bang, clunk . . . crack, crack' all day long! And then at sundown, 'bang . . . bang' as it started cooling and shrinking back."

The *Times* article mentions that the Moonliner was the theme of Tomorrowland, but it was more than that. The rocket became the universally recognized symbol of the dawning space age. In his novel *Moonglow* Michael Chabon writes, "In children's drawings, all houses have chimneys, all monkeys eat bananas, and every rocket is a V-2. Even after decades of stepped-back multistage behemoths, chunky orbiters, and space planes, the midcentury-modern *Enterprise*, the polyhedral bulk of Imperial star destroyers and Borg cubes, the Ortho-Cyclen disk of *Millennium Falcon*—in our deepest imaginations the surest way to the nearest planet remains a trim cigar tapering to a pointed nose cone, poised on the tips of four swept-back axial fins. By the time I became conscious of rockets . . . they had progressed well beyond von Braun's early masterwork, in design as in power, size, and capacity. But it was a V-2 that would carry me into the outer space of a fairground ride, that labeled the spines of the public library's science fiction collection. A V-2 was the 'weenie' or visual anchor of Walt Disney's Tomorrowland."

In its red-and-white livery, the Moonliner dominated the Disney future for more than a decade before being scrapped in 1966. Even after more than fifty years, to anyone who ever saw the rocket, Tomorrowland still feels a bit empty without it.

30

Through the Castle Gate

Only one wienie outdid the Moonliner to make a deeper impression on the national imagination, to nearly eclipse Mickey Mouse himself as the universally recognized symbol of the Disney empire.

The building at the end of Main Street ran through a number of names at its inception: Medieval Castle, the Fantasyland Castle, the Robin Hood Castle (Disney made a movie about him in 1952), and in an early *Disneyland* show Walt referred to it as Snow White's Castle. But in the end he named it after his cartoon feature then still in development.

Herb Ryman designed the Sleeping Beauty Castle, taking some of its features from Neuschwanstein, the Romanesque Revival palace built by Ludwig II of Bavaria in the 1860s to be a place where, the king said, the gods "will come to live with Us on the lofty heights, breathing the air of heaven"—the "Us" being Ludwig and his revered friend Richard Wagner.

As Ryman's conception of the castle advanced through a series of models, he worried that it was too literal a reflection of King Ludwig's god lure: "I didn't like it because it was such an obvious copy. People would say, 'Walt's men have no imagination of their own—they can't even create their own castle.'"

Still unhappy as the final model stood awaiting Disney's imminent judgment, he fretfully took hold of a cluster of spires, lifted them free, reversed them, and set them back down. This alarmed Dick Irvine and Marvin Davis, who were standing by. "Dick said I'd better put it back.

Walt would be back any minute. At that moment, Walt was standing behind me, hands on his hips."

He advanced on the model scowling, then stopped and stood staring at it. Ryman's impulsive intervention had made it look warmer: more of a fantasy, less of a fortress, it had gained a stronger power to charm. Disney approved it at once.

As with the Main Street buildings, the Sleeping Beauty Castle uses forced perspective to appear much taller than its seventy-seven feet. The ramparts are fiberglass, but the gleaming tops of the many spires apparently are the genuine article. Ryman pushed Disney to cover them with twenty-four-karat gold leaf, and Walt sneaked this costly modification past his brother at the expense of a later quarrel. It might have heartened Roy to know that the cost would be amortized by gold leaf's virtue of requiring little maintenance to retain its shine.

When it was finished, John Hench, the laureate of the park's psychology, thought it distilled all that made Disneyland special: "Take Sleeping Beauty Castle, for instance. Most people walk up to this point and take a picture. In fact, more pictures are probably taken right here of that castle than anything else perhaps in the world. But if you walked up and asked a guest WHY he likes the castle . . . WHY is it worth photographing? . . . He could never tell you. He'd probably stammer out something like 'Because it's just beautiful.' And yet, when he gets back home and shows his pictures, the feeling will never be the same that he experiences simply standing there.

"The fact is, as we stand here right now, there are literally hundreds of stimuli etching an impression . . . and an experience in our minds through every one of our senses. Probably the most conscious and obvious stimulus is visual . . . we are looking at that castle and we think it is beautiful. Yet consider the factors that are playing on our sense of vision . . . the colors . . . the lighting, the shapes and designs. There is a static nature about the castle structure itself that makes you think its been standing there for centuries. And yet there is motion . . . the motion of those flags, and the trees around us made by the wind. The movement of people, vehicles and boats, water, balloons, horses, and the white clouds passing by overhead.

"Look at the top of the castle. At the base of the highest tower are a series of tremendously detailed gargoyles which you can barely see from the ground. And yet they are part of our 'magic formula.' They are part of a thousand little tiny details we are looking at right now but don't consciously perceive. Individually they are nothing. Collectively, they add up to a visual experience that the guest can't find anywhere else."

That visual experience was to continue beyond the castle's portcullis, where a fairy-tale village, all warm, honey-colored old stone and half-timbering, would house the Fantasyland dark rides and shops. That would happen, but not before a whole generation had passed through the park. The castle had eaten up much of the initial Fantasyland budget, and those rides would have to operate in a series of sixty- by one-hundred-foot prefabricated metal boxes.

The WED team got around this by fronting the buildings with Masonite flats cut and painted to look like tents, boldly striped, topped with banners, the whole effect suggesting a medieval tourney. This was cleverly done (it sufficed perfectly well for thirty years), but George Whitney Jr.'s lifetime in the amusement business told him what the sequence of small rooms encased in sheet metal would mean to the visitor. He wrote in a cautionary memo, "The heat that builds up in the building points to the fact that we must consider some sort of ventilation. This could be eliminated however, if we changed the ride from 'Snow White' to 'A trip through Hell,' in which the heat would be a natural prop."

———

Ventilation would not be a problem with what, next to the castle, was Fantasyland's most impressive attraction.

Back in 1939, Disney had been giving close thought to amusement parks, both because he was taking his young daughters to the Griffith Park merry-go-round, and because he was developing for his feature cartoon *Pinocchio* the snare for bad boys called Pleasure Island, a masterly evocation of that brimstone breath of the sinister every traditional park occasionally emanates.

He had two brothers, Bob and Bill Jones, at work making models of Pleasure Island's septic diversions, and he started talking to them about parks, describing a couple he'd visited recently. "Things could be done better than this," he said. "A park should be designed for total family enjoyment. Besides a merry-go-round, there could be other rides, but they should all be safe and attractive. The grounds should be landscaped, clean and well maintained. These are my thoughts on the subject. . . . See what you can do to develop them, and I'll check [in] with you every few days."

Making a two-dimensional amusement park proved challenge enough, and Disney dropped the idea for years; but it's telling that he gave the carousel primacy in his imaginary park. He would have one in his real park, too, the only ride there not designed specifically for Disneyland.

While construction was under way, Disney described Fantasyland to a reporter, saying, "In the middle will be King Arthur Carrousel, with leaping horses, not just trotting, but all of them leaping!" This was unusual for a carousel; most had a combination of stationary horses ("standers") and leaping ones ("jumpers") that rose and fell with the motion of the overhead crankshafts to which they were attached.

Disney's ideal, though, was the Griffith Park machine, and all its horses were jumpers, sixty-eight of them set flank-to-flank in four concentric rows. It was—and is—superb; and when Disney asked Ross Davis, its owner, about finding one just like it, he learned that it was the sole remaining carousel with four-abreast jumpers.

He had struck up a friendship with Davis during his days visiting the park with his daughters. Now he told him he needed the best carousel he could get, and commissioned him to find it. Davis had many contacts in the amusement world—his family had been in the carousel business since the turn of the century—and his inquiries led him to Toronto, where Sunnyside Amusement Park was about to be extinguished by a new expressway. Sunnyside was home to a carousel made in 1922 by the Dentzel Company of Philadelphia. It wasn't all jumpers; in fact, it wasn't all horses, but rather was a "menagerie" merry-go-round with a mixture of cats, deer, rabbits, giraffes, and a chariot or two among the chargers.

Davis liked it though, and in October of 1954 Disney bought it on his recommendation, sight unseen, for $22,500, close to a quarter million today—just the sort of expenditure the amusement park consultants saw as tearing up money. J. O. Davis, Ross's son, said, "When we got it, it had horses three abreast and the outer row was all standers. Walt wanted his carousel to be four abreast, all horses, all jumpers like our Griffith Park machine. I worked on repainting and repairing the horses, and we took unused figures [animals] in payment for our efforts. We worked on the figures, and Arrow Development did all the engineering. This meant new crankshafts to operate the four rows of horses, but the platform remained the same."

In the WED shops, they converted standers to jumpers—by grafting on freshly carved legs—until they ran out of horses. Disreputable old Coney came to the rescue when it revealed a hoard of figures made by the master carver Charles Looff, who had started his carousel-building career in Brooklyn, and George Whitney was able to pry some additional ones loose from his father's Playland.

In the end, Disney acquired eighty-five jumpers; the carousel holds seventy-two of them, with the surplus being constantly renovated and substituted as part of a maintenance program that continues to this day.

Bruce Bushman was assigned the task of designing the canopy for the King Arthur Carrousel (Disney insisted on the French double "r" spelling; perhaps it sounded more satisfactorily Old World to him). As the name suggests, Disney wanted a medieval appearance, but Bushman was reluctant to do away with Dentzel's elegant 1920s carvings on the rounding board that encircled the top of the ride. He came up with a happy compromise, designing a tall, sharp-peaked canopy that preserved the rounding board while from a distance drawing attention only to the plunging steeds beneath it. Here again, the tireless Mel Tilley had his way: the canopy looked like taut canvas, but it was aluminum—which was fine in this role, as it wouldn't be asked to collide with other carousels.

Thrust back into the merry-go-round business, Ed Morgan and Karl Bacon also got the commission to build the King Arthur Carrousel's neighbor, the Mad Tea Party ride, loosely drawn from *Alice in Wonderland.* Disney had never cared for the film. "I got trapped into making" it, he said, "against my better judgment and it was a terrible disappointment. I always liked the Tenniel illustrations in Alice but I never exactly died laughing over the story." He added a thought that could have saved many another movie: "It's terribly tough to transfer whimsy to the screen."

Still, he saw in the Mad Hatter's party the potential for a popular attraction. In it, three turntables, each holding six teacups, revolve clockwise, set in a single, far larger turntable that rotates in the opposite direction. Every teacup has a center wheel that the riders can turn to spin themselves faster.

Dana Morgan, Ed's son, who now runs an amusement ride manufacturing business of his own, was a boy (a very fortunately situated boy, one thinks) when the park was being built. "I remember that before Disneyland opened, they had the tea party ride at the plant. The building wasn't big enough to build it inside, so they built it outside. At that time, they only had one teacup on it. I rode it a lot then. I think I was almost certainly the first kid to ride it. I was a guinea pig, used to see if a kid was strong enough to turn it, and could stand it without throwing up after riding in it."

As it turned out, the teacups probably caused the most severe nausea in those who had to maintain them. Although the Mad Tea Party was close to being a conventional amusement park ride, not even Dumbo would cause its operators more trouble.

31

THE PERFECTIONIST AT WORK

Walt Disney was omnipresent. Van Arsdale France wrote, "A bicycle was the preferred means of getting around 'The Site.' Unfortunately, our bikes had a habit of breaking down. Back then, things didn't get done by procedure. We used a certain amount of guilt, bluff, friends, grease, and lies. One trick was to use Walt's name. For example, 'Please repair Walt's bike' would get immediate action—and who was to know that Walt never rode a bike?"

How he *did* travel from roundhouse to jungle to Main Street was something of a mystery. "Although he didn't ride a bicycle, Walt managed to amaze me by the way he'd get around 'The Site' by walking. One day I saw Walt at one end of the park-to-be. I was driving. But, by the time I got to the other side of the park, he was already there. I guess it was due to his days on the farm and delivering papers, because he could cover a lot of distance on foot, without seeming to be in a hurry."

Not only was he a ubiquitous presence, he was an all-seeing one. To C. V. Wood's continuing exasperation, he wouldn't cut corners, and spotted any attempt to do so. "I wanted to put plastic railing up on top of the houses on Main Street," said Wood, "and [Walt] wanted real wrought iron. Forty feet in the air—nobody could tell the difference."

One day, crossing the railroad tracks, Disney realized what had been nagging him about them. The ballast! The trains were built to five-eighths scale, but the rocks on which their tracks lay were full-size; this roadbed could carry the mighty 20th Century Limited. Disney picked up one of the stones and turned to a nearby workman. "That's not to scale. It gives the wrong appearance." The ballast got re-crushed.

"Look," Disney said around this time, "the thing that's going to make Disneyland unique and different is the detail. If we lose the detail, we lose it all."

Another thing that was to make Disneyland different was its cleanliness, which Disney had stressed from his earliest plans. Now, walking through acres strewn with the already rusting leavings of heavy construction, he worried about the litter to come. He ordered that only ice cream bars with flat sticks be sold—"nothing with round sticks, people trip on them." Not that there'd be much time to find one to trip on: Disney was determined that no rubbish should stay on the ground for more than a couple of minutes. Having hired American Building Maintenance to keep the park tidy, he quickly realized he wanted a higher standard of cleaning than the company offered: he took as his models luxury hotels and ocean liners. Having spent hours discussing his gospel of cleanliness with American Building's foreman, Chuck Boyajian, he sent him off to spend a weekend haunting the lobby of a "top-notch" hotel watching how unobtrusively refuse was spirited away. Disneyland's janitorial department became "Custodial Guest Services," and Boyajian proved so satisfactory a student that he and his crew would keep the park immaculate for the next quarter century.

Disney used hot dogs to plot the placement of trash cans. He happily ate with the construction crews, from the site's food trucks—they were universally known as roach coaches—and his favorite fare was frankfurters (Mickey Mouse's very first spoken words, in the 1929 cartoon *The Karnival Kid*, were "Hot dogs! Hot dogs!"). Disney would bring a frank away from a lunch wagon and pace off the distance it took him to eat it. At the point where he finished, he indicated that a receptacle should be planted to receive the wrapper.

Disney was often dissatisfied with things as he found them; his preferences changed from day to day, sometimes from hour to hour. When he had introduced the park in miniature to the American television audience with "The Disneyland Story," taking the viewers "past the railroad station, down the steps, and across the band concert park," that park was of course equipped with a model bandstand.

By spring the real one was standing in Town Square. One Sunday

Van Arsdale France brought his daughter to see the site, and they came upon Disney at the bandstand. "Walt was standing there just looking at it. At the risk of interrupting his thoughts, I introduced my daughter. He was gracious, as he always was to children, but definitely preoccupied. Sort of talking to himself, but also to us, he said, 'There's something damned wrong with the location of that bandstand.' Leaving him alone with his thoughts, my daughter and I left.

"The next morning I was on Main Street and saw the bandstand being moved."

It had been interfering with the view down Main Street to the castle; but a new location in Adventureland made no sense. France said "it was moved to about seven different places, before and after opening." Disney never could find just the right spot; today the bandstand is adding its fin de siècle charm to the Roger's Gardens nursery in Newport Beach.

Naturally the landscaping came under Disney's scrutiny. As Bill Evans summed up his own role during the spring of '55. "We got pretty good at moving trees."

"All through the construction phases, Walt would be out there every weekend, and we would take a kind of ritual hike on Saturday. He would make comments of a general nature, with nothing in detail about the landscaping. Once in while we'd be walking along with Joe Fowler and Dick Irvine and Walt, with all the troop strung along behind us, and Walt would turn to Joe Fowler and say, 'Joe, that tree looks a little close to the walkway, doesn't it?' And then he'd turn around and he'd say, 'How about moving that tree, Bill?' And this was a fifteen-ton tree. The next day it would be ten feet further away."

That Disney said "nothing in detail about the landscaping" did not mean it satisfied him. He thought the Evans brothers were making a good jungle, but worried that their work along Main Street lacked imagination.

He wasn't looking merely for greenery in his park. The plantings should be more than decorative; they had to help set a mood, and serve as half-subliminal signals that the visitor was moving from one land to its neighbor.

Capable as they were, the Evans brothers had come up through the nursery business. Disney wanted to find someone who had a highly specialized education; someone who could envision plants as a crucial element in a cinematic whole.

He went to Welton Becket, the architect friend who had told him no architect could design his park. Becket said he did know somebody, an unusual person with an unusual background, who might be right for the job.

32

RUTH'S ROLE

Ruth Shellhorn had decided to become a landscape architect when she was fifteen years old. She'd been born in Los Angeles in 1909 to parents who were unusually forward-looking for the time. When she showed herself to be good at math and possessed of strong artistic leanings, they backed her as she advanced toward a profession almost devoid of women. There was no talk of secretarial school or home economics; she enrolled in the Oregon State College School of Landscape Architecture.

Shellhorn flourished there, winning the highest grades in the school, but felt she also needed solid architectural training, and transferred to Cornell's College of Architecture in 1930.

Her parents sold their house to keep Ruth in Cornell, but the money ran out right before her final year. She left just four "units," as the school's academic jargon put it, short of her degree. (Cornell discovered seventy years later that she had in fact completed enough units to qualify for *two* degrees, and she became bachelor of architecture and bachelor of landscape architecture in 2005, while she still had a year of life left to savor the dilatory triumph.)

Once out of school, she got increasingly good jobs despite the buffetings of the Depression, and at the end of the decade she made a happy marriage, to Harry A. Kueser, a banker successful enough to retire in 1945 and run her back office with the sure hand he'd brought to his financial career. That year she began working with Welton Becket to landscape Bullock's department store in Pasadena.

Glimpsing a future in which shopping would become a brief vacation rather than a mundane chore, Shellhorn created a verdant little oasis full of shade and color. More Bullock's stores followed, and when she took on Fashion Square, where several architects had been commissioned to build stores, each in a different style, she tied the assemblage together with just the sort of subtly varied plantings that Disney was seeking.

When his emissaries first sounded her out, her immediate response was "I don't do amusement parks."

Still, in early March she visited the studio, where Dick Irvine—who had nearly as complete a grasp of what was wanted as did Disney himself—showed her the drawings and the models. Each of the lands, he explained, had its own art director, and Disney was worried that this might lead to a lack of coherence in the park; the place, he said, had to "hang together."

Shellhorn was intrigued. Irvine told her about the Evans brothers, saying that Disney was "satisfied enough" with their work, but that they "couldn't spend enough time in the studio." This was diplomatic to the point of opacity: what Irvine meant was that the brothers were good at planting things on the site, but lacked the vision to help much in the park's overall planning.

Shellhorn signed on. Her initial charge was to design the plantings at the park's entrance, along Main Street, and in Tomorrowland. Her duties expanded quickly, almost violently.

She wrote, "Even at the time of my introduction to the project in March, there were no buildings started in Tomorrowland, just one in Frontierland, and only parts of the Main Street section and the Castle were in evidence. . . . W.E.D. designers were tackling the problems of developing site plans for the various areas involving circulation, organization, tree placement and planting. The Plaza especially was presenting many problems, as from it radiated all five sections of the park. Many schemes had been advanced, but none had been selected, and time was growing short.

"It was at this stage of progress that I was engaged by W.E.D. to work with the Art Directors as Consulting Landscape Architect until the opening of the park, and to act as liaison officer between the Studio and the Evans organization on the site. It was thought, at first, that this consultation work would take only a portion of my time, but such was not the case. The Art Directors and their staffs had so much work to do in the designing of their buildings and other features of the park that, after the first week on the project, it became evident that more than consultation work was required, and I was asked to restudy and design the Plaza area. From this, the site planning of one section led to another until every part of the five 'Lands' involving pedestrian traffic was studied— as to circulation, paved and planted areas, tree placement, and in some cases as in the Plaza, the outline of the water courses."

At first, she worked at her home or in the Disney Studio. Then, on March 23, she drove down to Anaheim, touring the site in a Jeep before walking it alone until dusk began to fall.

She was appalled by what she saw.

Disney had started out with a crew of surveyors. They'd hammer in their stakes, and in the rough-and-tumble of the speedy construction, a truck or bulldozer would unknowingly grind them to splinters hours after they'd been driven. The sites would be surveyed again, and again the stakes would disappear. Disney got tired of paying the surveyors, and in their place took to waving toward the planned location of a grove or walkway and telling Goff, "Just eyeball it, Harper." The result, to the eyeball of a professional architect, was that almost nothing was quite right.

A few days after her visit Shellhorn wrote in her diary, "I'm really scared about Disneyland. . . . So much I don't know and trying to design and not being sure I'm on the right track. And the rush of time." A little later: "Feel lower than a worm. This AM am discouraged over the Disneyland project—so big, so much to figure out."

But she was tough; she knew how she could help; and the project had got its hooks in her. By mid-April she had come to realize that she couldn't manage the work from the studio. She began commuting to the site, and entered what became a daily ordeal: "the wind-blown dust, the heat, the terrific fatigue of walking miles during the day and working far into the night on plans as the pressure increased, the tremendous activity of the many trades all working at breakneck speed, the dashing carryalls, the whistling cranes, the constant hammering, sawing, and digging."

She discovered right away "that a number of trees had already been planted in many of the areas to be restudied or designed, their location based on earlier conferences or plans. . . . It was necessary to determine the exact location of those planted trees, and to determine the variety, size, and number of unplanted specimen trees purchased for the project, before proceeding with the planting of the areas. It was necessary to move a few trees to new locations."

This brought Shellhorn into closer contact with the Evans brothers than either she or they desired. Though they held the title of "landscape architect," here was a bona fide one, a woman, giving them orders. By the end of the month she was insisting that she stake out the trees herself, and inspect each before it went in the ground, while her stern sense of professionalism had her protesting to construction bosses about their faulty grading.

The Evans brothers griped about her to Disney, and in May he spoke with her. She was, he said, "as stubborn as Wade Rubottom," the art director in charge of Main Street. But he surprised and briefly buoyed her by adding, "I have absolute confidence in your ability."

All her planning was sound, and her designs would make it into the park almost unchanged. It was Shellhorn who had planted the first doubts in Disney about the peripatetic bandstand, and he trusted her.

This did not, however, make her daily life any easier. In the hard-pressed all-male freemasonry of the park workers, she was largely excluded. She became known as "Mother Shellhorn"—which meant: an officious biddy—and at lunch, she said, she was an "orphan," eating alone. At the end of the day, when Woody would gather some of the crew in his office to enjoy a few belts of what he called "the old loud-mouth," Shellhorn was never included. In her diary she wrote bitterly about Jack Evans, "So to heck with it. I can see how Jack has gotten to his dirty work with the men for their attitude now that I'm a little 'filly' who doesn't know how to handle a big job."

She did know how to handle this big job, though, and she kept on doing it as her tasks grew ever larger.

She had started by working on the space between the station and the castle. Her main concern, baldly stated, was crowd circulation, but that does not suggest the hundred astute little touches that would keep people moving. Shellhorn wanted the visitor in a perpetual state of mild suspense, and accomplished this with what park designers called "progressive realization," a sort of botanical striptease in which enticing details briefly show themselves beyond the foliage, then again retreat from view.

Visitors entering Disneyland would first come upon Town Square, its benches set outside of the pedestrian flow in the shade of Brazilian pepper trees. And as this America reflected the bumptious patriotism of the songwriter George M. Cohan's era, along concrete walkways tinted a subdued crimson—the warm rose hue of aged brick—was a "Grand Old (floral) Flag:" red, white, and blue perennials lapping up against hedges heavy with white blossoms.

Here was a place where one could tarry indefinitely amid the amiable bustle of an eternally sunny 1910 full of marching bands and popcorn vendors, were it not for the castle sending its romantic summons down the double row of Chinese elms that Jack Evans had planted along Main Street.

Shellhorn liked the elms (they had, she said, "character") but not where most of them stood. Some partially blocked the entrances to the shops, but, more important, they failed to help the castle become the visual magnet it should.

She employed horticultural stagecraft to make a beckoning mystery of the building. As one approached, a grove of trees would conceal all but the gold sparkle of the turret-tops; a bit farther on a slice of battlement would offer a martial frisson; and the visitors would be moving at a speed partially set by the width of the walkways (counterintuitively, people walked faster when the path narrowed) until they reached the Plaza Hub and could see the castle whole.

The plans for the building itself were already solidified, but Shellhorn made its setting more imposing by increasing the height of the berm that rose on either side and covering its slopes with pine and cedar (to mimic the Northern European fir and spruce that girdle Neuschwanstein, but would quickly die of thirst and heat in Southern California) planted so tightly that they would grow in what she called "drifts." When they reached maturity, they would frame the castle with a forest dense and mysterious as the ones through which fairy-tale figures flee ogres.

All of Disneyland was in those days a welter of big changes being made at the last moment, but Shellhorn's were especially extensive—some not changes at all, but new designs laid on ground that had not yet even been surveyed—and every one involved Jack and Bill Evans. Occasionally she worked with the brothers in something like harmony. The castle moat was to be inhabited by black and white swans. When Shellhorn proposed planting junipers along its banks, Bill Evans happily agreed: the birds were the avian equivalent of the cartoon billy goat that eats everything from laundry to hubcaps, but the juniper, Bill allowed, was "swan-proof."

The truer reflection of the relationship came when, in mid-June, an editor at *Landscape Architecture*, a quarterly journal influential not only among landscape planners but throughout the architectural profession, asked Shellhorn to write about her work on Disneyland. Circle C, WDP's iron lid, covered all that came out of the park, and Dick Irvine had to approve the article. He told Shellhorn he needed to clear it with the Evanses. He approached them somewhat nervously, knowing the overlapping title they shared with her, which had helped keep peace in the park, might cause trouble in the public arena.

And so it did. Irvine had to tell Shellhorn, "Jack said it was OK"—as long as she "was billed as his assistant."

As Shellhorn added anger to exhaustion, she took to calling Jack Evans the "*patrón*"—that is, a lazy grandee who let others do his work—and wrote, "I feel I was being used. The *patrón* "gets the publicity and I do the planning."

Her sense of isolation deepened: "I feel so strongly that Irvine has no love for me at all and is very chummy with Jack." But she stayed the course, her very competence aggravating her fellow managers.

33

UNION TROUBLES

Tempers were fraying all over the site. One day Disney told his brother, "I've got to have more money, or I can't open the park."

Roy had heard this same demand until he was sick to death of it. He'd always responded by finding the money, but this time he had a different answer: "Well, I'm not going to give it to you. You've spent enough. And enough is enough."

"Okay," Disney said, "I'll sell my name to some banks I know, and I will make my own money."

Roy came up with more cash. C. V. Wood said that at this point his "biggest function was keeping Walt and Roy from each other's throats." Always more closely allied with Roy than with Walt, and not shy about declaring his own paramount importance to the project, Wood may have been exaggerating the friction between the brothers; but with just weeks to go, quarrels sparked and fumed everywhere, exacerbated by endless unanticipated difficulties.

———

One that Disney probably did anticipate, given how bruised he still remained from the studio strike of fifteen years earlier, was with the unions. Van Arsdale France said that as far back as January, Fred Schumacher had been worrying both about attempts to organize the park, and C. V. Wood's complacency on the subject. "Van, I'm trying to get Woody to face up to the union situation, but he insists we aren't going to have any union!" France took no satisfaction in turning out to be right: "Since Disneyland was a totally new concept of entertainment, there was a certain logic in starting out without any unions. It was not to be."

The American Guild of Variety Artists got wind of the Jungle Ride, and claimed the boats' skippers' monologues fell under their jurisdiction: the boatmen were giving a professional performance, and must be paid union scale as performing artists.

The Teamsters, never timid and certainly not in 1955, went after Owen Pope and his animals. Pope had hired a man named Jack Montgomery to train his pack mules. After beginning as a working cowboy, Montgomery had spent most of his life in Hollywood, riding as an extra in Westerns while they grew in prestige and popularity during the late thirties and forties.

His daughter, Diana Serra Cary, a writer and once a popular child star known as "Baby Peggy," went to visit him, and saw that he had his hands full. "A trader named Pope provided the raw material in the form of thirty or so stubborn, temperamental and completely unbroken bronc mules gathered from some godforsaken corner of the Texas range."

The mules, however, were not the problem on the day of her visit. "Going into Frontierland I located the mule corral, but as I started to enter through the gate I overheard an argument and sensed trouble was brewing." Montgomery was leaning against a hitching rack, and he wasn't happy. "I stopped short of making my presence known, for I could tell by Father's expression he was furious—rolling a Bull Durham cigarette very slowly, a sure sign he was trying to give his temper time to cool down."

The objects of his dissatisfaction were "two young men in blue jeans, flat-heeled boots, and wearing country boy 'straw Stetsons' with the side brims curled tight as paper cones."

One of them was saying, "This is our kind of job, that's clear on the face of it."

Montgomery answered slowly, but not hesitantly. "The mule rides are strictly for the children. It has nothing to do with labor unions, loading and unloading produce or merchandise or anything of the kind."

The other man replied. "Not in our book! Any time you load a kid on a mule and take him off it again, that's Teamsters' work and we aim to see that Teamster members get it!"

Cary wrote, "The stand-off between three grown men in the center of a miniature corral was absurd, and yet it was cunningly real as everything else I had observed at Disneyland."

Montgomery was through talking. He stared at his two adversaries until one of them said, "And just don't you forget that, old-timer. We mean to take over all the loading in this park, and the sooner you get that straight the better."

Finally stared down, the two drugstore cowboys took their leave. Cary asked her father, "Well, what was all that about?"

"Just a bunch of goddammed union toughs determined to get a slice of the cake. Come on, I'll show you around."

The Orange County plumbers and asphalt layers, though not particularly sore at Disney, went out on strike. This endangered three highly important elements of a place designed to receive multitudes: toilets, drinking fountains, and paving.

"We had all the plumbing on hand," said Joe Fowler, "and we couldn't get it installed." But here the Teamsters were more accommodating than they had been with Montgomery. "We had a wonderful relation with labor," Fowler said, and when he explained his plight to the Teamsters, he remembered them promising him, "Now, if the plumbers won't put this in, we're not going to have this park defeated. We'll put it in for you."

Armed with that pledge, Fowler went to the plumbers: "All right, tell you what we'll do now. We'll guarantee you that whatever the settlement on your ultimate finishing of the strike, we will pay you the same thing. Now, under those circumstances, will you put it in?"

The plumbers agreed, but time was now so short that Disney was faced with a choice between installing toilets and water fountains. He went with the former.

Absurd internecine squabbles between chapters of a union that was already established at the Disney Studio caused constant problems. The sixty-year-old International Alliance of Theatrical Stage Employees, Moving Picture Technicians, Artists and Allied Crafts of the United States, Its Territories and Canada (which was known by an equally unwieldy acronym: IATSE) had a chapter in Burbank and one in Orange Country, and the two chapters had been at loggerheads long before work on Disneyland began.

Each lived in the bitter certainty that its rival was stealing away jobs, and on the site fistfights occasionally broke out between Burbank and Orange County members. When Arrow finally shipped the Casey Jr. Circus Train to Burbank, Ken Anderson said, Bruce Bushman had given it "a beautiful paint job. It was done up at the studio, but was done by union artists; it wasn't Disney artists. Each color of enamel was beauti-fully finished." The gleaming result then went to Anaheim, where it was greeted with fury by the Orange County IATSE members. "They just looked at it and said, 'We will have to redo that.'" It was *their* preroga-tive to paint the rides. "And they sandblasted the whole damn train. They took all the paint off. Then they painted it themselves. They used our colors, what I had done in a thumbnail. It turned out pretty good, but not like the original. The original was really great."

Matters went more smoothly with the newcomer unions. "The agreement which was reached was as unique as Disneyland itself," wrote France. "There were established unions for most of the people, but it was difficult to know how to categorize someone who would guide a Jungle cruise boat. . . . This problem was settled with the understand-ing that if our young ride operators wanted a union, we would recom-mend the Teamsters. If they didn't want a union, we couldn't force them to sign up, however, most who wanted a job at the park felt it was the prudent thing to do."

The final contract between Disneyland and organized labor included twenty-nine unions (one of them, which represented the farrier who shod Pope's horses, contained a single member). France wrote that "when the full impact of the negotiations was understood, Walt was mad as hell."

He was especially peeved when the Inland Boatmen's Union declared that the *Mark Twain* belonged in the hands of their pilots, even though it required no piloting at all, as it would, like the Jungle Cruise boats, be guided by underwater rails.

But the *Mark Twain* itself worried Disney far more than the Inland Boatmen's agitations. The stern-wheeler needed a river to ply, and the winding course for the Rivers of America (a few hundred yards each of the Mississippi, the Columbia, the Missouri, and the Rio Grande) had long been dug.

As the time to fill it approached, Disney's engineers said they needed a big, costly pump to deliver the water from the wells. He shook his head. "No, just cut a flume to the river and turn the water on." The engineers unfolded maps and explained that the water needed to flow uphill, and wouldn't do that. Try it anyway, Disney insisted.

They did, and it worked. Disney had carefully gone over his acreage months earlier, when its orange trees still stood; he'd talked with the farmers about irrigation, and he'd seen how they managed it. He knew the surveyors' maps were wrong.

The difficulty, it turned out, lay not in getting the water in but keeping it there. "We had a hell of a time with the design of the river so that it would hold water," said Fowler. "We did all the research work on that damn thing, all different types of plastic lining." In late spring he had a section blocked off for his initial test. At first the water rose obligingly toward the banks. Then Bill Evans's "ball-bearing sand" started to drink it up. After a few hours, Fowler was looking at a steaming runnel of damp earth.

The admiral was hard to rattle, but this scared him. He treated the riverbed with soil stabilizers and again filled his test section. Again the water quickly seeped away.

"And finally we found that simple clay was the real answer. We built a section of the river, dammed it up, and it worked fine. So then we got busy and lined the whole river with it, with clay." This seemed to do the job, but Fowler couldn't be entirely sure: there was no way to adequately test it.

That was because the Rivers of America were joined to the jungle river, which had made perfect sense when they were designed, as a single water and filtration system would be easier to maintain than two separate ones. But it meant that the Rivers of America could not be filled without also filling their tropical counterpart, where crews were still at work laying the track and wrestling animal statues into place.

Fowler did what he could, filling the larger river to just below the mouth of the sluice that led to the jungle. The riverbed held, but it contained only a fraction of the water it needed to be fully operational, and who knew how it would handle that additional tonnage? Fowler would have just one shot at filling his waterways before opening day.

34

"We're Not Going to Make It"

Opening day. July 17 had seemed close enough back in February; now, in June, the date's proximity was excruciating, and once the plumbers and asphalt workers went on strike, even the indefatigable C. V. Wood began to lose heart. He went to Fowler. "We might as well postpone until September. We're not going to make it by July."

"Woody, we *have* to make it" was all the discussion Fowler allowed. "Course I'd been sort of indoctrinated during the war. I had been working right under limits, I had twenty-five private shipyards and by doggie, we had to make dates!" Fowler knew the seventeenth was about as late as they could delay and still have the summer vacation season to begin to chip away at their mountainous debt.

A few weeks earlier, Fowler, Wood, and the Disneys were still hoping they'd finally set a ceiling on the cost of the park. Then, Fowler said, there came "a man named Dean in the Bank of America. . . . This was in April and we're still talking eleven million. And we walked down Main Street and Mr. Dean looked on all sides and he turned to Roy and he said, 'Roy, you know if ever I have seen anything that appeared to me to be a little bit of variance . . .' The banker glanced back at the dry riverbed. 'I think we're looking at fifteen million rather than eleven.'" That is just a hair under $140 million in today's dollars, and the spending was only accelerating.

During that dispiriting seminar with the amusement park owners, one of them had said, "Now, Mr. Disney, you should never pay over twenty-five thousand for a ride. I mean anybody who does that should have his head examined." Disney's spinning teacups alone looked to be coming in at something like one hundred thousand, and they were still in pieces four hundred miles away in the Arrow factory. "And God knows," Fowler said later, "some of our things cost way into the millions."

And there was the asphalt. Fowler learned that "all the hot-asphalt plants in Orange County went on strike. And for my last roads I had to haul it all from San Diego. Jesus, what a cost!"

Meanwhile, as more and more workers were drafted into overtime, many were earning $1,000 a week, twelve times the average wage of a laborer.

Disney asked Fowler for a personal loan, and got it.

The shortness of money reflected itself in the plants Bill Evans was buying for the park: they arrived smaller and smaller. And still there were rank, blowing swaths of weeds on the northern side of the berm. Disney had an idea about that: "I'll tell you what do, Bill. You know all those fancy Latin names for plants. Why don't you go down there and put some Latin names on those weeds?" Annual ryegrass, barnyard grass, and chickweed were ennobled with little plaques: *Lolium multiflorum*; *Echinochloa crus-galli*; *Stellaria media*.

———— * ————

Much was unfinished, and much that was finished didn't work right. Bob Gurr was on hand for the first trial steam-up of the *E.P. Ripley*. Of course Disney was in the cab. "Walt opened the throttle a bit but nothing happened. A bit more and the new locomotive glided forward." Glided in silence.

"No, no, no!" said Disney. "Go fix it!"

A steam engine was supposed to *sound* like a steam engine: no hiss and chuff, and half its character disappeared.

Ed Lingenfelter knew what was wrong. He told Gurr "that locomotives have machining clearance tolerances expressed as 'either tight or loose 64th of an inch.'" The Disney machinists had found so broad a specification ludicrous. "Seems the studio machine shop did a fine job and revised some of the tolerances to thousands of an inch. After all, the shop did build precise movie cameras." That camera-worthy precision meant that the *Ripley* did its work, but with a barely audible whisper.

Gurr said that Lingenfelter "got a big laugh out of the effort to disassemble the tight parts and open them up." That was accomplished by Friday, June 17, when Earl Vilmer told Disney, "We'll have Number Two steamed up tomorrow morning around eight o'clock if you're ready to try her out."

"I'll be there," Disney said.

For all its virtues, steam requires a lot of attending to. When Disney arrived at eight, Vilmer and his crew had been stoking and oiling the *Ripley* for three hours. Disney took his place on the engineer's seat, eased open the throttle, and, said Gurr, "the locomotive clunked and clanked out of the barn just like a proper locomotive should, using just a tiny bit of throttle. Vilmer and all the steam freaks in attendance smiled and nodded in their conservative silence."

Disney shared the cab with a three-foot-tall Mickey Mouse doll, and he drew to a stop several times on his circuit of the park so the two of them could pose for press photos. The studio's publicity staff, having absorbed the boss's gospel of fidelity to detail, had outfitted Mickey in the same checked shirt his creator was wearing.

At the end of the run, Disney said, "At least we'll have the railroad operating on opening day."

He took the locomotive back out on an unscheduled trip a few days later. The studio had received a letter from an East Coast mother whose seven-year-old son was dying of leukemia. The boy had two wishes: to meet the children's comedian Pinky Lee and to ride on the train whose progress he had been following on the *Disneyland* show. The boy would probably not have the stamina to make it to the opening, and his family had set out driving cross-country in the hope that he might be granted a preview. When they arrived in California and called the studio, they were asked to come to the site on Saturday morning.

There, Disney appeared, introduced himself, and said to the boy, "I understand you want to see my train—well, let's go." He picked the child up, carried him over to the locomotive, lifted him into the cab,

and drove him around the park, explaining where all the wonders her-
alded on TV were going to be.

Afterward, Disney returned to his car, reached in, and took out a
gold-framed cel from *Lady and the Tramp*, which had just opened, and
gave it to the boy. "Well," he told the parents, "We really saw the place;
he liked my train."

After the family had driven off, Disney noticed that Bob Jani, who
had just joined the company as head of Guest Relations, had been
watching the visit, and gave him a curt order: "No publicity."

———

It started to rain, and rarely stopped as 1955 revealed itself to be the wet-
test year Anaheim had seen in a decade. The frequent downpours added
more complications to the ceaseless pandemonium of the site.

So did Disney. With just weeks to go, he decided to strengthen
Tomorrowland's meager offerings by adding a walk-through attraction that allowed visitors to explore the *Nautilus*. A fanciful evocation
of mid-Victorian machinery might seem an anachronistic intruder in
the world of tomorrow, but Captain Nemo's vessel had, after all, been
driven (in the movie, if not the book) by atomic power, and the film
ended with what appeared to be a nuclear explosion. Moreover, Harper
Goff had tried to ensure that the sculptural fillips on the ship's workings
looked true to the 1860s without descending into the jocose decorative
excesses of what he called "sewing-machine Gothic."

The highly detailed set was still fresh, and little had to be built anew.
But the giant squid had been designed to show Captain Nemo battling
it amid the obscuring scud of a gale. Now it had to be persuasive to a
dawdling onlooker.

"Hey, Ken, we've got another problem here," Disney said, collaring
Anderson. "Are you all finished with Toad?"

"Well, pretty much."

"I want you to go up to the park and see Bob Mattey. I want to put a
giant squid, a ninety-foot squid, that goes in this window on this thing
in *20,000 Leagues Under the Sea*."

Anderson said, "We had two weeks to do it. . . . Bob Mattey had already made the squid once, for the picture, so he knew how the hell to do it. So I went up and talked to Bob. And Bob was working on the squid. It was just a big rubber squid or a plastic squid—it wasn't colored or anything. We moved it down to Disneyland." The *Nautilus* "had the iris window facing into it with this big squid in this underwater cavern, and it was moving slowly around. It had to move its tentacles and be alive."

The creature was big enough to require an ancillary building, a tin shed that went up quickly, and as quickly became known to the workers painting and patching tentacles within it as Squid Row.

Disney had asked Anderson about Mr. Toad's Wild Ride because it, too, was making trouble. Anderson had built a full-scale mock-up in Burbank while Arrow was working on the attraction itself. "I got the whole thing with the track and everything all laid out duplicating the track that would be done at the park. We had the ride ready to show Walt. We showed Walt the whole thing. He liked it. He thought it was pretty good. So I had the word to go ahead, and found out the track was a different size."

That is, the track already laid in the park "was supposed to be the same track, and it wasn't. That meant the whole thing had to be refigured. Refiguring means everything: the timing from here to here because of a certain gag. And the way this thing would work, everything was timed. I finally got it refigured to the new dimensions. And when it came out it was smaller than what we had at the studio. That made it even tighter; it was a very tight thing to figure. But we did."

Peter Pan's Flight also caused difficulties, though fewer than it should have, as it was the most elaborate and unusual of all the dark rides. Its nine seven-foot-long fiberglass pirate galleons ran not on floor tracks but lofted themselves through the Darling children's nursery to follow Peter out into the skies over nighttime London and then on to Never Land.

The machinery that carried the ships was not built by Arrow. That contract went to the Cleveland Tram Rail Company, which had no experience with amusement rides, but had long been making aerial track systems that freed up factory floors by moving industrial materials overhead. The layout lifted the ships—each outfitted with a one-horsepower motor—by their masts and carried them along a single rail hung from the ceiling. Carefully placed sails prevented the riders from seeing the equipment above them as the ships circled Big Ben beneath a starry sky at a height of nineteen feet, then descended to the mountains of Never Land and Captain Hook and his pirate crew. The problem was that the track, designed for industrial use, made a deafening industrial clatter, and no sooner had it been installed than it had to be redesigned.

The Snow White ride, which performed flawlessly during tests on the Arrow grounds, showed weaknesses as soon as it got to Anaheim. The problem with the cars, Ed Morgan said, was that "they had three wheels, two in the back, one in front. This allowed you to go around very sharp corners. Those cars have a little step. It wasn't intended as a step. They gave us sketches for the shells, and we did the machinery to fit inside the shells that we made. The shell had, behind the back seat, a kind of edge on it. What happened was that the operating people, when it came to the station, discovered that ledge. They would jump on it and ride the cars into the station from the last door as they came out of the dark. The heavy guys would, with the leverage of their weight, lift the front end of the track. So the carriage that steered the thing was now running loose. . . . We discovered that these kids were jumping on, and they didn't know what they were doing, of course. They were derailing all the cars. In the meantime, they wrecked the carriages on some of them."

All was not well inside the ride, either. As the cars buzzed from one chamber to the next, air cylinders swung open the doors before them. That was the plan, anyway. Morgan was still indignant years later when he remembered, "Disney used Stanley hinges—regular door hinges, of all things, in something like that! Just like your house door hinges. The cylinders were mounted real close to the hinge point. It turned out that the cylinders were not strong enough to open the doors fast enough so the cars wouldn't hit them." The obvious remedy was more air cylinders, which were quickly installed alongside the weaker ones. "They finally got enough power," but this meant "that they were uprooting all the hinges, and the doors were falling on the track!"

Among this stew of failures, one great success. With the Jungle Cruise finally finished, Joe Fowler at last was able to fully test his rivers. He filled them all, from the Rio Grande to the Amazon, and every riverbed held.

During these penultimate days, Fowler took to living on the site in one of the old farmhouses. So did Disney, in the more comfortable quarters of the compact—five hundred square feet—apartment overlooking Town Square, built for him in the firehouse, decorated with Eastlake furniture and lit with the soft glow of turn-of-the-century lamps. Of this pied-à-terre, his daughter Diane said, "Mother collected cranberry glass and cranberry is the color that dominates the apartment, a microcosm of cranberry red in a little Victorian hideaway. It was really a very cozy, family place. Very private. It was just for them. . . . There's a proper, old-fashioned door-bell on the front door—the kind you twist to make it ring. There is a set of cups and a jar bearing the name 'Tom and Jerry,' a brandy and rum punch. Dad's shower had multiple jets to help him soothe his back when it flared up from an old polo injury."

———

By now the workforce had grown from some eight hundred to fifteen hundred, many of its members pulling down those thousand-dollar-a-week wages, today the equivalent of bringing home half a million dollars a year. In early July they found themselves having to lay pipe and hammer down roof shingles amid a thicket of new obstacles. The television crews were moving in.

Those crews were the reason Disneyland had to spring to life on July 17 and not a day later. From the beginning of the ABC partnership it had been understood that the park's opening would be the subject of the most ambitious television broadcast yet attempted in America. The network had already bought $40,000 worth of newspaper ads for the ninety-minute broadcast, and had sold out every advertising spot back in March.

This televised spectacle, all of it live, was in the hands of the ABC producer Sherman Marks. A nervous man by nature, Marks early realized that his worst anxieties would be surpassed. He had wanted to start setting up equipment and staging rehearsals in May, but so little was yet built to rehearse around that he couldn't do anything until the last days of June.

As the scope of the job became clearer, he started hiring: there would be five control rooms—Central, Main Street, Frontierland, Fantasyland, Tomorrowland—each with its own director. And each of those directors needed a staff. That meant more personnel than ABC had, so Marks began arranging to borrow technicians from his rivals CBS and NBC.

Just as the show required more people than ABC could supply, so did it demand more hardware than ABC possessed. Marks ransacked the country to acquire cameras and sound systems from Chicago and San Diego, San Francisco and Seattle, until he had enough equipment to run twelve television stations. Twenty audio mixers came in, ten PA talk-back systems, sixteen miles of cable. In New York, ABC was pretaping dozens of shows so the network wouldn't have to shut down once its equipment had been sent west.

Six cameras were flown to Anaheim from Manhattan, five from San Francisco, four from NBC, two from KCTV, two from CBS. . . . By the end, there would be twenty-nine, overseen by four segment directors, a musical director, four assistant directors, scores of technical people, all guarded by a crowd control team eighty strong.

Spindly perches went up for the cameras: the one on Main Street was sixty feet tall; the most ambitious was a scratch-built cage that dangled scarily from a 110-foot crane so it could hold something like parity with the towering TWA Moonliner. These stationary fixtures were joined by thirteen forklifts, each able to maneuver a camera above the crowds.

The show was to begin with a parade up Main Street, followed by dance numbers, celebrating the opening of each land. The dancers rehearsed for weeks on a Hollywood stage; when they finally got to Disneyland, they found they had to stumble through their routines with mud underfoot and workers sawing and hammering all about them.

Miriam Nelson, the show's choreographer, was able to find enough room next to the mule stables to rehearse the musical number "Bang! Goes Old Betsy." (Fess Parker would be there, of course; Old Betsy was

Davy's rifle.) The evening after the first run-through she got a note from Disney: "Please have your dancers cover up a little more because the workmen are all stopping to watch them."

Construction and film crews were mutually hostile as soon as they met, because each got in the other's way. The workmen moved already-laid cable to put down track for rides; cameramen set up shop in half-finished buildings. When a segment director berated a worker for interfering with his vantage point, the man said, "Don't worry. You'll have plenty of action to shoot. We'll be pouring cement."

Nor were the segment directors happy with their boss; the strain so told on Marks that he began to treat them with suspicion bordering on paranoia. One said that he was "obviously a madman. He had no business to be in that position. He was nominally in control. And I say nominally because he was a madman who refused to share any information with his subdirectors. . . . It was bizarre." Walter Schumann, the musical director, was struck down by a heart attack and would watch the ceremonies from his hospital bed.

Some of the segment directors threatened to quit. So, in those frantic days, did Ruth Shellhorn. Planting the huge floral portrait of Mickey Mouse that lay outside the park, on the ground sloping up to the railroad station, she got into such a fierce quarrel with Wade Rubottom, the art director Disney had said was as stubborn as she, that Dick Irvine had to push the two apart before they came to blows.

Irvine was so pressed that when he heard he had to approve some surveyors' plans, he said that if he couldn't be found right away, just "sign my name" to them and keep on with the work.

Even the boss seemed exhausted: when Anderson came to report that for once a ride was working properly, he went away with a weird non sequitur he never forgot: "You know, goddammit Kenny, I don't understand you guys. Your hobby, you're running with the girls out at the mill. I don't understand that hobby." Disney pointed at the tumult around him and said, "*This* is my hobby. What could be more fulfilling? Why don't you get a hobby like this?"

John Rich also got a sting from Disney's exposed nerves. An assistant director at NBC, Rich had, to his surprise, been borrowed to direct the

Main Street parade on opening day. He was more surprised to find that "when I arrived, Main Street was still an unpaved stretch of California dirt." Nevertheless, he went to work. "Having turned over my center of operations to the technical crew for wiring, I then spent much of my time selecting camera positions on rooftops and plotting the parade route."

The film crews ate with the workers, "so one day when the whistle blew for lunch and I headed for the mess tent, someone fell into step with me."

"You going to lunch? I'll walk with you."

Rich said, "Sure," and "then realized that my companion was none other than the great man himself, Walt Disney. Still in my twenties, I was awestruck to find myself walking with this semi-mythical figure, and I struggled to think of some way to strike up a conversation. After a moment, I ventured, 'You know, Mr. Disney—'"

The figure spoke. "Call me Walt," Disney's ritual request upon meeting someone, and perfectly sincere (although it would have been a foolhardy freshman animator who took it for an invitation to treat him as an equal). Recently he had begun to add, "The only mister around here is Mister Toad."

Rich "couldn't do it. I started again, assuming that the message proclaimed on a familiar poster of the period—'For the children of the world, we present Disneyland'—was a safe subject."

He said, "Mr. Disney, this is a wonderful thing you're doing for the children of the world."

Disney responded with testy suspicion. "What did you say?"

"This park, what you're doing here—is great for children."

"Don't you know anything?" snapped Disney. "Kids don't have any money."

Everything about this response is unusual: the gratuitous insult, the open worry about money, and what might be seen as cynicism about the entire project.

The harsh rejoinder would have startled Joe Fowler, who said, "In all my association with Walt, I never heard him raise his voice." It had a strong effect on Rich: "If I had harbored any doubts about the American system of capitalism, that remark forever dispelled them."

Despite the young director's disenchantment, it would be absurd to assume that Disney was in this enormous enterprise solely for the financial rewards. Ward Kimball once said, "If you want to know the secret of Walt Disney's success, it's that he never tried to make money." And if ever there was a potential get-poor-quick scheme it was the inchoate Disneyland of early July 1955.

35

TEMPUS FUGIT

Disney was neither too worried nor too distracted to ignore his thir-
tieth wedding anniversary. A few weeks before the opening, an
invitation went out to three hundred people announcing a "Tempus
Fugit Celebration."

> **WHERE**: Disneyland . . . where there's plenty of room . . .
> **WHEN**: . . . Wednesday, July 13, 1955, at six o'clock in the
> afternoon . . .
> **WHY**: . . . because we've been married Thirty Years . . .
> **HOW**: . . . By cruising down the Mississippi on the *Mark
> Twain*'s maiden voyage, followed by dinner at Slue-
> Foot Sue's Golden Horseshoe!
>
> Hope you can make it—we especially want you and, by
> the way, no gifts, please—we have everything, including a
> grandson!
>
> Lilly and Walt

Slue-Foot Sue's Golden Horseshoe recreated a saloon from Gold Rush
days, designed by Harper Goff—for the second time, as he'd already
done a nearly identical one for the 1953 movie *Calamity Jane*. The
Horseshoe would have infuriated the clientele of its Old West ancestors because it was to serve no liquor. Disney had early decided against
selling alcohol in his park: "No liquor, no beer, nothing. Because that

brings in a rowdy element. That brings people that we don't want and I feel they don't need it. I feel when I go down to the park I don't need a drink. I work around that place all day and I don't have one. After I come out of a heavy day at the studio sometimes I want a drink to relax."

But there would be plenty to drink this night.

The host awaited his invitees near the front gate with Jack Sayers. "By six o'clock, nobody had shown up," said Sayers. "Walt was not a patient man. We paced and smoked together, and he kept asking me, 'Where are they?' I think he blamed me for the fact that everyone was late!" One reason they were late was that Disneyland, for the last time in history, was difficult to find.

Eventually the guests arrived, were driven in surreys along a still unpaved Main Street, and rolled into Frontierland, where they disembarked to eat and drink in the Golden Horseshoe until it was time to board the *Mark Twain*.

Joe Fowler got to the party early, and he went not to the saloon but directly to the riverboat. "I had brought the *Mark Twain* around from the dry dock on the day before the party. First time she had been on the track. And she never went around the track completely until the night of Walt's . . . party."

This man who had calmly shouldered immense responsibilities when the whole nation was threatened couldn't quite shake his worries about a new amusement park. "So I had a dream and I very seldom carried any of my problems to bed with me, but in this particular case . . . God, there she was at the dock and we were gonna have all of the dignitaries and so forth, and the damned river was dry. Something had happened. We had a big leak. All the water disappeared." Living as he was on the site, Fowler didn't have to go far to reassure himself: "I think I was the most relieved man in the world when I got up that morning and found that we had the river."

A residue of anxiety made him want to take plenty of time to check the *Mark Twain* before her maiden voyage. To his dismay, she looked ratty: "I'll have to admit there were a lot of shavings and things around." Some woman had preceded him aboard, and she, too, had noticed the slovenly state of the decks. "Here, get this broom," she said. "Let's get this place cleaned up. It's terrible."

Fowler knew an order when he heard one. He took the broom and started sweeping. "That's the first time I met Lilly," he said.

Admiral Fowler and Mrs. Disney had made the boat presentable by the time the first guests came aboard. Their host circulated among them as the stern-wheeler steamed around Tom Sawyer's Island, which the Rivers of America ringed. Mint juleps were circulating, too, and Disney had several of them; the silent, stately progress of the boat, the Dixieland band jubilating on its promenade deck, the gusts of admiring laughter—and, of course, the juleps—put him in a state of slightly dazed euphoria.

The short voyage over, the passengers returned to the Golden Horseshoe to watch a Western revue. Disney was seated in the balcony, where, his daughter Diane wrote, "People below started to notice him. 'There's Walt,' they said. And with that, Daddy was off. He started to climb down the balcony, and every little bit of comment or applause would just keep him onward." Diane worried he might fall, but he made it safely to the stage, where "he just stood there and beamed. Everyone started saying 'Speech! Speech!' But there was no speech forthcoming. All he did was stand there and beam. Then everybody applauded and said, 'Lilly! Lilly! We want Lilly!' So Mother got up on stage, figuring, 'If I get up there, I can get Walt down.' Well, that wasn't the case."

Seeking reinforcements, Lillian pulled Diane and her sister, Sharon, onto the stage, "and still nothing happened. Dad was just planted there, and he was loving every minute of it."

Diane was relieved when "someone must have sensed our plight, because the band started to play and Edgar Bergen came up on stage and started to dance with me and some others came up and danced with Mother and Sharon. Everybody started dancing, and my father was gently elbowed into the wing. He was loving every minute of it, just grinning at people."

Later, "everyone was worried about Dad's driving home. They were trying to steal his car keys and everything, but I just said, 'Daddy, can I drive you home?' He said, 'Well, sure, honey.' No problem at all. He was meek and mild and willing. He just climbed in the back seat of the car. He had a map of Disneyland, and he rolled it up and tooted in my ear as if it was a toy trumpet. And before I knew it, all was silent. I looked around and there he was, with his arms folded around the map like a boy with a toy trumpet, sound asleep."

Diane loyally concludes the account of her father's happy evening with "I know he didn't have too much to drink, because the next morning he didn't have a hangover. He bounded out of the house at seven-thirty and headed for Disneyland again."

———

Three more days, and the park would open. "Actually there were no 'days,'" France wrote of that molten interval. "Hours and days all melted together like an Einstein conception of time." Trying to recall those days and hours later, he could put no chronology to them: "It was a bouil-labaisse of memories."

Among the other duties that piled on him, France had been assigned to make some order beyond the park's berm. "The *outside* of Disney-land was also a disaster area." The job's pressures reflected themselves in the approach to clearing the land for the parking lot. The Peltzer house, at the north end of where the lot would be, had housed the McNeil Construction company, whose work was all but done. "It had to be torn down before the grading and surfacing of the parking lot could begin. Rather than simply using a bulldozer somebody suggested that we have a house wrecking party. Woody approved, with the thought that it might be a good way to release some tensions before the final pre-opening push. Somebody provided liquor. How and why nobody was hurt amazes me." In a bacchanal of vandalism chandeliers were wrenched from ceilings, windows punched out, banisters uprooted, walls smashed to excavate the plumbing inside them. France said he served as a "Safety Engineer," but what safety he promoted was vestigial. "Eventually, somebody dropped a match and the fire department was called."

At some point Disneyland acquired an address: 1313 Harbor Boulevard. Why? Any number along the street's 1300 block, 1301 to 1399, was available, and it was evidently Disney's choice. Was it a sardonic jape to tease fate with a pair of unlucky thirteens? France said, "The best I've been able to find out is that it was the license plate on Donald Duck's car." But Jim Denney, a student of Disneyland, has come up with the most persuasive theory: "What's the thirteenth letter in the alphabet? M! Put two M's side by side and what Disney character do you think of? That's right, it all started with a mouse."

It does seem strange that Disney might have been courting bad luck, for plenty of it was coming his way already.

The landscaping budget had run out; the Evans brothers' supply of ever-smaller plants dried up entirely, and workmen began to spray dead grass with green paint.

Fowler reluctantly brought his boss news about Casey Jr. The game little engine had crested a formidable grade in *Dumbo*, but she wasn't going to when Disneyland opened. Fowler said that Disney "loved" the train, "and just before we opened, this was the first time the train had come back, down from the studio, and we ran it around and it was top-heavy."

Fowler said, "Walt, I'm sorry, but we just shouldn't run that train for the public until after we get some keepers on it so that going around the curve or if she's loaded on one side or the other, it won't tip over. Otherwise, very frankly, it would be very dangerous."

"All right, Joe," said Disney, and walked away. Fowler "heard afterward he was very disappointed. But that's all he said."

Tomorrowland was still the sparsest of the kingdoms. It had acquired a seventeen-foot-tall Clock of the World—sponsored by Timex—that promoted itself with the tepid enticement "Do you want to know what time it is in Tokyo, or New York? Paris or Cairo? Walk around this stately column, and you can read the time of day in any city in the world." A projected Mars ride—with a surprising glimpse of futuristic dystopian realism: it was to be inhabited by "Interplanetary Penal Colonists"—had fallen through. An auditorium whose video screens would simulate a voyage to and around the moon had been built, but the show itself wasn't ready. Disney had several buildings thickly hung with balloons in the hope that the festive touch would help disguise the fact that they were half-empty.

The big, immobile pirate ship that housed the Chicken of the Sea Restaurant was complete, but only half-painted: the side that would face visitors was gleaming black and red; the other, pale fragrant lumber.

As the evening of July 16 came on, Disney was well aware of all the shortcomings, and he knew his crews were at work fixing what could be fixed. Still, he withdrew from a dinner for his corporate sponsors to roam the grounds.

He found John Hench in the Rocket to the Moon theater; no progress there. On the other hand, a half-ton elephant that had been slowly sinking into a tropical riverbank had been stabilized and was ready to wave its trunk at the Jungle Cruise launches tomorrow.

When he arrived at the King Arthur Carrousel, he was pleased to find the horses handsomely finished, each one frozen in mid-leap awaiting its rider. But the merry-go-round's housing was shabby, and needed a night's work. His presence made the painters self-conscious, and their pace slackened. Disney told them to hurry up: "My insurance money is paying for this."

On Main Street, he noticed colors that should be brighter, or different altogether. Well, at least the Main Street Station looked fine; and the ballast before it was the right size.

Beyond the station, Van Arsdale France was irrigating the morale of the men installing curbing on West Street and painting lines on Harbor Boulevard. "To keep the crews going, I went out and bought several cases of beer and would drop by with these incentives."

Disney went looking for something that he could do to help, and found it in the *Nautilus* exhibit, where Ken Anderson was painting the oceanic backdrop of the giant squid. He joined in. "We got the whole damn thing done in one day and night," said Anderson. "Walt was busy with us, too. He wanted to get the thing done for the opening of the production. So we did. We finished that thing up and we got it going, got it working, and colored, but we were drained."

Disney and Anderson left Squid Row together and drifted down

Main Street to Town Square, where a workman brought the news that the wires had been cut on the Toad ride.

When he got to the ride, Anderson discovered that several other Fantasyland attractions were also down. The severed connections represented a final spasm of petulance in the IATSE civil war, but this was mere mischief rather than true sabotage: nothing had been cut, only unplugged. "I went through the wires," Anderson said, "and, with some help from the electrician, we got them fixed so that everything worked."

Disney went to his apartment over the firehouse to try for some sleep. It probably would not come easily: he had even more at stake now than on the eve of the premiere of *Snow White*.

Thinking about that night years later, Van Arsdale France wrote, "The opening of Disneyland was different from anything I . . . or anyone I know, for that matter . . . had ever encountered.

"The test flight for a totally new airplane is a thrilling experience. Lives and reputations are at stake. I'd observed ten thousand people bursting into a spontaneous cheer at the test flight of a B-24 bomber. But the date of the flight can be postponed until everything is favorable.

"Broadway plays open in a small town . . . and can be radically changed before they hit the big time. Movies can be tested, cut and altered in sneak previews.

"But Disneyland was right there in Anaheim . . . and could not be tried out in other hick towns." Every part of Disney's new world had to run smoothly from the first hour.

Disney went to bed listening to the far-summoned asphalt at last being poured in Town Square, very much aware that in a few hours he might be at the center of the most public humiliation in show business history.

36

DATELINE: DISNEYLAND

The climactic episode of Disney's television show was a special that aired under the title of *Dateline: Disneyland*. The United States contained 169 million citizens on July 17, 1955, and 90 million of them watched it. That was 54.2 percent of the population—a larger proportion than would see the final episode of *M*A*S*H*, or any Super Bowl, or even the moon landing.

Of course Walt Disney was the star, but an operation of this size needed more than one host, and Disney had gone to his friend Art Linkletter, who was then as popular as Johnny Carson or David Letterman or Jon Stewart would be to later generations.

As Linkletter remembered it, Walt opened his request with "Art, this is a difficult moment for me, because I would like to ask you to be the master of ceremonies of the opening, and work with me, but I don't know how to approach you."

"What do you mean?"

"Well, you don't have an agent! Why don't you have an agent like everybody else I talk to?"

"Well, Walt, you know me—I'm my own business man, I've always done it, never had an agent, and I make my own deals."

"Well, let me begin by telling you, as you know, we've had many cost overruns, I've had to borrow money against my studio—I can't really afford to pay you what you're worth."

Linkletter brushed this aside. "Pay me union scale. That's fine with me."

"Scale! A couple hundred bucks?"

"Yeah! This is a big community event—it's a national event—in fact it's a world event. And I'd like to be a part of it! And we're good friends."

Then Linkletter's commercial instincts tempered his charitable ones. Showing how well he could manage deals on his own, he said, "Of course, once I have you in my debt, you'll be happy to give me the photo concession at Disneyland for the next ten years. I'll pay your standard concession fee if you'll let me handle all the film and cameras sold at the park."

Disney accepted at once. Forty years later, Linkletter wrote, "Surprisingly, the net returns from this valuable concession made me the highest paid broadcaster for that one show in the history of television." Walt went on to tell him that they'd need at least two more hosts, "and they'll have to be good ad-libbers." Linkletter was among the best. "I had been doing the opening of world's fairs for many years before Disneyland. I'm an ad-libber, so chaos is made for me. I love the catch-as-catch-can atmosphere. I love interviewing people who don't even know they're on the air. That's my business. So this show was made to order." It wouldn't be entirely spontaneous—"we had a kind of a rough working script"—but "the four of us showed up with no rehearsals, of course."

As for the cohosts, Linkletter said, "I chose two friends to assist me. One was actor Robert Cummings, who had just appeared with Grace Kelly in Alfred Hitchcock's *Dial M for Murder*. The other was a charming actor named Ronald Reagan (I understand he later went into government work)."

Linkletter was a sound choice. John Rich, the director in charge of the Main Street parade, said the show gave him problems, "although Art Linkletter was not one of them. He had asked me if he could station himself on a balcony overlooking Main Street."

"Is it the balcony that features that big Kodak Film sign?"

"Why yes, how did you know?"

"Someone told me you own that concession."

Linkletter laughed, and Rich said, "It's okay with me, if you're comfortable standing there." Rich believed he would have been comfortable standing anywhere: "Linkletter was a superb ad-lib commentator. He could have stood on his head and delivered a wonderful broadcast."

The future president proved more difficult. "Although I disagreed with most of his agenda once he entered politics, [Reagan] was one of the most affable people I ever worked with." But he "arrived a bit late, and then asked to see the script."

Rich was surprised. "There's no script. It's a parade."

"I know, but what do I say?"

"Well, if I were describing it, I might offer something like, 'Here comes Mickey Mouse, there goes Minnie, this looks like Pluto . . .'

"But Reagan was not to be denied, and we finally provided him with written 'talking points' about the Disney characters he would see."

Reagan would deliver his talking points with smooth, unstuffy dignity, but Disney was right about wanting agile ad-libbers: no show ever needed them more. *Dateline: Disneyland* has plenty of gaffes, but not nearly so many as one would expect from such a sprawling, quickly mounted exercise.

Disneyland workers who were there would always remember July 17 as "Black Sunday," although thanks to what can justly be called heroic efforts on the part of the television crews, remarkably few of the mounting calamities spilled over onto the screen, and today the broadcast remains a lively and engaging record of what the very first of Disneyland's visitors experienced.

After Tinkerbell scatters her pixie dust, as she had at the start of every preceding show, *Dateline: Disneyland* opens not with Art Linkletter, or Ronald Reagan, or Walt Disney, but with an important-looking man sitting behind of a typewriter in a room crowded with people busy handing papers back and forth to one another.

"How do you do everyone—this is Hank Weaver. For the past year this signature has announced the opening of *Disneyland* the show. Now it announces the opening of Disneyland the place. The people and eyes around the world are focused on these one hundred and sixty acres here in Anaheim, California.

"This afternoon, Disneyland, the world's most fabulous kingdom, will be unveiled before an invitational world premiere, and you, our guests. Art Linkletter will be your host, and with ABC crews and cameras on the spot will guide you through this truly magic land.

"You're now in the press room of Disneyland, which is equipped to service over one thousand members of the worldwide press here to cover this truly great event. And to start the proceedings we take you to the entrance of Disneyland and your host, Art Linkletter."

The floral Mickey fills the screen, looking bright even in monochrome and complete despite the ill feelings the flowerbed ignited during its creation. A jolly voice exclaims: "That's not Art Linkletter! That's Mickey Mouse, the inimitable little character that started this whole story with Walt Disney twenty-five years ago, perhaps the most popular motion picture star in Hollywood."

The camera pans up to Linkletter, looking relaxed in a light-colored suit and holding a microphone.

"I'm standing here on the railroad tracks with helicopters roaring overhead and cars parking by the thousands, and I'm in front of the big Disneyland and Santa Fe railroad station. And down these tracks in just a couple of seconds will come Walt Disney himself, barreling in in a railroad train built to five-eighths miniature size.

"Well, this job in the next hour and a half is going to be a delight. I feel like—well, I feel like Santa Claus with a seventeen-million-dollar bundle of gift packages all wrapped in whimsy and sent your way over television with the help of twenty-nine cameras, dozens of crews, and literally miles and miles of cable.

"Now, of course this is not so much a show as it is a special event. The rehearsal"—a sketchy effort, rushed through earlier in the day— "went about the way you'd expect a rehearsal to go if you were covering three volcanoes all erupting at the same time and you didn't expect any of them.

"So, from time to time, if I say, 'We take you now by camera to the snapping crocodiles in Adventureland,' and instead somebody pushes the wrong button and we catch Irene Dunne adjusting her bustle on the *Mark Twain*, don't be too surprised—it's all in fun, and that's what we're here for. . . .

"In fact, I think I'll get off the tracks right now and go over and meet some of the people waiting for the train to come in. And since this is a family affair, I thought you might be interested in seeing the rest of the Linkletters."

There are six other Linkletters, and he asks them what they hope to see first. Six-year-old Diane wants to go "to the great big castle where Sleeping Beauty is"; for eight-year-old Sharon, it's Davy Crockett in Frontierland; ten-year-old Robert is looking forward to "a boat trip down the Congo"; and finally fully grown Jack says, "I want to see Bob Cummings."

"Oh, Bob Cummings!" snorts Linkletter in mock disgust.

A chuckling Cummings appears, and Linkletter explains, "You know, Bob's going to help out here in jumping all over the grounds describing the various things—and where do you go first?"

"Well, I go down on Main Street here and go into an old-fashioned car called a Premier, and I'll be seeing you in a couple of minutes."

He lopes off while Linkletter calls (the informality slightly jarring, given what history has in store), "Ronnie Reagan, come on in!"

Every bit as agreeable as Rich remembered him, Reagan says, "Yeah, how about that son of yours? I've been buttering up to him all morning hoping he'd say that about me."

"Isn't this a riot, today?"

"Oh, it certainly is."

"And Ron, your first job is down here in the Town Square."

"Right out here in front of the depot, yes."

"We have lots to do. Get busy!"

Reagan leaves, and Linkletter, building some mild suspense, again announces the imminence of the *E.P. Ripley*, approaching on "a mile and a quarter track, and it's a trip that's out of this world because inside that circle is a brand-new eighth wonder of the world. First there's Adventureland, yes, a visit by boat to remote and adventurous regions of the world." There follow quick introductory glimpses of all the lands, and then we are shown the "tremendous parking lot, where twelve thousand cars can be parked—twenty-four thousand if they pave over the first twelve thousand and park the others on top of them."

The comic parking conceit over, the scene shifts, but no *E.P. Ripley* yet. Instead we're at the main entrance, "And coming in the gate we see all kinds of families—Hey, Danny Thomas! Hey, how are ya?—that's Danny and his gang, and representatives of the press, thousands are coming in and they're going through the magic tunnel on foot because no car can enter here. And, like Alice in Wonderland, as you go on through that tunnel past the Disneyland Santa Fe [Railroad], you find yourself in a bygone time, another world. The clock has turned back half a century and you're in the main square of a small American town. The year—nineteen hundred."

The camera surveys the square while a band plays "In the Good Old Summertime." The buildings look just as they should—as if they've been doing business here for decades—and Shellhorn's and the Evans brothers' trees might have shaded this prosperous town for generations. "Let's take a look around—there's the city hall, quaint and dignified with its post office, the place where the citizens of the town gather to hear gossip and exchange the latest news of the day. Fire station—aha, that's of special interest to the volunteer bucket brigade—horse-drawn engine and up-to-date hose and chemical wagon are a source of real local pride. Then here's the car barn housing the horse-drawn streetcar, a great boon to speedy transportation, and that little old streetcar will be going up and down Main Street here in Disneyland about every ten or fifteen minutes, day in and day out. It goes by a whole flock of very interesting and quaint little stores. . . .

"The old-time music shop should be in there somewhere. If you were courtin' a gal, that's where you'd buy your mandolin or banjo and start tuning it up for the Sunday canoe ride—Oh! You kid! Twenty-three skidoo! . . .

"And if you were daring, you might go out with your girl for a ride in an 1898 Locomobile, the hot rod of its day. Is that one coming up Main Street? Why, yes, and Bob Cummings is aboard! Take it away, Bob."

The Locomobile's birth has been anticipated by a year, but Cummings is there: "Here I am down on Main Street. I've got my whole family, my lovely wife, Mary, and my daughter, Melinda, and Bob.

"You know, this is a Main Street, ladies and gentlemen, just like my grandma used to tell me about back in Joplin, Missouri. Sometimes she had a whole penny for herself to spend on Saturday night. Now all these stores are different—for instance, now right over here's the Candy Palace. Now, that's where Grandma probably got those licorice whips and the jujubes . . ." There follows a lengthy catalog of antique confectionery before Cummings winds up with "Whaddya say, Art?"

"Thank you, Bob Cummings, for that word picture. But right now, we gotta get back here. The *E.P. Ripley* is rolling around the Santa Fe and Disneyland Railroad track with Walt Disney at the controls.

"In the cab with him, you may be surprised to know, is the governor of the State of California and the president of the Santa Fe, Mr. Gurley himself."

There has been a shift of engineers: "Now if you look on down the track you see Mickey Mouse there at the controls. And that's an exact duplicate of the engines that ran over fifty years ago. You can see the conductor there with his brass buttons glistening in the sun."

The conductor looks at home, as well he might: it is Commodore Vanderbilt "Hunky" Wood, C. V.'s father, who had spent his working life as a brakeman and conductor on the Santa Fe.

"Hello, Walt!" Linkletter calls as the train pulls to a stop, "Hello, Governor!"

Hands are shaken all around, and Linkletter asks Disney how the run went.

"Fine! Fine! The governor had her around through Frontierland, and then Fred Gurley, there, he took her around, and then I picked her up and brought her in—highballin' in!"

Disney had become so anxious in the days leading up to the opening that at one point he told his wife and daughters to stay at home and spare themselves what he feared would be a sordid failure; he didn't "want any of you women out there. It's going to be a mess, and I don't want to worry about you, too." But the dark premonitions have lifted: now he seems to be completely at ease and hugely enjoying the moment. When Linkletter introduces "Mr. Gurley, the president of the Santa Fe," and Gurley interjects, "*And* of the Santa Fe and Disneyland," Disney offers a jovial correction: "*Vice* president of the Santa Fe and Disneyland."

Linkletter says, "You gentlemen have lots to do down in the square, so we'll see you at the dedication. . . . And after a few words from your sponsor, Ronnie Reagan will take it away for the dedication ceremonies to Disneyland."

Reagan, in Town Square, says, "All activity on Main Street has ceased. Those carriages lined up for the parade to follow are full of celebrities. Walt Disney, Governor Knight, the mayor of Anaheim and other dignitaries are talking to the three chaplains representing the Protestant, Catholic, and Jewish faith. And now Walt Disney will step forward to read the dedication of Disneyland."

Disney, rid of his engineer's cap, is in a new business suit bought for the occasion. "To all who come to this happy place, welcome. Disneyland is your land. Here age relives fond memories of the past, and here youth may savor the promise and challenge of the future. Disneyland is dedicated to the ideals, the dreams, and the hard facts that have created America—with the hope that it will be a source of joy and inspiration to all the world. Thank you."

Back to Reagan: "The military chaplains representing the various creeds are present, but all were agreed there would be no—"

He is interrupted by the Protestant chaplain: "I have known Walt Disney for many years and have long been aware of the spiritual motivation in the heart of this man who has dreamed Disneyland to being. Let us join with him, then, in dedicating these wonder-filled acres to those things dear to his heart and ours, to understanding and goodwill among men, laughter for children, memories for the mature, and aspiration for young people everywhere. And beyond the creeds that would divide us, let us unite in a silent prayer that this and every worthy endeavor may prosper at God's hand. Let us bow in prayer."

A moment of silence, then "Amen."

Reagan says we've just been listening to "Walt Disney's nephew, the Reverend Glenn Puder," and that is the beginning and end of organized religion in Disneyland.

Elias Disney was a member of the Congregational Church, occasionally even delivering a sermon (his wife remarked that he was "a pretty good preacher" because he "did a lot of that at home, you know"), but brought to his faith the grimness he did to so much else in his life, and religion never seemed to take too strong a hold on his son. When Diane Disney said she wanted to attend a Catholic school, and her father enrolled her in one, his sister sent him a worried letter: What if the girl became a convert? Walt replied, "I think she is intelligent enough to know what she wants to do, and I feel that whatever her decision may be is her privilege. . . . I have explained to her that Catholics are people just like us and, basically, there is no difference." The important thing, he said, was to "create a spirit of tolerance" in Diane. There is no church on Main Street.

"And now," says Reagan, "it's the honorable Goodwin Knight, Governor of California." The governor says Disneyland "is a wondrous community with all the charm of the Old World and all the progress and ingenuity of the New World," and "all built by American capital and American labor . . . and as we dedicate this flag now we do it under the knowledge that we are the fortunate ones to be Americans, and that we extend to everyone everywhere the great ideals of Americanism, brotherhood, and peace on earth goodwill to men."

Drumroll; the flag sails up its staff; and Reagan says, "At any moment now a flight of planes from the 146th Fighter-Interceptor Wing of the California Air National Guard will be over . . ." We hear them, but don't see them. The solemnities concluded, Reagan announces, "And now the parade is on! And here we go to the roof of a Main Street building and Art Linkletter."

Art ballyhoos his franchise right out of the gate: "And here we are, my son Jack and I, up on the second floor of Main Street by the Eastman Kodak camera shop, where you can buy and rent all the film and cameras, and we're looking down on the United States Marine Band coming up Main Street. The color guard has just passed—massed armed forces color guard for all the four armed services—and behind the Marine band comes the grand marshal's 1903 Pierce with Disney and Governor Knight. . . .

"This is a real cavalcade of Disneyland characters, the Disneyland Band, directed by Vesey Walker—uh, Tommy Walker—and there's Mickey and Minnie Mouse and all of the gang cavorting up and down.

Dumbo and Pluto and Donald Duck and all the other characters are from the Walt Disney costumes created for Harris' Ice Capades, which is on tour with Peter Pan right now around the United States."

Disney was lucky to have that show to draw on, as time and money had both gone before costumes could be run up. Not that it matters at this particular moment, as we see none of the characters Linkletter has reeled off.

That wasn't Linkletter's fault. "They had arranged a monitor for me to look at, so I would know what the cameras were looking at, because they were somewhere else covering the parade from another angle. But by the time that the show was on in the late afternoon, the sun was shining right into the monitor—so I couldn't see what the camera was covering!"

"So I'd say something like 'now here comes Mickey Mouse,' and they'd be on a band! And the director of course realized pretty soon that I couldn't follow the cameras, so the cameras had better follow me! So as I would talk about something, they would search it out."

The crews had gotten the hang of it by the time Fess Parker showed up.

"Now here comes the Frontierland and of course who would be there at the front but Davy Crockett, Fess Parker, beard and all. And Davy Crockett has a scout—Buddy Ebsen's there, too. Annie Oakley, [and] the hostess girl for the Carnation Ice Cream Pavilion here on Main Street, is riding with them. The Conestoga wagons have Governor Frank Clement of Tennessee riding aboard. And there's Annie Oakley coming up now. And the buckboard stagecoach with Gale Storm and Danny Thomas and his family—he's a popular fella with all the crowd!"

"Well, I guess we've got more parade than we can handle today. Bob Cummings, you better take it away, wherever you are.

Cummings is ready: "Yessir! Okay, Art Linkletter, thank you very much. You did a wonderful job there describing that.

"I'm at the head of the parade now, and my job here is to more or less give you an orientation process, because I am standing at about the center of this giant hundred and sixty acres of Disneyland." He explains the four lands, then says, "Standing here has been one of the most exciting moments of my life. I think, ladies and gentlemen, that anyone who's been here today will say, as the people did many years ago when they were at the opening of the Eiffel Tower, 'I was there.' "

Cummings is overridden by a portentous sponsorial voice: "In just one minute we will start our exciting trip to Frontierland, the Old West, and Davy Crockett."

There follows a silent and unexplained shot of an untended horse-drawn ice wagon, which, in its casual workaday authenticity, almost suggests that the era of President William McKinley has given a spectral wink of approval to Disney's mimicry; and then we find Walt in front of the gates of the Frontierland stockade. They are closed.

"Before you enter this realm," he says, "I'd like to read the dedication, which will be inscribed on a plaque. 'Frontierland: It is here that we experience the story of our country's past—the color, romance, and drama of frontier America as it developed from wilderness trails to roads, riverboats, railroads, and civilization—a tribute to the faith, courage, and ingenuity of our hardy pioneers who blazed the trails and made this progress possible.' "

Reagan takes over: "And this is Frontierland. Inside this stockade, Walt Disney has created a frontier village that could have been carved out of the wilderness a hundred years ago by the pioneers themselves. [The gates swing open.] The flag flying over the stockade has thirteen stars, commemorating America's first period of independence. [A rattle of musketry.] And that volley signals the arrival of a wagon train with the first visitors to travel through the gates of time and into our very historic past.

"And now, inside Frontierland to Art Linkletter."

Who says, "Well, here they come into Frontierland, Conestoga wagons, riders, and all off the big Main Street parade, they're going on into the stagecoach country. Yessir, there's little Annie Oakley, and there are the special horses, five-eighths size, bred by Walt Disney"—here a ubiquitous guest engenders further excitement—"and Danny Thomas! The cameras are in the other direction, Danny! Yeah, there they go, and kids, there goes the Wells Fargo stagecoach with Gale Storm and her kids inside and, uh, what do you think of this, Robert?"

His son says, "Great!"

"Looking for anything special?"

"Davy Crockett."

"Well, Davy Crockett oughta be around here someplace. In the meantime, let's take a little look around. Over here's where the little burros and horses are, and that's the Davy Crockett Museum—what do you think of that, Sharon?"

"Oh, it's fine, but where's Davy Crockett?"

Having received the unsatisfactory answer that "he's out someplace where the Indians are," Robert is not to be diverted by: "Now there's the frontier trading post. Isn't that exciting, Robert?"

"Yeah, it sure is. But I still don't know where Davy Crockett is!"

"Well, I'll tell you what we're going to do. I'm going to give you this gun, Robert." He hands him a pistol. "You point it up in the air, and when you fire it, that'll bring Dave-ee-ee Crockett!"

Robert squeezes the trigger. "There it goes! Now everybody look over in that direction, and I think we're going to see Davy Crockett very shortly."

The ballad begins to play, and Davy and George Russel canter up, ready with a tall tale that wouldn't air today.

"Hi, Davy. And Russel, too. Come on over here, fellas. You're a little late getting in. Must have been some trouble on the trail someplace. Hiya, Fess—what happened?"

Fess looks grave. "We'd have been here sooner but we took a shortcut through the Painted Desert."

Russel adds, "Yeah, too much paint, too—*war paint*!"

"Indians?"

Russel nods: "Them redskins was just itchin' to lift our scalps."

"What did you do?"

Davy says, "Well I got out Old Betsy, but before I could draw a bead on the chief, Georgie here spilled his canteen on my gunpowder."

Russel elaborates. "Yeah, then when I grabbed for my tomahawk, danged if the head didn't come right off in my hand. So there we was— no dry gunpowder, no tomahawk, and all the time the redskins was creepin' closer and closer, and their hot breath was breathin' down the backs of our necks."

Linkletter is worried. "Oh, you were a goner, Davy! What'd you do?"

"Nuthin'"

"Nothing?"

"We just let those Injuns breathe away until their hot breath dried out that gunpowder, and Old Betsy took over."

"Aw! What a story!"

Russel says, "Tell us another story, Davy." Instead, Crockett begins to sing a song: "One day I took my leave from town, I aimed to grin a wildcat down . . ."

This is the introduction to "Bang! Goes Old Betsy," another George Bruns hit, but with lyrics by "Gil George," the pseudonym of Disney's clever nurse, Hazel George. Dancers in generic pioneer garb throng Davy, then swirl into a production number in which men and women swing rifles, do-si-do, and tumble over one another. Despite her rehearsal difficulties, Miriam Nelson, the choreographer, has pulled it off flawlessly.

The number ends with Parker singing, "I can travel far and wide with Betsy by my side," and Cummings is back, standing in the Golden Horseshoe. "Yessir, this is Bob Cummings again. Now, Art Linkletter has just gone down to the landing to give a wonderful send-off to the riverboat *Mark Twain* on its maiden voyage, but before we join him, I'd like to have you see Slue-Foot Sue's Golden Horseshoe. It's really the showplace of the frontier. . . . So come on, let's go inside and see what happens, huh?

"Well, I tell you Slue-Foot Sue's boasts the longest little bar in the whole wide world, with the tallest glass of soda pop. Now of course you begin to see the interior and there's the stage, and the orchestra, just like in the old, old days. Aren't they gorgeous, those girls doing the can-can?"

We're not given much time to appreciate the can-can before Cummings says, "Oh, that whistle you hear, ladies and gentlemen, means that the *Mark Twain* is ready down at the dock. We don't want to miss the launching ceremony, so come in, my friend Art Linkletter."

The can-can music shifts to "Good Old Summertime," and there is the *Mark Twain*, her decks already crowded. Linkletter says, "Walt Disney has built this great big, beautiful, authentic stern-wheel paddleboat from keel to smokestack, a quarter of a million dollars' worth of boat that hasn't been built in America in fifty years—loaded with gay and carefree happy passengers, a band playing up there on the second deck, which is the grand salon deck, all paneled in special wood, ready for the parties of the year. . . .

"But right now, it's my pleasure to introduce the lovely lady and famous star who Mr. Disney has asked to christen the *Mark Twain*. Ladies and gentlemen, Miss Irene Dunne."

"Hello, how are you?" says Dunne, quickly adding an unscripted "My, it's listing."

"It's listing a little because it will be shoving off in a moment."

The boat was not listing because it was about to cast off, but because it had been badly overloaded. This was the fault of Tim O'Brien, one of the hundreds of recently hired young Disneyland workers. He had been posted at the "holding pen" where passengers awaited their turn to board. "They gave me a clicker and told me to let people in until the pen was full. The boat would come in and let one group off and we'd put the other group on. No one was sure just how many people would fit so they said to try and keep it between two hundred to three hundred." But the day was boiling with interesting events, the crowd was talkative, and O'Brien began to chat with his guests while automatically punching his clicker and paying it little attention.

Later, after his distraction led to trouble, his supervisor asked how many he'd let aboard. O'Brien blithely replied, "About two hundred fifty." His boss said, "Well, better keep it at about two hundred." When the man had gone O'Brien fished the clicker out of his pocket. "I looked and was shocked to see I'd put 508 people on the boat. I never told anyone until now." "Now" was 2005, the park's fiftieth anniversary year.

Irene Dunne probably knew Linkletter had no idea what was causing the list. She had been chosen to christen the *Mark Twain* because she'd starred in the 1936 movie *Show Boat*, but her nautical experience ran deeper than that.

She tells Linkletter, "Well, this is an authentic stern-wheeler—did you know that?—one hundred and five feet long."

"How do you know all this?"

"Well, you see, my father used to be supervising general of steamships in America, and my grandfather used to build boats like this. . . . I can almost see him standing up there now with the captain alongside of him, just as though it were the greatest place in the world."

"Well, Miss Dunne, you're holding a very special bottle here in your arms."

"Yes, I am—you see, this bottle contains water from all the leading rivers in America . . . so with these precious waters I'm going to christen this boat the *Mark Twain*."

She smashes the bottle on a deck bollard; Linkletter says, "And the boat is christened! And it starts on its daily trips up and down the rivers of the world—of America, that is. Thank you, Miss Dunne. And now, ladies and gentlemen, I've got other places to go, and the commodore, Admiral Joe Fowler, up in the wheelhouse looks like they're getting ready to shove off, so I better—Goodbye, Irene, goodbye everybody— Have a good ride. Take her away, Admiral. Goodbye! Have a good trip!"

We shift to Reagan standing before a fence by the riverbank, the boat a couple of hundred feet beyond his back. "I have a wonderful view of the *Mark Twain* as she gets ready to start on her maiden voyage. The *Mark Twain*—a proud symbol of the romantic era when whole cities grew out of the river ports. Churning paddle wheels brought new people, new customs, and new industries to these fabulous ports— Pittsburgh, St. Louis, and Natchez. And the riverboat even brought a new kind of music up the river from the city where the blues were born, where the Dixieland style was king—New Orleans."

Bob Cummings appears in front of a Dixieland band. "Ah, yessir folks, this is Bob Cummings again. Isn't this great! It's the real thing all right. Right now, we're in a street just like in New Orleans—old New Orleans created by Walt Disney for you. And standing here behind me is probably the most famous little Dixieland band in the world—the Firehouse Five Plus Two, and they're in exactly the right place because New Orleans is the spot where this beat was born—the barrelhouse, the blues—so take it away Firehouse Five, burn it up, boys!"

The Firehouse Five Plus Two was made up of members of the animation department, led by Ward Kimball, who liked Dixieland music enough to teach himself the trombone so he could perform it (Harper

Goff was the banjoist). The group was more than an in-house hobby, becoming popular enough to cut more than a dozen successful albums.

They blast away through another production number, a Mardi Gras fantasy, not as tightly choreographed as "Betsy." A dancing Aunt Jemima billows past (Aylene Lewis, who will soon take up her duties as hostess at the Aunt Jemima Pancake House), and then things get strange.

The camera lifts to a long second-floor balcony, populated by young women holding fans, who drape themselves over the familiar ironwork looking—can this possibly be the intention?—for all the world like prostitutes soliciting custom. The illusion is underscored by the music: the Dixieland bounce has been replaced by a trumpeter growling through a slow drag.

The moment is broken back at street level by the Firehouse Five roistering through the crowd, which contains another surprise. Bob Cummings seems momentarily to have forgotten his lovely wife, Mary, for here he is, back to the camera, in a deeply carnal embrace with one of the dancers. He jumps away and swings around, wiping his mouth, while the dancer, scowling and evidently abashed, flees the camera.

Was this racy vignette all part of the act? Perhaps a plug for Cummings's new television situation comedy, risqué at the time, in which he plays an amorous bachelor? If so, it's violently out of tune with the rest of *Dateline: Disneyland*; if not, Cummings turns out to be no mean ad-libber himself.

"Oh—heh, heh, heh—well, folks, as you can see, I'd like to stay here at the Mardi Gras forever. But there's a Disneyland train leaving from the Western Station right away, and we don't want to miss that. It's taking us to more exciting lands, so take it away on the train, Ronnie Reagan."

"Thanks, Bob. This is the Western railway station"—a steam locomotive pulls in—"and this is the *C.K. Holliday*, and it's on its way now leaving Frontierland and going a hundred years into the future to Tomorrowland."

Disney is back: "I'll read these few words of dedication. 'A vista into a world of wondrous ideas, signifying man's achievement—'" He stops, shakes his head. "I thought I got a signal."

This is the only time in the show when he stumbles slightly, but he smiles and begins again: "Before our preview of Tomorrowland, I'd like to read these few words of dedication. 'A vista into a world of wondrous ideas signifying man's achievement, a step into the future with predictions of constructive things to come. Tomorrow offers new frontiers in science, adventure, and ideas. The atomic age, the challenge of outer space, and the hope for a peaceful and unified world.'"

A flight of pigeons clatters into the sky, masquerading as doves. Cummings, offscreen, says, "Those doves are, I hope ladies and gentlemen, harbingers of peace for the world of tomorrow. And now, here in Disneyland, the year is 1986. 1986—that's way ahead, and that's when Halley's Comet will flash past the earth again, and the time of its arrival will be recorded on a futuristic clock like this one here, which tells you, incidentally, at a glance that exact time of any spot on the earth. Yes, this is Tomorrowland, and it's not a stylized dream of the future, but a scientifically planned projection of future techniques by leading space experts and scientists."

Drums and bugles, ruffles and flourishes, and Disney's friend George Murphy, the actor and future senator, says, "The flags now being unfurled are the official colors of the forty-eight states of this nation. [C. V. Wood had seen to it that the Texas flagstaff was a few inches taller than all the others.] It's appropriate that the Eagle Scouts handle the ceremonies, because these boys represent the citizens of the future. The world of tomorrow belongs to them."

Art Linkletter is back. "Now we're in Autopia, about a mile of superhighway adventure, with all the kids lined up and little gasoline-driven automobiles that go whistling around the various freeway and highway convolutions at eleven miles an hour. These are gasoline driven, and the kids can drive to their hearts' content with their parents or without their parents."

There is a small traffic jam; most of Bob Gurr's sports cars are working at the moment.

"Now, the entire Autopia goes by a lake and by canals, there's scenic features, and look who's riding in the various cars! Coming down the road here is my old friend Don DeFore, Ozzie and Harriet's next-door neighbor—comin' right by—Hello, Don! Good to see ya!—Keep on going! Frank Sinatra! Hello, Franco. Who's driving? Frankie—"

"My son, yeah."

"Don't hit this man. Look who hit who—Sammy Davis Jr.! Hello Sammy."

"Now, these all have aluminum bumpers completely around them, as you might see over here, so they can't hurt anybody, and they have governors on them—they only run eleven miles an hour." Then comes the era's inevitable joke about those hapless creatures who a few years earlier had been building Flying Fortresses: "And of course the women drivers are given a little special space, just as they are on the highways."

"Well, we've got a lot more celebrities coming up. Come up here, Gale. I want you to see one of the prettiest gals in the world, Miss Gale Storm, and her little boy. We've been waitin' for you, honey. How was the ride?"

Gale Storm thinks it "was the greatest ride I ever had."

"Thank you. Well, we ought to go down to the boat landing. Ronnie Reagan, are you there? Take it away!"

"Well, thank you very much, Art, and here on the lake of Tomorrowland we have boats made out of fiberglass, and they're as strong and safe as anything afloat. And I have two customers right here, Bonita Granville and Jack Wrather."

"Hi, Ronnie," both say. "How are you?"

"Just fine. I haven't seen you since we left the bus this morning here."

"Well," says Wrather, "we had a nice ride out, and we've had a big day here."

"Oh, boy! And did you see it all in one day?"

"Oh, that's impossible—it's a fabulous place!"

Wrather had a reason for stressing the necessity of taking more than a day to see the park: he and Granville were building the Disneyland Hotel.

Disney had the land for a hotel—sixty acres on West Street—but no money left to put one up. He knew it was needed: Anaheim's two motels and five hotels still offered a total of eighty-seven rooms.

The preceding November, Jack Wrather had written to C. V. Wood proposing to build a motor hotel, lavish by the standards of the time, especially designed to accommodate families.

Wrather had no experience in the hotel business, but he'd begun to tire of the businesses he did know. He started out as a successful oil wildcatter, but "I was a major in the Marines during the war. While in the South Pacific, I made up my mind to try something after the war as far removed from the oil business as possible." Once home, he became a successful movie producer. His first film *The Guilty*, starred Bonita Granville, whom he went on to marry. He branched out into television production, but now that, too, was starting to bore him.

"It was 1954 when I got a call that Walt was putting in something very special out there in Anaheim, and I was asked if I would be interested in building a hotel next to it. I had heard a little bit about the Disneyland plans, but when they told where it was being built, all I could exclaim was 'Anaheim! Oh, God! Anaheim!'" But "I stayed with Walt and Roy for several days and they [were] convinced of what they were going to do down there in Anaheim, but we started an analysis of the area on our own, anyway. There were only two or three in my organization then, and we did a rather thorough study of Anaheim until we convinced ourselves statistically, psychologically, and every other way that although it was mostly orange groves, the area was one of the growingest in California and the United States. We didn't want to just depend on Disneyland, because no matter how fantastic a project or idea it was, nobody in those days knew just how it was going to go, really, or how long it was going to last."

C. V. Wood drafted a generous ninety-nine-year lease that stipulated a thousand dollars per month rental during construction, doubling upon completion, 2 percent of the gross on the first half million and 1½ above that, and $25,000 a year to use the word "Disneyland"—not only on this hotel, but on any other one Wrather might build in Southern California. This was unusual: Disney always kept a tight hold on his name, and that he would allow Wrather access to it reflects how much he wanted his park served by a good hotel that was currently beyond his means.

Wrather agreed to the terms, and in the last days of 1954 hired as his architects Disney's old colleagues Pereira & Luckman. (The firm hadn't suffered greatly from losing the Disneyland business: begun in 1950 with ten employees, it now had a staff of more than four hundred, at work designing the NASA Space Center in Cape Canaveral and the Los Angeles International Airport.) In mid-March, with Roy Disney and C. V. Wood looking on, Wrather, Granville, and Charles Pearson, the mayor of Anaheim, took hold of a gilded three-handled shovel and broke ground.

Now, on *Dateline*, Reagan goes to the business at hand: "And that gets me around to the other point. You're sort of interested in the hotel arrangements here, aren't you?"

Wrather says, "We're building the Disneyland Hotel, which is right at the exit to Disneyland Park." Bonita adds, "You and Nancy gotta bring the kids and come out and stay with us."

"When're you going to open?"

"We're opening part of it in September, and the rest in January, Ronnie."

This is wishful thinking: the hotel would open on October 5, but with just seven guest rooms completed. Thereafter, work went quickly: in a few months there were 104 rooms in five two-story buildings; within the year another 96 opened, costing from $9 to $22 a night (not a cheap tariff in 1955 (the equivalent of $85 to $210 today); rooms at New York City's Plaza Hotel also started at $9 a night).

"We shall be there in September," says Reagan, "And in the meantime, why don't you have a boat ride?" Then he remembers the rest of the plug: "You know that this is a good chance to tell the people that this is a ten-million-dollar hotel [it was a three-million-dollar hotel] with a swimming pool and everything and that you can take two or three days."

The scene shifts abruptly back to Tomorrowland, where Danny Thomas has joined Linkletter for a colloquy on technological progress. The latter says, "The conquest of space, exploring the future, and the unknown up in the universe is probably the last big challenging problem left to man, Danny."

"It just about is—as a matter of fact, I'm absolutely flabbergasted at this fantastic place—"

Linkletter gestures to the building behind them. "And I would say that this is one of the most exciting—Captain Barton, come over here. This is Danny Thomas, Captain Barton. He's in charge of our two rocket ships. What are their names?"

Captain Barton—tall, friendly—says, "*Diana* and *Luna*."

"Oh, after the moon. And are you blasting off very shortly?"

"Just a few seconds, I'd say."

"Danny doesn't want to go."

Thomas, pretending horror, says, "You mean that this thing really goes up?"

"You don't want to leave the earth, Danny?"

"No, I certainly do not."

"Well, I think you've been out of this world for years, kid." General guffawing, then: "Captain, you go aboard the ship, and we'll contact you in a minute."

The captain leaves while Linkletter explains to Thomas, "You see, there're two ships, they each accommodate about a hundred and thirty people. As a matter of fact—you there, Captain Barton?"

"Yeah."

"Ready to blast off?"

"Yeah."

"All right, well take it away—let's take another look at what it looks like."

The attraction was far from ready because, John Hench said, "some disgruntled electrician sabotaged the electrical work. The control mechanisms in there had to be rewired; on opening day we had to show filmed portions of the ride on television." Captain Barton reappears, now wearing a vaguely martial jump suit. "I'd like to give you some idea about the rocket ship itself, and explain some of the more interesting highlights of our operation here." He points to a cutaway drawing. "Now, this'll give you a pretty good idea of the rocket ship in which you'll be traveling to the moon. Now, here is the captain's cockpit, and here are the crew's quarters. And this is the passenger section. In this section are two television screens—one above and another one below. Now, when the flight gets under way you'll be able to see by watching the upper screen what's ahead of you, and by watching the lower screen you can see what you've left behind.

"This chart shows the flight path of the rocket ship *Star of Polaris*, which will be taking off shortly for the moon. Now, this is a typical flight path and approximates the one of your own trip."

Now comes a crackle of loudspeaker announcements, while we see a nicely done animation of the Moonliner with fuel lines dropping away from its hull: *Clear field preparatory for takeoff. . . . Attention blast-off crew—attention blast-off crew—report to space dock three. . . . Attention fire control crew—attention fire control crew—report to space dock one. . . . All field personnel take blast-off stations. . . . Field control to tower—field has been cleared for takeoff.*

The scene shifts to the control room, where a man at a console says, "Check tower to captain rocket ship TWA *Star of Polaris*—you've been cleared for takeoff, Captain. Stand by."

"Captain *Star of Polaris*. Alrighty [that folksy chirp does seem to be what the captain is saying]."

A siren begins its ululation.

"Starting countdown. Fifteen seconds, X-fourteen, X-thirteen . . ." and on down to: ". . . X-one—Fire!" Celestial music, while the space-port dwindles below.

"This is Captain Barton again at Disneyland operations. I'm switching you back to the rocket *Polaris* for more highlights of this space trip. During the time I've been speaking, we've risen another ten thousand feet. We're assuming our flight course, which will take us over the Arctic Circle. You'll find most of the polar cap will be in shadow, or nightside. In a few moments we'll be one thousand and seventy-five miles high, and pass the orbit of the Space Station Terra."

But we are not to see Space Station Terra. Instead the camera cuts to the spires of Sleeping Beauty Castle, then moves down to Disney, sitting in front of the moat: "And now the plaque reserved for last. A few words of dedication for the happiest kingdom of them all—Fantasyland. Here is a world of imagination, hopes, and dreams. In this timeless land of enchantment, the age of chivalry, magic, and make-believe are reborn, and fairy tales come true. Fantasyland is dedicated to the young and the young at heart, to those who believe that when you wish upon a star your dreams do come true."

We see the castle full-on, drawbridge raised, with a group of children in the foreground. "This is Ronald Reagan again, and I'm very happy now to show you these young people. Since Disneyland opened, these children have been eagerly waiting to cross the moat for a wondrous trip through the Disney imagination. They'll be the first children to enjoy the Fantasyland rides, every one of which recreates the adventures of characters Walt has immortalized in film."

The drawbridge slowly lowers as an enormous voice commands, "Open the Fantasyland castle in the name of the children of the world!"

What at first looks like perhaps twenty or thirty children turns out to be a seemingly limitless swarm. As the choreographer, Miriam Nelson, remembered, costumed Disney characters were "given a specific direction to lead the children to specific rides. The characters couldn't believe their eyes when, as they rushed through the gate, there were hundreds of screaming children. So instead of beckoning the children, the children chased the Disney characters."

JoAnn Killingsworth, one of Miriam Nelson's dancers, who had been chosen to be Snow White, said, "Basically, my stage direction in Fantasyland was to 'run pretty,' and I tried my best. When the drawbridge dropped, we all feared we would be trampled by the children and didn't realize there would be so many of them or that they'd be so excited."

There are five hundred of them; driven from Anaheim church schools earlier in the day, they've been waiting in twitchy anticipation in their stifling buses. They scramble to the King Arthur Carrousel, and the Mad Hatter teacups—which spin beneath superimposed images of the tea party from the film—and finally to Peter Pan's Flight and a welcoming Linkletter: "It's the Peter Pan fly-through—and you go on in there, kids—they ride in pirate galleons that hang on a monorail."

Strictly speaking, it *is* a monorail, in that the ships hang from a single beam, but the ride had nothing to do with the monorail that was to come to the park, and nobody ever referred to it by that name. As early as May 1954, the United Press had run a story about Disneyland that included the mention of "an overhanging monorail car [that] can whiz visitors over the project." The word had been in the air, it had the glint of futurity to it, and Linkletter picked it up.

"Hi there, ya having fun?—and you're gonna get a ride through here on a pirate galleon hanging on a monorail and it flies first of all out through a moonbeam scene out over London town. . . . Well, they're loading up on these pirate galleons and it looks as if this is going to be one of the most exciting rides of all. . . . You're going to come back here in a minute. Right now Bob Cummings is—where is he?—he's at the Snow White ride. Bob—come on in!"

Now the show begins to get scattered—there's a quick, pointless shift to Bob Cummings, and then back to Linkletter, who announces a commercial because that's "who's paying the bill." The bill paid, we're back with Linkletter at the Casey Jr. Circus Train: apparently in working order despite Fowler's worries, it's setting out with Jerry Colonna at the throttle.

Next comes an inane sequence in which Bob Cummings, sitting aboard the Chicken of the Sea Pirate Ship, talks with Bobby Driscoll who, five years earlier, had starred in the Disney movie *Treasure Island*. Bob and Bobby agree that neither had ever expected anything like this, and isn't it just wonderful, until Cummings, straining a bit, says, "You know, looking at Fantasyland from where we are at this spot is simply fantastic—you can see the whole thing. Oh"—in clear relief—"I see Art Linkletter!"

Linkletter is in front of Mr. Toad's Wild Ride. Cummings realizes he is in difficulties, and reports with cheerful malice, "Art is looking for a microphone, he's looking all confused. He's standing over there in front of Mr. Toad's Wild Ride, and I think if he ever gets a microphone we'll be able to talk to him because he's waving his arms, as if something's gone wrong for just an instant. . . ."

Something *had* gone wrong. Linkletter said, "I went to Fantasyland to do a standup in front of Mr. Toad's Wild Ride. They told me, 'When you get there, the mike will be waiting for you. Well, the microphone was there, all right, but they had left it under a pile of lumber. I couldn't find it! Ninety million viewers saw me waving my arms, scrambling around, looking under trash barrels for my microphone. I eventually found it, and the show went on."

Cummings calls, "Now here he comes with his microphone—he's coming out—Art Linkletter!"

Reunited with his mike, Linkletter says, "Mr. Disney's great picture *Wind in the Willows* inspired this ride—Mr. Toad, on a nineteen hundred and three automobile, and believe me, this ride is the wildest of them all. . . . This is a ride that not only should parents go with children but the parents' parents should go with the parents."

Danny Thomas makes yet another reappearance (One critic complained of the show, "Precious time also was wasted in plugs for various Hollywood personalities. The personality plug is rapidly becoming one of the most tedious things on television."), and then Linkletter says, "Bob Cummings, up on the pirate ship, we're back to you, boy."

Cummings seems unhappy; perhaps he's had enough of the pirate ship and Bobby Driscoll. "Aw, you're waiting for me? Oh, thank you— everyone is waving at Bob Cummings over here so I think I'm back on. I'm on the top of the pirate ship, the Chicken of the Sea Pirate Ship, sitting right up here with Bobby Driscoll, and I think I can see coming now two of the most important people here at Fantasyland—the real star of it is Mickey and Minnie Mouse—and they're on their way, ladies and gentlemen. I can see them coming. There they go, and they're going into the Mickey Mouse Theater, a beautiful movie house which will have a continuous performance for children who visit Fantasyland."

As Mickey and Minnie enter the theater, they're replaced by a gout of children. Cummings says, "And out from inside the theater come the Mouseketeers." This is a preview of the *Mickey Mouse Club* show, which won't air until October, and Cummings doesn't quite know what these youngsters are. He explains only that we're seeing "a group of talented boys and girls, and I guarantee that many a future star will be coming out of this group." The mouse ears are still in the future; they're wearing Western costumes and cowboy hats, and launch into a dance ending with a roll call, which lasts quite a while, as there are twenty-five of them. When the final Mouseketeer has yelled out his name, it's back to Disney and Linkletter, standing in front of the castle.

"Well, Walt, it seems to me we've been everywhere, haven't we?"

"Well, I hope so—I don't know."

"Didn't we miss something?"

"Seems like it."

"A whole land?"

Disney slaps Linkletter's arm. "Adventureland!"

Linkletter, enthusiasm still intact after ninety draining minutes, exclaims, "That's my favorite! Let's go over there. Bob Cummings or somebody oughta be waiting to let us see that."

"Well, we better hurry," Disney says, "We haven't got much time."

They don't. The show has only a couple of minutes left to run, and Adventureland gets short shrift.

"Bob Cummings, ladies and gentlemen, again. We're now at the beginning of a true-life adventure into a still uncharted and untamed region of our own world—a Tahitian village where you can experience a slice of life as it exists in the paradise of the Pacific. An African trading post, the spearhead of civilization in these primitive lands."

The brief look at the Jungle Cruise has been filmed in advance. As we see the launch of *Mekong Maiden*, Cummings speeds his narrative along. "Now we're all loaded, I believe—yes, Captain, you can take her off. We're ready for a ride down the tropical waterways of the world. Now, you just can't believe it, folks—the colors are so unbelievable. The banks are lined with exotic foliage flown here from the far corners of the earth."

To the sound of jungle drums, the launches chug past the thick greenery, their passengers pointing at giraffes and elephants. But not for long. "Well, folks, this has been but a brief glimpse of this marvelous, marvelous network of Adventureland. But we haven't time now. We have to take you back to see how the rest of the visitors at Disneyland are doing."

There are only two visitors: Disney and Linkletter, again in front of the castle.

"Walt, you've made a bum out of Barnum today." Disney grins, and Linkletter reminds him, "We've got to go."

"I know, but I just want to say a word of thanks to all the artists, the workers, and everybody who helped make this dream come true."

Linkletter says, "Let's go into Fantasyland and have some fun. Goodbye, folks." He throws a comradely arm around Disney as they turn and walk away toward the castle.

37

DATELINE BEHIND THE CAMERAS: BLACK SUNDAY

Beyond that drawbridge, nobody was having much fun.

Joyce Bellinger, who had been hired ten days earlier to work aboard the *Mark Twain*, said of opening day, "I always remember that I was out there the night before. It was really a mess, you know. There was paint all over, and tools, and drop cloths. The windows were still covered with paint. Everybody was running around. And there were knives and hammers. The ticket booth for the *Mark Twain* wasn't even half finished. And we thought, 'My gosh! How are they going to be able to open it for the press and all the celebrities and everybody who's going to be here the following day?' So we came back the next morning, and it just sparkled. Everything was clean and beautiful, and it looked just simply great."

But she got there at eight in the morning. Most of the guests that day would have agreed with C. V. Wood: "It was a madhouse!"

The day's chief problem revealed itself early: the sheer mass of people drawn by Disney's ten-month advertising campaign.

This was the "Press Preview Day," by invitation only, and it had been carefully planned. The company issued eleven thousand invitations, with staggered entrance times. Each guest was to spend three hours in the park, with the last group arriving at 5:30. Nobody paid the slightest attention to the times. Many of the tickets offered entry to a guest "and party." A gatekeeper remembered, "One person got off his huge bus with his *party*. With one ticket." Moreover, the tickets had been printed long enough in advance to serve as models for a thriving traffic in counterfeits.

Some visitors got in without tickets, fake or real. Wood said, "We even found a guy who had built a ladder and flopped it over the barbed-wire fence back where the stables were. You could just walk up and over real easy. He was letting people in for five damn bucks a head."

The park's official tally had attendance at 28,154, but that seems suspiciously precise. Many of the employees believed the number much greater; Ken Anderson put it at fifty thousand.

One studio man, armed with a perfectly legitimate ticket, summed up the experience of almost everyone on the 17th: "Except for the fact that we can say we were at the opening, it was most disappointing in that neither [our] children nor ourselves could get near any rides, nor places to eat."

Not that getting to a restaurant would ensure something to eat; some of the concessions ran out of food by noon. Adding to the discomfort, the temperature quickly climbed to over one hundred degrees and stayed there. This made the lack of drinking fountains all the more apparent. "Instead," said Van Arsdale France, "we had young men carrying water on their backs . . . our version of Gunga Din. Along with other bad publicity, we were accused of depriving our guests of water to force them to buy Coca-Cola and Pepsi."

The toilets that Disney had chosen over the drinking fountains also had problems. "Even with the restrooms," wrote France, "they were totally inadequate for the needs of the people. The lines were almost as great at these facilities as they were for the attractions. And, since Walt did not want big signs saying 'MEN' and 'WOMEN' on his theme stages, they were hard to find. As a result, there was confusion in Fantasyland where they were named 'PRINCE' and 'PRINCESS.' Some people thought they were attractions. On Main Street the restrooms are hidden behind our flower display. One guest asked for restroom directions for her child, and was told "behind the flowers" . . . and took the direction at face value . . . and went . . . behind the flowers."

Trouble started at the gate. The newly laid asphalt was still so soft that Dick Nunis remembered seeing it suck women's high-heeled shoes off their feet, with Frank Sinatra's wife being one of the victims; and many visitors came away with their clothes bearing the indelible imprint of wet paint. Because the park was opening by degrees, one land at a time, crowds built up everywhere. "Christ, we had them packed on Main Street like sardines," said Wood. "They were bitching. They were mad."

Animators from the studio had been drafted to take part in the ceremonies. "My group," one of them wrote, "had been assigned to the *Mark Twain* riverboat. We gaily tripped up the plank and wandered around. It was still hot, and the passengers were all sweating on the crowded boat. There was no bar, fountain, no water aboard, and no way to jump ship after you were on because some so-and-so had removed the gangplank."

They'd been sweltering there for hours by the time Art Linkletter and Irene Dunne showed up.

Tim O'Brien, the negligent overseer of the holding pen, first knew there was trouble when he heard the boat's whistle give the two short blasts of the agreed-upon distress signal. The *Twain* was on the far side of the island, and when a maintenance crew arrived in their motorboat they found her with the list that Irene Dunne had noticed now so pronounced that the lower deck was awash.

A passenger yelled, "The boat is sunk!" The boat was fine, but had jumped its track and was stuck. Scores of people would have to wade ashore before it could be refloated. At first nobody wanted to: the turbid waters looked bottomless. But that effect had been achieved with dye, and the river was only two feet deep where the *Twain* was stranded. Gradually, holding their shoes aloft, passengers began to make for the bank. It took half an hour to lighten the ship enough for a diver to reset the stern-wheeler.

Passengers also had to be taken off those canal boats that Linkletter had mentioned. This was an attraction that shouldn't have been running at all. Although it was designed to send guests gliding past the miniature buildings of Storybook Land, the model shop had yet to produce a single one of them. Instead, the boats wound their way through the bare brown gully that operators had named the Mudbank Ride.

This was the only ride Jack Lindquist, his wife, and their five-year-old son got near. Lindquist was there because he had headed his advertising firm's successful effort to sell Disneyland a Kelvinator promotion (the "Foodarama" refrigerator in Tomorrowland, which, it boasted, could hold 166 pounds of meat), and he wasn't having a good time. "As we were being pushed along by the crowd, we saw the Canal Boats of the World in Fantasyland. They were barge-like boats piloted by an operator sitting in the back. My son, David, wanted to go on them, and I thought it was a great idea. I watched somewhat nervously as David sailed away with around forty other kids on board. The boat was supposed to return about five minutes after it took off; but after fifteen minutes, David hadn't returned." Other boats came in but not his. "Then, half an hour passed. Still no David. I thought I had sent my firstborn on a voyage to hell and that he'd never return." Forty-five minutes later, "four guys wearing waders slogged through the water pulling David's boat with ropes. . . . As I stood in this sweaty, sticky mass of humanity, I grew more disenchanted by the minute with the supposed 'happiest place on earth.'" David got off, "sweat rolling down his face," and immediately asked, "Can we go home now?" That was enough for Lindquist, too: "We walked around for a few more minutes, and then we got in the car and drove to Knott's Berry Farm for a chicken dinner."

Fantasyland was beset with crises. The most dangerous came while Fowler was trapped aboard the riverboat during its derailment. "I was in the cabin of the *Mark Twain* with Irene Dunne. And we were marooned there for an hour and a half. She was perfectly delightful, but because of the crowds we couldn't get off. Then I finally got a call when I hit the beach that we had a problem up in Fantasyland, and we did. We had a gas leak. And you could smell gas coming up through the courtyard there somewhere. The question was, 'What the hell will we do? Will we close up and get everybody out of the park?' I got hold of the fire chief and we decided we'd rope off the area."

Fowler and the fire chief found the leak, and got a plumber to fix the broken line. "I don't think half a dozen people knew it because . . . nobody could get in."

The day's only mortal danger had been defused, but one by one the Fantasyland rides began to fail. As Ed Morgan and Karl Bacon of Arrow had already predicted, the Snow White cars were regularly derailed by their half-trained operators. The Dumbo ride was still oozing its "shaving cream," and to keep its elephants aloft, Morgan and Bacon had to rely on a stalwart colleague. Karl: "We used a fellow by the name of Paul Harvey on-site. We left him there to—" Ed: "—milk the elephants!" Karl: "While they were loading, he'd go out there and drain the system and put in clean oil. We elected him . . ." Ed: "He was a wonderful employee, and we just left him there on opening day. It was a mean thing to do. They were actually operating the ride, and he was in the inner enclosure. He's draining fluid and putting fluid back in between time of load and unload. Disney was insistent that the ride would run because we had so many problems in the early days."

He also insisted that Casey Jr. perform. The little circus train would not be fully operational until the end of the month, but Fowler had made some emergency repairs he believed would serve for a couple of circuits of the track. Jerry Colonna didn't think so. The comedian, who had often loaned his piercing slide-whistle voice to Disney cartoons, stood by dressed as an engineer and scheduled to take the throttle. Morgan and Bacon, who had built the engine, were on hand, and Ed said, "On opening day, the guy with the bulgy eyes, Jerry Colonna, was supposed to drive the train, but he . . . just chickened out. He looked at that hill and said, 'No!'" The ABC crew, minutes away from having to cover the departure, looked to Morgan, but he was too big for the engineer's costume. He pointed to his smaller partner. Morgan said, "Karl looked at me, and I said, 'Yes, you can do it.'" So Bacon suited up, Colonna agreed to ride on the tender, and they made the run without injury.

If Paul Harvey, the elephant milker, had the worst job that day, Bob Gurr's came close, and got bad early. "About half the Autopia cars were taken from the ride and moved to an offstage area next to the Main Street town square for the opening day parade. The first sign of trouble appeared as I started the cars using a kick starter on the engine while holding the rear engine hood open. The day was getting hotter and hotter and the cars began to vapor lock and stall after idling in the heat for 15 minutes or so. Just as the cars were to join the parade I ran from car to car to restart the stalled engines as the drivers were itching to go."

At this point Disney added to Bob Gurr's difficulties. He came by with Gale Storm and introduced her to Gurr, whose pleasure in meeting this "gorgeous red-haired movie star" evaporated when Walt said, "Bobby will mind your boys for the day."

So, wrote Gurr, "now I'm to babysit two kids in addition to herding forty sick cars."

"The drivers moved the cars after the parade to the Autopia ride where we got them all back on the track to await the official Autopia ride opening later in the day. I was delighted to watch the happy faces of the little guests as they finally got to drive a 'real gasoline car' at Disneyland. But my delight turned to dismay as car after car suffered a variety of failures."

Gale Storm's two sons "clung to me wherever I had to rush to, helping the ride operators to rescue dying cars. Of course we did a lot of driving trips on the ride ourselves—I wasn't gonna miss out on the fun. The boys pointed out a short black guy with an eye patch and hollered 'get 'im' . . . obviously a friend of theirs. We whacked the guy clear off the track and up into the weeds. He gave us a startled look."

That was Sammy Davis Jr. Gurr "wanted to apologize to him till the day he died, but never caught up with him."

"As the number of functioning cars dwindled, the guest queue line got longer and longer. Soon, some guests were jumping the fence, running up the track, and commandeering the returning cars. The ride operators were outnumbered to try and stop this Autopia feeding frenzy."

And there were casualties. "As some cars were suffering faulty speed governors, drivers could go fast enough to jump curbs, spin out, and drive back down the track where head-on collisions took place. The original cars did not have padded steering wheels. I took a couple of kids to first aid, one with his hand full of teeth."

People were storming other rides, too. In Fantasyland, an employee said "there were so many people that they had to close the carrousel a few times because guests climbed over the chains and we couldn't control them." Some passed their children over the heads of the crowd to get them mounted.

Keith Murdoch, the Anaheim city manager who had been aboard from the park's earliest days, found the opening "such a mess that I went home and watched it on TV."

In the midst of all this, *Dateline: Disneyland* soldiered on, the TV monitors shimmering in the white fog lifting from tubs of dry ice that kept them cool enough to function. Although remarkably little of the mayhem is visible in the show, the hosts were well aware of it. Ronald Reagan had to scale an eight-foot fence to reach Frontierland on time, and even Disney had trouble getting around. Linkletter wrote, "On one occasion, Walt was going from one place to another, and he was going up an alley shortcut, and there was a guard there. He said, 'You can't go through here.' And Walt said to him, 'Do you know who I am?' And the guard said, 'Yes, Mr. Disney, I do, but I have my orders—nobody can go through here.' And Walt said, 'Well, *I'm* going to go through here. If you get in the way, you know what's going to happen to you!' And he walked right by."

Davy Crockett, unperturbed by hostile Plains warriors, was shaken by the crowds. As soon as his appearance was over, he found a young publicist whose nametag read Marty Sklar, and begged him, "Marty, help me get out of here before this horse kills somebody!" Sklar said, "I did manage to help Fess Parker (and his horse) reach a backstage area. The rest of the day was a blur."

Ken Anderson spent it in a daze. The night before, after he'd left Disney to attend to Mr. Toad, "I went on the rides over again more than once, but I spent a good deal of the time walking through the rides and checking out the painting and all the works. I was so damn tired I had been working straight through for two or three days and nights. And I was just asleep on my feet."

He found a patch of ground, and "was sound asleep for the opening of the park. I must have slept for about an hour because I was woken up again by some of the workmen saying, 'What in the hell are you doing?'"

He joined the swelling crowd. "I wandered around and met the people. I was amazed at the number of people. . . . We weren't prepared for them. We didn't know anything about lines. We didn't know anything about anything. We just had these attractions and 'wouldn't you like to go?' And sure, they were piling in like crazy. . . .

"It must have been a disaster, but it happened so fast, and there was so much of it, and they were all around you, you didn't know it was a disaster."

The press knew. The park had broken one of the cardinal rules for entertaining reporters: get them drunk. Harper Goff, visiting the press room, was set upon by two newspapermen who griped to him about Disney's stinginess: "Dumb bastard! Where's the liquor?"

Goff apologized, explaining that Anaheim law said Disney needed a special permit to serve alcohol, but the reporters were welcome to bring their own.

"Where's the nearest liquor store?"

Goff had no idea.

His indignant questioner said, "I'm going to sit down here and say that a father and mother with two kids came and left and it cost them two hundred dollars. Everything is *so* expensive."

"I'll make it worse than that," the other reporter promised. Walt "always thinks he's had good press, but he'll learn."

Just how much Disney was aware of the tumult is unclear. Certainly he was in the middle of it—an employee even saw him running an arm-load of emergency toilet paper to one of the restrooms—but reports differ, with some having him buoyant and confident, others anxious and downcast. Apparently after the telecast he sought out C. V. Wood and berated him, as if his general manager could have controlled the chaos better.

As the long day began to wane, a guest said, "Everything was broken down." That was true enough; at one point or another every ride save for the jungle boats had been out of commission. "The place looked like a cyclone had hit it."

What might have distressed Disney most were the drifts of trash. Chuck Boyajian and his crew had done their best, but the volume was overwhelming. Toward the end, they were simply piling it up behind the Main Street buildings, making heaps of garbage that attracted the harsh attention of the Health Department: "This is either gone, or you're not open!"

As soon as the throng began to thin, Bob Gurr went looking for Gale Storm, and gave her back her children.

"Returning to the Autopia ride, I found it shut down, the ride operators nursing bloody shins from kick-starting dead cars all day. A few said they had been run down by wild drivers.

"At last I had a chance to survey the mess the Autopia cars were in; distorted bumpers, rear wheel bearings shot, axle and brake damage. . . . Many of the remaining thirty-seven cars were in sad shape—just after only one day???!"

Brooding over the results of "the real testing," he "had a long, hot, sad drive home that night, only to return to Disneyland the next morning to face the regular public."

Van Arsdale France, in his role as traffic coordinator, had struggled through an even longer day, albeit one that gave him a privileged aerial view from the Goodyear Blimp, which he shared with Anaheim's chief of police, who remembered seeing automobiles backed up "halfway to L.A." in what was the worst traffic jam in Orange County history.

Now, fifteen hours or so later, France was back on the ground, trying to disperse all those cars, armed with a useful piece of highway patrol wisdom: "I was taught one thing about directing traffic. When, as was to happen, people were trying to drive home in many directions, and trapped in long lines, they would ask how to get to Los Angeles, San Diego, or any other place. There is, I was taught, only one reply . . . 'Straight ahead, sir.' We could only hope they would eventually find their way home."

Thinking it over, he wrote, "It was total confusion . . . both on camera and behind the scenes. But, it was the celebration of the birth of a dream."

The shell-shocked Ken Anderson, still on his feet and making his exhausted way through the shambles, also nursed an ember of optimism: "We had a park. It was a start."

38

Damage Control

Members of the press enjoyed their first look at Disneyland no more than anyone else had, and much of the coverage was brutal.

H. W. Mooring of the *Los Angeles Tidings* filed early and set the tone: "WALT'S DREAM IS A NIGHTMARE. I attended the so-called press premiere of Disneyland, a fiasco the like of which I cannot recall in thirty years of show life. To me, it felt like a giant cash register, clicking and clanging, as creatures of Disney magic came tumbling down from their lofty places in my daydreams to peddle and perish their charms with the aggressiveness of so many curbside barkers. With this harsh stroke, he transforms a beautiful realm into a blatant nightmare."

One headline decried "THE $17 MILLION DOLLAR PEOPLE TRAP THAT MICKEY MOUSE BUILT," where "irate adults cursed Mickey, Minnie, Pluto, Snow White and all the Seven Dwarfs."

Everyone complained about the lines, and the crowds. All that children would remember, a reporter said, was "a forest of baggy pants and summer skirts." The *Orange County Plain Dealer* agreed: "Children were probably the most disappointed, because of the inability to get near the rides. Tears were evident on many tykes' faces because they couldn't take a ride in a covered wagon or enter the magic realm of Fantasyland. . . . Many of the rides in Fantasyland, designed primarily for children, operated only a short time and were occupied mostly by adults."

Another correspondent "saw Davy Crockett and Annie Oakley and 47 children with running noses looking for lost mothers. Anything else we saw was purely accidental. We don't have x-ray eyes, which is what you need when 30,000 people are standing in one place looking at each other's backsides."

Cora Ulrich of the *Santa Ana Register* was slightly less damning, and offered an arresting simile: "Many citizens of Anaheim are beginning to regard the opening of Disneyland with dismay and 'mixed emotions'—the kind the man had when he pushed his mother-in-law over the cliff in his new Cadillac."

The majority of those first-day visitors shared the feelings of a brief newspaper report that concluded, "Everyone agreed it had been one of the most unpleasant days of his life."

At least the columnist Sheilah Graham ended on a generous note. Her love affair with F. Scott Fitzgerald during his last years may have reminded her that the vexatious and the marvelous sometimes travel together: "To sum up, Disneyland was a disappointment . . . but don't be discouraged, boys and girls—Walt Disney has always been a smart trader, and I'm sure there'll be some changes made."

There would indeed be some changes made—year in and year out forever after—but on Monday morning, July 18, Roy Disney wasn't thinking about any of them. He had a more immediate concern. Sure, the park had been crowded yesterday: everything was free. Now, though, came the official opening, not just to the parasitic press and a handful of TV stars, but to the vast American public. Reminiscing at a park veterans' reunion in 1968, he said, "What if we opened the gates and nobody came?

"Well, on opening day I left the studio and headed down the Santa Ana Freeway. I was so worried. After getting out of Los Angeles the traffic began to get heavy." That didn't encourage him: "It could have been people going to the beach."

With the freeway still unfinished, he became mired in ever-thicker traffic, and "it must have taken more than an hour to finally get to the Disney parking lot." Well worth the aggravation, though, because he found it already "jammed." The press of traffic had forced the attendants to open three hours ahead of schedule.

One of them recognized Roy and hurried over, obviously troubled.

"Mr. Disney, people have been stalled on the freeway and getting into our parking lot. Children are peeing all over the lot."

Roy "looked around at all of these people who were coming here to pay to get in. With a great sense of relief, I said, 'God bless 'em, let 'em pee.'"

Walt, a few hundred yards away in his firehouse apartment, had been sharing his brother's worry. Then the park opened, and he saw a steady flow of people filling Town Square and starting out along Main Street toward the castle.

He moved closer to the window. "Paying guests," he said, blowing them a kiss. "I love you."

He left the firehouse for a second round of opening ceremonies, less stressful than yesterday's, but far from pro forma. The *Los Angeles Times* said, "The man Disney was everywhere on Opening Day. He was at the front gate greeting customers, at the heliport to welcome arrivals, at a drugstore to officiate in a dessert contest, at the administration building to iron out ever-present problems and circulating through the crowds signing autographs."

He also would have met the first paying guest. That visitor did not get ticket number one; Roy had made sure to buy it earlier. But thereafter, the policy was first come, first served.

First come was a twenty-two-year-old student at Long Beach State named Dave MacPherson. He worked on the school paper, and reportorial zeal put him on his motorbike for a ten-mile ride to the park. "I decided I wanted to be the first on line. The first person to go into the park who wasn't a relative of Walt's or some celebrity. The first regular guy to go in through the front door."

He got there shortly before 1 a.m., having bested his closest competitor by a full hour. Taking up a post next to one of the two ticket booths, he settled in to await the park's opening at ten o'clock that morning.

MacPherson's vigil must have seemed to him like the sort of dream one has when coming down with a cold: a restless, uncomfortable ennui troubled by peculiar interruptions. When dawn began to color the eastern sky, he heard the shrieks and trumpetings of wild animals as the Adventureland staff tuned up the Jungle Cruise menagerie.

By full daylight, a crowd of six thousand had built up behind him. Weariness doubtless made him more anxious than usual, but the anxiety turned out to be justified.

"Well, I had thought that perhaps someone might try to get ahead of me at the last moment. So I had prepared a sheet to the effect that I was first, and had last-minute workers and security people sign it. Sure enough, about five minutes before the gates opened a woman and two little kids tried to get in front of me. So I pulled out the sheet (like a miniature Declaration of Independence!) and showed it to her. It was like Dracula seeing the light shining on the cross and she slunk back!"

The usurper foiled, MacPherson entered the park and at once ratified Disney's wisdom in choosing toilets over drinking fountains. After being on his feet in the same spot for nine hours, he needed the former far more than the latter, and "the first thing I did was go to the restroom."

This also seems to have been the most exciting thing he did that day. "I can't remember buying anything or seeing a parade, but as I recall, the attractions had very long lines that first day! It was hot and humid, and . . . I have no real sharp memories of the various parts of the park. I was very tired from being up all night, so I went briefly around to see at a glance, so to speak, the entire layout. I needed to get some rest because I wasn't thinking straight."

Although he remembered only a dazzle of heat and crowds, his pilgrimage paid off: "I was the most popular guy in the college after the students found out."

In later years, MacPherson had the opportunity to observe the park more clearly. On its fiftieth anniversary, the Disney publicity department tracked him down. He was seventy-two then, retired after a lifetime spent practicing the journalism he'd studied at Long Beach State. He'd been living in Utah for the past twenty years, having become disenchanted with what he called "Quakafornia." But he still returned there to visit Disneyland on the lifetime pass his long-ago nocturnal adventure had won him.

With the sole exception that money was at last coming in rather than going out, Disneyland's second day was like the first, right down to another gas leak. It was in Fantasyland again, discovered when a workman dropped a cigarette on it. By the time C. V. Wood got there, he could see a pale blue skirt of flame wavering along one of the castle walls.

Fantasyland hadn't yet opened, and save for the unwelcome presence of press photographers waiting for the first children to arrive, the courtyard was deserted.

Fowler arrived a few minutes later and, working with the fire control crew, found the leak and capped the ruptured pipe responsible. While this was going on, Wood pulled off a piece of salesmanship as impressive as any that won the most valuable sponsorships he'd brought in. He persuaded all the press people that there was no story here, and the memorable photograph of Sleeping Beauty's Castle hovering on the verge of fiery extinction at the moment of its birth does not exist.

Although no wienie exploded that day, many rides broke down. The elephants and teacups had already shown themselves almost impossible to keep running, and Bob Gurr had fewer and fewer cars to send out on Autopia. Less dangerous than the fire, but more peculiar, was a last-minute plumbing error that revealed itself when the sprinkler system in front of a snack bar on New Orleans Street began watering its lawn with orange juice.

There had been a healthy gate—26,007 visitors paid for admission, and every ride they went on—but many of the newspaper stories echoed those that followed the press opening twenty-four hours earlier. The Los Angeles *Mirror-News* ran a prodigious headline of Civil War–era length: "CROWDS GRIPE OVER LONG WAITING LINES EVERYWHERE—DISNEYLAND, ORANGE COUNTY'S NEW $17 MILLION PLAYGROUND, WAS A LAND OF GRIPES AND COMPLAINTS AGAIN TODAY, AS A HUGE MILLING THRONG OF 48,000 PEOPLE HAD THE PLACE BULGING AT THE SEAMS."

One of his close associates said that when Disney saw the sour reviews, he "wanted to shoot himself," but if so, such desolate moments were fleeting. He knew better than anyone that the park had opened perhaps less than 80 percent finished, and the hard work ahead did not frighten him; hard work never had.

What dismayed him most was the tender spot the thirsty reporter had poked when he complained to Harper Goff in the newsroom: "It's *so* expensive."

The Disney company had made careful calculations about this all-important issue and had figured out that a day in Disneyland would cost a family of four nine to ten dollars.

The reporter who felt caught in Mickey's "17-million-dollar people trap" heard a disgusted father on the way out with his family say that at least the miserable day had "saved me $500 in never being pestered to go back." A columnist named Eve Starr wrote, "The Disney people are making a point of saying that tourists can go through Disneyland without spending more than $2.00 per person. That is probably true, but it would be like taking a reformed alcoholic on a tour of a brewery." Dick Whittinghill, a popular West Coast radio personality, said he faced a dilemma: he could either take his children to Disneyland, or send them to college.

Possibly more damaging was the Los Angeles *Mirror-News* correspondent who did not seem to indulge in hyperbole when he tallied the cost for a family of four: "The total would be $32 if they went on every ride and ate and drank for a dollar apiece."

The park wasn't cheap—it never has been, nor could it have survived in anything like its current form if it were—but that $32 translates into about $300 in today's dollars, which struck people as a huge toll for an amusement park.

Those opening day customers paid a dollar to get in and fifty cents for their children. All the sponsored exhibits and the Golden Horseshoe were free; everything else required a ticket. Kiosks throughout the park sold them, already graded in the alphabetical ranking that would endure for years: "A" was good for 10 cents, "B" for 25, "C" for 40.

The arrangement was simple and rational, except that this was an all-cash business, and thus involved handling floods of small change. In its early days, Walt Disney's serene Main Street and his lordly riverboat alike rode on the knockabout finances of a traveling carnival.

"We collected money at the main gate," said Joe Fowler, "and we had our security boys with guns escorting them over to this big vault we had in the administration building where we kept our funds until the armored car from Bank of America could pick it up. We had no bank in the beginning." At the kiosks, the ticket sellers would toss the money into buckets, which runners regularly arrived to grab and take to City Hall. The bills would be counted, but the millions of coins were roughly assessed by weight.

Disney immediately set about making sure those buckets kept being filled. The most obvious task was to get all the equipment working properly. Joe Fowler helped see to that: "I didn't leave Disneyland for ten days from the day we opened."

Next, finish the uncompleted attractions (the *Nautilus* exhibit, for instance, had not yet opened despite Disney's and Ken Anderson's night-long efforts). And, saddled with debt though he was, Disney shocked both his brother and ABC by announcing that he intended to put 16 percent of the revenue back into the park.

Most important, he and Wood vigorously courted the press, inviting reporters on privately escorted tours, using Walt's celebrity and Wood's unquenchable affability to win Disneyland a second chance. The two men were frank about having opened prematurely, and cheerful but thorough in pointing out the swift-moving improvements.

Sheilah Graham had said Disney was a sharp trader, and his wooing of the press was indeed sharp, and most effective. In mid-August, the San Rafael *Daily Independent Journal* ran an article under a headline that, while not understating the price, said Disneyland was worth the money: "Marin Family 'Does' Fantasy Land in 10 Hours for $29.65, Likes It."

Having paid the 25-cent parking fee, the reporter, a Marin County resident named Chapin A. Day, his wife, and their two children, aged eight and eleven, "walked through the gates into a tunnel under the Santa Fe and Disneyland Railroad tracks and left reality behind."

The story goes on with much that would have made Disney happy, especially in its insistence that Disneyland was not only a lot of fun, but something new.

"Circling the park in the railroad train, we oriented ourselves. Here we first noted the thing which impressed us ever more deeply as the day went on—the care and quality of materials which has gone into everything.

"Disneyland is not shoddy. It is not a carnival of concessions at the beach. It is not false fronts and makeshift rears. It is carefully built by experienced workmen. Details are not forgotten and materials are of the highest obtainable quality.

"To match this perfection, the 1,000 or more employees at Disneyland are of the finest character. Although it was a hot day and smog stung our eyes the men and women who operated the rides, sold tickets or dispensed food were without exception courteous and helpful. . . . They alone are a tribute to Walt Disney."

As for the rides, they "are both unusual and enjoyable. They also are crowded, and in mid-afternoon it is not unusual for there to be a two and a half-hour delay to ride in the tiny cars of Autopia, or an hour and a half in line before Peter Pan [to this day, Peter Pan generates the longest lines in Fantasyland]. . . .

"The rivers of the world is the most elaborate and most expensive (50 cents adults, 35 cents children), but you'll probably enjoy it even after the wait in line. . . .

"Not all the work has been completed. The 105-foot sternwheeler *Mark Twain* splashes around the half mile-long rivers of the world [he means Rivers of America] carrying some 300 passengers. But right now one river looks much like another and all of them resemble an artificial stream in Southern California—but it's fun."

The food: "What's there to eat? Practically anything you want. . . . We ate hot cakes, but could have had anything from fried chicken to tacos or hot dogs. . . . You can get a full dinner in the swank Red Wagon Inn for from $3.50 down. Or munch chicken at the Plantation Inn for $1.50. Or you can have a 35-cent hamburger and a 10-cent cold drink."

The overall cost: "Our whole family went on every ride there was. . . . In all, the bill for admission, parking and rides, but excluding food items and trinkets purchased, came to $22.05, in our case happily, on the house. Food and trinkets, including three sets of gift earrings and seven cents in a penny arcade, cost $7.60, a grand total of $29.65 for 10 wonderful hours [$278.99 today].

"This may sound like everything costs money. It doesn't. Fully half of the time, or perhaps even more, we were inspecting things, seeing exhibits and the wonders of the park which cost nothing. We could have done more. We went on more rides than the children needed or would have been satisfied with. It would have been no trick to cut our expenses by $10. Below that it would have been harder."

The Day family verdict: "Disneyland is an experience. It can well be the high point in the vacation of any family."

The increasingly warm press began to help, but the stock market—far beyond the reach of any blandishments from Walt and Woody—did not. Before July 17, shares of Walt Disney Productions were trading for just below $60. A week later, they'd dropped 15 percent; two weeks later, another 10.

But the people were coming, 161,657 of them during the first week. Then, in mid-August, a heat wave clamped down on Southern California, and one early Disneyland employee said, "You could shoot a cannon through most areas and not hit anybody." An exaggeration: five hundred thousand visitors—half of all the tourists in Southern California at the time—showed up during that withering month.

Yet even on days when the baking Main Street was nearly deserted, the work never slowed. "I ran my ass off," said one pioneer employee. "I lost fifteen pounds in the first sixty days You never walked; you got behind the scenes and you ran. There was always a fire to put out. I went fourteen straight months without a day off."

Bob Gurr worked as hard as anyone in those heat-tormented days, and, as with most of the early recruits, his duties kept multiplying.

At the beginning, Autopia gave him more than he could handle. By the end of the first week his highway had just two cars still able to travel it, and he was touched to see the patience of the children who mutely endured three-hour waits to take the wheel of one of them.

"I had been repairing cars with my own tools since Disneyland repair folks were fixing the more important rides. Rather than test a couple of cars to destruction ourselves before finalizing the design, we now had thirty-seven test cars in various states of ruin. This meant that when I determined the cause for a failure and designed a fix, we had to repeat it thirty-seven times!"

Disney got to him toward the end of the week, and watched the two survivors gallantly rasping around the track. He "sat expressionless looking at the whole mess." When he spoke, it wasn't to complain or rebuke.

"Bobby, whaddaya need?"

"Some mechanics and some repair equipment."

Disney walked away, and "a little later an old tractor was dragging a small shed on wooden skids toward me along the service road next to the railroad tracks."

The driver—as overworked as anyone else that season—scowled down from his seat. "Where do you want the damn building? Walt said to get it over to Autopia right away."

For the first time, Gurr's freeway had a garage, but better still: "Two mechanics showed up with toolboxes, and we all went to work trying to get a few cars running. They would fix while I would think."

Naturally his first thoughts were about Autopia: "So many things were not lasting more than a few days the way kids were bashing the cars together." He'd known from the start the aluminum bumpers were worthless, but he hadn't foreseen that what called itself "the recessed hub safety steering wheel" would "be extracting little teeth daily."

Gurr redesigned the bumpers and had the studio machine shop make them out of aluminum's more dependable ancestor, steel; and he got a local company to supply "a mold so that the hard rim steering wheels could be padded with a molded-on big fat foam rubber cover."

These improvements had been simple, but in getting his cars running properly, Gurr found himself struggling through a small-scale recapitulation of the entire evolution of the automobile. The engines vibrated so violently that they shook off their carburetors; the clutches began to disintegrate as soon as they went to work; "the timing belt from the chain drive shaft would jump grooves and cause a violent chatter which loosened up even more parts." Rear axle bearings regularly broke, jamming the brake drums against the brake shoes, "thus locking the car on the track," while the unrelenting weather stalled the cars with the vapor lock that had been a problem on opening day. The only immediate solution was to continually kick-start them, so "you could always recognize the Autopia ride operators: they had bloody shins."

Gurr admitted that "a lot of the car was just dumb engineering on my part." His brake linkage worked well enough as long as it was constantly slathered with oil, for which he had made no provision. "Richfield Oil sponsored the ride and had a 300-pound guy, Tiny Snell, who had this big oil squirt can. When Disneyland accused him of not oiling the cars enough, he went up and down the line grabbing each car by the side bumper, yanked it on its side, then slammed them back down."

Watching this burly show of indignation, Gurr realized, "Oil was not the problem, lack of engineering was the problem." He also understood he was "getting a very revealing mechanical design education" courtesy of what he called "The Disneyland College of Experimental Engineering."

Once he had his Autopia vehicles in order, he was sent over to the Mad Hatter, which seemed to spin its cups loose from their moorings every day. The park's welders spent their first two hours each morning playing their torches on the ride's fractured underside. This brought Gurr into contact with Karl Bacon and Ed Morgan, who had built the teacups. He quickly established a camaraderie with the two men that didn't allow for any bruised amour propre. "They were never upset that Roger Broggie had me redesigning their products. We were both interested in getting it right for Walt."

The teacups made a lot of work. "I spent hours laying on my back underneath the ride when it was running, watching all the parts in motion until I had an idea of what the cure should be. I drew up plans for a new Tea Cup structure and wheel support system, it was built and reinstalled in early 1956. It's still the only Disneyland ride I've never been on, but under a lot."

Gurr and all the other mechanics "built up an enviable expertise in keeping troublesome rides in operation. There was really no way to stop and rebuild things during that first summer season . . . just weld and fix, weld and fix. Long-term improvement would have to wait until fall when all our young guests were back in school and we could catch our breath."

They were also learning how the park itself functioned. "As the hot summer of 1955 wore on, Disneyland steadily improved everything. Since we really did not quite know what to expect of the guests, and the guests did not quite know what Disneyland was about, we learned together. All kind of things people do and don't do gave us a big education in refining a multitude of operational details.

"Some of these refinements were easy to implement, like where shade is needed, how queue lines should work, and how ride operators can be trained to handle any human situation.

"But training machinery to behave was a whole 'nother deal."

That a lot of the machinery had never before existed made maintaining it that much harder. The Jungle Cruise animals that stood in the water were "just miserable to keep running," as even small amounts of sand getting into them "would literally grind lots of steel parts into junk." Moreover, the fake wildlife was already under attack by the real thing. Jim Harmon, who worked in Tomorrowland from its earliest days, said, "I remember how, during the course of a season the ants would eat the real fur off the animated birds and animals." Also, "At that time the sound speakers in the Rivers of America were hidden in false rocks and the gophers would fill the speakers with earth. They sent me into combat with the critters."

As soon as Bob Gurr had his Ferraris and the teacups behaving, he got dispatched on a detour into antiquity. Main Street was set in an America where the motorcar was beginning to make its presence felt, and along with his horsecars Disney wanted a few examples of the interloper. The cars that took part in the *Dateline: Disneyland* parade were all fifty-year-old veterans, and at first he planned on furnishing the street with actual early automobiles. Broggie and Gurr, however, both believed the old machines would not stand up to the daily demands of Main Street service, and Gurr suggested what he paradoxically called "authentic reproduction antiques."

He would design a turn-of-the-century exterior, and fill it with easily maintained off-the-shelf parts. He built a tonneau that had a Ford

Model A front end (Model A and T parts will be available until the end of time), a Jeep differential, brakes from a 1952 Mercury, and steering gear from a 1950 Chrysler Imperial. The car was powered by a Hercules engine made to drive water pumps: it was simple and sturdy, and its two cylinders provided the bark and shudder common to the cars of 1910. Gurr would build many such vehicles, and when a friend supplied one of them with a persuasive radiator emblem proclaiming it a "GURRMOBILE," he was delighted: "I used to get a kick out of guests who would tell others how they remembered the old Gurrmobiles that were built in Los Angeles years ago."

———

At one point in that disheveled season, Disney came upon Ed Morgan and Karl Bacon together. It must have been a moment when all the Fantasyland rides were working, because he had no complaints. Instead, he asked, "How did you boys come out on the Fantasyland rides?"

They had put in fixed bids on all of them, and with the intangible value of the experience gained making such brand-new devices subtracted, the partners were still in the red on every one.

Bacon told Disney so.

He replied, "I don't want you to lose money on my work. I'll cover your costs."

"And," said Karl, "he did."

Disney went further. "We couldn't have done it without you boys. What else can I do for you?"

Morgan remembered answering, "Nothing, it's just been a pleasure working with you."

Only afterward did it occur to him that "we could have probably received a concession such as hats or popcorn. They also gave stock at that time because they were broke. We should have taken stock instead of being paid." Well, not everyone can be Art Linkletter.

39

SOMETHING WORTHWHILE

A long with keeping the original rides running, Disney began making additions.

One of the first was to improve the dismal Canal Boats of the World. The boats were noisy, uncomfortable, and unreliable, and there was nothing to look out at but dirt. The sheepish operators were telling their passengers, "The miniature landscaping is so small you can't see it."

Combining his love of models with his life's work, Disney decided on a landscape of buildings from his films: Pinocchio's Italian village and Cinderella's French one, the houses of the Three Little Pigs, Toad Hall, and, down by the river, Ratty's home beneath a tree stump.

All were to be built on a one-inch-to-the-foot scale, with detailing that would have satisfied Mrs. Thorne: although visitors couldn't walk among the buildings, if they did, and peered into, say, Geppetto's shop windows, they'd have seen toys on display behind the thumbnail-size panes. To Alice's Wonderland neighborhood went the English church with the intricate stained-glass window, the elements of which Disney had once inadvertently scattered about the model shop. Cottages and castles would be set in an equally finely crafted living landscape of miniature plants and trees. Ken Anderson conceived and rendered the buildings, and sent his drawings to Fred Joerger and Harriet Burns to be expanded into three dimensions.

This tranquil "kingdom within a kingdom," as a Disney publication called it, served as a counterpart to the Fantasyland rides, which by their nature had to be all action and peril. (One small boy came out of the walk-through that opened in Sleeping Beauty Castle in 1957 with the memory of Maleficent the witch still so fresh that he seized the skirt of an attendant and warned her, "Lady, you better not go in there." "Why not?" "Because it'll scare hell out of you!") What came to be called Storybook Land contained no such terrors, instead offering a respite on placid green waters where all the sights revealed themselves with leisurely charm.

This was one of Disney's favorite attractions, and it remains many visitors' best-loved today, testament to his genius for carrying off an unlikely concept (a small-city business district) that manages to chime with how people occasionally like to envision their world, their past, and themselves.

He almost always got it right at Disneyland. But in these germinal days, a nostalgic pleasure of his youth both failed him and brought him into violent confrontation with C. V. Wood. He wanted a circus, and the cast of a new television show gave him enough of an excuse to mount one.

————

Toward the end of *Disneyland*'s first season, Walt had called Bill Walsh to announce, "I'm taking you off the evening show." The producer said that was great news: "doing an hour show every week was murder." Disney, amused, said he was shifting him to one that ran "an hour every *day.*" And "with children."

Walsh found himself in charge of *The Mickey Mouse Club*, which featured youngsters who would be known as Mouseketeers. He started interviewing excited preadolescent candidates while he planned a variety show with a different theme each day. He was a good sport about it, asserting that although "kind of hysterical," the work "was fun because we'd have meetings in the mornings with the kids, then we'd have the writers, then we'd have the guys who did the sets and costumes . . . and about three in the afternoon we'd shoot it."

What they shot first aired on October 8, 1955, when America got an explanation for those capering little buckaroos who had puzzled Bob Cummings during *Dateline: Disneyland.* Three-quarters of the television sets in America were tuned to ABC at five o'clock during the weekday evenings that followed: *The Mickey Mouse Club* was as big a hit as *Davy Crockett*, and more durable. A few weeks later the Nielsen report had the show "completely dominating regular daytime television," and within a year it had gained an audience of nineteen million.

Walsh, as baffled as he'd been by the Crockett fad, had no idea that seven million of those viewers were adults. Stopping by a bar one evening, he was amazed to see "at five o'clock all the drunks would stand up with their hand over their heart and sing the Mickey Mouse Club theme song."

The grown-ups in the show both came from the Disney Studio. Jimmie Dodd, in the music department, had an unforced friendliness that got him the job of host. Timeless show business custom demanded he have a comic sidekick. Roy Williams had spent twenty-six years as a studio artist, when one day he caught Disney's eye and won his unflattering approval: "He looked up at me and said, 'Say, you're fat and funny-looking. I'm going to put you on and call you the Big Mooseketeer.' The next thing I knew I was acting."

The Big Mooseketeer contributed more than being a foil for Jimmie Dodd. For *The Karnival Kid*—the 1929 cartoon where the mouse first finds his voice to yell "hot dogs"—Williams had animated a sequence in which, by way of tipping his hat to Minnie, Mickey doffs the top of his head, ears and all.

The vignette stayed with Williams for a quarter century, and once he was embroiled in the birth of *The Mickey Mouse Club*, he devised a skullcap equipped with those two black circles that are recognized the world around. Disney had great luck with hats that season: his park was soon selling twenty thousand Mickey Mouse ears every day.

As filming of the show's first season neared its end, Disney planned to use his popular—and now temporarily at liberty—Mouseketeers as an additional draw for the circus he'd been planning. After all, *The Mickey Mouse Club* had featured every Thursday as "Circus Day," so this was a perfectly natural extension.

C. V. Wood didn't think so. He was feeling the weight of the park's debt as fully as Disney did (it was busy helping wreck Wood's marriage), and he did not have his boss's whole-souled vision to lighten the burden. When Disney told him about this new venture, he reacted violently.

What possible addition to the park, he wanted to know, could be more expensive than a circus—especially since Disney was sure to apply the same perfectionism he had to the decorative architectural ironwork that should have been plastic.

Disney said the circus would be insurance against an ebbing cash flow if attendance dwindled during the Christmas season, as it always did at Knott's Berry Farm. Wood found the idea ridiculous: What kind of insurance was an attraction that would cost more to mount than it was likely to bring in? He began lecturing his boss on the necessity of making a profit.

Perhaps the only thing Disney enjoyed less than receiving testy instructions from a subordinate was having one of his ideas dismissed untried. Wood knew that as well as any of Disney's employees did by now, but he wouldn't let up, and the two men stood glaring at each other through a haze of mutual anger their shared exhaustion must have made all the more bitter.

Wood got in the last word: "No, Walt. There ain't no way. We don't need no six-hundred-thousand-dollar fucking circus right now. Period."

Disney walked away from the fight. Wood called Roy to get an ally in the dispute, but Walt's brother had long since ceased saying no in Disneyland financial controversies. Wood gave up: "Jesus Christ, Roy, if you tell me to do it I guess I don't have any choice."

He didn't, and the Mickey Mouse Club Circus opened just before Thanksgiving. Joe Fowler said, "My God! If I ever see a circus again, it'll be twice too soon. . . . All superimposed on everything else we had. And how [Walt] loved it! And it was a damned good circus, too. But my God, the problems."

The problems didn't come from the acts; Disney hired the best, and signed on two seasoned circus owners to manage them. The first performer he acquired was Professor George Keller, who had been traveling with a squadron of big cats that he billed as Keller's Jungle Killers (for their Disneyland appearance, the name was declawed to become Professor George Keller and His Feline Fantastics).

Keller really was a professor, head of the Department of Visual Arts at Teacher's College in Bloomsburg, Pennsylvania. His subsequent career began when a school friend, remembering Keller's oft-expressed fondness for circuses, and especially for their animal acts, played an expensive and potentially lethal practical joke.

One day in 1932 Keller got a call from the Bloomsburg railway express office: "Get down here right away." He found awaiting him "a wooden crate on the floor, and the head of a full-grown mountain lion was sticking up through the top. He had chewed a hole in the wood big enough to poke his head through." Keller's frat buddy had painted on the crate, "HERE KELLER—Train This."

Keller did, in his garage, and, thus emboldened, over the years acquired leopards, lions, panthers, and tigers. In 1950 he left teaching to travel with an act that was filmed for *The Mickey Mouse Club*, which brought him to Disney's attention.

Like any proper circus, the Mickey Mouse Club Circus was held outdoors under canvas. Actually, under vinyl, but in circus tradition Disney promoted the $48,000 red-and-white big top as the largest striped tent ever made. Colors notwithstanding, it was undeniably large; the bleachers beneath it could accommodate 2,500 spectators.

The circuses of Disney's youth announced their arrival in town with the gaudiest parade they could mount, and even the most modest ones had a few lavishly carved and gilded wagons containing the animals.

Disney, scrupulous as ever, found and restored nine of these magnificent behemoths. The opening day parade up Main Street provided a grisly portent of the show's fortunes. Among the wagons was a beauty from the once-famous Carl Hagenbeck Circus. It held a tiger and a panther, separated by a wooden partition. The wagon had been built in 1905, and the years had told on it. Halfway to the tent, the tiger managed to batter a hole in the partition, and thrust a paw through. The panther chewed it off.

The ever-present, ever-vigilant Fowler was on hand. "My boys tackled the panther with two-by-fours to get him off, and by the time we finished we had destroyed fifteen thousand dollars' worth of cats."

The circus, which required a separate admission fee, usually played to stands less than a quarter full. With his Main Street, Disney had taken something familiar and worked an imaginative change on it. His circus was too literal an embodiment of a familiar tradition to lure people away from the fresh pleasures of the park.

Fowler said that was the "first time we learned this lesson. People came to Disneyland to see Disneyland. They weren't interested in a circus. . . . People just wanted to see Disney and Disneyland." As Disney finally admitted, the show "is not unique enough to be in the park."

The circus died with the year, having lost perhaps $125,000 (Van Arsdale France thought it was as much as $400,000), but Disney liked Keller and his cats, and kept their act going for several months. And the lion tamer got another benefit from his Disneyland engagement. When he had checked into the Disneyland Hotel on November 18—one of its earliest guests—he was greeted at the reception desk by Ginny Lowry, a singer who was moonlighting there between engagements. He married her.

———

The failed circus did not put much of a dent in the park's larger success. The fierce summer days gave way to September's milder ones, and before the month was out the millionth visitor had stepped onto Main Street.

That guest would not have suffered the poorly managed lines and the malfunctioning rides that marred the first weeks. Just as the plantings were flourishing (technicians attending the Jungle Cruise audio equipment already had to carry machetes to clear away the foliage around the speakers), so was the rest of the park. A travel writer from Maine paid it a terse down east tribute: "Disneyland is a commercial proposition from start to finish, so don't go with an empty pocketbook, but it's worth all you care to spend." He wasn't alone; an early survey showed that 93.7 of the visitors felt they got their money's worth.

That satisfaction reflected itself in the revenues. In 1954, when the park was under construction, the company had brought in $11 million; in 1955, with it up and running, the take was $24.5 million. Walt Disney Productions had not been in so sunny a state since the heady months following the release of *Snow White*.

After its first weeks, Disneyland faced no real threat of failure. Now the work lay both in refining the park and, just as important, defining it. Van Arsdale France wrote of the staff in these early days, "There were many who were just out for a buck or who just needed the job. But Disneyland had a way of making true believers out of many people who might have been cynical at the beginning."

One of those converts was Jack Lindquist.

During Disney's prosperous September, he felt his park had become sufficiently mature to require an ad manager.

The job went to Lindquist, whose Kelvinator connection got him invited to opening day, where he'd seen his son kidnapped by the canal boat voyage, and left in disgust. So he surprised himself when he took the advertising manager job the moment it was offered. "I was shocked by my own response, but I think it goes back to opening day. Even though it was a debacle, I still remained totally intrigued by Disneyland itself."

He had to win the approval of Card Walker, who was in charge of the company's advertising. "I was plain awed to meet a Disney executive. Here I was, a 28-year-old kid who had done okay working at an ad agency, but had never met anybody big from an important corporation."

The two spoke for about forty-five minutes. "Card said he understood my responsibilities as a husband and father but $135-per-week salary was tops." This represented "a measly $10-per-week increase and a 70-mile commute each way. I would have to sell my home and buy a new one in a pretty unfamiliar area. But what the heck? Disney might look good on a resume in a few years. So I rolled the dice and gave my two-weeks notice."

His welcome from Walt came at a distance, and was not warm. "Two days later I got a call . . . telling me that Card had spoken to Walt, who informed Card that the ad manager's job at Disneyland was budgeted at $125 a week, and he would not go higher." (In fairness to Disney, he wasn't the tightfisted one: months later Lindquist learned that Walker himself had put on that $125 cap.)

There were other irritants. Lindquist discovered that, like any shop clerk in the Main Street era, he had to work till noon on Saturdays, and his first day on the job, September 26, was scary. He opened his desk drawers to find them "stuffed with $53,000 in unpaid bills." Nobody else would take responsibility for this alarming cache, and Lindquist had to wade right into the maddening task of finding out what the bills were for, and which were legitimate. No wonder that "I started at Disneyland slightly disappointed and skeptical."

But he was young and resilient, and so were his new colleagues. "We were all in our twenties. We were very confident and anxious to prove ourselves, to make more money, to get promoted, to be recognized, and to be accepted. And we were all intrigued, fascinated, captivated, and committed to this wonderful new place. Maybe we didn't know totally why, but we all knew we were lucky to be working at Disneyland at this point in our careers. We became good friends. We worked. We played together. We horsed around together. We drank together. We ate lunch at Harley's Green Tent, a lunch wagon in the backstage area that served as an employee cafeteria."

His office in City Hall gave him a view of the infant Disney traditions—the band marching down Main Street in the mornings, the flag retreat ceremony in Town Square at day's end—and Disneyland began to seep into his spirit. As the year declined toward December, Lindquist was well embarked on the journey that would lead to him becoming the park's first president.

During his four months he had found that he liked Disneyland best late at night, when he felt "alone in my own little city." In those peaceful hours, he was happiest on Main Street. The various lands "have their own character and personality when empty," but "Main Street is the most magical and pristine."

On Christmas Eve in 1955, his day's work done, he took a walk along Main before heading home. It was early evening, carolers were moving through the park, "and on this night, with the garlands strung between the lampposts, the wreaths strung in all the store windows, and the huge Christmas tree in Town Square, the atmosphere drew me in."

As he strolled past the quiet, glowing buildings, "a family caught my attention, and as the mother, father, and their ten-year-old son and younger daughter walked down Main Street, I followed them. They were dressed neatly but not stylish; the father and son wore overalls. The mother wore a cotton dress and coat. They all held hands."

When the family paused at the Christmas tree in Town Square, Jack saw the girl tug her mother's arm and heard her say, "Mom, this really was better than having Santa Claus."

Lindquist realized "that Santa wasn't bringing them presents. The parents must have told their children that if they went to Disneyland, Santa couldn't bring presents."

For the new advertising manager, "this one brief moment proved to be my most meaningful memory of the park because it symbolized what we mean to people: We are not a cure for cancer, we are not going to save the world, but if we can make people that happy for a few hours a day, then we are doing something worthwhile."

40

PLUSSING

The new year dawned auspiciously for Disney, with his park regularly drawing crowds 50 percent above the most optimistic projections. He needed more room, and more attractions.

First, though, he wanted to do some housecleaning among the staff. Shortly after opening day, he had collared Wood to ask, "C.V., do you know there are *pay* toilets in *all* the park's restrooms."

Wood said he didn't; he'd had a lot going on.

"C.V., I want you to see that they're removed before tomorrow. It's terrible—like inviting guests into your house and then having them pay to use the bathroom."

The hostile question was an augury. Woody said, "I knew I was in big trouble because he'd never called me C.V. before."

It's entirely possible Wood *did* know about the pay toilets: he was looking to make the park money however he could, and he didn't miss much.

That small contretemps reflected greater friction between the two men. Buzz Price said, "Walt didn't like Woody. He was too fast-moving for Walt. C.V. was capable of making a very fast deal. He wasn't corrupt, he was just fast-moving. Walt didn't trust him."

Price was always fond of Wood; but in some matters, like the kickbacks, he probably *was* corrupt. Roger Broggie's son, Michael, was perhaps closer to the mark when he said, "C.V. was not only devious. He was also very bright. He could keep a lot of what he was doing secret." There was a manipulative, almost sinister energy in his whooping, devil-may-care glad-handing and his big Texas howdys.

Disney, the least effusive of men, had tired early of the Lone Star bluster. "Wood and Walt did not get along," wrote Price. "It was not hard to see why. Walt was not amused when it came to off-color jokes. Walt's morals were conservative. Wood on the other hand was fast and loose with the ladies and told yeasty off color stories. He was a bit of a con man, albeit a charming one. Walt reacted to him the way the farmer reacts to the fast talking city slicker. It was a completely immiscible personality conflict."

Moreover, Disney had watched Wood hiring Texans, along with his Bomber friends, to build what was looking more and more like a private fiefdom. Disneyland had only one boss, and that boss did not welcome what he saw as growing infringements on his authority.

Van Arsdale France believed "it was inevitable that Walt and Wood came to the parting of the ways. They were both men of strong convictions, and at times the convictions went in opposite ways." France remembered Disney being asked what he thought was his greatest accomplishment. "To be able to build an organization—and hang on to it." France saw that "to a great extent, Woody was developing his *own* organization . . . with his Texans—this was a threat."

In January, Walt told Roy, "Fire him."

"So in one week," France wrote, "Wood was holding his regular meetings as usual . . . with an office crowded every minute of the day. And, just about overnight, he was out as General Manager, and Jack Sayers was in the job."

On Wood's last day, Sayers and France went to say goodbye. The office was strangely quiet, France remembered: "The sycophants and favor seekers were gone." The men shared a few glasses of the Old Loudmouth, and then Woody went off down Main Street for the last time.

France noticed that after his "departure, many Texans immediately learned to speak good English, and several stayed on to do important jobs."

———

Others followed Wood. Gabe Scognamillo, who'd had contentious dealings with Disney when he held the unenviable job of designing amorphous Tomorrowland, got fired, as did Wade Rubottom, who had quarreled with Ruth Shellhorn over the Main Street plantings.

Ruth Shellhorn left, too. Despite her thorny relations with the Evans brothers and other contractors, and all those lunches she'd had to eat alone, she'd hoped to stay on. Her work had been superb from beginning to end, and it seems strange that she was cut loose. Except that this was the mid-1950s, and she wasn't one of the boys. She went on to an increasingly successful career, leaving the park a valuable legacy. Seven decades later, Disneyland visitors are still shaded, beguiled, and comforted by what she built.

———

The park was developing customs that would jell into what might be called its personality. Although only twenty-one, Marty Sklar played a significant part in forming them.

He was the UCLA junior who had rescued Fess Parker from the crowd on Black Sunday. After that summer, he returned to school to graduate, and immediately rejoined the park as part of its embryonic publicity team.

His office was in the Town Square police station, just to the left of Lindquist's in City Hall. A small incident there "influenced much of my future Disney career—and, I believe, had a key role in communicating to the public about Walt Disney's Magic Kingdom."

One day Sklar neglected to lock the door after entering his office, and moments later visitors were exploring the station house. "Suddenly I was confronted by questions about the park. . . . As I pondered the half-dozen questions those early guests asked, it occurred to me that this was a prime source of useful information for those of us charged with making the public aware of what Disneyland was all about. . . . From that open-door day forward, whenever I was in the police station office, my front door was never locked."

Not long after, Sklar was hanging around the main gate eavesdropping on the customers when he got "the biggest surprise." Again and again he heard, "I want to go on the Jungle Cruise, the Rocket to the

Moon, and the *Mark Twain* Riverboat—*but I don't want to go on any rides.*"

What? The park's main draw was its rides. Then Sklar understood: "Walt had done such a great job of telling his television audience about Disneyland that the public had separated its offerings from the old amusement parks. . . . In their minds, the whips, shoot-the-chutes, whirl-a-gigs, and lose-your-lunch thrills of those amusement parks were the *rides*—which Disneyland did not have."

Armed with this insight, Sklar led his colleagues in inventing "a new vocabulary to describe what you would encounter at Disneyland." "Ride" was replaced by more stirring synonyms: "The key new terms were *adventures*, *experiences*, *attractions*, and of course *stories*."

Year after year Sklar stood guard against the humdrum monosyllable: "I was the last word on the copy issues for publicity and marketing . . . and my red pen eliminated the word 'ride' wherever I found it."

As late as 2008, he was still fighting the term: "When we only describe our attractions as 'rides' we fall into the category of Six Flags, Knott's, Universal, etc. describing their stuff. We should rise above them (because our stuff does!) and describe what we do as 'attractions, adventures, immersive experiences, and of course stories.' . . . When you are creating Disney Magic, the words to describe it should support the magical experiences!"

Only Mr. Toad was allowed to keep his Wild Ride's original name: to this day, it flaunts its exception on the facade of Toad Hall.

The use of such genteelisms percolated throughout the park. If the rides needed more elegant bynames, so did much else. As Van Arsdale France had decreed in the very first classes of what became Disney University, "customers" were to be called "guests"; those who sold them ice cream or settled them into the Autopia cars, "hosts" and "hostesses." Many labels were drawn from the theater. On even the busiest days, the close-packed guests would form not a crowd but an "audience." Ticket takers and ride operators did not have jobs, but "roles"; they were "cast members," and when they escaped their audience for a break, they took it "offstage," usually in the "backstage" area. (Any musical performance that smacked of the still-suspect rock 'n' roll received the slightly emetic cognomen of "humdinger.")

The park as a whole was "the show," which the audience first entered through the "outer lobby" (the parking lot), then by passing beneath the tracks (no freshly coined euphemisms attached themselves to nineteenth-century railroading nomenclature) into Town Square (the "inner lobby"), which led to "center stage" (Main Street, and all the lands).

The theater metaphor had weight behind it because the hosts and hostesses *were* actors, playing a demanding daylong role of being unfailingly kind, friendly, humorous, concerned, and delighted to see any of the thousands of audience members who happened onto their part of the stage.

———

This drive to distinguish Disneyland from its plebeian rivals soon spread to the fundamental issue of money. Every attraction demanded a ticket, and every ticket was sold separately. This meant that visitors constantly had to reach into their purses, their pockets, their wallets; the adult guest perforce continually had cash in mind.

Van Arsdale France wrote, "We had a major price increase resistance in 1955. The rumor was that it cost $40 to visit Disneyland. . . . To combat that rumor, Ed Ettinger, head of public relations, came up with the idea of a ticket book. Then we could advertise: 'Admission and eight rides for $2.50.' Ed worried and said, 'I'll either be a goat or a hero.' He was a hero."

The books were introduced as a monthlong promotion in mid-October, and stayed for a quarter century. They changed the experience of Disneyland more than might be expected of a small sheaf of scrip.

What they replaced was the faintly oily oblongs of thin pasteboard familiar to any county fairgoer. Instead, the buyer got a trim little booklet, nicely printed by the Globe Ticket Company, with pastel leaves that granted entry to the attractions, which were, as before, graded from "A" to "C." The booklets offered discounts on the prices of all the rides, but more important, the visitors' easy deployment of them after the initial purchase whispered that these attractions were theirs to enjoy free.

The forty-dollar rumor didn't frighten off many guests. Three and a half million had come by the time 1955 turned into 1956, which would bring four million more. That 13 percent increase was good, and Disney was determined to keep it growing by what he called "plussing," his term for improving what was already there and making constant additions. Introducing one of his television shows, he began, "It has been said that Disneyland will never be complete—in fact, *I* said it."

In fact, Marty Sklar said it.

Sklar—who would stay at Disneyland for fifty years and become head of Imagineering after it evolved from WED—got off to a strong start by writing copy Disney liked. He went on to perfect a voice that the boss adopted as his own.

Years after Disneyland embarked on its never-ending expansion program, Sklar articulated what was happening in a statement that is now usually attributed to Disney himself.

"The way I see it, Disneyland will never be finished. It's something we can keep developing and adding to. A motion picture is different. Once it's wrapped up and sent out for processing, we're through with it. If there are things that could be improved, we can't do anything about it anymore. I've always wanted to work on something alive, something that keeps growing. We've got that in Disneyland."

Right away, the park grew an Indian village, inhabited by true Native Americans drawn from as many as seventeen tribes. (When, in 1957, the Soviet press reported that Frontierland was holding Indians in captivity to amuse the capitalist visitors, Chief Riley Sunrise retorted, "Captivity my eye! How many Russians make a hundred and twenty-five bucks a week?")

Under the pressure of time, Disney condescended to buy an off-the-shelf German amusement company ride called the Roto-Jet. After some hasty cosmetic changes, its cars, which revolved around a central tower, entered Tomorrowland service in early April 1956 as the Astro-Jets, the first significant addition to the park.

This perfunctory attraction soon was joined by an ambitious and entirely house-built one. Considering how much he had just spent on his park, the Rainbow Caverns Mine Train shows Disney at his boldest. He put out half a million dollars for another train ride, largely the work of Harper Goff, with locomotives designed by Roger Broggie. They were electric, to Disney's frustration; he'd wanted more live steam, but in a rare interference with Disneyland operations, Orange County authorities decreed that as the steam engines already running there were still unlicensed, he had to make do with them.

Pulling a string of six ore cars that seated ten people each, the engines—there were four of them—departed Rainbow Ridge, a Gold Rush–era California mining town, to traverse a desert made romantic with Coyote Rock, Dead Man's Spring, Horse Thief Canyon, and the like. Its taupe-and-pink geology included a natural bridge that carried the pack mules over the tracks, and Balancing Rocks, boulders that rolled back and forth on seesawing horizontal stone shelves but never quite fell. After passing the Devil's Paint Pots (sand craters filled with bubbling blues and mauves), the trains entered the cool darkness of what the publicity department called "an unforgettable spectacle of multicolored waterfalls deep inside the mysteries of Rainbow Caverns."

Disney thought the spectacle unforgettable enough to require the advent of a "D" ticket, and the mine train ratified the spend-money-to-make-money adage by establishing a pattern that would hold throughout Disneyland's early years: every new attraction boosted attendance by 10 percent.

That desert also gave a hint of how strongly the park was already acting on the national consciousness when, in 1958, William Belknap Jr., writing for the *National Geographic* about the "flaming yellow, tan, brick red, and orange" rock formations of Bryce Canyon, said, "My wife summed it up best. 'It all looks like something by Walt Disney.' " The park had been there for three years, the canyon for sixty million; that the latter should bring to mind the former, rather than the other way around, is remarkable.

Disney kept plussing in large ways (a sky ride, the first of its kind in America, whose 2,400-foot cable carried pairs of visitors in aluminum buckets between Fantasyland and Tomorrowland) and small (a misguided effort to interest women in Tomorrowland by getting the Crane company to create "the Bathroom of Tomorrow," which featured yellow and gold fixtures created by the industrial designer Henry Dreyfuss).

The most impressive—and enduring—additions, ones that brought the park to its maturity, came in 1959.

"By the spring of 1958," Bob Gurr wrote, "Walt had built his WED Enterprises into a pretty big design powerhouse. He was starting to get some very expensive ideas. . . . Looking back in recent years, I'm still amazed at how much work was done so fast back then in 1958–9. I think this was Walt's golden time in building Disneyland. When you look at all the complicated civil engineering, the massive amounts of concrete work, to say nothing of engineering from scratch . . . totally new rides, this was unprecedented in the theme park industry."

41

THE MOUNTAIN AND THE MONORAIL

After excavating Sleeping Beauty Castle's moat, the earthmovers had left behind a twenty-foot pile of dirt. In a surprisingly feeble attempt to make this heap of detritus appealing, the park leveled off the top, installed a few picnic benches, and called it Holiday Hill.

Nobody went there, but it did offer a recreation that would prove as popular as Disneyland itself in the years to come. Bob Gurr wrote that although Holiday Hill was "just a lump . . . one of the gardeners was growing marijuana on top, and had been growing it for about a year before Bill Evans, the landscape architect, went up there." It tickled Gurr that what remains Disneyland's most visible feature "started out as a marijuana farm."

Despite his initial rejection of conventional amusement park attractions, Disney had been thinking that perhaps he did need something that went faster than Mr. Toad's motorcars. When one of his regular tours of the park with Joe Fowler brought them to the guestless crest of Holiday Hill, he said, "You know, Joe, why don't we make some snow and have a toboggan ride here?"

Fowler said it was hot in Southern California, so the snow would melt; melting, it would cause severe drainage problems; and a sopping attraction would be all but impossible to maintain. Of course, Disney knew all this. His only response was to begin calling the unsightly mound "Snow Hill."

Around that time, one of his lieutenants, crossing between Fantasyland and Tomorrowland, came upon him in an unusual posture of repose, sitting on a bench staring into empty air. The man knew his boss well enough to interrupt his reverie: "What are you looking at?"

"My mountain."

He found it in 1958, when he spent a week on the set of *Third Man on the Mountain*, a film about a young man determined to scale the slopes that had killed his father. The fictitious mountain in the movie is called the Citadel, but it was the Matterhorn that Disney had in mind, and during his stay in the shadow of its canted peak, he sent home an order Napoleonic in its decisive brevity. Victor Greene, one of his art directors, received a postcard: on the front, a photo of the Matterhorn; on the back, a two-word message—"Build this."

Nobody thought Disney was kidding, and work started immediately. It began in the model shop, thrown into the unwelcoming arms of Harriet Burns, who "thought the Matterhorn was crazy. I said, 'Good grief, a Matterhorn in the middle of Disneyland!' We just thought, well gosh, there's a *real* Matterhorn, so why would you want to bring it here?"

Fred Joerger was tied up with another project, and Burns had to start in alone, with little to guide her. "I worked with Vic Greene," she said. "We had some pictures from *National Geographic*, a double-page spread from *Life* magazine, and a couple of postcards."

She made the first, foot-high model in clay, "like a birthday cake, in layers so if one layer was wrong we could take the layer out and put a new layer in." That small model was succeeded by larger ones until she had "a big guy on a big platform." With Joerger now on the project, they made several casts from the big guy, and "sent one down that was all shaped up. We painted it. We did everything—all the trees, all the planter pockets, all the plumbing. It looked good."

However good it looked, this seems a casual beginning for what would become the tallest structure in Orange County, and the most complex.

Designed on a one-hundredth scale (Switzerland's Matterhorn: 14,700 feet; Disney's Matterhorn: 147 feet), the new structure was, like most big, modern buildings, built on a steel frame. Unlike any other modern building, few of the 2,175 girders making up that frame were the same length. They supported a jigsaw of plywood cladding frosted with concrete shaped into Alpine cragginess and artfully tinted. John Hench believed the coloring was the mountain's most important element: "That guests accept the notion of a miniature Alpine peak covered with snow in the middle of Southern California is a triumph of the Imagineer's art. The key effect that makes the illusion persuasive is the astonishingly realistic silvery-white blue-shadowed snow."

Fine so far, but the mountain had to *do* something. Joe Fowler told Ed Morgan and Karl Bacon to build a roller coaster in it. Actually, two roller coasters to handle the expected traffic; they would career down from the peak in rival spirals.

The partners worked under strictures no roller-coaster builder had ever before confronted. The traditional coaster's wooden trellising might be as high or as long as its builders wished. This one had to fit inside an eccentric skyscraper.

"We had to bridge the distances between the supports they gave us," said Morgan. "They gave us a preliminary draft on the building. However, we started to build the ride before they were very far along with the building. They gave us ten months to design the two rides in the building." Bacon, a long way out from sawing holes in warplane gas tanks, said, "In working on the layout, the goal was [to] establish the friction slope for the ride, taking into account the various radii, inclines, and dips."

Arrow could build the track, and cram it into the mountain, but how could it satisfy Disney's further demand that it simulate the smooth surge of a bobsled run? Ever since the first modern roller coasters had started buffeting people at Coney Island in the 1880s, they had been close cousins to any railroad, their metal wheels running on metal rails. The ride was jarring—that was part of the point—but it wouldn't do for what Disney had in mind.

In three words, Morgan described how Arrow solved the problem: "Steel tube rail."

Tubes could be bent into tighter turns than could regular track, but that was only part of their virtue. Morgan said, "We sure weren't going to run steel wheels on a steel rail." Too noisy.

Rubber was the obvious solution, but the partners thought they could do better. "Polyurethane came from Germany as spoils of war after World War II," said Morgan, "and DuPont bought the rights from the federal government. Polyurethane rolls with a lot less effort than rubber does. A rubber tire deforms differently and loses more energy to heat than polyurethane. . . . We were conducting tests on small six- or eight-foot long pipe sections. We were loading them and running them twenty-four hours a day. We were doing the same with nylon and other things."

They liked the polyurethane wheels best, "but we had our necks out a long, long way, because DuPont said, 'We just don't know.'" Then the company pledged, "off-the-record, that they would help us if we got into a real bind." Working with DuPont, Arrow developed a wholly satisfactory wheel.

The sled that would run on those wheels was the child either of Arrow or Bob Gurr. Both claim authorship. Arrow says the Disney people were too busy to take on the car; Gurr says he did, and all by himself: "I patterned the guest seating design after the Swiss bobsled arrangement. This allowed folks to snuggle together, a plan that later proved delightful to young couples. We sent my bobsled sketches up to Arrow for them to mock up a full-size car shape."

Morgan and Bacon claim they never saw any such sketches. The old maxim holds that success has many fathers, but failure is an orphan. The Matterhorn bobsleds were a complete success, and the Alpine plunge remains as popular today as it was when it opened.

More than that, the ride transformed the outdoor amusement industry. Rather than lurching along on top of the tracks, the cars nestled between them. Sklar said, "It was a totally new kind of roller coaster. You're in the ground, you actually feel like you're part of the earth."

And the heavens. The continuous tubing allowed coasters to hit well over one hundred miles an hour, and corkscrew their riders through steel lariats four hundred feet high.

The revolutionary advancement took a decade to begin to spread, but today every nation with an amusement park has a descendant of Ed and Karl's bobsleds.

With the Matterhorn finished, a weary Fowler pleaded, "The next time, Walt, we have to build a mountain, let's let God do it." The Matterhorn had cost its builder $1.5 million ($14 million now), but it was only part of his plans in that exorbitant season.

Disney had always wanted a monorail; the word had been in the air from the park's beginning, which is why Art Linkletter misused it in connection with the Peter Pan ride. Disney had seen one for the first time in the early 1950s in Germany, where the Wuppertal Suspension Railway had been carrying passengers over an eight-mile route above the Wupper River since 1901 (and still does, despite the intervention of two world wars). Walt was immediately won over, but not Lillian. The cars hung beneath the rail, swaying from side to side to a degree that gave Mrs. Disney motion sickness.

Disney still wanted a monorail, and so did the Swedish industrialist Axel Wenner Grenn, a millionaire many times over from his investment in Electrolux. At the end of World War II he found himself with a fortune in German holdings, which the struggling government would not let him bring back to Sweden. "He got mad," said Bob Gurr, "and arbitrarily picked a project and said, 'Okay, we will improve the monorail, and we'll spend the money until it's gone.'"

The money lasted until 1958, when his Alweg (an acronym formed from his name) company had a prototype running three miles outside of Cologne. That summer, Walt and Lillian were motoring through Germany when they came to a strange-looking bridge spanning the road— and, crossing the bridge, a monorail train. Disney, astonished, braked to a stop. Bob Gurr, who soon would be consumed by monorails, said, "I've often thought that ten seconds either way and Walt would have driven right by and never have seen that thing. To my knowledge, at that time there had been no publicity for this train that anybody had ever seen."

Disney immediately dispatched Joe Fowler and Roger Broggie to Cologne, followed, a few weeks later, by Gurr. He was impressed by the improvement the Alweg represented over the Wuppertal Suspension Railway. "Rather than have a metal beam that was hollow, with all the truck equipment inside of it, they ran this as a regular rubber-tired vehicle on top of the beam, with side wheels along the beam. This became known as the 'German saddle bag' method," because the cars straddled the track.

The problem with what would be billed as Tomorrowland's "train of the future" was that the Alweg cars were boxy and drab. Gurr remembered thinking, "What in the world am I going to do with this ugly loaf of bread with a slot in the bottom sitting on a stick?"

Working around the constraints imposed by the beam and the motors, he started to design a train acceptable to the imagined aesthetics of the future. "I knew that the way you can make something look slender is to put some 'tumblehome' (an automotive design term [and, centuries before that, a shipwright's] meaning 'tuck it in' or 'curve it' to improve the appearance) on it. Something just plain and straight can look terrible, but with a little shaping, it gets to look good."

He got the train looking good—low and sleek, with the appearance of speed even when it was at rest—"but then I wondered how I'd hide the ugly open front on the thing."

A movie serial of his youth helped him. "I remembered how much I had enjoyed Buck Rogers and Doctor Zarkov riding around in their rocket ship with their big windshield and portholes and big fin along the top, and the blaster nozzles out the back. Now Buck's rocket had always landed on a planet or asteroid someplace by skidding down to it. The ship would land in the sand on its runners, like a sled. So I thought, 'Hey . . . that'll do it!' and I brought the skirt around in front like Buck Rogers' rocket, and it hid the slot perfectly."

Gurr made a presentation drawing showing two of his reconfigured trains gliding past each other on their "beamways," and "brought it to a meeting in the Animation building. I put the drawing up on the wall, and Walt walked in and just looked at it. His eyes lit up and he reached out and tapped it and said, 'Bobby, can you build that?' And I said, 'Yeah. . . .' Walt just looked around at everybody and said, 'Okay.' And that was it . . . end of meeting."

Gurr took his plans to Cologne in early November of 1958. "We did the whole thing in three weeks while the Germans had worked on theirs for years . . . but that was what it was like around Walt."

The meetings with the German engineers were stormy. Back in Burbank, WED had changed not only the shape of the cars, but a good deal more. "What we planned to build was not the inner workings of the Alweg Monorail, but something based upon available parts that we could purchase in Los Angeles." For all its innovative zeal, WED had a saying: "Don't invent it, just go buy it."

Gurr felt some sympathy when "the guy from Mannheim was sent home in a fury." After all, "from their viewpoint, they had spent years (and millions of Marks) getting the technology to where it worked so that Disney's Roger Broggie (a film technician) and Bob Gurr (an Autopia car sketch artist) could do a different monorail and made theirs look bad."

Theirs wouldn't look so bad if Disney's didn't get built. The spring of 1959 was busy everywhere in the park, but especially so with the monorail. When the outside contractor for the cars fell behind schedule, Broggie moved every half-completed shell to a studio sound stage and said, "Bob—you are now the production manager."

The man who, a few years earlier, had only wanted to draw cars found himself responsible for hastening the birth of a brand-new kind of engineering. "There was no time at this stage to make any more drawings. I knew what I wanted to do anywhere along the train, so I'd tell a guy, 'Okay, here's what I want!' and I'd make a sketch, walk over and tape it on the side of the car close to the place where the work was needed. I'd go back to the desk, and the next guy was waiting there. The machine shop was about four hundred feet away, and I'd write out requisitions for parts, and a guy on a bicycle would run over there, and they'd get the parts purchased and run them back and put them in a box by my stand. Everybody was cooperating, and everybody was trusting each other, but nobody knew what the design was until it was done."

As the tempo increased, Gurr had a rope stretched across the sound stage door; only those working within were permitted to cross it.

One day Disney came by with Mickey Clark, his "finance guy." Gurr met them at the rope, and they spoke briefly. As the two left, Clark turned back and said to Gurr, "Walt doesn't understand how you do this, but here—" He handed him an envelope.

Back inside the sound stage, Gurr opened it, "and there was a thousand dollars in there. I thought to myself how much Walt wanted the Monorail finished, but while I had the rope up he wouldn't come in there."

Disney didn't entirely keep his distance. At one point he ordered the monorail's driver moved out of sight. "I don't want any passengers lookin' down the greasy neck of a motorman." Gurr guessed he was remembering one of the less nostalgic aspects of life back in Marceline: "I'm sure Walt was thinking about how it was on the streetcars, where the motormen always had dirty necks."

Precast concrete pylons sprouted 110 feet apart throughout the park, some as high as thirty feet above it, some only five feet off the ground. They were knit together along their tops by the beams holding the rail that would feed six hundred volts of current to each train's quartet of hundred-horsepower motors.

The motors that drove the train of tomorrow were a relic of Main Street yesterday. Gurr wrote that "Lee Adams (the chief engineer at the studio) was a Westinghouse guy, and he had access to some used Westinghouse DC [direct current] motors that were really cheap! There were still a lot of streetcars in those days, which were simple DC equipment, and it was easy to buy parts and stick them together."

Despite the reliability of equipment in use for half a century, "the Monorail did not make an actual trouble-free lap around the track until the night before Walt was to introduce his new monorail system on live TV."

42

DISNEYLAND '59

Disney was going to do it again. Despite his sometime dictum that "you can't top pigs with pigs," he planned to celebrate his expansion of the park with another hour-and-a-half live television show, Art Linkletter and all.

If *Dateline: Disneyland* introduced an ambitious, not-quite-ready newcomer, *Disneyland '59* was a statement that all the early promises had been kept.

The show aired on June 15, and opens just where *Dateline* left off: Walt and Art are standing in front of Sleeping Beauty Castle.

Linkletter speaks first: "Well, Walt?"

"Yeah?"

"How do you feel?"

"Like an expectant father—nervous, but wonderful."

For some reason they synchronize their wristwatches, and Linkletter says, "This kinda reminds me of something we did four years ago."

And so it does, but with a loftier guest list. Linkletter makes the introductions at the outset from the main reviewing stand, where the audience includes the consul general of Switzerland ("Come to see who stole the Matterhorn") and some high navy brass, who are there to dedicate the third new attraction, a submarine ride in which eight craft patterned on America's new nuclear fleet explore "liquid space." In 1955 Linkletter was excited to spot Danny Thomas as a visitor; now he introduced Vice President Richard Nixon, who would officiate over the monorail's first run.

Unlike *Dateline*, *Disneyland '59* comes off without a hitch (save that the flag planted atop the Matterhorn is Norwegian and not Swiss). It is also not nearly as interesting.

Perhaps that was inevitable. This show is not an urgent plea to come admire the new baby, but a complacent declaration of success. Almost half of it is given over to a triumphal parade, opening, somewhat strangely, with a band playing the Confederate anthem "Bonnie Blue Flag," while a pageant of nations begins with Japan (parasols) and Austria (lederhosen). Spain comes by in a crackle of castanets, then Mexico, then Scotland (bagpipes, highland fling), the Firehouse Five Plus Two, Bob Gurr's cars from the greatly enlarged Autopia (it's a surprise to see Dennis Hopper driving one of them). Elaborate floats herald the new attractions: a city whose skyscrapers are connected by a web of monorail tracks carrying working model trains; the Matterhorn, sharing its float with a rocking bobsled; a submarine accompanied by "Anchors Aweigh" played by the San Diego Naval Training Center Band.

More than forty minutes have passed before we get to see the first of the new attractions. After a brief shot of the traffic jams the transportation of the future will do away with, Disney says, "To open the first operating monorail system in America, it is our good fortune to have our friend and fellow Californian, the vice president of the United States, Mr. Richard Nixon, and his charming family."

Nixon is a gracious guest. "Well, thank you very much, Walt. I have to say this has been one of the most exciting and interesting days I've ever had in my life. And I'm sure that's true of all the others who are here and plan to participate in these various ceremonies opening these wonderful new exhibits which we have here. I think you'll be interested to know, and I know that our television and radio listeners will be interested to know, that when my wife and I were planning this trip and talking it over with our daughters, we asked what they wanted to do most when they came to California, and they said, 'We want to see our grandmother and go to Disneyland.'"

After speaking about the park's universal appeal, Nixon concludes, "Now of course comes the time for the dedication, and although you and I, the adults up here, are probably just as interested in riding in this as the children, since the first monorail system is the system of the future, and since Disneyland is a place children love above everybody else, I think it would be nice if our two daughters, Patricia and Julie, cut this ribbon, and if they would like to do that we'll step back and let them do the job."

The girls are handed an outsize pair of scissors and, with a little assistance from Walt, cut the monorail loose. Guests climb aboard and we get a glimpse of another veteran of '55—Bob Cummings, whose marriage has apparently survived *Dateline: Disneyland*, as his lovely wife Mary is with him.

The doors shut, and the train, looking entirely modern and efficient, glides away along its beamway into a transportation future that has yet to arrive.

The submarines are next. Admiral Charles C. Kirkpatrick tells Disney, "As a matter of fact, the navy has been interested for some time in the proceedings that go on here today, and we have considerable rooting interest in Disney's peacetime fleet. . . . We believe that the underseas of the world have great potential for peace, and for the benefit of all mankind."

These irreproachable sentiments are followed by an eight-mermaid water ballet, and the fleet sets sail, its submarines cruising past the sunken city of Atlantis, under the polar ice cap, and through the caresses of a giant squid.

Then it's time for the Matterhorn, with mountaineers scaling its crags, followed by an eternity of Swiss folk dancing.

As in 1955, Disney opens the new attractions to a throng of waiting children, and all ends tidily.

———

The additions were an instant hit, so popular that they required an alphabetical advance in the ticket books. The new E-ticket soon made its way into the language. After Sally Ride became the first American woman astronaut to go into space, aboard the shuttle *Challenger* in 1983, she reported, "This is definitely an E-ticket." The tickets had been dropped the year before in favor of all-inclusive pay-one-price "passport" system still in place today, but everyone knew what she meant.

A few years after the new ticket was issued, some of the Jungle Cruise skippers, who tended to be an impertinent lot, issued a subversive F-ticket, which was "GOOD FOR CHOICE OF ONE: MAIN STREET: WALK DOWN MAIN STREET (ONE WAY); TOMORROWLAND: DRINKING FOUNTAIN ATTRACTION, TRASH CAN ATTRACTION; FANTASYLAND: MEN'S ROOM ATTRACTION (CLOSED AT DUSK); FRONTIERLAND: VIEW BIG THUNDER WORKERS EATING LUNCH, POPCORN WAGON GUEST CONTROL; ADVENTURELAND: INHALING AND EXHALING OXYGEN RIDE; BEAR COUNTRY: SIT DOWN ON REAL WOODEN BENCH."

The quick adoption of the E-ticket phrase suggests that *Disneyland '59* was superfluous, at least as far as promoting the park went. Four years into Disneyland's life, virtually every American knew what it was, and even those who had never set foot there had a good idea of what to expect when they did.

Ripples from Disneyland's impact continued to widen. Its closest predecessor, the Coney Island of 1910, exercised enormous influence on the outdoor amusement industry, but this new park was leaching into quadrants of American life that had nothing to do with dark rides and roller coasters.

The year 1958 had seen the first mention of the now universal term "theme park." Since then, there have been many contenders for the laurels of being the first one. All such claims are fragile. Knott's Berry Farm, for instance, had put up a ghost town next to its chicken restaurant in 1940, but only launched a themed attraction—the Calico Mine Ride— four years after Disney's Rainbow Caverns began spilling its chromatic waterfalls.

There is no real contest here: the name "theme park" was not invented to describe Knott's Berry Farm (or a plaintive runner-up, the 1946 Santa Claus Land), but Disneyland alone; immediately taken up by the trade publications, it often alternated in their pages with "Disneyland-style park."

"Theming" had begun its imperial progress. David Younger's 2016 book *Theme Park Design*, the most authoritative study of the subject, begins not with amusement parks, but by presenting a roster of "Attraction-Scale Themed Attractions" that includes "Themed Casinos,

Themed Clubs & Bars, Themed Hotels, Themed Restaurants, Themed Shows, Themed Stores," and on and on to "Corporate Visitor Centers, "Retail Entertainment Centers," "Cruise Ships," "Hospitals[!]," and "Zoos, Aquariums, and Safari Parks."

The fully realized Disneyland of 1959 was also making itself felt overseas, having become, as one newspaper put it, "an instrumentality of American foreign policy." The U.S. Department of State issued a statement saying, "In a very meaningful, sincere manner, Walt sold America and Americana to foreign dignitaries. . . . Walt Disney and Disneyland in a very real way may have contributed to better understanding and a friendlier attitude on the part of world leaders toward the United States."

43

"Do You Have Rocket-Launching Pads There?"

In his monorail dedication speech, Nixon, after speaking of his family's enthusiasm for the park, went on to say that this zeal was shared not only by "young people all over the country, but it's true of the diplomats who've come to Washington from other lands. I remember President Sukarno [of Indonesia] also wanted to come to Disneyland, and has been here, as you know, the king of Belgium, the king of Morocco. From all over the world, people, whether they're adults or children, want to come to Disneyland to see America—the past, the present, and the future. And so, consequently, I just want to take this opportunity to say what a fine job Disneyland has been doing in letting all of us for just a brief few hours have an interlude in our rather busy lives, and to participate in a feeling about the traditions, the dreams, the hope, of this great country of ours."

Disney also played the amiable guide to Prime Minister Nehru and the Shah of Iran. When King Baudouin of Belgium wanted to know why the Matterhorn had holes in it (for the Skyway cars to pass through), his host briskly replied, "Because it's a Swiss mountain."

Harry Truman joked that he didn't dare get aboard the Dumbo ride for fear of being seen enjoying himself in a Republican symbol. Dwight Eisenhower had no such concerns. Senator John F. Kennedy borrowed a room in City Hall to meet with the president of Guinea.

Marty Sklar witnessed a close call with President Sukarno: "Although the park worked closely with State Department security for all these visits, somehow the 'Western bad man' in Frontierland—who performed

341

fast-draw duels daily with the sheriff using pistols that made a loud noise when blanks were fired—did not get the word about the head of state's visit. When 'Black Bart' started to go into his act, and reached for the gun in his holster, he realized just in time that there were at least half a dozen weapons pointed at him—and none of them had blanks."

The most famous foreign visit never actually took place. Soviet premier Nikita Khrushchev arrived for an eleven-day tour of the United States in September of 1959, saying he wanted to see Hollywood and Disneyland.

Two years earlier the Soviet Union had given America one of its greatest Cold War shocks by launching Sputnik, the two-foot globe that was the first artificial satellite. Clearly visible as it crossed the night skies, its batteries flung down a derisive radio chirp.

This started the Space Race—poorly, for America, as our first attempt to match Sputnik a month later with a televised Vanguard launch ended in seconds when the rocket exploded. We eventually did better (Vanguard 1, put in orbit six months later, is the oldest satellite still in space), but tensions between America and Russia remained high, and the Los Angeles police, worried about providing security in the park, warned against Khrushchev's visit.

When the Communist first secretary got to Los Angeles, Frank Sinatra greeted him and showed him around the Twentieth Century-Fox studios. He saw a dance sequence from *Can-Can* being shot, and then went to lunch, where Bob Hope remarked to Mrs. Khrushchev that she shouldn't miss Disneyland. She told Sinatra, "It's the only place I really want to see here." He said, "Why, Disneyland is the safest place in the world. I'll take you myself if you want to go." He then leaned over to David Niven and muttered, "Tell the old broad that you and I will take her out there this afternoon if she wants to go that badly."

But even the combined star power of Sinatra and Niven couldn't prevail. When Khrushchev learned this, he gave an angry speech, and one can feel some sympathy for his indignation, which he laced with sharp humor.

"Just now I was told I could not go to Disneyland. I asked, 'Why not? What is it? Do you have rocket-launching pads there?' And just listen—just listen to what I was told—to what reason I was told. 'We,' which means the American authorities, 'cannot guarantee your safety if you go there.' What is it? Is there an epidemic of cholera there or something? Or have gangsters taken over the park that can destroy me. Then what must I do? Commit suicide?"

Bob Hope tried to take the sting out of the impasse by saying, "I know why they were afraid to let Mr. Khrushchev into Disneyland. They have the only United States trouble-free rocket there."

Instead, the first secretary and his family were driven around several shopping centers and the UCLA campus. He was told he could stop and explore anything that caught his eye, but he sat silent in the car in a black sulk.

Disney was also unhappy about the non-visit, and so was Lillian. Walt said, "We've had a lot of dignitaries down there and he was one that Mrs. Disney wanted to go down and meet. So, she was disappointed he didn't come."

Disney had planned for his guest, selecting "places where we'd take pictures with Khrushchev and I had one that was my favorite." He wanted the party to pose in front of the new submarines. "I'd be pointing to Mr. Khrushchev and say, 'Well now Mr. Khrushchev, here's my Disneyland submarine fleet. It's the eighth largest submarine fleet in the world.'"

44

Suing God in Heaven

Despite the reverberations of international glory, Disneyland had already been afflicted by those two incubi of any great success: lawsuits and opprobrium.

The first suit was brought against the park three days after it opened. As might have been expected, Autopia was to blame. The boy that Bob Gurr took to the nurse with a handful of teeth worried only about getting back on the ride as soon as possible. The parents of a girl who cracked two teeth caroming off the curb were not so easily placated. They sued—and lost, as would most of the thousands of plaintiffs who were to follow.

From the start, Disneyland looked like easy pickings: here's a place where everyone is friendly and wants only the best for you, and, being a child of Hollywood, it's awash in money.

But Disneyland's lawyers do not prepare for court by wishing upon a star. W. Mike McCray, the park's attorney for its first three decades, had been picked by Disney from a local firm because he was young—thirty-one—and cheerful, with none of the chill gloss of the corporate about him. He was also shrewd and implacable. As he summed up his philosophy of representing Disneyland, "If we think we are not in the wrong, we're going to fight. It's the only way to keep fifty lawsuits a year from becoming five hundred. It took a long time for people to realize that we meant business."

The park has always defended itself ferociously: a case against it has a 4 percent chance of getting to court and ending in a victory. Part of that record reflects the sympathies of Orange County jurors reluctant to bite the hand that has so generously fed them; and, by and large, the jury system tends to work. A great many of the suits brought against the park have been generated by the rawest opportunism. Possibly the most bizarre came from the family of a man who was mauled to death by his neighbor's pet African lion. While its owners were away watching imitation ones on the Jungle Cruise, their real example escaped its cage and went into the neighboring yard. The neighbors called Disneyland and demanded the park get the intruder's keepers on the phone. There was no way to do that, and the lion's owners returned to grim news—but not, amazingly, a lawsuit, which instead got leveled against Disneyland. The case was dismissed.

Few suits have been as lurid as the lion attack. Most involve falls, although the continuous attempts to prevent them have always been extraordinary. A dropped ice cream cone, once spotted, is guarded by a cast member warning passersby against a potential slip until the cleaner arrives, almost at once, to do away with the death trap.

The suits that proved hardest for the park to win involved animals. McCray said, "We used to shudder when we saw a mule train case coming."

As vanished generations of U.S. Army muleskinners could have told Disney, their charges are indomitable and tireless, but also a still-surviving simile for stubbornness, always ready to reward their feeder with a bite that, if not of lion caliber, is painful enough.

Much as Disney wanted the pack mules in his American West, the animals were forever shedding their riders, and the park lost every resulting personal injury case that went to trial.

A mule was also responsible for one of Bob Gurr's keenest professional disappointments. Disney's interest in lifelike automata—which would evolve into the human figures of what he called Audio Animatronics—began with animals. As with almost every new park development, Gurr had a hand in designing them, and created one that he believed was his masterpiece: "The walking mountain sheep was absolutely the greatest animation I ever did. Not only was it convincing to humans, even the line ride animals on the Mule Pack ride thought it was real, too."

All too real. "The sheep was staged so that it would pop out from behind a big rock right near the passing guests. . . . The first day we turned it on, the very first guest-carrying mule came to where the sheep was waiting. It went into action, and so did the mule!" It reared, lost its footing, "and fell down the slope into the river, taking all the other mules and guests with it, as they were all roped together into a train. Everyone got a dunking."

The mule's handlers gave it a week to recover, then took it back on the trail. "When he came to the sheep's location, he stopped and would not budge any farther." The park shut down Gurr's walking sheep "that day and it never ran again." But he was able to find some wan solace: "Of course, it never wore out either."

The other animals made trouble, too. The elegant small-scale stage-coaches were, like their century-old prototypes, top-heavy, and the horses that pulled them were easily scared by the whistle of the mine train that shared the desert with them.

Two years after the park opened, the whistle frightened one horse, whose panic made the whole team bolt, tipping over the stage, tumbling the riders off its roof, and dragging the pile of people inside for two hundred yards. Three passengers sued; Disney shut down the ride. This began a gradual diminution of working animals in the park.

Barring the occasional electrical crisis, Peter Pan's galleons always showed up on their tight schedule, and steam transportation, in the hands of those who knew what they were doing, had been reliable since the railroads replaced the canals. Mules and horses weren't so easily man-aged, and today the only Disneyland ride still pulled by animal muscle is the Main Street horsecars, with their big, calm, patient, unflusterable Shires and Percherons.

As the capsized stagecoach indicates, not all the claims against Disneyland have been frivolous. Three months after the park opened, a woman on the Toad ride, passing the tower of gyrating barrels that always threatened to topple, was hit by a shower of them when they really did. She won her case.

Still, suing Disneyland is usually a losing proposition. A woman named Sandra Varely, rear-ended on the Autopia ride, suffered back injuries that required $120,000 worth of surgery. Her lawyers improved what already seemed a watertight case by getting a change of venue from Orange County. Even so, the jury took less than two hours to find for the park. Her husband said, "The situation with Disneyland, to put it bluntly, is that you can't sue God in heaven."

45

A Perfect Fascist Regime

That kernel of toughness in Disney's Elysium represented something darker to many critics, who began to believe that the spotless park was polluting the whole culture, or, at the very least, infantilizing it. In his 1968 critical and biographical study, *The Disney Version: The Life, Times, Art and Commerce of Walt Disney*, Richard Schickel writes, "The word 'dream' is often associated with Disneyland, particularly by its promotion and publicity people. It is, as they have it, 'Walt's Dream' and a place that awakens the desire to dream in the visitor. But the quality of the dreams it represents is most peculiar—no sex and no violence, no release of inhibitions, no relief from real stresses and tensions through their symbolic statement, and therefore no therapeutic effect. It is all pure escapism, offering momentary thrills, laughs and nostalgic pleasures for the impressionable; guaranteed safety for that broad spectrum of humanity whose mental health is predicated on denying that there is any such thing as mental ill health or, indeed, a mental life of any significance."

That was one of the gentler complaints. A decade earlier, when the park had been open for only three years, Julian Halevy, a critic and screenwriter, went there and wrote about his visit for the *Nation*. Beginning with a wildly reductive description of the place—"the amusement park advertised throughout the world as Disneyland is a collection of Midway rides, concessions, hot-dog stands and soft drink counters, peep-shows and advertising stunts for big corporations"—Halevy goes on to say, "As in the Disney movies, the whole world, the universe, and all man's striving for dominion over self and nature, have been reduced to a sickening blend of cheap formulas packaged to sell. Romance, Adventure, Fantasy, Science are ballyhooed and marketed: life is bright-colored, clean, cute, titivating, safe, mediocre, inoffensive to the lowest common denominator, and somehow poignantly inhuman. The mythology glorified in TV and Hollywood's B films has been given too solid flesh. By some Gresham's law of bad art driving out good, the whole of Southern California and the nation indivisible is affected. The invitation and challenge of real living is abandoned. It doesn't sell tickets. It's dangerous and offensive. Give 'em mumbo-jumbo. One feels our whole mass culture heading up the dark river to the source—the heart of darkness where Mr. Disney traffics in pastel-trinketed evil for gold and ivory."

Like Halevy, the historian Mike Wallace finds the entire operation inimical, as is suggested by the scornful title of his 1996 book *Mickey Mouse History*. The essay in it of the same name carries an epigraph consisting of definitions from *The American Heritage Dictionary of the English Language*.

> **Mick-ey Finn** (mĭk'ē fĭn') *n. Slang.* An alcoholic beverage that is surreptitiously altered to induce diarrhea or stupefy, render unconscious, or otherwise incapacitate the person who drinks it. [Origin unknown.]
>
> **Mickey Mouse** *adj.* **1.a.** *Slang.* Unimportant; trivial . . . **b.** *Slang.* Irritatingly petty . . . **2.** *Slang.* Intellectually unchallenging; simple . . . **3.** *Music.* **a.** Blandly sentimental.

That pair economically summarizes much of the animus toward the park. The hostility goes further though: Disneyland is puerile yet also menacing and somehow all-commanding—a Circe's Isle that robs its visitors of free choice, saps their intelligence, and fools them about the essentials of life itself.

In his Olympian 1961 *The Image: A Guide to Pseudo-Events in America*, the historian Daniel J. Boorstin finds the park so completely pseudo that he gives it the merest swipe in passing. Of the fake and meretricious, "Disneyland in California—the American 'attraction' which tourist Khrushchev most wanted to see—is the example to end all examples. Here indeed Nature imitates Art. The visitor to Disneyland encounters not the two-dimensional comic strip or movie originals, but only their three-dimensional facsimiles."

One critic has called Disneyland "a small-scale model of a perfect fascist regime." The novelist and playwright Paul Rudnick puts this more amusingly when he has his alter ego Libby Gelman-Waxner quote her (highly precocious) seven-year-old son exclaiming upon entering Main Street: "Oh my God! We're trapped in a production of *The Music Man* directed by Leni Riefenstahl."

The Third Reich comparisons are extreme, but not much more so than Halevy's "heart of darkness" polemic. The critic Greil Marcus, however, who has always been leery of modish intellectual trends, writes in his essay "Forty Years of Overstatement: Criticism and the Disney Theme Parks," "that many of these attacks are prompted by 'spite,'" which "is not a good posture to practice criticism—an angry defensiveness, a fear that somehow one's faculties or tools of analysis are not up to the job disguised as contempt for the job itself."

Marcus finds this most clearly expressed in something that has given itself the brief, tone-deaf title *The Project on Disney*. "Here, courtesy of three academics and a photographer-essayist who pretend to be working collectively . . . is the Anhedonic School of Disney Criticism without doubt or restraint." One of the project's contributors writes, "I always approach culture as a consumer." She's an unusual consumer, for "I don't find shopping pleasurable." She calls Walt Disney World—but of course she means Disneyland, too—"the quintessential enactment of the hysterical bourgeois subject."

Marcus is calm throughout the essay, but this gets his back up, and he offers an astringent reply: "Your notion of culture is vastly impoverished; your notion of pleasure must be inconceivably refined; you're probably in the wrong business; speaking of hysterical, speak for yourself, sister."

46

THE GREATEST PIECE OF URBAN DESIGN

The park has also found influential defenders, sometimes in surprising quarters. The art historian and critic Vincent Scully (the celebrated American architect Philip Johnson called him "the most influential architectural teacher ever") acknowledged what he saw as the park's fundamental saccharine lie: " 'When you wish upon a star your dreams come true' makes a lovely fiction for a while, especially when it is sung in front of Cinderella's Castle with the magic animals capering about, but it is, after all, pure bullshit in the long run. When you wish upon a star you die like everyone else."

But despite Disneyland's failure to bestow immortality on its customers, Scully respected it. Walt Disney, he said, condensed "Classic and Romantic garden types into a new unity, one never quite seen before it. It was a special kind of American Amusement Park. . . . Disney formed it into a new architectural program, one of the few in American history where many buildings could be arranged in relation to each other to shape a whole place." Quite a place: "The 'Magic Kingdom' seems to build the very structure of myths, with themes from the depths of the American consciousness, sinuously intertwined. . . . We are swept away in the American myth."

In 1963 James W. Rouse, the architectural planner who developed South Street Seaport in Manhattan, Baltimore's Inner Harbor, and Boston's Faneuil Marketplace, startled his colleagues with the keynote speech he gave to the Urban Design Conference at Harvard. "I hold a view, that may be somewhat shocking to an audience as sophisticated as this: that the greatest piece of urban design in the United States today is Disneyland.

"If you think about Disneyland and think about its performance in relation to its purpose, its meaning to people—and more than that, its meaning to the process of development—you will find it the outstanding piece of urban design in the United States.

"It took an area of activity—the amusement park—and lifted it to a standard so high in its performance, in its respect for people, that it really has become a brand-new thing. It fulfills all the functions it set out to accomplish un-self-consciously, usefully, and profitably to its owners and developers.

"I find," Rouse bravely concluded, "more to learn in the standards that have been set and in the goals that have been achieved in the development of Disneyland than in any other single piece of physical development in the country."

The novelist Ray Bradbury went even further, attributing to the park a spiritual element. "Disneyland liberates men to their better selves. Here the wild brute is gently corralled, not used and squashed, not put upon and harassed, not tromped on by real-estate operators nor exhausted by fog and traffic." For Bradbury, Disney "has proven once again that the first function of architecture is to make men over, make them wish to go on living, feed them fresh oxygen, grow them tall, delight their eyes, make them kind." As for Halevy, Bradbury mourned his parched soul, declaring him "one of those who, for intellectual reasons, refuse to let go and enjoy themselves. I feel sorry for him. He will never travel in space, he will never touch the stars."

Yet Disneyland has been more than an inimitable—and thus sterile—exemplar, a place whose benefits one may enjoy only by going to Anaheim. When Halevy said "the whole of Southern California and the nation indivisible is affected," he meant it as a warning of encroaching moral calamity. But Disneyland has remade the way Americans live in agreeable ways that range from the small courtesies of people running checkout counters to the planning of airports, from unexpected bursts of flowers surrounding shopping malls to allowing an easier, more interesting progress through those malls, and so on right along to the buildings we inhabit and the streets that they stand on.

———

In his bleakly titled *The Geography of Nowhere: The Rise and Decline of America's Man-Made Landscape*, the historian and social critic James Howard Kunstler writes of Disneyland, "The underlying message of Main Street U.S.A.—for the grownups, anyway—was that a big corporation could make a better Main Street than a bunch of rubes in a real small town.

"And Walt was right! Through the postwar decades Americans happily allowed their town to be destroyed. They'd flock to Disneyland . . . and walk down Main Street, and think, *gee, it feels good here.* Then they'd go back home and tear down half the old buildings downtown and pave them over for parking lots, throw a parade to celebrate a new K Mart opening—even when it put ten local merchants out of business—turn Elm Street into a six-lane crosstown expressway. . . . They'd do every fool thing possible to destroy good existing relationships between things in their towns, and put their local economies at the mercy of distant corporations whose officers didn't give a damn whether these towns lived or died. And then, when vacation time rolled around, they'd flock back to Disney World to feel good about America."

In fact, Disneyland's Main Street was having the opposite effect. Rather than simply serving as a haven for the nostalgic, it was putting an impress on downtowns all across the country.

In their splendid 1984 guide, *The City Observed: Los Angeles*, Charles Moore, Peter Becker, and Regula Campbell get to the park just thirty-five pages in. "What may come as a surprise is how richly Disneyland offers us insight into many layers of reality. People often use Disneyland as a synonym for the facile, shallow and fake, just as they use the term 'Mickey Mouse' to signify the egregiously trivial. It just doesn't wash: this incredibly energetic collection of environmental experiences offers enough lessons for a whole architectural education in all the things that matter—community and reality, private memory and inhabitation, as well as some technical lessons in propinquity and choreography."

That education begins on Main Street, which, for all its whimsy, is an archetype of something not whimsical at all. In his 1996 book *Main Street Revisited*, the architectural historian Richard V. Francaviglia writes that "the period from the 1870s until just after the turn of the century has such a strong effect on the popular mind because many Main Streets were built up as virtually intact assemblages of buildings . . . during this era. As earlier buildings were remodeled to match new construction, American small town streetscapes took on a very stylized, and highly standardized, appearance by the 1880s. . . . Viewed in context, then, the Victorian-era commercial storefront should be recognized as the first truly national building form in the history of American architecture."

This was the form that Disney chose for the introduction to his park, no sylvan country road but a new urban arrangement that has moved artists as diverse as Edward Hopper and Charles Burchfield and the photographers Berenice Abbott and David Plowden. Hopper simplified; Disney elaborated; but both left work that has changed the way we see. Speaking of the park as a whole, Francaviglia says, "In world history, few places this small have had such a powerful effect on so many people."

That small place has had a lasting effect on Medina, Ohio, whose revival Francaviglia closely studied. Medina's nineteenth-century downtown was sharing the general decay that blighted most American cities in the late 1950s and early 1960s. Then the directors of the Phoenix Bank changed their minds about pulling down their Victorian headquarters in favor of building something on the outskirts of town. Instead, they spent a million dollars restoring the bank. The refurbishment affected the whole district. Nearby merchants, many of whom had visited Disneyland, followed suit, one saying their town had "something as good as, and perhaps better than, Disneyland, for it was really historic and original." Medina's Second Empire Courthouse also dodged the wrecker's ball to be restored, as did dozens of less imposing buildings. Medinans came to call the rebirth "Main Street USA," a telling term, because there is no Main Street in Medina.

Today Medina's restored downtown is humming with such commercial vigor that "charm" is too feeble a description.

In 1977 the National Trust for Historic Preservation launched its Main Street Program, which has so far rehabilitated nearly 300,000 buildings, investing $79 billion in the process, while creating 640,000 new jobs and 144,000 new businesses. These revitalized districts are home to enterprises that would have confounded their turn-of-the-century ancestors—sushi bars, Apple stores—but they draw their strength directly from historical memory and old aspirations. Mike Wallace informs those *Mickey Mouse History* readers who may have grown up in Candyland that the turn-of-the-century era "also included depressions, strikes on the railroads, warfare in the minefields, squalor in the immigrant communities, lynching, imperial wars, and the emergence of mass protests by populists and socialists." But Francaviglia finds an equally valid truth in Disney's confident architecture. "Such landscapes are at once optimistic and didactic; they embody the belief that people can be instructed to develop such values through instructional (if entertaining) experiences. In this regard, such landscapes are indeed educational as well as entertaining, and it should be remembered that Walt Disney was, above all, a tremendously successful educator—which may help explain academicians' disdain for him."

Walt Disney isn't the sole inspiration for the heartening Main Street trend, but he is the least appreciated one. And his long-ago vision is still at work: "In creating Main Street with its emphasis on detail, form, and pedestrian scale," Francaviglia writes, "Disney anticipated postmodern design trends that would reshape the American landscape for two generations after his death."

47

THE FIRST GOODBYE

Disney would not see the revivified Medina, nor any of the other main streets that were yet to catch their second wind from his model.

After 1959 he still kept watch over Disneyland, but had his attention drawn away by substantial distractions: creating exhibits for the 1964 New York World's Fair and planning his huge Florida project, Walt Disney World and Epcot. In Disneyland he had to make do with fewer than a couple hundred acres; Disney World would require ten thousand.

He never got to visit the new park; nor, of course, the others now sewn around the globe, in Paris, Tokyo, Hong Kong, and Shanghai.

After the fair, he went to work on what would become two of Disneyland's most enduringly popular attractions in the years ahead, the Haunted Mansion and Pirates of the Caribbean.

Disney had decided as early as 1957 that he wanted a haunted house in his park, but it got off to a slow start because nobody could agree on what the house should look like. The WED artists pushed for the popular conception of such a place: a forbidding ruin with rotting pillars and skewed shutters. Disney didn't want something gloomy and decayed in his park. And as it was initially planned as a walk-through, there seemed no way to herd enough visitors along its ghost-haunted corridors in a day.

Pirates, too, started at about the same time, also as a walk-through, and slowly evolved into a large forty-foot mock-up that Disney liked. Both attractions were well along by the fall of 1966.

Disney's pace never slackened, but the cough that had alerted his colleagues to his approach for as long as anyone in the studio could remember got worse. He had made sporadic attempts to give up smoking, but none took, and he continued to burn every Chesterfield down to his knuckles.

In early November, he went into the hospital for tests, and the doctors discovered a walnut-sized growth on his left lung. He had surgery the following Monday, and lost the entire lung.

Two weeks later he was back at work. Rolly Crump, who had joined WED in 1959, said, "All we knew was that he went into the hospital, and that supposedly there was something wrong with his back that had to do with an old polo injury. That's the only thing we heard. Then the next thing, I remember seeing Walt. He came over one day and he looked terrible. His eyes had already started receding, and I thought, 'Jesus Christ, this man's sick.'"

A couple of weeks after that Disney was talking with Marc Davis, one of his favorite animators, of whom he had said, "Marc can do story, he can do character, he can animate, he can design shows for me. All I have to do is tell him what I want and it's there. He's my Renaissance man!" John Hench was with them, and Dick Irvine, and they all examined a mock-up of an improved moon-trip attraction. After a while Disney said to Irvine, "I'm getting kinda tired; do you want to take me back to the studio?" As he walked to the door, he turned and said, "Goodbye, Marc." It was the first time Davis had ever heard him say goodbye.

His end-of-day scotch and massage sessions with Hazel George had become increasingly important to him. The two called the massage room a name drawn from the Uncle Remus movie: the Laughing Place. Just after he'd wished Davis farewell, he showed up and said to Hazel, "Well, here we are in the Laughing Place." He paused. "There's something I want to tell you—" That was as far as he got; they wept in each other's arms. Then he left Hazel George, and his studio, forever.

———

Around nine o'clock on the morning of December 15—ten days after Disney's sixty-fifth birthday—Marty Sklar heard the WED paging system barking his name. Card Walker wanted to see him right away. " 'Walt's dead,' Card said the moment I entered his office. 'Write the statement Roy will sign and we'll distribute it to the press and our employees. You've got an hour.' "

Sklar began the first of the hundreds of tributes that would follow: "The death of Walt Disney is a loss to all the people of the world. In everything he did, Walt had an intuitive way of reaching out and touching the hearts and minds of young and old alike. His entertainment was an international language. . . ."

That night on CBS the newsman Eric Sevareid said Disney "was an original; not just an American original, but an original, period. He was a happy accident; one of the happiest this century has experienced; and judging by the way it's been behaving in spite of all Disney tried to tell it about laughter, love, children, puppies, and sunrises, the century hardly deserved him.

"He probably did more to heal or at least to soothe troubled human spirits than all the psychiatrists in the world. There can't be many adults in the allegedly civilized parts of the globe who did not inhabit Disney's mind and imagination at least for a few hours and feel better for the visitation."

He had wanted a private funeral, and got one: just the family interring his ashes at Forest Lawn Memorial Park the day after his death.

The persistent myth about his corpse having been frozen to await medical advances that could resurrect him, foolish even by urban legend standards, reflects the hold he had on the public imagination, even on its trust. Ward Kimball may have started the rumor. If so, he did it more out of wish than of mischief. Thirty years later Kimball said, "I always tell people that if anyone was going to be cryogenically frozen, doesn't it seem like something Walt would be interested in? He was always interested in experiments, always interested in science. . . . Was he frozen? I wouldn't put it past him and that's my answer. I like to keep it floating out there."

48

Beautiful?

In the park, the light in the window of Disney's firehouse apartment burns all night long, every night of the year. This memorial is joined along Main Street by ones to his lieutenants.

The street's shop windows bear the names of those he worked with over the years, with whimsical businesses ascribed to them, the lettering done in scrupulous turn-of-the-century style, reverse painting on glass, lots of gold:

FOUNDED 1955
PRICE IS RIGHT LAND COMPANY
ANAHEIM ORLANDO
CALL ON OUR NUMBERS MAN FOR THE BEST PRICE!
HARRISON "BUZZ" PRICE
FOUNDER & FINDER
WE NEVER SAY "NO"
"YES" MAKES MORE CENTS!

ID SOMNIATE ID FACITE
MAIN STREET COLLEGE OF ARTS & SCIENCES
EST. 1852
MARTIN A. SKLAR
DEAN
INSPIRING THE DREAMERS AND DOERS OF TOMORROW

(The Latin phrase means "Dream It, Do It," Sklar's longtime slogan and
the title of his autobiography.)

J.B. LINDQUIST
HONORARY MAYOR OF DISNEYLAND
"JACK OF ALL TRADES
MASTER OF FUN"

THE ARTISANS LOFT
HANDMADE MINIATURES
BY
HARRIET BURNS

ELIAS DISNEY
CONTRACTOR
EST. 1895

(Walt's father.)

UNITED AUDIT
BOOKKEEPING
ACCOUNTS AUDIT
ROYAL CLARK, MGR.

(Mickey Clark, who handed Bob Gurr the envelope with a thousand
dollars in it.)

PLAZA SCHOOL OF ART
INSTRUCTORS
HERBERT RYMAN JOHN HENCH PETER ELLENSHAW

LEADING THE RACE TO THE FUTURE
METEOR CYCLE CO.
OUR VEHICLES PASS THE TEST OF TIME

FAST FAULTLESS AND FADLESS
BOB GURR
DESIGN IMPRESARIO

ROYAL CARE CO.
WE KEEP YOUR CASTLE SHINING
CHUCK BOYAJIAN
PROP.

KEN ANDERSON
BAIT CO.

(A joke of Disney's: Anderson, a dedicated fly fisherman, disdained bait.)

VAN ARSDALE FRANCE
FOUNDER AND PROFESSOR EMERITUS
DISNEY UNIVERSITIES

"CAN DO"
MACHINE WORKS
MECHANICAL WONDERS
LIVE STEAM ENGINES
MAGICAL ILLUSIONS
CAMERAS
ROGER BROGGIE
SHOPMASTER
"ADVISOR TO THE MAGIC MAKERS"

EVANS GARDENS
EXOTIC & RARE SPECIES
FREEWAY COLLECTIONS
EST. 1910
MORGAN (BILL) EVANS
SENIOR PARTNER

DAVY CROCKETT
COONSKIN CAP SUPPLY CO.
FESS PARKER
PROPRIETOR

ORIENTAL TATTOOING
BY PROF. HARPER GOFF
BANJO LESSONS

(Goff had wanted to put a tattoo parlor on Main Street; Disney thought it would be sleazy.)

OPEN SINCE '55
DISNEYLAND
CASTING AGENCY
"IT TAKES PEOPLE TO MAKE A DREAM A REALITY"
WALTER ELIAS DISNEY
FOUNDER & DIRECTOR EMERITUS

There is no window for C. V. Wood.

As soon as he left Disneyland, Wood founded a consulting company, and set to work building rival amusement parks. They would, he told the press, be better than Disney's, and there would be thirty-five of them.

Hubris had set in. Billing himself as the "Master Planner of Disneyland," Wood said, "Walt made wonderful movies and invented Mickey Mouse, but he didn't know anything about theme parks." His promotions erased Walt entirely: Disneyland had been built by "the team of C. V. Wood and Roy Disney."

Wood did build successful parks—among them Six Flags Over Texas—and brought London Bridge to Arizona, stone by stone, before his near-lifelong consumption of three packs of cigarettes a day killed him in 1992.

Of all his projects, the one most closely patterned on Disneyland was Freedomland, set down on a four-hundred-acre site in the Bronx. Built within a vast outline of the United States, it strove to outdo Disneyland, while drawing on its elements. Here, too, were the American frontier, the future embodied in "Satellite City," not one but two stern-wheelers built by Todd's East Coast shipyards, a sky ride, a narrow-gauge live-steam railroad. There were spectacles Disney never attempted. The Chicago fire erupted hourly, and dark rides traveled through the 1906 San Francisco earthquake and the swirling cone of a Kansas twister.

Freedomland opened in 1960 to much publicity and a crowd of 63,000. I got there soon after, an eager thirteen-year-old who, living just a half hour away, was able to return several times. I always tried to have more fun there than I did. I couldn't understand the source of the disappointment that accompanied me every time I left, but looking back across the decades, I realize that my every visit was haunted by my memories of Disneyland. I believe I always felt that the park was *insincere*. The self-proclaimed Master Planner of Disneyland was not the master of Disneyland: Freedomland tried hard, but it was Disneyland without Walt Disney. It closed after five seasons.

Disneyland's most distinguished alumnus has to be Steve Martin. His family moved to Orange County shortly before the park opened two miles from his home, and in his memoir, *Born Standing Up*, he remembers his excitement: "Two-inch headlines announced the event as though it were a victory at sea."

When a friend told him the park was hiring youngsters to sell guidebooks, he rode his bicycle out and was immediately hired. He was ten years old then; he worked at the park for nearly a decade.

In Merlin's Magic Shop, "tricks were demonstrated in front of crowds of two or three people." He got very good at those magic tricks, and picked up much that would nurture his career. After graduating from high school, he "halfheartedly applied to and was accepted at Santa Ana Junior College," and also got lured away from his longtime employer by the competition, Knott's Berry Farm.

Delighted to have won his new job, he nonetheless felt desolate on his last day in the magic shop. "I stood behind the counter where I had pitched Svengali decks and the Incredible Shrinking Die, and I felt an emotional contradiction: nostalgia for the present. Somehow, even though I had stopped working only minutes earlier, my future fondness for the store was clear, and I experienced a sadness like that of looking at a photo of an old, favorite pooch."

He said his goodbyes, stepped out into Disneyland's bright twilight, and encountered a person whose sensibilities could not have been more different from Walt Disney's.

A guard stopped him and asked—politely, of course—if he would use the side exit, as a photographer was at work nearby.

He did, and paused to watch a small, slim, brown-haired woman "aim her large-format camera directly at the dramatically lit castle, where white swans floated on the moat underneath the functioning drawbridge."

Forty years later he was able to buy the picture he saw being made that evening.

"The photographer, it turned out, was Diane Arbus. I try to square the photo's breathtakingly romantic image with the rest of her extreme subject matter, and I assume she saw this facsimile of a castle as though it were a kitsch roadside statue of Paul Bunyan. Or perhaps she saw it as I did: beautiful."

———

I'd like to think Diane Arbus wasn't viewing the castle with irony; ironic or not, the photograph she took that evening, with a swan glowing on the dark surface of the moat, would have pleased its builder. However she saw it, I find that castle, as Steve Martin did, beautiful. Or, rather, I accept it as beautiful, which is not quite the same thing. It has so lodged in my mind's registry of beauty—like a familiar tree or lake or cat—that when I last visited Disneyland I scarcely noticed its pastel ramparts.

But Main Street continues to startle me with its playful magnificence. Not just because of the adroit architectural history its designers worked into it, but for the message it radiates; despite the fact that behind those alluring facades lie acres of T-shirts and stuffed Goofys pleading for your money, the street still says what Walt Disney hoped it would.

On opening day in 1955, many of the people seeing Main Street for the first time remembered the actual main streets this one embellished, and the era it summoned.

Those visitors who had known both Main Streets are all dead now.

But Main Street still mirrors a belief in the possibility of an America where all is prosperous and convivial, a national—to use a threadbare word encoding a thousand disappointments—community.

Its author once said, "The Disneyland park is a sort of monument to the American way of life." But monuments commemorate past actualities. Disneyland, a tireless commercial dynamo, is nonetheless also a sincere attempt to point the way toward a better future.

Like America, the park will, as Walt Disney often repeated, never be finished. Tomorrowland was always the least coherent of the lands, but the idea, if not the place, was perhaps closest to his heart. He had a lifelong belief in a bountiful and magnanimous tomorrow.

———

The Town Square lights coming on at dusk looked just as good to me in 2018 as they had in 1959, easing my gloomy wonder that sixty years had disappeared since Uncle Win and I had together watched them shine.

I'd been about to leave the park, but just before I reached the exit the *E.P. Ripley* pulled into the Main Street Station and stood there sizzling, as pretty an embodiment of the zenith of America's industrial age as one could ever hope to see.

The *Ripley* drew me up the station stairs to take a final circuit of the park.

I was too late. The train was moving away, the locomotive's bell tossing its fading silver notes back to the few of us left on the platform.

But I knew what Walt Disney understood and had brought about: that another engine—perhaps even a better one—was just a stop or two down the line.

The photograph that Steve Martin saw Diane Arbus taking at the end of his last day working for the park: *A castle in Disneyland, Cal.* (1962).

AFTERWORD, AND A
NOTE ON THE SOURCES

There are twelve Disney parks in the world today, but the original, in Anaheim, is the only one Walt Disney ever saw, for which he supervised the entire design, and one can sense his presence there more strongly than at any of its descendants.

Much of this comes from Disneyland's greater intimacy. The Florida Main Street is larger, the buildings isolated and monumental; they're fun to look at, but they feel impersonal by comparison. In Anaheim, one can easily imagine Disney pacing off the storefronts and mandating that the street corners be rounded rather than square, hence subliminally more welcoming.

When I was there last year conducting research (perhaps too inflated a term for a trip to Disneyland) on this book, I found that Main Street had temporarily been done away with.

After sixty-three years, the horsecar tracks needed to be replaced. As with everything at Disneyland, this was done with great consideration for the visitor. The plywood panels that enclosed the work—which, of course, ran from Town Square to the Hub—were so neatly joined and nicely finished that they might have been meant to stand forever. They'd been painted a soothing hue and enlivened with signs that both explained what was going on within and offered a well-illustrated history of urban surface transportation. But however nicely finished and decorated, there was no getting around the fact that a twelve-foot-high barrier had cut Main Street laterally in half. With only one side visible at a time, the street looked like a movie set, as though the temporary structure had infected the facades it faced with a similar impermanence.

The traffic—equine and motorized—was gone, and all the sight lines were spoiled.

As that street had moved my earlier self more than anything else in the park, I was disappointed. But then I realized that I was receiving an important lesson in the strength and intelligence of Disney's vision.

He had seen his Main Street not just as a cheerful thoroughfare that led to his other offerings, but as an autobiographical statement: everything that lies beyond has been nurtured and informed by this conception of my youth, and America's.

And sure enough, with the effect of that passage from the real world to his world nullified, the park lost coherence. The lands no longer seemed part of a working whole, but isolated congeries of diversions. Take Main Street away and Disneyland, although still superior to its imitators, is diminished.

So I turned on my heel and went right home. Just kidding. I still had a good time, and given my interest in the park at that moment, a useful one. Disneyland is as aware of its own relatively brief history as Colonial Williamsburg is of its ancient (by American standards) one. On a truncated side street there is a wall holding a drinking fountain, wholly unremarkable, save that its few square yards preserve the experiments with various composition bricks during the park's frenzied birth. The slightly differing textures of the mismatched bricks—in a place where *nothing* is mismatched—are an unobtrusive monument to the hard-pressed days when Disney feared his realm wouldn't be completed on time, and most onlookers believed the over-ambitious project was bound to fail.

The entire thriving park is testament to its enduring success, but that, too, is memorialized in subtle ways. In the New Orleans Square depot (the one from *So Dear to My Heart* that Disney had to recreate after Ward Kimball refused to return the original) the telegraph sounder clacks out in Morse fragments of Walt's opening day address: "To all who come to this happy place, welcome. . . ."

The park makes more direct historical efforts. If you're going there, and its past interests you, do sign up for a tour called "Walk in Walt's Disneyland Footsteps." I found it delightful. Our guide (whom I would like to thank here by name, but alas my corrupt handwriting often becomes unintelligible even to me after a week or so) took us through those precincts of the park that have least changed since its opening, including a visit to Disney's firehouse apartment, perfectly preserved right down to the little refrigerator, which still holds those old, dimpled aluminum ice trays.

Under her seemingly effortless intervention, we were able to jump the line to the Alice in Wonderland ride, which Disney enjoyed far more than he had his movie (and so did I). Afterward, we were served a good lunch under the shade of the trees Ruth Shellhorn so adeptly deployed in Town Square.

———

I had never planned to write a book about Disneyland. I was working on another subject that I tried to persuade myself was promising, but that more and more felt like a particularly dreary homework assignment. While I was glumly pursuing this task, I came across, in the infinite attic of the Internet, a book by Sam Gennawey called *The Disneyland Story: The Unofficial Guide to the Evolution of Walt Disney's Dream*. Huh, I thought, this sounds sort of interesting. So I bought it, and here I am.

When I'd done enough initial reading to come up with a plausible proposal, I sent it to my invaluable agent, Emma Sweeney, and asked if she thought this might work. Emma is a Southern California girl, and she remembered many trips to the park when the frosty fingertip of the Matterhorn rising above Orange County signaled that the goal was close. She suggested I stick with Disneyland, as did my generous, patient, and altogether brilliant editor, Colin Harrison. I was also buoyed by the enthusiasm and the shrewd suggestions of his colleague Sarah Goldberg.

So Disney it would be. My previous book had been about the Civil War, and I went in thinking that I was unlikely to encounter anywhere near so much published material on this subject. Instead, I found to my surprise—mixed with a blend of pleasure and alarm—that there is an immense body of literature about not only Walt Disney, but Disneyland itself. The bibliography will suggest the extent of this plenitude, but there were scores—perhaps hundreds—of books I couldn't get to.

Janet Wasko must have felt something of the same when, getting ready to write her *Understanding Disney*, she found that "a recent search of the amazon.com website identified 2,922 books with 'Disney' in the title." And that was just Amazon, and twenty years ago to boot.

The older I get, the more persuaded I become that the term "amateur historian" is too dismissive for one who, engrossed in a subject, however "minor," tracks down every living person who knows anything about it and pursues each printed reference. This certainly holds true with Disneyland, which has a passionately dedicated following. Its students range from those who want to place Disney and his works in the broadest socioeconomic context to, say, Ken Pellman and Lynn Barron, who devoted years, I'll bet, to learning how the park is kept so immaculate.

So many of these books and articles proved useful—and often stimulating—that it is impossible to begin to offer my gratitude to more than the merest fraction of them here.

One I must mention, however, is Todd James Pierce's *Three Years in Wonderland*. Just as the unruly C. V. Wood tried to erase Walt Disney from Disneyland, so Disneyland has little to say about Wood. Pierce has done a masterly job of coloring in this blank page in the park's copious histories.

Of the many biographies of Disney, Neal Gabler's is the longest and fullest. Apparently it didn't please the Disney family—who had granted the author full access—but I found it thorough and fair-minded. Steven Watts's *The Magic Kingdom* is a less traditional biography, casting a wide net to draw in all the ways that Disney has affected our culture. He weaves together his themes without any visible strain, and the result is as entertaining as it is enlightening. Michael Barrier's *The Animated Man* is, as its title hints, especially strong on Disney's animation, but contains much good information on Disneyland as well.

––––––––

As for the park itself, I am fortunate that the Walt Disney Family Museum in San Francisco has issued a set of three CD-ROMs containing the first twenty-four issues of the *"E" Ticket*, a magazine devoted to Disneyland's past that ran for two decades. Its cumulative history is unusually comprehensive even in this well-tilled field, for it contains whole issues given over to single attractions, very good on the hardware and enriched by interviews with the people who invented the rides and built them.

Interviews: Didier Ghez has conducted hundreds with Disney veterans, and so far published more than twenty volumes of them. Equally prolific is Jim Korkis, whose huge volume of work on Disney I mentioned earlier in the book. The vigorous, continuing study that people bring to Walt and his legacy is reflected in his *How to Be a Disney Historian*, which includes a section called "Good Advice" in which it is dispensed by no fewer than fifteen of them.

Bob Gurr, the subject of much Disney history, published a vivid, high-hearted memoir called *Design: Just for Fun*. Although it came out less than a decade ago, it seems to be nearly as rare as the Book of Kells and costs, when you can find it, as much as an advanced iPad. Karen Crane, the Century Association's resourceful librarian, came to my rescue, securing the loan of a copy from, I believe, Yale. Equally useful to me—and free as the air—was the Disney material on YouTube. It let me watch the entirety of *Dateline: Disneyland*, as well as *Disneyland '59*, which was believed lost until just a few months ago. (*Dateline* has been shorn of commercials, but they're all there in '59, and it is oddly comforting to discover that back in television's first so-called golden age, they were as frequent and interminable as they are during the final hour of any morning show in today's second.)

After I'd drawn on all these resources, and Colin and Sarah had read the manuscript—making many improvements—it went to the copy editor. I've always been fortunate in the copy editors that Scribner has assigned me, but even among that exceptional lot, Richard Willett shines. Although he had to read my text on an accelerated schedule, he went through it with a care and acuity that would have taken me a good half year, and saved me from errors large and small (in the latter category, for instance, he was able to correct my improper hyphenation of the "Wheels a-Rolling" pageant's title).

———

George Orwell said, "Writing a book is a horrible exhausting struggle, like a long bout of some painful illness." I haven't found it quite that harrowing (perhaps because all my subjects have been softened by the buffer of the past, which, for all the horrors it contains, is never quite as scary as the present), but like every writer I've had my occasional fraught doldrums, when the terrible two-word question looms: "Who cares?"

At such times, friends are far more important than finding *le mot juste*. So: my warmest thanks to Ellen Feldman, historian and novelist, who was willing to read this in its mangy manuscript form, and to Stacy Schiff, André Bernard, Geoff Ward, Rick Brookhiser, Ed Sorel, and two excellent Freds, Allen and Smoler, who offered me valuable encouragement and advice while never once confirming my suspicion that none of them wanted to learn more—or anything—about the history of Disneyland. And finally, I must once again express my warmest gratitude to Sal and Falco, proprietors of the incomparable Volare Italian restaurant, who offered me the comfortable haven in which much of this book was written. Volare is at 147 West 4th Street in Greenwich Village: go there.

I'm wonderfully lucky that my wisest and most encouraging friend is also my wife. Carol, who enjoys fantasy even less than she does garlic, cheerfully went with me to Disneyland the moment I'd decided to write about it, and brightened my spirits all the time I was working on the book. Not to mention that she also kept me fed and housed throughout.

BIBLIOGRAPHY

Adams, Judith A. *The American Amusement Park Industry: A History of Technology and Thrills.* Woodbridge, CT: Twayne Publishers, 1991.

Alcorn, Steve. *Theme Park Design: Behind the Scenes with an Engineer.* Scotts Valley, CA: CreateSpace, 2010.

Amendola, Dana. *All Aboard: The Wonderful World of Disney Trains.* Glendale, CA: Disney Editions, 2015.

Anderson, Paul F. *Jack of All Trades: Conversations with Disney Legend Ken Anderson.* Theme Park Press, 2017.

Apgar, Gary, ed. *Mickey Mouse: Emblem of the American Spirit.* San Francisco, CA: The Walt Disney Family Foundation Press, 2015.

———. *A Mickey Mouse Reader.* Jackson: University Press of Mississippi, 2014.

Baham, Jeff. *The Unauthorized Story of Walt Disney's Haunted Mansion.* Theme Park Press, 2014.

Ballard, Donald W. *Disneyland Hotel: 1954–1949: The Little Motel in the Middle of the Orange Grove.* Self-published, 2011.

Barczewski, Stephanie. *Magic Kingdoms: A History of the Disney Theme Parks.* Theme Park Press, 2016.

Barrier, Michael. *The Animated Man: A Life of Walt Disney.* Berkeley: University of California Press, 2007.

Belknap, William, Jr. "Nature Carves Fantasies in Bryce Canyon." *National Geographic* (October 1958).

Boorstin, Daniel J. *The Image: A Guide of Pseudo-Events in America.* New York: Atheneum, 1987.

Bradbury, Ray. "The Machine-Tooled Happyland." *Holiday* (October 1965).

Bright, Randy. *Disneyland: Inside Story.* New York: Abrams, 1987.

Broggie, Michael. *Walt Disney's Railroad Story: The Small-Scale Fascination That Led to a Full-Scale Kingdom.* Virginia Beach, VA: Donning, 2006.

Brown, Gloria. *Images of America: Medina.* Mount Pleasant, SC: Arcadia Publishing, 2007.

Bryman, Alan. *Disney and His Worlds.* Abingdon-on-Thames, UK: Routledge, 1995.

Burnes, Brian, et al. *Walt Disney's Missouri: The Roots of a Creative Genius.* Kansas City Star Books, 2002.

Canemaker, John. *Walt Disney's Nine Old Men & the Art of Animation.* Glendale, CA: Disney Editions, 2001.

Carosso, Vincent P. *The California Wine Industry 1830–1895: A Study of the Formative Years.* Berkeley: University of California Press, 1951.

Cary, Diana Serra. *The Hollywood Posse: The Story of a Gallant Band of Horsemen Who Made Movie History.* Boston, MA: Houghton Mifflin, 1975.

Chabon, Michael. *Moonglow.* New York: Harper, 2016.

Chicago Railroad Fair: Official Guide Book and Program for the Pageant "Wheels a-Rolling." 1948.

Chytry, Josef. "Disney's Design: Imagineering Main Street." *Boom: A Journal of California* (spring 2012).

Comras, Kelly. *Ruth Shellhorn.* Athens: University of Georgia Press, 2016.

Cotter, Bill. *The Wonderful World of Disney Television: A Complete History.* New York: Hyperion, 1997.

Cross, Gary. *Consumed Nostalgia: Memory in the Age of Fast Capitalism.* New York: Columbia University Press, 2015.

——— and John K. Walton. *The Playful Crowd: Pleasure Places in the Twentieth Century.* New York: Columbia University Press, 2005.

Crump, Rolly. *It's Kind of a Cute Story.* Baltimore, MD: Bamboo Forest Publishing, 2012.

Dallas, Alastair. *Inventing Disneyland: The Unauthorized Story of the Team That Made Walt Disney's Dream Come True.* Theme Park Press, 2018.

D'Arcy, Bob. *A Walk in the Park: Reflections of Disneyland's First Host.* Irvine, CA: Bonaventure Press, 2018.

DeGaetano, Steve. *The Disneyland Railroad: A Complete History in Words and Pictures.* Theme Park Press, 2015.

———. *The Ward Kimball: The Story of Disneyland Engine No. 5.* Theme Park Press, 2015.

Denney, Jim. *Walt's Disneyland.* Anaheim, CA: Writing in Overdrive Books, 2017.

De Roos, Robert. "The Magic Worlds of Walt Disney." *National Geographic* (August 1963).

Disneyland: Dreams, Traditions and Transitions. Disney's Kingdom Editions, 2000.

Dunlop, Beth. *Building a Dream: The Art of Disney Architecture.* New York: Abrams, 1996.

Eliot, Marc. *Walt Disney: Hollywood's Dark Prince.* New York: Birch Lane Press, 1993.

The "E" Ticket. Nos. 1–24, 27–29, 33, 35, 39, 41, 43, 44 (1986–2006).

Finch, Christopher. *Walt Disney's America.* New York: Abbeville Press, 1978.

Findlay, John M. *Magic Lands: Western Cityscapes and American Culture After 1940.* Berkeley: University of California Press, 1992.

Flores, Russell D. *Seen, Un-Seen Disneyland: What You See at Disneyland, but Never Really See.* Garden Grove, CA: Synergy-Books, 2012.

Fox, Mike. *The Hidden Secrets & Stories of Disneyland.* Self-published, 2016.

Francaviglia, Richard V. "History After Disney: The Significance of 'Imagineered' Historical Places." *Public Historian* (autumn 1995).

———. *Main Street Revisited: Time, Space, and Image Building in Small-Town America.* Iowa City: University of Iowa Press, 1996.

France, Van Arsdale. *Backstage Disneyland: A Personal History.* Self-published, 1980.

———. *Window on Main Street: 35 Years of Creating Happiness at Disneyland Park.* Nashua, NH: Laughter Publications, 1991.

Gabler, Neal. *Walt Disney: The Triumph of the American Imagination.* New York: Knopf, 2007.

Gennawey, Sam. *The Disneyland Story: The Unofficial Guide to the Evolution of Walt Disney's Dream.* Birmingham, AL: Keene Communications, 2014.

Ghez, Didier, ed. *Walt's People: Talking Disney with the Artists Who Knew Him.* Volumes 6 (2008), 10 (2017), 22 (2019). Theme Park Press.

Gibson, Weldon B. *SRI: The Founding Years.* Los Altos, CA: Publishing Services Center, 1980.

———. *SRI: The Take-Off Days.* Los Altos, CA: Publishing Services Center, 1986.

Giroux, Henry A. *The Mouse That Roared: Disney and the End of Innocence.* Lanham, MD: Rowman & Littlefield, 1999.

Goldberg, Aaron H. *The Disney Story: Chronicling the Man, the Mouse & the Parks.* Quaker Scribe Publishing, 2016.

Goldenson, Leonard H. *Beating the Odds: The Untold Story Behind the Rise of ABC.* New York: Scribner, 1981.

Gordon, Bruce, and David Mumford, eds. *A Brush with Disney: An Artist's Journey Told Through the Words and Works of Herbert Dickens Ryman.* Redlands, CA: Camphor Tree Publishers, 2000.

———. *Disneyland: The Nickel Tour.* Redlands, CA: Camphor Tree Publishers, 1995.

Green, Amy Boothe, and Howard E. Green. *Remembering Walt: Favorite Memories of Walt Disney.* Glendale, CA: Disney Editions, 1999.

Gurr, Bob. *Design: Just for Fun.* APP-GurrDesign Publishing, 2012.

Haden-Guest, Anthony. *The Paradise Program: Travels Through Muzak, Hilton, Coca-Cola, Texaco, Walt Disney, and Other World Empires.* New York: Morrow, 1973.

Hahn, Don. *Yesterday's Tomorrow: Disney's Magical Mid-Century.* Glendale, CA: Disney Editions, 2017.

Halevy, Julian. "Disneyland and Las Vegas." *The Nation* (June 7, 1958).

H. C. Evans & Co. *Park and Carnival Equipment.* Chicago: H. C. Evans, 1932.

———. *The Secret Blue Book.* Chicago: H. C. Evans, 1932.

Heimbuch, Jeff. *Main Street Windows: A Complete Guide to Disney's Whimsical Tributes.* Orchard Hill Press, 2014.

Hench, John. *Designing Disney: Imagineering and the Art of the Show.* Glendale, CA: Disney Editions, 2008.

———. *The Imagineering Field Guide to Disneyland: An Imagineer's-Eye Tour.* Glendale, CA: Disney Editions, 2008.

The Imagineers. *Walt Disney Imagineering: A Behind the Dreams Look at Making the Magic Real.* New York: Hyperion, 1996.

Jackson, Kathy Merlock, and Mark I. West, eds. *Disneyland and Culture: Essays on the Parks and Their Influence.* Jefferson, NC: McFarland, 2011.

Keller, George. *Here Keller—Train This.* New York: Random House, 1961.

Kharlamov, M., and O. Vadeyvev, eds. *Face to Face with America: The Story of Nikita S. Khrushchev's Visit to the U.S.A.* Honolulu: University Press of the Pacific, 2003.

Kinney, Jack. *Walt Disney and Assorted Other Characters.* New York: Harmony Books, 1988.

Kipen, David, ed. *Dear Los Angeles: The City in Diaries and Letters 1542–2018.* New York: Modern Library, 2018.

Koenig David. *More Mouse Tales: A Closer Peek Backstage at Disneyland.* Irvine, CA: Bonaventure Press, 1999.

———. *Mouse Tales: A Behind-the-Ears Look at Disneyland.* Irvine, CA: Bonaventure Press, 1995.

———. *The People v. Disneyland: How Lawsuits & Lawyers Transformed the Magic.* Irvine, CA: Bonaventure Press, 2015.

Korkis, Jim. *Call Me Walt: Everything You Never Knew About Walt Disney.* Theme Park Press, 2017.

———. *How to Be a Disney Historian.* Theme Park Press, 2016.

———. *More Secret Stories of Disneyland: More Trivia Notes, Quotes & Anecdotes.* Theme Park Press, 2018.

———. *The Revised Vault of Walt.* Theme Park Press, 2012.

———. *Secret Stories of Disneyland: Trivia Notes, Quotes & Anecdotes.* Theme Park Press, 2017.

———. *Secret Stories of Extinct Disneyland: Memories of the Original Park.* Theme Park Press, 2019.

———. *The Unofficial Disneyland 1955 Companion: The Anecdotal Story of the Birth of the Happiest Place on Earth.* Theme Park Press, 2016.

———. *The Vault of Walt: Unofficial, Unauthorized, Uncensored Disney Stories Never Told.* Theme Park Press, 2010.

———. *The Vault of Walt: Volume 2. More Unofficial Disney Stories Never Told.* Theme Park Press, 2013.

———. *The Vault of Walt: Volume 3. More Unofficial Disney Stories Never Told.* Theme Park Press, 2014.

———. *The Vault of Walt: Volume 4. Still More Unofficial Disney Stories Never Told.* Theme Park Press, 2015.

———. *The Vault of Walt: Volume 5. Still More Unofficial Disney Stories Never Told.* Theme Park Press, 2015.

———. *Walt's Words: Quotations of Walt Disney with Sources!* Theme Park Press, 2016.

Kruse, Kevin M. *One Nation Under God: How Corporate America Invented Christian America.* New York: Basic Books, 2015.

Kubersky, Seth, et al. *The Unofficial Guide: Disneyland 2018.* Birmingham, AL: Adventure KEEN, 2018.

Kunstler, James Howard. *The Geography of Nowhere: The Rise and Decline of America's Man-Made Landscape.* New York: Simon & Schuster, 1993.

Kurtti, Jeff. *Disneyland from Once Upon a Time to Happily Ever After.* Glendale, CA: Disney Editions, 2010.

———. *Disneyland Through the Decades: A Photographic Celebration.* Glendale, CA: Disney Editions, 2010.

———. *Walt Disney's Imagineering Legends and the Genesis of the Disney Theme Park.* Glendale, CA: Disney Editions, 2008.

Lantzer, Jason. *Dis-History: Uses of the Past at Walt Disney's Worlds.* Theme Park Press, 2017.

Lindquist, Jack. *In Service to the Mouse: My Unexpected Journey to Becoming Disneyland's First President.* Orange, CA: Chapman University Press, 2010.

Linkletter, Art. *I Didn't Do It Alone: The Autobiography of Art Linkletter as Told to George Bishop.* Ottawa, IL: Caroline House, 1980.

Longstreth, Richard. *The Buildings of Main Street: A Guide to American Commercial Architecture.* Lafayette, LA: The Preservation Press, 1987.

Madden, Scott M. *The Sorcerer's Brother: How Roy O. Disney Made Walt's Magic Possible.* Theme Park Press, 2017.

Maltin, Leonard. *The Disney Films.* New York: Popular Library, 1983.

Marcus, Greil. "Forty Years of Overstatement: Criticism and the Disney Theme Parks." In Marling, *Designing Disney Theme Parks.*

Marley, David John. *Skipper Stories: True Tales from Disneyland's Jungle Cruise.* Theme Park Press, 2016.

Marling, Karal Ann, ed. *Designing Disney's Theme Parks: The Architecture of Reassurance.* New York: Flammarion, 1997.

Martin, Steve. *Born Standing Up.* New York: Scribner, 2007.

McEvoy, J. P. "McEvoy in Disneyland." *Reader's Digest* (February 1955).

McLaughlin, Robert. *Images of Modern America: Freedomland 1960–1964.* Mount Pleasant, SC: Arcadia Publishing, 2015.

Menen, Aubrey. "Dazzled in Disneyland." *Holiday* (July 1963).

Miller, Diane Disney. *The Story of Walt Disney.* New York: Dell Publishing, 1957.

Moore, Charles, Peter Becker, et al. *The City Observed: Los Angeles.* New York: Vintage Books, 1994.

Moran, Christian. *Great Big Beautiful Tomorrow: Walt Disney and Technology.* Theme Park Press, 2015.

Mosley, Leonard. *Disney's World.* New York: Stein and Day, 1985.

Mumpower, David. *Disney Demystified: The Stories and Secrets Behind Disney's Favorite Theme Park Attractions.* Theme Park Press, 2016.

Nichols, Chris. *Walt Disney's Disneyland.* Los Angeles: Taschen, 2018.

Nielson, Donald. *A Heritage of Innovation: SRI's First Half Century.* Menlo Park, CA: SRI International, 2004.

Pearson, Harlan C. *Tilyou's Gravity Steeplechase and Amusement Exposition, Surf Avenue, Coney Island, N.Y.* Concord, NH: Rumford Printing Company, 1900.

Pellman, Ken, and Lynn Barron. *Cleaning the Kingdom: Insider Tales of Keeping Walt's Dream Spotless.* Garden Grove, CA: Synergy-Books, 2015.

Penfield, Bob. *The Last Original Disneylander: Stories & Secrets from the Last to Retire of the First to Be Hired.* Bonaventure Press, 2016.

Peri, Don. *Working with Disney: Interviews with Animators, Producers and Artists.* Jackson: University Press of Mississippi, 2011.

———. *Working with Walt: Interviews with Disney Artists.* Jackson: University Press of Mississippi, 2008.

Pierce, Todd James. *Three Years in Wonderland: The Disney Brothers, C.V. Wood, and the Making of the Great American Theme Park.* Jackson: University Press of Mississippi, 2016.

Price, Harrison. *Walt's Revolution! By the Numbers.* Orlando, FL: Ripley Entertainment, 2003.

The Project on Disney. *Inside the Mouse: Work and Play at Disney World.* Durham, NC: Duke University Press, 1995.

Reynolds, Robert R. *Roller Coasters, Flumes and Flying Saucers: The Story of Ed Morgan and Karl Bacon, Ride Inventors of the Modern Amusement Parks.* Jupiter, FL: Northern Lights Publishing, 1999.

Rich, John. *Warm Up the Snake: A Hollywood Memoir.* Ann Arbor: University of Michigan Press, 2006.

'Round the Beaches: Official Souvenir, Program & Guide; Dreamland . . . Luna Park . . . Brighton Beach . . . Manhattan Beach . . . Coney Island (June–July 1907).

Rydell, Robert W. *All the World's a Fair: Visions of Empire at American International Expositions, 1876–1916.* Chicago: University of Chicago Press, 1984.

Schickel, Richard. *The Disney Version: The Life, Times, Art and Commerce of Walt Disney.* Third edition. Chicago: Ivan R. Dee, Inc., 1997.

Schmidt, Chuck. *Disney's Dream Weavers: The Visionaries Who Shaped Disneyland, Freedomland, the New York World's Fair, and Walt Disney World.* Theme Park Press, 2017.

Shellhorn, Ruth. "Disneyland: Dream Built in One Year Through Teamwork of Many Artists." *Landscape Architecture* (April 1956).

Silverman, Stephen M. *The Amusement Park: 800 Years of Thrills and Spills, and the Dreamers and Schemers Who Built Them.* New York: Black Dog & Leventhal, 2019.

Smith, Dave. *Disney A to Z: The Official Encyclopedia.* Third edition. Glendale, CA: Disney Editions, 2006.

Smothers, Marcy Carriker. *Eat Like Walt: The Wonderful World of Disney Food.* Glendale, CA: Disney Editions, 2017.

Snow, Richard. *Coney Island: A Postcard Journey to the City of Fire.* New York: Brightwaters Press, 1984.

Snyder, Chuck. *Windows on Main Street: Discover the Real Stories of the Talented People*

Featured on the Windows of Main Street, U.S.A. Glendale, CA: Disney Editions, 2009.

"Sound Effects Add Realism to Disneyland." *Radio & Television News* (August 1956).

Strodder, Chris. *The Disneyland Encyclopedia: The Official, Unauthorized, and Unprecedented History of Every Land, Attraction, Restaurant, Shop, and Event in the Original Magic Kingdom.* Santa Monica, CA: Santa Monica Press, 2008.

Sullivan, William. *From Jungle Cruise Skipper to Disney Legend.* Theme Park Press, 2015.

Surrell, Jason. *The Disney Mountains: Imagineering at Its Peak.* Glendale, CA: Disney Editions, 2007.

Telotte, J. P. *Disney TV.* Detroit: Wayne State University Press, 2004.

———. *The Mouse Machine: Disney and Technology.* Champaign, IL: University of Illinois Press, 2008.

Thie, Carlene. *Disneyland's Early Years Through the Eyes of a Photographer.* Ape Pen Publishing, 2003.

———. *Disneyland . . . The Beginning.* Ape Pen Publishing, 2003.

———. *A Photographer's Life with Disneyland Under Construction.* Ape Pen Publishing, 2002.

Thomas, Bob. *Building a Company: Roy O. Disney and the Creation of an Entertainment Empire.* New York: Hyperion, 1998.

———. *Walt Disney: An American Original.* New York: Simon and Schuster, 1976.

Van Eaton Galleries Presents Walt Disney's Disneyland: An Exhibition and Auction. Sherman Oaks, CA: Van Eaton Galleries, 2017.

Virgintino, Michael R. *Freedomland U.S.A: The Definitive History.* Theme Park Press, 2018.

Wallace, Mike. *Mickey Mouse History and Other Essays on American Memory.* Philadelphia: Temple University Press, 1996.

Wasko, Janet. *Understanding Disney.* Cambridge, UK: Polity Press, 2001.

Watts, Steven. *The Magic Kingdom: Walt Disney and the American Way of Life.* Columbia: University of Missouri Press, 1997.

Williams, Pat. *How to Be Like Walt: Capturing the Disney Magic Every Day of Your Life.* Deerfield Beach, FL: Health Communications, 2004.

Wilson, Alexander. *The Culture of Nature: North American Landscape from Disney to the Exxon Valdez.* Hoboken, NJ: Blackwell Publishers, 1992.

Younger, David. *Theme Park Design & the Art of Themed Entertainment.* Inklingwood Press, 2016.

Zinsser, William. *American Places.* The Akadine Press, 2002.

Illustration Credits

Map, pages iv–v: University of Southern California (USC) Libraries
Frontispiece: Hulton Archive/Getty Images

1. Office of War Information/PhotoQuest/Getty Images
2. Keystone-France/Gamma-Keystone via Getty Images
3. Gene Lester/Archive Photos/Getty Images
4. Alfred Eisenstaedt/The LIFE Premium Collection via Getty Images
5. Alfred Eisenstaedt/The LIFE Picture Collection via Getty Images
6. Author's Collection
7. Author's Collection
8. Earl Theisen/Getty Images
9. Bettmann/Getty Images
10. Bettmann/Getty Images
11. USC Libraries
12. Allan Grant/The LIFE Picture Collection via Getty Images
13. Bettmann/Getty Images
14. Loomis Dean/The LIFE Picture Collection via Getty Images
15. Loomis Dean/The LIFE Picture Collection via Getty Images
16. Loomis Dean/The LIFE Picture Collection via Getty Images
17. Loomis Dean/The LIFE Picture Collection via Getty Images
18. USC Libraries/Corbis via Getty Images
19. Paul Popper/Popperfoto via Getty Images/Getty Images
20. Author's Collection
21. Gene Lester/Getty Images

page 371: © The Estate of Diane Arbus, courtesy of the Fraenkel Gallery, San Francisco

INDEX

ABOUT THE AUTHOR

Richard Snow spent nearly four decades at *American Heritage* magazine, serving as editor in chief for seventeen years. He has been a consultant on historical motion pictures, among them *Glory*, and worked on numerous documentaries, including the Burns brothers' *The Civil War*. Snow is the author of nine books, among them two historical novels and a volume of poetry. His previous book, *Iron Dawn: The* Monitor, *the* Merrimack, *and the Civil War Sea Battle That Changed History*, received the Samuel Eliot Morison Award for distinguished naval literature. He was awarded a John Simon Guggenheim Memorial Foundation Fellowship in 2012.